Civil Society and the Market Question

Also by K. B. Ghimire

Forests and Livelihoods: the Social Dynamics of Deforestation in Developing Countries, co-authored with Solon L. Barraclough (Macmillan, 1995)

Land Reform and Peasant Livelihoods: the Social Dynamics of Rural Poverty and Agrarian Reform in Developing Countries, editor (ITDG, 2001)

Social Change and Conservation: Environmental Politics and Impacts of National Parks and Protected Areas, co-edited with Michel P. Pimbert (Earthscan, 1996)

The Native Tourist: Mass Tourism within Developing Countries, editor (Earthscan, 2001)

Travail, Culture et Nature: le développement local dans le contexte des parcs nationaux et naturels régionax de France, co-authored with Andréa S. Finger-Stich (L'Harmattan, 1997)

Civil Society and the Market Question

Dynamics of Rural Development and Popular Mobilization

Edited by

K. B. Ghimire
UNRISD

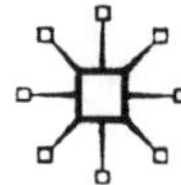

First published in 2005 by
PALGRAVE MACMILLAN
Houndmills, Basingstoke, Hampshire RG21 6XS and
175 Fifth Avenue, New York, N.Y. 10010
Companies and representatives throughout the world.

PALGRAVE MACMILLAN is the global academic imprint of the Palgrave Macmillan division of St. Martin's Press, LLC and of Palgrave Macmillan Ltd. Macmillan® is a registered trademark in the United States, United Kingdom and other countries. Palgrave is a registered trademark in the European Union and other countries.

ISBN-13: 978–1–4039–4915–8
ISBN-10: 1–4039–4915–8

This book is printed on paper suitable for recycling and made from fully managed and sustained forest sources.

A catalogue record for this book is available from the British Library.

Library of Congress Cataloging-in-Publication Data

    Civil society and the market question : dynamics of rural development and popular mobilization / edited by K.B. Ghimire.
      p. cm.
    Includes bibliographical references and index.
    ISBN 1–4039–4915–8 (cloth)
     1. Rural development – Developing countries. 2. Agriculture, market forces and state – Developing countries. 3. Peasantry – Developing countries. 4. Rural poor – Developing countries. 5. Non-governmental organizations – Developing countries. 6. Civil society – Developing countries. 7. Developing countries – Economic policy. I. Ghimire, Kléber.

HN981.C6C58 2005
338.1′09172′4—dc22   2004063293

10 9 8 7 6 5 4 3 2 1
14 13 12 11 10 09 08 07 06 05

Printed and bound in Great Britain by
Antony Rowe Ltd, Chippenham and Eastbourne.

*In memory of Solon L. Barraclough
who continues to inspire many of us*

Contents

List of Tables, Figures and Boxes

Tables

Figure

Box

Preface

The United Nations Research Institute for Social Development (UNRISD) initiated a major programme of research on Civil Society and Social Movements in the late 1990s with the aim of contributing to a better understanding of the ways in which civil society is being constructed in various political contexts. The programme has focused on the new challenges emerging in the triangular relationship between multilateral institutions, national governments and civil society at various levels. It has sought to analyse some important contemporary social movements both in rural and urban contexts, in which alliances are increasingly forged across social groups for defending or improving access to resources, income and services. In one project, the Institute has carried out research on the role of civil society organizations in agrarian reforms and their positions to markets and land reforms. The present volume is an outcome of this research project. One of the paradoxes of the recent neoliberal reforms has arisen from their attempt to engage civil society in development projects and service delivery, and the simultaneous groundswell of civil society opinion and activism critical of structural adjustment programmes, the policies to privatize vital public services and liberalize the agricultural sector, and the domineering role of transnational corporations (TNCs) and lending institutions. And in light of (and, at times, in lieu of) weakened states, many civil society organizations have sought to directly influence market outcomes in favour of the poor and to blunt their negative thrust. But what is the actual ability of civil society organizations and initiatives to influence the role of the market in agricultural development within neoliberal reforms?

Drawing on case studies on Asia, Africa and Latin America, the present volume critically looks at how civil society organizations in diverse contexts are able to assist poor cultivators and agricultural workers to improve their productive asset base, working conditions and group power through influencing the market mechanism. The work brings out the heterogeneous and ambiguous character of civil society positions and responses to market reforms in agriculture. 'Market advocates' support market-based economic activities and welfare in rural development; 'market sceptics' express misgivings about the possibility that the market mechanism can resolve rural poverty and inequality but at the same time are prepared to collaborate with mainstream development institutions; and 'market opponents' try actively to oppose such institutions and construct radical alternatives. More crucially, none of these three perspectives seems to have the ability to significantly influence the philosophy and functioning of the market.

Ironically, in their focus on the market many of these organizations run the danger of being on the other side of neoliberalism and its tendency to fetishize the market. These fears are prompted by a perceptible tendency within many of these movements to try to explain many of the contemporary socioeconomic processes and outcomes in rural areas merely by markets. Markets have no independent and prior existence from other social institutions and arrangements. They are firmly embedded in their societies and polities, and what they ultimately do depends on this embeddedness.

The prime message of the book is that forceful and unrelenting social mobilization within civil society is crucial to giving added voice to peasant producers and rural workers, as well as raising the visibility of their conditions and indicating potential solutions. Many of the challenges to the 'market' will be waged outside the 'market' itself and will involve high levels of self-organization among the rural populations and coalitions that go beyond rural societies themselves.

I would like to take this opportunity to thank the governments of Denmark, Finland, Mexico, Norway, Sweden, The Netherlands, United Kingdom and Switzerland for their generous financial support to the core activities of the Institute.

Thandika Mkandawire
Director, United Nations Research Institute
for Social Development (UNRISD)

Notes on Contributors

Nyangabyaki Bazaara passed away in August 2003. He was the director of the Centre for Basic Research in Kampala, Uganda. Articles by Dr Bazaara include 'The limits of agricultural reforms in contemporary Uganda', in *News from the Nordic African Institute*, No. 3, October 2000 and 'The bumpy road to constitutionalism in East Africa: a review of the experience', in *CBR Bulletin*, Vol. 2, No. 1, August 2000. He is also author of 'Mixed results in Uganda's constitutional development: an assessment', in Kituo Kya Katiba, *Constitutionalism in East Africa: Progress, Challenges and Prospects in 1999* (Kampala: Fountain Publishers, 2001).

Saturnino M. Borras Jr. is a political activist who has been deeply involved with rural social movements in the Philippines and internationally since the early 1980s. He is currently a Fellow at the Rural Development, Environment and Population Studies Group of the Institute of Social Studies, The Hague, The Netherlands. He has written articles on land reform and peasant movements, some of which have been published in academic journals including the *Journal of Development Studies, Development and Change, Journal of Agrarian Change*, and *Journal of International Development*. He is author of the book *The Bibingka Strategy in Land Reform Implementation: Autonomous Peasant Movements and State Reformists in the Philippines* (Quezon City: Institute for Popular Democracy, 1999).

Ray Bush teaches politics at the University of Leeds. He is an editor of the *Review of African Political Economy*. Recent publications include *Economic Crisis and the Politics of Reform in Egypt* (Boulder, CO: Westview, 1999) and he is editor of *Counter Revolution in Egypt's Countryside: Land and Farmers in the Era of Economic Reform* (London: Zed Books, 2002). He researches the political economy of Africa and the Middle East. He is currently working on a book exploring the persistence of poverty in the global south for Pluto Books where he is also a series editor of Third World in Global Politics.

K. B. Ghimire, a development sociologist, is Research Co-ordinator for the programme on Civil Society and Social Movements at the United Nations Research Institute for Social Development, Geneva. Throughout the 1990s he led research projects in the area of environmental change, tourism and land tenure reforms. His publications include: *Forests and Livelihoods* (co-authored with Solon Barraclough) (London: Macmillan, 1995), and *The Native Tourist* (London: Earthscan, 2001). He is also editor of *Land Reform and Peasant Livelihoods* (London: ITDG Publishing, 2001). He holds a PhD from the University of East Anglia, UK.

Manzurul Mannan is a social anthropologist and a faculty member at the Independent University, Bangladesh (IUB). Prior to joining the university, he worked as researcher, development manager and trainer in NGOs and development agencies. He has published articles widely in international journals and chapters in books on NGOs, culture and development of Bangladesh. His current research is on the ethnography of NGO and development institutions, markets and poverty, globalization and indigenous populations. He is author of several research articles on rural development and agrarian change in Bangladesh, including 'South Asia's experience in land reform: NGOs, the state and donors', in K. Ghimire (ed.), *Whose Land? Civil Society Perspectives on Land Reform and Rural Poverty Reduction* (Rome: IFAD/The Popular Coalition to Eradicate Hunger and Poverty/UNRISD, 2001); and 'The state and the formation of a dependent bourgeoisie in Bangladesh', *South Asia Journal*, Vol. 3, No. 4, April–June 1990.

Nora McKeon studied history, political science and sociology at Harvard University and the Sorbonne. Now an independent consultant, she worked for many years with the Food and Agriculture Organization of the United Nations. Her areas of work and study include reactions of African rural producers to the impact on their livelihoods of structural adjustment and international trade agreements; capacity building of rural peoples' organizations, and interaction of civil society organizations and social movements with governments and intergovernmental institutions. She has written and lectured extensively on these topics. Her recent publication includes *Peasant Associations in Theory and Practice* (co-authored with Michael Watts and Wendy Wolford; Geneva: UNRISD, 2004).

Leonilde Servolo de Medeiros is professor in the Post-Graduate Programme on Development, Agriculture and Society (CPDA) of the Federal Rural University of Rio de Janeiro (UFRRJ) Brazil. She graduated in Social Sciences at the São Paulo University (USP) and obtained a PhD at the Campinas University (Unicamp). She has written books and articles about Brazilian rural social movements and, more recently, about land settlements and agrarian reform policies. Her current interest of research lies in the Rural Landless Movement (MST) and the family farm producers' trade union movement. She is the author of *Movimentos Sociais, Disputas Políticas e Reforma Agrária de Mercado no Brasil* (Rio de Janeiro: CPDA/UFRRG and UNRISD, 2002).

Stephan Suhner is an independent researcher based in Berne and the Political Representative of the Working Group Switzerland Colombia ASK, a Swiss NGO dedicated to the promotion of human rights and peace in Colombia. He was educated at the University of Berne and his current research interests are in the fields of rural development, foreign investment and conflict in Colombia and on war on drugs and alternative development. He is the author of *Resistiendo al Olvido: Tendencias Recientes del Movimiento Social* *y de las Organizaciones Campesinas en Colombia*, co-published by UNRISD, Geneva and Taurus, Bogotá, 2002.

Henry Veltmeyer is Acting Coordinator of the International Development Studies (IDS) programme of St Mary's University (Halifax, Canada) and Professor of Development with the Doctoral Programme in Development Studies at the Autonomous University of Zacatecas (Mexico). He is the author of numerous books and journal articles on issues of world development, globalization and Latin America, including *Globalization and Antiglobalization: Dynamics of Social Change in the New World Order* (London: Ashgate, 2004) and, with James Petras, *Las dos Caras del Imperialismo* (Mexico: Editorial Migual Angel Porrua, 2004), *System in Crisis: the Dynamics of Free Market Capitalism* (London: Zed Press, 2003) and *Globalization Unmasked: Imperialism in the 21st Century* (London: Zed Press, 2001).

Neil Webster is Senior Research Fellow and Head of the Department of Development Research at the Danish Institute of International Studies, Copenhagen. Commencing with fieldwork for a PhD thesis on agrarian change in West Bengal while at Manchester University, he has studied and published on decentralization, rural development and local service delivery based on fieldwork in South Asia and elsewhere. His current research is on political interventions for rural development and poverty reduction in West Bengal and Nepal as part of a broader research programme in which Danish and Dutch researchers examine the local politics of service provision in Asia, Africa and Latin America. Recent publications include *In the Name of the Poor: Contesting Political Space for Poverty Reduction*, co-edited with Lars Engberg-Pedersen (London: Zed Press, 2002); and a co-authored book together with S. Folke, A. Cox and L. Schulpen, *Do the Poor Matter Enough? A Comparative Study of European Aid for Poverty Reduction in India* (New Delhi: Concept, 2002).

Abbreviations and Acronyms

AAA	Anti-communist American Action (Colombia)
A&D	alienable and disposable
ABRA	Brazilian Association for Agrarian Reform
ACABA	Consejo Comunitario General del Río Baudó y sus afluentes (Colombia)
ACBRA	Colombian Association of Beneficiaries of the Agrarian Reform
ACCIR	Association champenoise de coopération inter-régionale (France)
ACFODE	Action for Development (Uganda)
ACIA	Asociación Campesina Integral del Atrato (Colombia)
ACP	African, Caribbean and Pacific group of states
ADPES	Association pour une dynamique du progrès économique et social
AFDI	Agriculteurs français et développement international
ALCA	Latin America Tree Trade Agreement
ANCAR	Agence national de conseil agricole et rurale
ANDI	National Association of Industry (Colombia)
ANGOC	Asian NGO Coalition for Agrarian Reform and Rural Development
ANMTR	National Council of Rural Women Workers (Brazil)
ANUC	National Association of Usuary Farmers (Colombia)
AO	Administrative Order (Philippines)
AoA	Agreement on Agriculture
APCR	Association of Presidents of Rural Communities
ASAP	Agricultural Structural Adjustment Programme
ASIP	Agricultural Structural Investment Programme
ASOCODE	Asociación de Organizaciones Campesinas Centroamericanas para la Cooperación y el Desarrollo
ASPRODEB	Senegalese Association for the Promotion of Small Grassroots Development Projects
ATTAC	Association pour la Taxation des Transactions pour l'Aide aux citoyens (Association for the Taxation of Financial Transactions for the Aid of Citizens)
AUC	Autodefensas Unidas de Colombia
BADC	Bangladesh Agriculture Development Corporation
BISIG	Union of the Advancement of Socialist Thought and Action (Philippines)
BJP	Bharatiya Janata Party (India)

BRAC	Bangladesh Rural Advancement Committee
BSS	Bangladesh Bureau of Statistics
CA	Compulsory Acquisition
CAN	Confederação Nacional da Agricultura (Brazil)
CAP	Capability Enhancement through Citizen Action
CARET	Centre for Agrarian Reform, Empowerment and Transformation (Philippines)
CARP	Comprehensive Agrarian Reform Programme (Philippines)
CASE	Research Centre for Analysis of Social Exclusion
CBO	community-based organization
CBR	Centre for Basic Research (Uganda)
CDAs	community development associations
CDPs	Provincial Development Councils
CESAO	Centre d'études économiques et sociales de l'Afrique de l'Ouest (Burkina Faso)
CIDA	Canadian International Development Agency
CILSS	Comité permanent inter-états de lutte contre la sécheresse au Sahel
CIMI	Indigenous Missionary Council (Brazil)
CINEP	Companhia de Desenvolvimento da Paraíba (Brazil)
CIPA	Council on International and Public Affairs
CIRAD	Centre de coopération internationale en recherche agronomique pour le développement
CLOAs	Certificates of Land Ownership Awards
CMS	Coordinadora de Movimientos Sociales (Ecuador)
CNA	Confederação Nacional da Agricultura
CNASI	National Confederation of INCRA Employees
CNBB	National Conference of Brazilian Bishops
CNC	Consejo Nacional Campesino para la Acción Rural (Colombia)
CNCR	Comité national de concertation des ruraux (Senegal)
CNIA	Comité national interprofessionnel de l'arachide
COB	Central Obrera Boliviana
CODESRIA	Council for the Development of Social Science Research in Africa
CODHES	Consultoría para los Derechos Humanos y el Desplazamiento (Colombia)
CONAIE	Confederation of Indigenous Nationalities of Ecuador
CONCLAT	Conferência Nacional das Classes Trabalhadoras (Brazil)
CONFENIAE	Confederación de Nacionalidades Indígenas de la Amazonía Ecuatoriana
CONIC	National Council of Christian Churches in Brazil
CONTAG	Confederação Nacional dos Trabalhadores na Agricultura (Brazil)

CONVIVIR	Co-operatives of Rural Security (Colombia)
CPAR	Congress for a People's Agrarian Reform (Philippines)
CPI(M)	Communist Party of India (Marxist)
CPP	Maoist Communist Party of the Philippines
CPP	Popular Participation Councils (Bolivia)
CPPPs	Provincial Councils of Popular Participation
CPT	Comissão Pastoral da Terra (Brazil)
CSOs	civil society organizations
CUT	Central Única dos Trabalhadores (Brazil)
DAC	Development Assistance Committee (OECD)
DANE	National Administrative Department of Statistics (Colombia)
DAR	Department of Agrarian Reform (Philippines)
DARBCI	Dole Agrarian Reform Beneficiaries Cooperative Incorporated (Philippines)
DENIVA	Development Network of Indigenous Rural Population (Uganda)
DENR	Department of Environment and Natural Resources (Philippines)
DESER	Department of Rural Socioeconomic Studies (Brazil)
DFID	Department for International Development (UK)
DKMP	Demokratikong Kilusang Magbubukid ng Pilipinas (Democratic Peasant Movement of the Philippines)
DTW	deep tubewell
ECASA	Empresa Comercializadora de Alimento SA (Peru)
ECJ	Eduardo Cojuangco Jr. Company (Philippines)
ECLAC	Economic Commission for Latin America and the Caribbean
ECOWAS	Economic Community of West African States
ECUARUNARI	Confederación de los Pueblos de la Nacionalidad Quichua del Ecuador
EIA	environmental impact assessment
ELN	National Liberation Army (Colombia)
ENDA	Environnement et développement du tiers-monde
ERSAP	Economic Reform and Structural Adjustment Programme
EU	European Union
EZLN	Zapatista Army for National Liberation (Mexico)
FAO	Food and Agriculture Organization of the United Nations
FARC	Revolutionary Armed Forces of Colombia
FASE	Federation of Educational and Social Welfare Institutions (Brazil)
FCFA	Communauté financière africaine franc

FEDEGAN	National Federation of Cattle Dealers (Colombia)
FENAGIE	Fédération nationale des groupements d'intérêt économique de pêcheurs (Senegal)
FENSUAGRO	Federación Nacional Sindical Unitaria Agropecuaria (Colombia)
FIAN	Food First Information and Action Network
FIARA	International Fair of Agriculture and Animal Resources
FNRAA	Fonds national de recherches agricoles et agro-alimentaires
FONGS	Fédération des ONG Sénégalaises
FORUD	Foundation for Rural Development (Uganda)
FUT	Frente Unitario de Trabajadores
GDP	gross domestic product
GFI	Government Financial Institution
GIE	economic interest groups
GLTF	Gender Land Task Force
GoE	Government of Egypt
GSS	Gonoshahajjo Sangstha (Bangladesh)
HIES	Household Income and Expenditure Survey (Egypt)
HIPC	heavily indebted poor countries
HYV	high-yielding variety
IBASE	Brazilian Institute of Socioeconomic Analysis
ICARRDD	International Conference on Agrarian Reform and Rural Development (Philippines)
ICCI	Instituto Científico de Culturas Indígenas
ICIC	Iniciativa Civil para la Integración Centroamericana
IDB	International Development Bank
IFAD	International Fund for Agricultural Development
IFDA	International Foundation for Development Alternatives
IFIs	international financial institutions
ILO	International Labour Organization
IMF	International Monetary Fund
INCORA	Colombian Institute of Agrarian Reform
INCRA	Instituto Nacional de Colonização e Reforma Agrária (Brazil)
INESC	Institute of Socio-Economic Studies (Brazil)
INI	National Indigenist Institute (Mexico)
INTRAC	International NGO Training and Research Centre
IPS	Institute for Policy Studies
IRRI	International Rice Research Institute
ISI	import-substitution-industrialization
IUB	Independent University Bangladesh
IUCN	World Conservation Union
IUPERJ	Instituto Universitario de Pesquisas do Rio de Janeiro (Brazil)

KADU	Kenya African Democratic Union
KANU	Kenya African Nationalist Union
KASAMA-KA	Federation of People's Organizations in the Countryside (Philippines)
KFA	Kenya Farmers Association
KKK	Kilusang Kabuhayan at Kaunlaran (Marketing Coordinating Center established during the Marcos regime)
KLA	Kenya Land Alliance
KMP	Kilusang Magbubukid ng Pilipinas (Philippines)
KNFU	Kenya National Farmers Union
KPCU	Kenya Planters Cooperative Union
LBP	Land Bank of the Philippines
LE	Egyptian pound
LFG	Left Front Government (India)
LGED	Local Government Engineering Department (Bangladesh)
LLP	low lift pump
LSE	London School of Economics and Political Science
MALR	Ministry of Agriculture and Land Reclamation (Egypt)
MAS	Movement for Socialism (Bolivia)
MCAR	Municipal Councils of Agrarian Reform (Colombia)
MCRD	Municipal Councils of Rural Development (Colombia)
MEPF	Special Ministry of Funding Policy (Brazil)
MFR	Maisons familiales rurales (Senegal)
MINGA	Managing Natural Resources, Latin America and the Caribbean
MIRAD	Ministry of Agrarian Reform and Development (Brazil)
MISA	Ministry of Insurance and Social Affairs (Egypt)
MISR	Makerere Institute of Social Research (Uganda)
MLAR	market-led agrarian reform
MNCs	multinational companies
MOIR	Independent Revolutionary Workers Movement (Colombia)
MST	Movimento dos Trabalhadores Rurais sem Terra (Brazil)
MuCARRDS	Municipal Consultations on Agrarian Reform and Rural Development (Philippines)
NACLA	North American Congress on Latin America
NAFTA	North American Free Trade Agreement
ND	National-Democratic Movement ('Nat-Dem') (Philippines)
NDC	National Development Corporation (Philippines)
NDF	United Front (Philippines)
NEAD	Núcleo de Estudos em Agricultura e Desenvolvimento (Brazil)
NEM	neoliberal economic model
NEPAD	New Economic Partnership for African Development

NGOs	non-governmental organizations
NLF	National Land Forum
NOVIB	Oxfam – Netherlands
NPA	New People's Army (Philippines)
NPA	Nouvelle politique agricole (Senegal)
NRA	National Resistance Army (Uganda)
NRM	National Resistance Movement (Uganda)
NSP	New Social Policy
ODA	official development assistance
ODI	Overseas Development Institute (UK)
OECD	Organisation for Economic Co-operation and Development
OLT	Operation Land Transfer
ONCAD	Office national de la commercialisation et de l'assistance au développement (Senegal)
ONIC	National Indigenous Association of Colombia
OTBs	Organizaciones Teritoriales de Base
PAKISAMA	National Movement of Farmers' Associations (Philippines)
PARC	Presidential Agrarian Reform Council
PARCode	People's Agrarian Reform Code (Philippines)
PARRDS	Partnership for Agrarian Reform and Rural Development Services (Philippines)
PBDAC	Principal Bank for Development and Agricultural Credit
PCB	Brazilian Communist Party
PEACE	Philippine Ecumenical Action for Community Empowerment
PhilNET-RDI	Philippine Network of Rural Development Institutes
PHP	Philippines pesos
PKSK	National Federation of Organizations in the Countryside (Philippines)
PNRA	Proposal for a National Agrarian Reform Plan (Brazil)
PNUD	Programme des Nations Unies pour le Développement
PO	producers' organizations
PPI	Philippine Peasant Institute
PRA	Participatory Rapid Appraisal (Bangladesh)
PRIDE	Promotion of Rural Initiative and Development Enterprises
ProCARRDS	Provincial Consultations on Agrarian Reform and Rural Development (Philippines)
Procera	Special Programme of Credit for Agrarian Reform
PRONAA	Programa Nacional de Asistencia Alimentaria (Peru)
PRONAF	National Programme of Assistance for Family Agriculture (Brazil)
PRONASOL	Programa Nacional de Solidaridad (Mexico)

PROSANA	Proyecto de Seguridad Alimentaria Nutricional en la Provincia Arque (Bolivia)
PROSHIKA	Centre for Human Development (Bangladesh)
PRSPs	Poverty Reduction Strategy Papers
PSAOP	Programme of Agricultural Services and Producers Organizations
PT	Partido dos Trabalhadores (Brazil)
PVOs	private and voluntary organizations
RAFAD	Recherches et applications de financements alternatifs au développment
RDA	Rural Development Academy (Bangladesh)
ROPPA	Réseau des organisations paysannes et de producteurs agricoles de l'Afrique de l'Ouest
SAC	Colombian Agricultural Society
SAED	Société nationale d'aménagement et d'exploitation des terres du delta du fleuve Sénégal et des vallées du fleuve Sénégal et de la Falème
SAP	structural adjustment programme
SATEC	Société d'aide technique et de coopération (Senegal)
SDC	Swiss Agency for Development and Cooperation
SDO	stock distribution option
SINTRADIN	Sindicato Nacional de Trabajadores de INCORA (Colombia)
SLA	Sustainable Livelihoods Approach
SNV	Foundation of Netherlands Volunteers
SODEFITEX	Société de développement des fibres textiles
SODEVA	Société du développement et de la vulgarisation agricole (Senegal)
SOMIVAC	Société pour la mise en valeur de la Casamance (Senegal)
SONACOS	Société nationale de commercialisation des oléagineux
SONAGRAINES	Former subsidiary company of SONACOS responsible for collection and transportation of grains
SPFS	Special Programme for Food Security
SRB	Sociedade Rural Brasileira
STW	shallow tubewell
TDA	Títulos da Dívida Agrária
TMS	Tengamara Mahila Samity (Bangladesh)
TNCs	transnational corporations
TRAC	Transnational Resource and Action Center
TRENCOP	Tree and Energy Conservation Programme (Uganda)
UDR	União Democrática Ruralista (Brazil)
UEMOA	Economic and Monetary Union of West African States
UFRRJ	Universidade Federal Rural do Rio de Janeiro

UK	United Kingdom
ULA	Uganda Land Alliance
UN	United Nations
UNC	Uganda National Congress
UNCAS	Union nationale des coopératives agricoles du Sénégal
UNDP	United Nations Development Programme
UNESCO	United Nations Educational, Scientific and Cultural Organization
UNIBAN	Union of Banana Growers (Colombia)
UNORKA	National Coordination of Autonomous Local Rural People's Organizations (Philippines)
UNRISD	United Nations Research Institute for Social Development
UP	Union Parishad (Bangladesh)
URDT	Uganda Rural Development and Training
US	United States
USAID	United States Agency for International Development
USD	United States dollars
VLT	voluntary land transfer
VOS	voluntary-offer-to-sell
WB	World Bank
WTO	World Trade Organization
WUAs	water-user associations

1
Markets and Civil Society in Rural Transformation: an Overview of Principal Issues, Trends and Outcomes

*K. B. Ghimire**

Introduction

Neoliberal reforms are embedded in a paradox. Market[1] deregulation and free trade are obviously regarded as essential ingredients. Also integral to it are reform in political plurality and strengthening of civil society. Yet, a significant section of the political and civil society forces have tended to disagree with the very logic and consequences of market deregulation and free trade.

Pertaining to the reaction of civil society to neoliberal economic reforms, Desai and Said believe that this arises on mainly two fronts. First, 'it is reacting to market encroachment on both personal and public spaces: consumerism, atomisation, the erosion of public services, and nation state models of democracy'. Second, 'it is reacting to socio-economic consequences of capitalism such as poverty, inequality and instability' (Desai and Said, 2001: 64). The focal point of the present book consists of an examination of civil society enunciation surrounding the latter theme, with specific accentuation on agricultural or rural issues.

From the standpoint of recent civil society mobilizations at different venues coinciding with meetings of international financing and regional institutions, it is evident that many civil society groups have misgivings on the possibility of market mechanisms solving the current problems of rural poverty and social inequalities and in bringing about positive changes in the quality of life in rural areas. They are critical of both the substance and functioning of neoliberal market policies. As such, they are hostile to structural adjustment programmes, the policies to privatize vital public services and liberalize the agricultural sector, and the hegemonic role of transnational corporations (TNCs) and lending institutions. At times, they press for alternatives, and this is the case even when changing the fundamental nature and functioning of neoliberal economy policies has not been feasible. For example, they have commonly called for the cancellation of external debt and change in trade rules and barriers, favouring peasant agriculture, smaller enterprises and ecosystems in developing countries.

But, as can be expected, civil society is not monolithic. As will be explained later, some civil society organizations are simply content to implement neoliberal agricultural or rural development schemes. Others remain spectators, not knowing how to react. Yet others express reservations, but do not want to discard the present economic and political system altogether. And there are those that have seemingly decided to come to the fore and oppose the notion, *modus operandi* and effects of neoliberal agendas. This frequently makes it difficult for many civil society groups to find a common ground for building alliances and campaign for secure rural livelihoods and rights as well as trying out alternative proposals.

In addition to the horizontal divide, vertical fissures within a given movement may emerge. For example, leadership, which is usually made up of middle-class individuals with no worry about daily survival needs, can therefore afford to speak against the neoliberal market economy. On the other hand, the working population and their representative organizations at the local level may be more keen in using market means to enhance income opportunities and living conditions. As will be elaborated subsequently, this has for instance been the case with respect to the civil society movements surrounding the implementation of market-assisted land reform policies.

So what is the actual ability of civil society organizations and initiatives to influence the debate on the role of the market in economic development and social progress? Markets have existed in all societies in one form or another from the time of the existence of social institutions and arrangements, but when and how do they become detrimental to wider public interest? Should it be 'reformed within' or 'transformed' altogether? Are most civil society movements mainly limited to the 'popularization' of debate on the impending consequences of free market economy and 'retorting' to major financial institutions? What is the alternative to the dominance of a free market logic, and has anything distinctive been tried out? The language, comportment and actions embodied in many current civil society groups and mobilizations are not always translucent.

The task of the present book has been to highlight some of these critical issues. It aims specifically to scrutinize the ambiguities and complexities inherent in the actions of civil society organizations with respect to the use of market instruments in rural development, recognizing at the same time that the scope for civil society organizations and movements in rural transformation is genuinely consequential.

The book's structure is quite straightforward. This introductory chapter seeks to highlight some of the principal questions and debates involved with civil society and the market question. A major part of the book is based on detailed case studies from Asia, Africa and Latin America showing the dynamics of market-led agricultural/rural development, the role played by different institutions and social groups including civil society organizations and their accompanied outcomes especially with regard to the implications of improving rural livelihoods and reviving social mobilization.

Understanding the context of agricultural modernization, market forces and civil society

If we define 'civil society'[2] as being a social arena in which individuals and social groups are organized in shared actions to express their views and fulfil their interests, the interactions of civil society organizations and networks with market forces can probably be tracked from the epoch of state formations. Some scholars on agrarian transformation suggest that completely self-sufficient rural communities without trading a certain amount of food have 'probably always been a rarity since Neolithic times' (Stavenhagen, 1981: 85). Polanyi believed that the emergence of markets was 'the outcome of conscious and often violent intervention on the part of government' (Polanyi, 2001: 258). In the same way, Moore in his legendary book *Social Origins of Dictatorship and Democracy: Lord and Peasant in the Making of the Modern World* expounds on how the spread of the state's authority and intrusion of the market have gone hand in hand in various parts of the world since the fifteenth century, affecting 'the bonds of the peasants to the overlord, the division of labour within the village, its system of authority, class groupings within the peasantry, tenure and property rights' (Moore, 1981: 468). Central authority remained keen in extracting agricultural surpluses in the form of taxes, food or labour; at times it attempted to promote new technology with changes in tools and crop methods; and trade in agricultural products was considered auspicious and thus encouraged (ibid.).

In all these circumstances, market forces comprising traders and merchants had important stakes (see Myrdal, 1968: 1040 for references to South and Southeast Asia). They were frequently embedded in the state's power structure, but at times they were also in conflict of interest with central authorities (e.g., when a high level of trade levies and taxes were asked to support war efforts). In a similar manner, the role of various groups and associations in civil society – varying from irrigation committees to religious institutions – was considered crucial in facilitating the diffusion of new agrarian technologies, regular supply of taxes and food, recruitment for the army as well as free labour for public work. They were also important in executing voluntary operations, especially during drought, natural disasters or other types of emergency situations as well as being used in propagating rulers' erudite views and teaching, thereby seeking to legitimize the latter's social position. The reactions of 'civic' organizations and forces to state authorities as well as market forces varied widely from cooperation or indifference to, at times, open revolt, depending upon circumstances (e.g., Moore, 1981; Hagen, 1962).

But, as has been widely accepted, it was the expansion of European colonization from the sixteenth and seventeenth centuries onwards in Asia, Africa and Latin America that profoundly affected the existing agrarian structures, peasant welfare, as well as the rise of potent market forces. Both the spread of money economy and commercial agriculture became steadily widespread. Taxes were levied in cash; payments to workers were also paid in cash, and varieties of new commercial goods to be purchased in cash became more widely available (e.g., alcohol, cigarettes, clothes). This required peasants and rural workers to generate additional cash income, while prices of agricultural products began to fluctuate, depending upon national and international demands and speculations. Furthermore, this process led to the increased importance of the moneylending class and dispossession of peasants' lands. The consequence was stern, as Stavenhagen summarizes:

> Rural communities that have been drawn into the money economy have generally, on the whole, lost more than they gained: in India they lost their capacity to feed and clothe themselves; in Africa they lost their man-power; in Latin America their land and liberty (we may recall that 'land and liberty' was the rallying cry of the Mexican agrarian revolution). The money economy per se is no boon to agrarian communities. Most of the money earned through cash crops or wage labour is drained into pockets other than those of the worker or producer. (Stavenhagen, 1981: 90)

A majority of developing countries in Asia, Africa and Latin America obtained independence in the 1950s and 1960s taking on intact many of these trends. The logic of development frequently implied a maximum use of market mechanisms, and this was the case with both the right- and left-leaning national elites. Within the latter tradition in particular, 'planning' was seen as crucial for mobilization of resources for purposes of productive investment and their efficient use in economic development, and this was understood to happen within the framework of the market. Indeed, one authority in planning, Arthur Lewis, laid emphasis on the market factor by saying that 'the more the market is extensive, the more the possibilities of specialization are important' (Lewis, 1963: 76).[3] Third World governments in the 1960s, 1970s and 1980s had not been deficient in emphasizing the role of agricultural modernization, investment and trade, although some socialist governments had also sought to experiment regulation of markets to promote equality and prevent exploitation of farmers through trade. From the late 1980s, however, private investment, free trade and liberalization of the economy, combined with an attempt to downsize the intervention capacity of the state, have been proposed and tried out by leading financial institutions and donor agencies with acute impacts on employment, social well-being and inequality. This has been accompanied by a severe debt problem, instability in the financial system and shrinking foreign aid for many countries.

Suggestions and policy recommendations have not been lacking in order to tackle many of these negative impacts. Those who sought to promote free market economy in the first place assume that additional right policy measures are required to permit further 'optimum allocation of resources', insisting that 'participating in the market is the key to boosting economic growth for nations and to reducing poverty for individuals' (World Bank, 2001: 1; see also de Jonquières, 1997). Another view suggests that a 'new balance between public and private interest must be found' as 'too great a reliance on the "invisible hand" of the market is pushing the world toward unsustainable levels of inequality and deprivation' (UNRISD, 2000: viii; see also UNDP, 1993: 30). And there are those who believe the model is fundamentally deceitful, 'remunerating capital to the detriment of labour and thus moving wealth from the bottom of society to the top' (George, 2001: 9) and which 'can be challenged and replaced because its own failures will require this' (ibid.: 10; see also Cassen, 1997). In the same vein, some have called for greater localization of economic activities at the community level of production and consumption, thereby serving to deglobalize trade and investment (Bello, 2002: 113). Indeed, some sixty years ago Karl Polanyi had warned that the institution of liberal economy 'could not exist for any length of time without annihilating the human and natural substance of society' (Polanyi, 2001: 3).

With respect to agriculture, the central constituent of the economic activity in rural areas in most developing countries and increased trade liberalization have meant progressive elimination of various tariffs and other protective barriers, including removal of preferential treatment to local food products. This has been accompanied by cuts in government budgets for agriculture and rural development in line with structural adjustment programmes with severe implications for the institutional provision of production inputs, quality control, training, research and extension; peasant cooperatives have disintegrated; and many tenancy legislations that previously gave a higher degree of security to tenants and sharecroppers have been unravelled. Private investment in agriculture has been encouraged from abroad, especially from transnational agribusiness groups, frequently at the cost of national enterprises or labour rights. Land prices have been liberalized. In the same way, leasing of productive land by wealthier people has been simplified and 'contract farming' has popped up as a new form of tenancy or wage labouring.

These processes have had many implications for food security, employment and family welfare among the marginalized population groups, such as small farmers and rural workers. Furthermore, rural producers and workers have remained acutely susceptible everywhere to the inflow of cheap agricultural products, typically resulting in stagnant production and a decreasing domestic demand for food. Also, the spread of mass media promoting consumer ethics and the desire to purchase outside goods (including processed food) have put further economic strain on the lives of many groups of the rural population.

A more detailed account of the foundation and expansion of market forces in various agricultural contexts and recent trade liberalization measures and their associated effects is not feasible here. The key aspect to be shown in the above sketch is the broad parameters under which civil society could exist and how they could be modulated. It is clear that, in recent years, civil society has been seen by leading institutions as an integral part of the neoliberal development agenda. It is perceived to be a vital element for promoting and consolidating democracy; and it should contribute to improved account-ability and implementation of development initiatives aimed at fostering economic growth and social welfare. This has created a certain degree of political space for increased civil society visibility and activism. At the same time, any important attempt on the part of civil society to take up broad themes of social justice and people-centred development, with radical demands for reforms in world economic and political systems, has tended to bring it directly at odds with leading institutions and thoughts, as was hinted at the beginning of the chapter.

Civil society organizations (CSOs) have remained particularly active in pin-pointing the negative impacts of the present neoliberal world economic and financial systems on the agricultural sector, especially by organizing forceful events at international summits and conferences and utilizing more actively Internet technology. Increasingly, CSO movements and networks are com-bining their advocacy campaigns with distinct alternative proposals to change international trade rules and barriers for the benefit of Third World poorer agricultural producers and workers. For example, the Porto Alegre Global Social Forum, which is now organized as an annual event and brings together several thousand civil society advocates and groups to discuss many of the negative impacts of globalization processes, has brought to the forefront the issues of sustainable rural communities, dignified work and a healthy environment. The Via Campesina – an international radical agrar-ian movement with widespread links with global and regional agrarian organizations – for example, outlines the market policies within the agricul-tural sector requiring following fundamental changes:

- Ensure adequate remunerative prices for all farmers;
- Exercise the rights to protect domestic markets from imports at low prices;
- Regulate production on the internal market in order to avoid the creation of surpluses;
- Abolish all direct and indirect export support;
- Phase out domestic production subsidies that promote unsustainable agri-culture and inequitable land tenure patterns, and target support at inte-grated agrarian reform programmes as well as sustainable farming practices. (Via Campesina, 2001: 1)

But how effective are campaigns such as this in terms of producing tangible results, especially given the highly intractable position of powerful institutions and nations? Do civil society campaigns tend to remain largely a 'straw fire' intended to put across the main message during major events, or are they nevertheless able to sustain the momentum of their action and implement their main agenda? How cohesive are these movements; and how capable are they in creating wider alliances with like-minded people and institutions? It is clear that for any CSO movement to be considered successful, it should particularly be able to convince common people and grassroots organizations in rural and urban areas of its capacity to help improve sociopolitical and livelihood conditions, recognizing that the priorities of local people and their representative organizations are often specific and immediate.

Civil society: differing composition and visions

Meghnad Desai and Yahia Said regroup the recent global civil society movements as a response to the current financial sector or global capitalism in general in four categories: (a) isolationists (those calling directly or indirectly for the abolition of the global economic order; e.g., Friends of the Earth, Focus on the Global South, *Le Monde diplomatique*); (b) supporters (those supporting market expansion and global capitalism; e.g., Centre for Civil Society, India; *The Economist; The Wall Street Journal*; the Chamber of British Industry in the United Kingdom); (c) reformists (groups aiming to maintain the advantages of a capitalist model while mitigating its excess through regulation and redistribution; e.g., Oxfam, World Development Movement, Association pour la Taxation des Transactions pour L'Aide aux Citoyens (ATTAC); and (d) alternatives (those concerned with encroachment of the market in public life and creating space for alternatives; e.g., the Grameen Bank, the Zapatistas)[4] (Desai and Said, 2001: 65–75). Within developing countries, an echo of many of these movements can be heard and detected in major urban centres and capital cities. One major problem, of course, is the overlap in the composition and activities of these movements. As such, making explicit categories and placing certain groups under them is frequently flawed. Also, by their very nature, most social movements are short-term, if not sporadic (e.g., anti-globalization protests surrounding global summits); and the success of these movements in popularizing and implementing global issues of concern and specific initiatives at national and local levels is always relative, and to a great extent uncertain. This is even more blurred when it comes to rural areas.

Very broadly, there appear to be three groups of civil society movements as regards the issue of the market in rural or agricultural development.

1. *Market advocates.* A whole range of civil society groups ranging from agribusiness companies, microcredit organizations, non-governmental organizations (NGOs) promoting rural business, enterprises and income-generation

activities, farmers' cooperatives specialized in cash crop production and export, and so forth, remain strong campaigners for a market economy that promotes economic growth and liberalization. As such they are usually closely related to the funding projects of the dominant institutions like the World Bank, United States Agency for International Development (USAID) and a variety of other international development bodies as well as the government (see Bush, Chapter 6, for a discussion on the case of Egypt). At times, some market advocate NGOs may be providing services at a lower price than the commercial sector (e.g., the experience of the Grameen Bank and other NGOs in Bangladesh – see Mannan, Chapter 9) and improving the capacity of marginalized rural producer groups to cope with rapid withdrawl of state support services, indebtedness and price instability (see McKeon, Chapter 7, on adept work by the Fédération des ONG Sénégalaises [FONGS] and Comité national de concertation des ruraux [CNCR] in Senegal); these, as well as national agribusiness groups and enterprises, may also be concerned with trade barriers in industrialized countries and agricultural dumping in developing countries, thereby giving rise to potential alliances with militant global civil society forces openly campaigning for fundamental changes on these issues. But since market advocate groups strongly support free circulation of capital, freedom of investment and free trade, ideologically, it proves restricting for them to go against these very principles. Furthermore, at national and local levels, they are frequently directly at odds with radical civil society movements and networks on scores of other fundamental matters such as access to resources, development of land and water markets, wages and pricing, thereby making it highly difficult to build any stable coalition around international trade issues.

2. *Market sceptics.* Most civil society movements and networks tend to express misgivings about the possibility of the market mechanism resolving rural poverty and inequalities. They comprise community organizations, rural development organizations, peasants' associations, rural trade unions, environmental groups, indigenous peoples' and human rights advocacy groups, and so forth. These groups point to the negative impacts on income levels, working conditions, as well as physical environment of current trading and pricing policies of agricultural products, debt problems and the growing power of multinational agribusiness groups. At national level, they are critical of the reduction and privatization of vital support services to small farmers, removal of price protection policies, growing food imports, breaking of tenancy laws and liberalization of land markets. But they have frequently an ambivalent position in terms of the role of the state as, on the one hand, they pledge for the protection of the public sector while, at the same time, many of them participate in donor policies and projects that are commonly accompanied by an attempt to scale down state capacity.

On the whole, a majority of the civil society groups in this category have tended to avoid a direct 'confrontation' with donor agencies and the government both in terms of the approach to rural or agricultural development taken and specific projects initiated. Many structural problems of rural poverty are reduced to the question of providing credit or appropriate technology. For example, as Barraclough and Moss, examining the role of NGOs in promoting food security in Central America, note:

> Proposals for structural changes in land tenure and land-use planning, which are fundamental for food security, were barely heard at discussion tables and were replaced by more modest proposals to improve cultivation techniques on hillsides and to register land titles. (Barraclough and Moss, 1999: 18–19)

Obviously, there are other civil society groups which are actively animating networks, promoting greater documentation and exchange of opinions, and organizing meetings and protest rallies denouncing the negative effect of agricultural trade liberalization, exploitation and manipulation by multinational groups, official corruption and collision with landed classes, or delays in official redistribution of lands and so forth (e.g., Asian NGO Coalition for Agrarian Reform and Rural Development (ANGOC) in Asia, Asociación de Organizaciones Campesinas Centroamericanas para la Cooperación y el Desarrollo (ASOCODE) in Central America and CNCR in Senegal/West Africa). These groups find themselves in an intricate relationship with donor agencies and the government. While they protest against the negative effects of the current neoliberal economic policies on agriculture and rural living, they remain in agreement with donor policies with respect to a greater use of the market mechanism for rural or agricultural development, as well as on a variety of political reform issues, such as the promotion of Western-style democracy, rule of law, civil society, decentralization and efficient governance. They see the benefits of markets, but favourable conditions are not being created for rural people to take full advantage and equally share the benefits. They also argue that current market liberalization processes are detrimental to the local environment and cultural diversity.

3. *Market opponents.* Civil society groups, such as the Movimento dos Trabalhadores Rurais Sem Terra (MST) in Brazil, the Zapatistas in Mexico, the KMP (Kilusang Magbubukid ng Pilipinas) peasant movement in the Philippines, and similar radical and, at times, armed peasant associations in South Asia (e.g., the current Maoist movement in Nepal) could be cited as being examples of actively trying to oppose the economic and political hegemony of the neoliberal forces. In particular, they see the international market mechanism as highly exploitative of peasants and other working population groups. As such, they propose to build agricultural policies that would reflect national needs and peasant welfare. For example, in its agrarian model, the MST proposes, among others, that the development of agriculture should: (a) be aimed towards the internal market; (b) ensure increased income and productivity of family farms through pricing, subsidized rural credits and agricultural security; and (c) promote agro-industrial cooperatives in order to democratize access to the market.[5] In other words,

it seeks to discard the conception that agricultural policy should rely on export crops with foreign investment. Similar ideas and propositions relating to the promotion of a local self-help mechanism and solidarity measures, based on the development of cooperatives, agricultural funds and rural industries, are frequently being advanced as well as tried out in certain contexts in other countries such as Nepal in areas controlled by Maoist movements and in certain parts of India where radical left parties have remained strong.

While groups such as the MST, the Zapatistas and the KMP encourage reflection on the development and implementation of a locally or nationally autonomous agricultural policy, they are not seeking to de-link totally with the current modernization processes and world market economy. As a matter of fact, urbanized rural lifestyles and increased consumption of goods coming from cities and foreign countries are major problems that do not get as much attention in these movements. Indeed, rural movements that seek to totally disconnect with markets remain rare (examples may include spiritual, ecological and consumer associations).

We will see shortly, based on the information and analyses contained in different chapters in this book, how the perceptions and engagements of different civil society groups have had an effect on the key aspects of market relations affecting rural development. The short overview provided above on the three principal categories of civil society forces in rural areas is nevertheless sufficient to indicate that, on the whole, there are few civil society groups that actually reject the very notion of markets.

It should be noted that even academics and social thinkers from the left who, in the past, usually pronounced an inclination towards planning over markets, indicating the destructive effects of capitalist development in agriculture and free trade on food security and wider livelihood issues, are required to redefine the role of markets in rural economies, including methods of food distribution in urban areas. In other words, people's survival is better linked to the expansion in 'real markets'. As Mackintosh writes:

> Markets … have widely varying institutions and economic contexts, they operate on limited information, they involve and help to create a variety of social classes, power relations, and complex patterns of needs and responses. (Mackintosh, 1990: 47)

She suggests that in seeking to comprehend 'real markets', it is crucial to carefully consider the following four elements: (a) the terms under which people come to a market, especially the ownership of resources allowing select individuals to establish dominance over markets, while those lacking resources are required to participate in the market in vulnerable terms; (b) power and control of powerful individuals and companies over the terms under which markets operate, including the action of powerful governments; (c) class structure of traders and state action directing or controlling rural technical change and class formation; and (d) some markets are abrogated rather than developed, notably the creation of new forms of unfree labour through contract farming amid the rhetoric of market liberalization (ibid.: 51–2).

An analysis of markets that encompasses the issue of power structures, institutions, economic inequalities and complex patterns of local needs and responses is especially important as much of the discussion on the subject among donor agencies and governments centres around the problems of marketing of agricultural production, namely marketing organizations, storage, financing and transport (Mosher, 1966: 63–74; Morss et al., 1976: 194–201; IFAD, 2001: 173–7; FAO, undated). Indeed, the World Bank in its *World Development Report 2002* declares that 'marketing problems are the biggest institutional constraints to increasing agricultural productivity' and that 'the more open the market, the greater is the demand for effective formal institutions for farmers – from documented property rights in land to better access to credit' (World Bank, 2001: 32). The Bank, as well as many other donor agencies, fail to acknowledge even common problems of pricing affected by unfair competition, monopoly, trade barriers, price speculations and dumping of agricultural products. In particular, the (political and economic) difficulties linked to the lack of access to prime means of production – land and water – are not recognized when discussing marketing issues. Similarly, access to labour markets for poor rural producers and workers, especially the constraints associated with them, is seldom considered. Consequently, the solutions commonly prescribed on the part of donor agencies and governments have tended to involve development of adequate infrastructure, extension of credit to the poor, skill development, and access to information, thereby heavily relying on the involvement of the private sector.

This pro-free market approach, with little consideration of existing power relations, has acute consequences in terms of the scope for civil society participation. Despite a lot of hype on the promotion of civil society in rural areas, few donor agencies and governments are actually encouraging civil society forces to help transform rural power structures in favour of the poorer and weaker sections of the population (see, for example, Ghimire, 2002a: 249–70 for a discussion on the dismal role of leading international agencies in changing rural power structures through land tenure reforms). On the whole, civil society is expected to participate in the smooth implementation of market development projects focused on infrastructure building, credit provisioning, farmers' training, as well as providing information on markets and prices. Accordingly, civil society organizations that support this strategy are bolstered, which has been categorized above as 'market advocates'. In some cases, donor agencies and the governments themselves may be involved in establishing 'tailor-made NGOs', thereby seeking to show that they are helping to create and consolidate 'vibrant' civil society in rural areas as well as execute related programmes and projects through NGOs. The support to civil society forces belonging to 'market sceptic' and 'market opponent' groups, on the other hand, may be little or non-existent, unless they are able to prove a serious nuisance or creditable opponents requiring some compromise, cooption or respect.

A few illustrations on the market positioning of civil society organizations

Rural development entails access to means of production by the rural poor, protecting their labour rights and caring about their working conditions, as well as preventing their exploitation and manipulation by individuals and groups wielding political and economic power. It entails greater farm productivity, creation of new skills, jobs and income and increased household consumption capacity. This should go together with extension in education, health and social services. Overall, it should have a goal of reducing injustices and inequalities. And this would be feasible only when the class power of the rural poor is increased through meaningful participation in the political process, including creation and consolidation of powerful grassroots movements and initiatives. Market forces have a bearing on most of these aspects of rural development, with dynamics coming from global to local levels and involving interplay of various economic as well as non-economic actors and institutions. So how are civil society organizations seeking to reach out to the rural poor and campaigning for improved livelihoods and rights influencing the debate on rural development, in general, and market relations and expansion, in particular?

Land redistribution and market mechanisms

In line with the logic of bolstering economic liberalization, the use of a market mechanism is considered by leading donor agencies (especially the World Bank, USAID and the Food and Agriculture Organization of the United Nations – FAO) and governments to be the principal instrument for rural land redistribution and poverty reduction. The central formula of this perception has been to create vibrant land markets by transforming communally or collectively owned/used lands into private holdings (thereby allowing individual transactions of land), encouraging land sales among large landholders through desirable price offers, and introducing more flexible tenancy reforms permitting landowners to recuperate their lands more easily for sales or renting. Land-poor peasants and rural workers should thus take advantage of the increased availability of land in the market through purchase, and this would be supplemented by the provision of the necessary external financial and technical support. This approach has been implemented throughout Latin America, and in some African and Asian countries with bi-model agrarian structures, notably South Africa, the Philippines and Indonesia. But some elements of market-oriented tenancy reforms are being tried out in many other African and Asian countries with communal or smallholding land tenure systems (e.g., see Bazaara, Chapter 5, for a discussion on East Africa).

The effectiveness of this policy has been questioned on numerous grounds, namely that prospects for attaining a significant amount of land for redistribution through voluntary willingness on the part of landowners wielding political power are limited; and where some land has been sold by landowners after receiving attractive compensation, it is usually the more informed and wealthier individuals and groups in society that have tended to seize most of it (such as drug dealers in Colombia – as highlighted by Suhner in Chapter 3). On the other hand, the costs of land have been burdensome everywhere for poorer households seeking access to land, especially given volatile commodity prices and the lack of institutional production support services.

The market-led agrarian reform has turned out to be unsettling among civil society organizations. As expected, a few NGOs close to the World Bank and governments have been involved in selecting and training beneficiaries of the reform programme, but their political influence on the peasantry is minute. In limited cases, such as in Brazil, entirely new forms of peasant associations of land reform beneficiaries are created, thereby circumventing the influence of agrarian trade unions and other existent peasant associations (Medeiros, Chapter 2). Among the latter organizations, some have conceived the market-led agrarian reform measures to represent a window of opportunity around which social mobilization could be built, as well as to provide land to some needy poorer households. As elaborated by Borras, Medeiros and Suhner in their respective chapters (i.e., Chapters 8, 2 and 3), in the Philippines, Brazil and Colombia, for example – three countries with a significant experience in the recently implemented market-driven land reforms – several of these social movement groups have recognized a certain degree of land redistribution potential through the market path and have moderated their criticism of the government. At times they have also participated in the direct or indirect implementation of specific market-led land reform projects and programmes, although part of the leadership and some cadres have continued to express disquiet over this policy measure. In contrast, more radical rural social movements, such as the MST in Brazil, the Peasant Movement of the Philippines (KMP) (see also KMP, 2000) and National United Agricultural Workers Union/Federación Nacional Sindical Unitaria Agropecuaria (FENSUAGRO) in Colombia have openly opposed the initiative on the grounds that it undermines social movements and trade union actions for more sweeping land reform, although they are not totally opposed to building wider alliances and collaboration on a broad redistributive land agenda with the former groups.

This rift has been most acutely felt at the grassroots since it is at this level that rural trade unions and peasant associations are required to deal with a high demand for land among poor peasants and rural workers as well as the unrelenting power of the landowning elites, government officials and agribusiness interests. In some cases, individual members and local organizations are breaking the rank and file when the organizations' formal policies remain totally opposed to peasants and workers applying for land in market-led land reform programmes. This has increasingly become the case with the MST in Brazil (Ghimire, 2002b). On the other hand, as shown in the case study on Colombia, peasant leaders who try to act as mediator between landowners and peasants in the acquisition of land, thereby working in close contacts with government officials and landowners and at times receiving political protection and personal financial gains, often face the difficulty of protecting their credibility as leaders within their organizations (Chapter 3). These types of vertical divisions and tensions within a rural social movement are especially perilous in seeking to campaign for widespread land reform as there are already numerous horizontal divides among trade unions and peasant organizations.

While the civil society groups that have decided to participate in the market-led land reform programmes are not able to bring about any major redistributive changes in rural tenure structures, the overt antagonism to these programmes by the more radical groups has made forceful alliance around the land reform issue increasingly problematical. The rejection of market-led agrarian reform programmes by these groups primarily emanates from their political strategy to oppose neoliberal agricultural policies. However, the extent to which a market mechanism can be used in property transfer favouring poor rural producers and workers in concrete situations is yet to be decided and implemented by these movements.

Labour markets

Due to the combined processes of pauperization, agricultural modernization and a host of other factors leading to land loss by poorer cultivators, the population size of agricultural labourers has increased in most developing countries. Frequently, women and children are drawn into the local labour market under highly exploitative terms. As such, agricultural labourers frequently constitute the largest social group in rural areas. In Brazil, for example, permanent and temporary wage-workers comprised over 60 per cent of the agricultural population in 1984, and the number of people joining the ranks of permanent and temporary wage-workers nearly doubled between 1978 and 1984 (Pereira, 1992). This implies that, without strengthening the livelihood interests of this specific group of population, no significant achievement can be made in rural poverty eradication and grassroots empowerment.

The likelihood of obtaining land by a large and growing number of rural labourers through the recently initiated market-assisted land transfer mechanism is slim, as was indicated above. It is nearly impossible for an average agricultural labourer to be able to purchase land and other productive assets through wage labouring.[6] Under these circumstances, renting or sharecropping of land under exploitative and unsecure conditions may be the primary option available when seeking to maintain access to land. Or, alternatively, rural labourers may attempt to squat large private holdings and public areas, but the risks are multiple. Agricultural labourers are also usually discriminated against obtaining institutional credits in their efforts to improve their asset base because of the lack of safe collateral support. In general, rural labour opportunities remain limited, wages are low and work is highly seasonal. Furthermore, the impact of economic liberalization and, 'in the pursuit of "flexibility", agricultural employment has become precarious, with substantial increases in the number of migrant workers, day-labourers, and seasonal and temporary workers, all of whom suffer in terms of pay, social protection, housing, education and medical protection' (ILO, 2000: 32).

So the main question is: How are civil society groups helping rural labouring households to build up a secure source of livelihood in the context of evolving market liberalizations? It is evident that most of the rural social movements outlined above were directly related to the issue of access to productive land by poor rural workers in market-led agrarian reform programmes (e.g., Brazil, the Philippines). The role of civil society organizations could also prove valuable in providing the necessary information, contacts and financial means for acquiring land and other productive resources in agricultural frontier areas, government resettlement programmes, and as common property resources (forests, waste land, water bodies, grazing fields) by labouring households. They have confirmed an ability to make available credits and other essential agricultural inputs at affordable rates to labouring and land-poor households (see Chapters 9 and 7 for two prominent examples covered in this volume, namely Bangladesh and Senegal). Pro-market civil society groups and most donor agencies tend to emphasize the optimistic views of agricultural commercialization, agro-industrialization and export of cash crops on increased labour demands within rural areas (cf. IFAD, 2001: 171). As an integral part of this process, 'contract farming' between transnational agribusiness groups and small farmers is viewed as potentially creating wider employment opportunities within rural communities (cf. Glover and Kusterer, 1990: 2).

As could be expected, there are no common positions of civil society groups on rural labour issues. While a majority, in principle, recognize the need to improve labour conditions in rural areas, the specific approaches prescribed and implemented vary greatly. Many institutionalized labour unions or federations, for example, have a tendency to reduce most labour problems to social welfare issues, or even to a 'band-aid' type of answer, thereby avoiding engagement in issues of structural change (Moyo et al., 2000). These labour groups, as well as some rural development NGOs, identify agricultural commercialization and increased production of export crops as a potential solution to improving income levels of labouring people; as such they see no stigma in establishing closer links with agribusiness groups and donor agencies promoting agricultural liberalization and free trade.

Others indicate more unfavourable consequences, such as diversion of resources from staple food to cash crop production, monopoly power over peasant producers, health hazards and environmental problems (Moore Lappé and Collins, 1977; Bernstein et al., 1990). Yet alternatives proposed are not always tangible from the point of view of a desperate wage earner. This is also the case with contract farming, which may provide an important source of credit and other inputs and could provide a level of price guarantee. While independent farming is increasingly threatened in the absence of state production support or a household's increased economic marginalization, many civil society groups tend to reject in block this kind of farming or labour arrangement. This is especially the case with leadership, which is frequently based in urban centres and associated with foreign trade union federations or networks, but a local chain of command and activists working more directly with rural labourers and small producers are required to consider such possibilities more positively, including negotiation and resolution of plentiful labour conflicts in local areas. It is also at this level that civil society groups are the most valuable in helping poorer households with relevant information on job availability and useful contacts when considering migration or looking for seasonal or stable jobs in urban areas.

Dealing with uncertainty and vulnerability caused by the market

In rural areas, market mechanisms produce numerous uncertainties and vulnerabilities, calling for the attention of various institutions and social forces such as civil society organizations. For example, to continue with the labour market issues, it is clear that many rural and agricultural workers not only suffer chronic job shortages, including a high degree of seasonality and informality, but they also remain highly vulnerable to exploitation and repression from employers, ranging from traditional landowners to plantation owners, or regional/international agribusiness groups. This economic vulnerability is frequently linked to their political weakness. Thus the role of workers' unions and peasant associations is crucial in seeking to ensure that workers obtain minimum wages, acceptable working conditions as well as political voice. Indeed, a good number of contemporary trade union movements in countries like the Philippines, Brazil, and a host of other Latin American countries, have proved to be a persuasive force precisely because they have been able to combine demands for land reform together with rural labour conditions (see Chapters 8, 2 and 4, in their order of relevance).

The lack of credit and savings for poor peasants and workers, on the one hand, and a steady decline in the state capacity to help them with credit provisioning, on the other, has given enhanced prominence to rural development NGOs in the area of micro-financing. In East Africa (namely, Tanzania, Kenya and Uganda), there has been a boom in NGOs and grassroots associations specialized in offering credits to the rural poor for crop production, livestock-raising and small-scale trading activities with an impact on rural production and social structures (Bazaara, Chapter 5). Similarly, in Senegal, decentralized savings and credit programmes have been developed by farmers' federations and NGOs as an essential tool in helping to make small family farms viable, especially as previously existent state credit institutions were hastily discarded (McKeon, Chapter 7). In Asia, Bangladesh has recurrently been cited as a prime example of a successful NGO engagement to increase the economic power of the rural poor – especially women – through micro-credit. Increasingly, many NGOs are themselves operating as moneylenders and business entrepreneurs using market logics and creating links between local traders and multinational business companies. Indeed, in some cases, the NGOs themselves have become business entities entering into exploitative relations with local population groups (Mannan, Chapter 9).

Price fluctuations of agricultural commodities, caused by speculations and monopoly of internal and external commercial interests and export dumping of agricultural products by rich countries, have manifestly remained one of the common themes of civil society mobilizations at various levels. They also indicate the typical governmental policy of attempting to keep the price of agricultural produce low for peasant producers in order to guarantee inexpensive food to urban areas (see McKeon, Chapter 7). In addition to this, institutional privatization and deregulation measures have meant reductions in agricultural support services, including elimination of a price guarantee. On the other hand, the price of agricultural inputs such as seeds, tools and fertilizers has tended to increase – at times provoking popular rural uprising, such as the fertilizer crisis in Bangladesh in the mid-1990s, which was caused by the shortage and price speculation of fertilizer following the deregulation of the institutional distribution system (Mannan, Chapter 9). While some NGOs (especially related to left-wing thinking) rallied behind the peasants' cause, many others tended to see the problem essentially as an erroneous implementation of privatization/deregulation measures.

Increased debt among small producers is another issue of concern among civil society organizations. In some cases, small producers are indebted as a consequence of the sudden and sharp reduction in the institutional support services provided to them, or economic unviability and fraud within the production/marketing organizations that they have been associated with (e.g., cooperatives), thereby giving the opportunity to civil society organizations to negotiate the question of debt repayment with local or national authorities (see the case of Senegal in Chapter 7). Others may indicate the processes that result in increased peasant indebtedness. For example, Veltmeyer, referring to Mexico and Peru, asserts that recent market-led rural development policies have produced a drastic deterioration in the market situation of small producers who, forced to sell their production at prices below their cost of production, have accrued enormous unpayable debts and, in many cases, have been pushed into bankruptcy. Indeed, he argues that, in Mexico, the problem of debt has been a galvanizing factor in prompting one of the largest mass movements in its recent history of land struggle by a million highly indebted independent family farms (see Chapter 4). Peasant indebtedness has become especially acute where market-led agrarian policies have been introduced as 'beneficiary' driving households to acquire long-term credit for the purchase of land (Ghimire, 2001: 134–63; see also Borras, Chapter 8). In seeking to elaborate this problem in the case of Colombia, Suhner argues that market-led agrarian reform measures have not only pushed the peasants into a rising debt trap, but also NGOs and peasant representative organizations are widely divided on the issue – although persistent civil society mobilization around this topic has also compelled the government to take at least some 'alleviation measures' (Suhner, Chapter 3).

Awareness-raising and social mobilization around market issues

Civil society groups commonly take up awareness-raising and social mobilization activities, although this may occur in different forms, the expected outcome possibly varying depending upon their organizational philosophy, societal base and links with other forces. First, there are CSOs that emphasize the need to promote awareness-raising on market conditions by providing useful information with the prime goal of helping poor rural producers to better design a market-oriented production system. This group comprises NGOs as well as business and private sector entities involved in the provision of micro-credit, extension services, technology and so forth and works in direct partnership with donor agencies and government institutions, as has been pointed out earlier. As such, they often have easy access to official media or resources in order to be able to communicate their approaches, plans and perspectives through other means (e.g., publications, press, organization of training programmes etc.).

Other groups of CSOs, on the other hand, consider it necessary to make rural producers and other marginalized groups more attentive to the issues of markets affecting their livelihoods. Their task is made somewhat easier as increasingly the political action of the rural poor is directed at economic power at the local level (Webster, Chapter 10). These groups recognize the value of the market, but are concerned that it is not automatically favouring the interests of poor workers and peasants, given global and national power structures and, at times, narrow business interests. Accordingly, poor workers and producers should have access to what is realistically feasible in terms of production options, prices, etc., but they may have limited contact with official media; and, at times, they might collaborate with the government to accentuate the negative impacts of trade barriers on Southern agricultural products. This sort of alliance also makes it possible for CSO groups to get involved in organizing adapted workshops and training programmes, such as innovative national seminars and training courses for farmers in Senegal surrounding the issues of unfair competition of Northern agricultural products and the destabilizing role of the World Trade Organization (WTO) negotiation processes for peasant production, food security and employment (McKeon, Chapter 7). More importantly, the political space created by decentralization, participatory development and electoral freedom is being increasingly used to facilitate debate on the consequences of market liberalization, in general, or impact of agricultural or rural economic development approaches and projects in specific contexts (see Veltmeyer, Chapter 4, for a discussion on Bolivia; Mannan, Chapter 9, on Bangladesh; and Suhner, Chapter 3, on Colombia).

An underlying goal of many of these consciousness-raising activities is obviously to try and put political pressure on the privileged elites, landowning classes and wealthier business groups for broad structural changes favouring the interests of marginalized rural population groups. But more radical CSOs tend to argue that activities merely revolved around meetings and training programmes within a restrained policy framework of government and donor agencies and were frequently promoted through licensed NGOs, which can scarcely change existing power relations, emphasizing that peasant associations, rural trade unions, peasant cooperatives and other types of broad-based representative organizations should be strengthened. These organizations should represent a sturdy power bloc capable of negotiating major issues of economic enhancement and political power. In particular, peasants' and workers' representative organizations should be potent actors in preventing exploitation by traders, agribusiness groups, elites etc. (See Webster, Chapter 10, on a highly favourable outcome for the rural poor of formal political interventions of the left government and social movements of peasants, women and agricultural cooperatives through improved bargaining position in key markets and regulation of markets in West Bengal, India; Suhner, Chapter 3, on popular mobilization against land dispossession by drug dealers in Colombia; Borras, Chapter 8, on the exploitation and manipulation by agribusiness groups; Mannan, Chapter 9, on the increased weight of traders.) Their participation in direct actions to acquire assets (e.g., land), a greater share of their produce (especially involving sharecropping and tenancy arrangements), legitimate prices for their produce, and so forth, are seen as especially crucial for political conscientization as well as gainful livelihood opportunities (see Medeiros, Chapter 2, on the action by the MST in this area). In some cases, this may evolve into major peasant rebellion or war (Wolf, 1969; Huizer, 2001). Some contemporary examples include the MST in Brazil, the Zapatistas in Mexico, Maoists in Nepal, and the Philippines' left-wing peasant insurgents. Equally, the need to create wider alliances with local and outside forces has constantly been highlighted so as to become more effective in their advocacy campaigns and articulating their demands and strategies for influencing public opinion and government and donor policies. The evidence emerging from various chapters in this book, promisingly, tends to indicate that there is an observable emergent movement towards linkages among diverse organizations involved in popular resistance, involving peasant farmers, indigenous communities and workers in many parts of the Third World on the damaging impacts of neoliberal policies (see Veltmeyer, Chapter 4; Medeiros, Chapter 2; Suhner, Chapter 3; Borras, Chapter 8). This process has extended an added voice to marginalized communities and groups and raised the visibility of their condition, especially through the effective use of new information and communication technologies. But what concrete impact CSOs' awareness and social mobilization campaigns have on the actual functioning of markets in specific contexts is still difficult to say.

Conclusion

Drawing information and insights from various countries and regions covered in individual chapters in this book as well as relevant secondary sources, an attempt has been made in the above discussion to disentangle the different civil society reactions to the market question in rural development, first, by classifying them in broad categories, and then cross-examining their stance and functioning with respect to market-led land redistribution, labour markets, dealing with uncertainty and vulnerability caused by market mechanisms and raising of social awareness and mobilization around market issues. The evidence seems to suggest that there are three clearly identifiable civil society perspectives: market advocates, market sceptics and market opponents, even though a given civil society group or organization within a particular perspective may, at times, be combining its activities covering more than just one viewpoint. In the usual course of events, it is the middle ground retained by market sceptics that tends to attract attention from the two conflicting extremes (i.e., pro-market and market opponents), with market sceptics themselves occasionally moving from one extreme to another.

The precise ability of these three perspectives to influence the debate on the market in rural or agricultural development is, however, less evident. As has been explained earlier, the pro-market perspective is mainly concerned with promoting market-based economic activities and welfare in rural areas and remains favourably enthusiastic with regard to putting into practice the dominant approaches and methods of economic development endorsed by the leading funding agencies. The market sceptic approach, on the other hand, emphasizes the negative consequences of uncontrolled neoliberal market economy and argues for broader 'safety nets' and increased popular participation in decision-making. The market opponent perspective sees the present economic and social order as essentially abysmal, thus advocating resistance and widespread mobilization. Despite the fact that these divisions persist and, at times, even widen, by and large, neoliberal market development has opened space for civil society action across all groups. Predictably there is a good deal of financial resources and political backing from donors and governments to implement market-oriented agricultural/rural development projects through a direct involvement of pro-market civil society organizations, while market sceptic and market opponent groups are able to become better mobilized, calling for, respectively, 'adapted reform' in the current economic liberalization policies, or its total 'defiance'.

One aspect that appears especially noteworthy, however, is that an increased and, at times, highly militant mobilization and campaigns by the anti-neoliberal civil society group have sometimes strengthened the positions and demands of the more 'reformist' standpoint – for example, increased protection and welfare of marginalized population groups, debt relief, microfinance, fair trade, greater community participation in crucial decision-making, protection of the local physical environment and so forth. In any event, governments and donor agencies would find it easier to negotiate with 'reformist' groups than with those that frequently call for the rejection of the current system of neoliberalization and prioritize instead the use of political pressure and mass mobilization. Yet this latter force cannot be dismissed altogether by governments and donor agencies because of their ability to mobilize widespread public support and attract media attention – hence the need to attest that they are taking some of the issues into consideration by supporting more moderate calls and propositions emerging from radical CSOs.

In considering the market issue in agricultural/rural development, the core questions emerging are: Should one conceive of the rural society as going back to a primitive form of existence with minimum exchange relations? Should it be kept where it is? Or, should it try and catch up, taking advantage of the market economy? None of the three civil society perspectives actually suggests taking a U-turn in the modernization process, renouncing the potential gain to be made through improvement in technology, knowledge base, education, health and so forth. Their prime concern, even for the market opponent civil society groups, is basically to see how some of the most detrimental consequences of the modernization process could be disposed of. But how to go about this is not always clear. In particular, the extent to which it considers working inside the system has permanently proved to be an awkward question in civil society movements.

In this regard, one aspect that seems quite manifest is that by trying to remain outside the debate on the existing as well as the potential role of the market is not only providing the Bretton Woods, WTO, United Nations, bilateral donor agencies and associated intelligentsia with a free hand in fixing a (market-based) development agenda of their liking, but also making it highly problematical for civil society groups to exploit certain real possibilities. For example, the importance of cooperative ideals and projects is not sufficiently defended despite their highly established relevance in agricultural as well as urban economies. Even when there is international donor aversion to cooperative ideas, civil society groups could attempt to take progressive elements of governments and foreign funding on their side to harness different possibilities. In general, there have been no or few attempts to promote membership-based economic activities or enterprises among civil society organizations, thereby allowing them to stay autonomous from donor or government encroachment. In particular, a large number of civil society groups tend to stay away from developing and running commercial enterprises that would not only ensure their own economic base but also the economic interests of wider social groups that they are seeking to represent. It is clear that not all commercial activities need to be based on exploitative terms.

Second, one way of challenging the omnipotence of the market is to endeavour to make the rural population socially aware of the various possibilities of making the most of what is within their reach by way of achieving autonomous and self-help-oriented development. In particular, civil society groups could devise educational and awareness measures seeking to change the mindset that rural societies should mechanically follow an urbanized lifestyle and consumption behaviour. With less demand for cash for outside goods and development, the consolidation of a more solid household self-subsistence economic base would make rural living less vulnerable to market forces. This is obviously not meant to suggest that rural producers and workers should just make ends meet or live a 'primitive existence' without enjoying a higher standard of living. Indeed, any attempt to build an inward-oriented sustainable economy in rural areas must go hand in hand with improved provisioning in health, education and other vital socioeconomic services.

In all cases, it is plain that without forceful and unrelenting social mobilization within civil society there would be little prospect for giving added voice to peasant producers and workers as well as raising the visibility of their conditions and indicating potential solutions. Perhaps it is not in anyone's capacity to stop the market, but concerted efforts by more progressive civil society forces can certainly help to contest the hegemony of the 'unique thinking' and practice of neoliberal market policies, as has been discussed above. But how civil society organizations could prove advantageous for autonomous rural development, with improved terms of participation and enhancement of livelihoods of social groups hitherto excluded in diverse contexts, is still a vast and recalcitrant area that the present book can claim to address only partially.

Notes

* I am highly indebted to Anita Tombez for bibliographical control and communications with individual authors.

1. *The Penguin Dictionary of Economics* defines 'market' as 'the fundamental forces of supply and demand' (Bannock et al., 1981: 297). This mainstream neoclassical definition has been criticized on numerous grounds. First, there is no single market, but various sorts of markets depending upon the goods and services concerned, as

well as whether they are local, national or global markets. Second, even mainstream economists commonly recognize that the forces of demand–supply do not always work perfectly, given the problems of monopoly, externalities, lack of relevant information and that some public goods cannot be supplied by markets (*The Economist*, 17 February 1996: 66–7). Third, prices, profit and private property (which are considered vital ingredients of market economics) are intimately tied to power relations, interest groups and political institutions (cf. UNRISD, 2000: 12; Stiglitz, 2002: 139; Webster, Chapter 10). Finally, even ardent neoliberalists such as Soros now admit that 'markets are good at creating wealth but are not designed to take care of other social needs' (Soros, 2002: 5), thus they can be a source of 'increasing inequality and poverty' (UNDP, 1993: 30). A detailed explanation of the meaning and structure of markets in different contexts is neither necessary nor plausible in the present work. But some of these aspects have been brought up and analysed in relation to the dynamics in rural/agricultural economies and livelihoods later in this and several other chapters.

2. 'Civil society' is increasingly a catchphrase, but it is also hugely contested. Generally, non-state and non-market associative forces are seen to be civil society. Yet, if carefully examined, progressive interest groups within the state, such as public sector organizations, may prove resilient in demanding greater protection of welfare regimes; and, in any event, a strong and democratic state would help to facilitate the arenas in which civil society organizations can operate. Similarly, not all forces participating in the market would necessarily be unscrupulous. For example, NGOs operating shops and commercial outlets using 'fair-trade' principles could attest to being an important source of improved wages, prices and working conditions for some marginalized working population groups in urban and rural areas. In this book, socio-professional organizations and advocacy movements, such as civil and human rights groups, trade unions, NGOs and community voluntary organizations, environmental foundations, associations of peasants and indigenous peoples, academic centres and political parties that seek to promote peoples' rights, better living conditions and wider social awareness, are viewed as civil society. Even here a certain degree of care must be taken as day-to-day functioning of some of these organizations may not be fully democratic and they often remain vulnerable to manipulation by powerful elites, governments and donor agencies. It should also be noted that not all civil society organizations are truly 'civil' as some of them may be influenced by anti-social structures and ideologies (xenophobia, religious and ethnic extremism, etc.); and there are organizations in civil society which clearly represent a repressive and exploitative power structure, such as large landowners' associations, paramilitary forces, rich merchants and traders and agro-industrial groups. This problematic has been emphasized in several of the contributions to this book, highlighting civil society as more of a political space that exists between the state and its citizens, as well as opposing international unequal power relations.

3. The citation is taken from the French version of his book which reads as 'plus le marché est vaste, plus les possibilités de spécialisation sont importantes', so exact words may be different from his original writing in English.

4. The examples mentioned under all four categories of civil society movements are cited by Desai and Said and should not be regarded as the present author's stance.

5. See http://www.mstbrazil.org/EconomicModel.html

6. A study on Egypt, for example, suggests that in order to acquire one feddan (0.42 ha) of land, an adult male landless worker needed to accumulate all his

daily earnings for a period of 39 years, without spending anything on living costs (El-Ghonemy, 1999).

References

Bannock, Graham, R. E. Baxter and Ray Rees (1981) *The Penguin Dictionary of Economics*. Harmondsworth, Middlesex: Penguin Books.

Barraclough, S. and D. Moss (1999) *Toward Greater Food Security in Central America Following Hurricane Mitch: Rethinking Sustainable Rural Development Priorities*, a report commissioned by Oxfam America. Washington, DC.

Bello, Walden (2002) *Deglobalization: Ideas for a New World Economy*. London and New York: Zed Books.

Bernstein, Henry, Ben Crow, Maureen Mackintosh and Charlotte Martin (eds) (1990) *The Food Question*. London: Earthscan Publications.

Cassen, Bernard (1997) 'Pour sauver la société', *Le monde diplomatique*, May.

Desai, Meghnad and Yahia Said (2001) 'The new anti-capitalist movement: money and global civil society', in Helmut Anheier, Marlies Glasius and Marry Kaldor (eds), *Global Civil Society 2001*. Oxford: Oxford University Press.

The Economist (1996) 'State and market', 17 February.

El-Ghonemy, M. R. (1999) *The Political Economy of Market-Based Land Reform*, Discussion Paper No. 104. Geneva: UNRISD.

Food and Agriculture Organization of the United Nations (FAO) (undated) *Agricultural Marketing in FAO: Concepts, Policies and Service*. http://www.fao.org/waicent/faoinfo/agricult/ags/AGSM/program.htm

George, Susan (2001) 'The neo-liberal gospel', *South Bulletin 06*, 15 February, pp. 6–11. http://www.southcentre.org/info/southbulletin/bulletin06/bulletin6.pdf

Ghimire, K. B. (2001) 'Peasants' pursuit of outside alliances and legal support in the process of land reform', in K. B. Ghimire (ed.), *Land Reform and Peasant Livelihoods*. London: ITDG Publishing.

Ghimire, K. B. (2002a) 'Changing rural power structures through land tenure reforms: the current dismal role of international organizations', *Canadian Journal of Development Studies*, Vol. 23, No. 2.

Ghimire, K. B. (2002b) 'Social movements and marginalized rural youth in Brazil, Egypt and Nepal', *The Journal of Peasant Studies*, Vol. 30, No. 1, October.

Glover, David and Ken Kusterer (1990) *Small Farmers, Big Business*. Basingstoke: Macmillan.

Hagen, Everett (1962) *On the Theory of Social Change*. Illinois: Dorsey Press.

Huizer, Gerrit (2001) 'Peasant mobilization for land reform: historical case studies and theoretical considerations', in K. B. Ghimire (ed.), *Land Reform and Peasant Livelihoods*. London: ITDG Publishing.

International Fund for Agricultural Development (IFAD) (2001) *Rural Poverty Report 2001 – The Challenge of Ending Rural Poverty*. Oxford: Oxford University Press.

International Labour Organization (ILO) (2000) *Sustainable Agriculture in a Globalized Economy*. Geneva: ILO.

Jonquières, Guy de (1997) 'Des réformes qui ne sont pas allées assez loin', *Le monde diplomatique*, May.

Kilusang Magbubukid ng Pilipinas (KMP) (2000) *The World Bank's Market-Assisted Land Reform: Obstacles to Rural Justice*. Quezon City: KMP.

Lewis, W. A. (1963) *La théorie de la croissance économique*. Paris: Payot.

Mackintosh, Maureen (1990) 'Abstract markets and real needs', in Henry Bernstein, Ben Crow, Maureen Mackintosh and Charlotte Martin (eds), *The Food Question*. London: Earthscan Publications.

Moore, Jr., Barrington (1981) *Social Origins of Dictatorship and Democracy: Lord and Peasant in the Making of the Modern World*. Harmondsworth, Middlesex: Penguin Books.

Moore Lappé, F. and J. Collins (1977) *Food First: Beyond the Myth of Scarcity*. Boston: Houghton Mifflin.

Morss, Elliot, John Hatch, Donald Mickelwait and Charles Sweet (1976) *Strategies for Small Farmers Development*, Vol. I. Boulder: Westview Press.

Mosher, A. T. (1966) *Getting Agriculture Moving: Essentials for Development and Modernization*. New York and London: Praeger Publishers.

Moyo, Sam, Blair Rutherford and Dede Amanor-Wilks (2000) 'Land reform and changing social relations for farm workers in Zimbabwe', *Review of African Political Economy*, Vol. 27, No. 84, June, pp. 181–202.

Movimento dos Trabalhadores Rurais Sem Terra (MST). http://www.mstbrazil.org/economicmodel.html

Myrdal, Gunnar (1968) *Asian Drama: an Inquiry into the Poverty of Nations*, Vol. II. New York: Pantheon.

Pereira, A. (1992) 'Agrarian reform and the Rural Workers' Union of the Pernambuco Sugar Zone, Brazil 1985–1988', *The Journal of Developing Areas*, January.

Polanyi, Karl (2001) *The Great Transformation: the Political and Economic Origins of Our Time*. Boston: Beacon Press.

Soros, George (2002) *George Soros on Globalization*. New York: Public Affairs.

Stavenhagen, R. (1981) 'Changing functions of the community in underdeveloped countries', in Henry Bernstein (ed.), *Underdevelopment and Development*. Harmondsworth, Middlesex: Penguin Books.

Stiglitz, J. E. (2002) *Globalization and Its Discontents*. London: Allen Lane.

United Nations Development Programme (UNDP) (1993) *Human Development Report 1993*. New York and Oxford: Oxford University Press.

United Nations Research Institute for Social Development (UNRISD) (2000) *Visible Hands*. Geneva: UNRISD.

Via Campesina (2001) 'Our world is not for sale', *2001 Via Campesina Declaration on Food Sovereignty*. http://www.voiceoftheturtle.org/library/2001-11-1%20Peoples%20foodsovereignty-en.htm

Wolf, Eric (1969) *Peasant Wars of the Twentieth Century*. New York: Harper and Row.

World Bank (2001) *World Development Report 2002*. Washington, DC: World Bank.

2

Social Movements, the State and the Experience of Market-led Agrarian Reform in Brazil[1]

Leonilde Servolo de Medeiros

Introduction

The theme of agrarian reform has been present in Brazilian political debate, in a more or less intense fashion, at least since the beginning of the twentieth century, although over time it has assumed different forms and meanings. Its continual development has been mainly achieved through the actions of significant contingents of rural workers who have placed themselves, and made themselves recognized, in the public sphere through the struggle for land.

During the last forty years, the Brazilian countryside has been technologically modernized, agro-industry has become strengthened, the rural population has dramatically declined in relation to the urban, financial capital has also become orientated towards investments in land, strengthening even further the alliance between capital and landownership, new interests have been created and new actors have emerged from the struggle for land. The utopias that foresaw a socialist society have entered into crisis, obliging left-wing movements to rethink their demands and the meaning of their struggles. Nevertheless, none of these profound changes has excluded the demand for agrarian reform from political debate. It has not disappeared from the agenda of either organizations of rural workers or the civic entities which give them support. The dream of access to land continues to feed the imagination not just of recently evicted workers, but also, to the surprise of many researchers, of workers who are already part of the labour market, whether rural or urban, as has been shown in various recent episodes of occupation of land.

In the 1990s, the discussion about rural poverty, the growing importance of environmental questions and, especially, the intensification of land occupations has once again brought the land question to the fore. More recently, at the dawn of the twenty-first century, influenced by the policy of the World

Bank, a controversy has emerged about the possibility of land distribution using market mechanisms.

In this chapter, first we will present a short historical outline of Brazilian land policy, the way in which the debate about agrarian reform has developed and its inheritance. The next step will be to outline the context in which the proposal for access to land through market mechanisms emerged. Having done this, the reactions from civil society to the proposal and the main initiatives currently being undertaken will be discussed.

Throughout the chapter we will highlight the growing importance that connections between workers' unions and non-governmental organizations are gaining, both at the national and international level, in a typical example of what several authors have pointed to as constituting a global public sphere, where networks of social movements 'tend to connect subjects from different levels, from the most local to the most global' (Scherer-Warren, 1999: 17).

The agrarian reform debate in Brazil

The concentration of landownership and the exclusion of rural workers from access to land in Brazil has historical roots, originating in the colonial period, with the creation of an inequality of rights between landowners and rural workers, and a culture based on personal relationships, exchange of favours and dependency relationships (Martins, 1981). This has been consolidated in Brazilian law over time; the 1850 Land Law, the Republican Constitution of 1891, and the 1917 Civil Code all guaranteed the absolute nature of the right of ownership.

When the issue of agrarian reform entered the political agenda, it had to question this concept of property. In the first decades of the twentieth century, parts of the *tenentista*[2] movement spoke of the need for agrarian reform as essential to democratize the Brazilian political process, since this would reduce the power of the large landholders and their capacity to marshal votes. Politically defeated, all that remained of their proposals were government initiatives such as projects for the colonization of public lands, especially in the frontier regions, during the Estado Novo (a period of dictatorship which lasted from 1937–45). Rural workers remained marginal to the labour rights then guaranteed to urban workers. Nor was access to land, in the form of *arrendamento* and *parceria*,[3] regulated, rather, this was left to the mercy of the rules imposed by custom and the power of the large landholders.

Following the post-war redemocratization, the pressure of the reduced communist bloc managed to get the concept that 'the use of property is subordinate to the social good' (art. 147) written into the new Constitution, approved in 1947. Since then, the debate about the meaning, the limits and the potential of agrarian reform has centred on the question of the social function of property.

Until this time, although recurrent, land conflicts were fragmented and scattered. *Posseiros* (squatters) resisted in isolation the attempts of landholders, or their agents, to evict them to expand the agricultural frontier. *Colonos* and *moradores* questioned the rules of their contracts.[4] The rules of *arrendamento* and *parceria* also stopped being seen as 'normal' by rural workers (high percentages to be paid to the landholder; the obligation to leave the area after three years of use, leaving it with pasture; the possibility of the land being taken back at any moment, without any compensation for planting or improvements). These situations came to be seen as unfair, creating discontent and revolt (Moore Jr., 1987).

In the 1950s, the different forms of conflict which existed in the Brazilian countryside began to be unified through a common language, through the mediation of the Brazilian Communist Party (PCB), leading to the consolidation of the demand for labour rights and for changes in the landholding structure. For the Communist Party, agrarian reform was one of the necessary steps in a set of transformations through which the country had to pass in the 'democratic bourgeois revolution' stage. Central to this concept was the idea that the Brazilian countryside was marked by the existence of feudal residues (forms of personal domination, the requirement that workers paid for the use of land etc.), which prevented the free development of productive forces. From this viewpoint, an enormous range of social categories came to be referred to politically as 'the exploited masses of the countryside', or, more commonly, *peasants*. Landholders, irrespective of the type of product realized (coffee, sugarcane, cotton, cocoa, livestock etc.), or land use (raising of crops for export or for the internal market, livestock raising, and/or speculation), were all classified as *latifundiários* (large landowners) and seen as the main force to be combated.

The actions of the PCB in the countryside were aimed, on the one hand, at leading the more immediate struggles (better salaries, labour rights, supporting resistance on the land, demands for longer periods or the guarantee of continuity and the reduction of the costs of *arrendamento* and *parceria* contracts, the reduction of taxes and freight charges). On the other, it sought to stimulate the struggle for agrarian reform, which implied more profound transformations and broader political alliances. To achieve this, it was believed that the support of industrial segments, especially the so-called 'national bourgeoisie', could be counted on.

In the same context, and in opposition to the proposal defended by the PCB, other concepts of agrarian reform emerged. One of these had as its spokesperson the most important leader of the Ligas Camponesas de Pernambuco (the Peasant Leagues of Pernambuco), Francisco Julião, who believed that agrarian reform, by breaking the power of the *latifundiários* and introducing the peasant as a vital political actor, would constitute the first step in a socialist revolution in the country. Therefore, it would not be possible to count on the support of any part of the bourgeoisie for this struggle.

Disputing space with these forces, the Catholic Church took its position from the values and idea which were part of the Catholic tradition (shown, for example, in the defence of the small rural landholder as the basis of family stability), which, however, had suffered from the impact of the intensification of urbanization and import-substitute industrialization in the 1940s and 1950s. The Church was also influenced by nationalism and the idea of development characteristic of this period (Paiva, 1985: 14). It began to denounce the living conditions of rural workers and to advocate the need for pacific agrarian reform, through expropriations with fair compensation. From this perspective, it began to dispute the political leadership of rural workers, stimulating the creation of trade unions and the demand for social and labour rights (Carvalho, 1985).

The reasons for the vitality which the 'agrarian reform' banner gained in Brazil in the 1950s and 1960s can also be explained by more general Brazilian and Latin American political questions, marked by the Cold War context and the debate about the need to promote the economic development in the region, which signified stimulating industry and eliminating the structural obstacle to development represented by agriculture based on large landholdings with low levels of technological incorporation. It is important to bear in mind that the Cuban revolution had strong repercussions in Latin America and in Brazil in particular, whether being seen by significant countryside leadership groups as an example to be followed (such as Francisco Julião of the Peasant League), or, to the contrary, as a warning to the dominant sectors about the possible risks implied in the persistence of the existing forms of exploitation and misery. One of the political results of this process was the constitution of the Alliance for Progress, established on the initiative of the United States government, which encouraged Latin American governments to carry out preventative programmes of agrarian reform, in order to eliminate the concentration of landownership and to create a rural middle class, seen as a barrier against the penetration of communist ideas.

It was in this context that the meaning of some of the central concepts of the debate became politically established, defining the content of keywords, thereby making them into important references, still relevant even now. The most significant of these keywords is perhaps *latifúndio*, which became the equivalent not just of large holdings, technological backwardness and lack of productivity, but also the synonym for relations of power, oppression and the absence of rights (Palmeira, 1968).

Notwithstanding the international pressure, the land struggles developing throughout the country and the apparent consensus about the need for transformations in landownership, all the different projects for agrarian reform presented to the National Congress, which had a variety of political leanings, were successively defeated. The political ability of the large landholders was decisive in achieving this, since they were able to count on the support of the representatives of industry in their opposition to attempts to 'subvert' the 'sacred right of property'.

The institutional rupture of 1964, through the military coup, stifled the emerging demands of rural workers, but, to some extent, incorporated the criticism of the *latifundiários* coming from many social sectors. Shortly after the coup, the same National Congress which had blocked dozens of projects for agrarian reform approved a constitutional amendment which permitted payment for expropriated land with government bonds and suspended the requirement that the compensation be paid prior to the expropriation. The Land Statutes were also approved, thereby creating a legal space to make transformation in the landholding structure viable.

The Land Statutes classified rural properties as: smallholdings (holdings inferior to one rural land unit,[5] which are, therefore, incapable by definition of providing subsistence to the producer and his family); *latifúndios* by use (with a area between 1 and 600 rural land units, characterized by levels of use inferior to the regional average); *latifúndios* by size (with an area greater than 600 rural land units, independent of the type and characteristics of the production); and enterprises (holdings between 1 and 600 land units, characterized by a specific level of land use, rational exploitation, compliance with labour legislation and the preservation of natural resources). The objective of agrarian reform was the gradual extinction of smallholdings and *latifúndios*, considered to be sources of social tension in the countryside. The enterprise, which could be a family enterprise, became the ideal model of landholding. The way *latifúndios* would be replaced by enterprises was through expropriation (only in cases of social tension), progressive taxation and technical and economic assistance for production.

Through the Land Statutes some of the terms which had been politicized in the debate in the 1960s gained the status of legal categories, with relatively precise definitions in terms of area, the form and level of use, the nature of labour relations etc. This classification crystallized the stigma given both to *latifúndios* and smallholdings. The state had thus absorbed the demands which had appeared and controlled them, placing the demand for land within the parameters of a modernized agriculture capable of meeting the requirements of what was then considered as development.

Nevertheless, in the rearrangement of political forces that followed the coup, the idea of encouraging rural enterprises became restricted to supporting the technological modernization of large landholdings, through fiscal incentives and cheap and plentiful credit (Delgado, 1985). Land expropriations were ruled out, as was the modernization of labour relations. However, along with the transformations that were successful (increase of productivity, agricultural industrialization, a dramatic reduction in the rural population compared to the urban, the expansion of the agricultural frontier), the demand for land remained. In the context of intense repression, it was stifled, but did not cease to exist, fed by conflicts which occurred in a dispersed and isolated manner, especially in the Amazon region, where large tracts of lands were transferred through a variety of public policy mechanisms to private landowners, notably large enterprises from the industrial and financial sectors, which began to evict the workers who were living there as *posseiros* (squatters).

From the political point of view, the struggle found support in two currents of social thought: the left-wing communist tradition and that of the Catholic Church. Guided by this tradition and via rural trade unionism, a particular version of the Land Statutes was produced, centred on the demand for the expropriation of the areas of conflict.

Despite the repression, various trade unions influenced by the Catholic Church avoided state intervention (Palmeira, 1985). From this core a national trade union network was formed, gaining strength during the 1970s. During this period the main activity of CONTAG (Confederação Nacional dos Trabalhadores na Agricultura – the National Confederation of Agricultural Workers) was to bring together a group of previously dispersed and isolated unions, linked by common concepts whose central axis was the demand for labour rights and agrarian reform. The enormous variety of situations and the fact that many unions had been stimulated by forces linked to local powers resulted in the creation of a permanent tension throughout the 'links' of this network (unions and federations), between the weight of local political forces which tended to pull unions into the already existing mesh of different forms of domination, and the actions of CONTAG itself, which, through its campaign for already recognized rights, sought to create another network of relations and counterbalance the weight of local power.

At the end of the 1970s and the beginning of the 1980s, CONTAG became an important national reference through its campaign for rights that were already recognized by law but not respected. If its actions were inefficient in the sense of influencing the land policy of the military governments, it did play an important role in the socialization among rural workers of the demand for agrarian reform and the knowledge of the law which defined its shape, keeping the critique of the *latifúndio* alive. Through the actions of CONTAG, the question of the expropriation of *latifúndio* and of areas of conflict became the kernel of the demand for agrarian reform, resulting in it becoming, in a progressive manner, socially translated and understood in terms of the Land Statutes.

At the same time, during the 1970s, influenced by those parts of the Catholic Church linked to liberation theology, criticisms of CONTAG grew, whose mode of action was considered 'welfarist' and non-mobilizing. In 1975, the CPT (Comissão Pastoral da Terra – Pastoral Land Commission) was established, creating the conditions for the consolidation of a powerful network of influence. The CPT gave theological legitimacy to the emerging demands and to acts of resistance, provided training through the actions of pastoral agents and made space and infrastructure available for meetings and the creation of organizations, in a period in which the very act of meeting was considered suspect by the military regime (Novaes, 1997).

As a result, trade union 'oppositions' emerged, seeking to implement new forms of trade union action based on the mobilization of workers. These 'oppositions' played a leading role in most of the conflicts which emerged at the end of the 1970s and the beginning of the 1980s. The 'oppositions' established connections with the new networks, creating links with the so-called 'new trade unionism' developing in urban areas, especially the most industrialized part of São Paulo, as well as with the central questions of national political struggles (liberty and trade union autonomy, redemocratization, direct elections etc.). In 1983, when the CUT (Central Única dos Trabalhadores – Central Workers Union) was established, the presence of the 'opposition' rural trade unions was notable, creating a new area of conflict with CONTAG, which had aligned itself with another trade union confederation created at that time, the CONCLAT (Conferência Nacional das Classes Trabalhadoras – the National Conference of the Working Classes).

At this moment, conflicts multiplied and new actors emerged, including among others: the 'dam victims' (small landholders, squatters, leaseholders and *parceiros* who had lost their land due to the construction of large hydroelectric power stations to increase the energy generated for urban centres); *seringueiros* (rubber tappers) from the state of Acre, who resisted the destruction of the native rubber tree plantations and their substitution by pasture and the consequent destabilization of their way of living; and 'small producers', especially in the south of the country, who were excluded from the benefits of modernization, had either lost their land or believed that their children would have access to it only with difficulty, and who would create the group that would conform to the political identity of 'the landless' (Grzybowski, 1987; Medeiros, 1989).

In addition, other demands began to emerge, such as better prices for products and for agricultural credit among those small producers who had managed to advance technologically, as well as confrontations between these modernized segments and agro-industries over the prices for the products they supplied (chicken, pork, tobacco, grapes) and the conditions established in the 'integrated production' contracts. Rural employees, through mobilizations and strikes, showed the public the other side of modernization: precarious living and working conditions related to seasonal employment, low salaries, long working hours, lack of professional registration and the consequent absence of basic labour rights.

Within this scenario of expanding conflict, the question of agrarian reform was once again brought to the fore. Rural trade unionism, with its hegemony in CONTAG, made agrarian reform one of the principal demands of its Third National Congress held in 1979. From then on, it began to hold public events calling for the expropriation of land areas under conflict.

At the same time, independent of the trade union movement, land occupations began, forming the embryo of what would in 1984 be formally founded as the MST (Movimento dos Trabalhadores Rurais sem Terra – Movement of Landless Rural Workers). Land occupations appeared to be an alternative to pressurize the state, thereby creating a political front and attracting the attention of public opinion. Starting in Rio Grande do Sul at the end of the 1970s, they rapidly began to occur in Santa Catarina, Paraná, São Paulo and Mato Grosso do Sul, becoming the principal form of the struggle for land, and, even more than this, the central element in the creation of a political identity. Organizing principles developed around land occupation, based on the regimentation of entire families (and not just individuals), without any formal affiliation or association process, based rather on adherence and participation, and could begin at any time in any place and involve people from a wide variety of backgrounds, including those without any rural connections (Caldart, 2000).

This situation involved the strengthening of civil society, marked not just by the appearance of new demands and the reworking of already existing ones, but also by the multiplication of workers' organizations and support groups, strengthening the potential for action. Specifically in relation to the land question non-governmental organizations gained visibility. Through their actions these groups supported training programmes for rural workers and initiated support campaigns, such as the case of the National Campaign for Agrarian Reform.

The widespread popular mobilizations, both rural and urban, which took place at the end of the military regime and the beginning of the New Republic rekindled expectations for agrarian reform. At first, the Brazilian state absorbed the theme, but was shortly afterwards caught up in the contradictions generated by this commitment. The trajectory of the Proposal for a National Agrarian Reform Plan (PNRA) during 1985, and the Constituent process in 1987/88, revealed the continued force of powers which had previously appeared weakened by urban and industrial growth and demonstrated, both for the actors involved and researchers in the area, the complexity of forces which had emerged inside the different elements of the state.

The PNRA, the preparation of which had started at the beginning of the New Republic and which had counted on the active participation of well-known intellectual defenders of agrarian reformers as well as organizers and officials of rural trade unions, was symbolically presented to the public during the Fourth National Congress of Rural Workers, held by CONTAG in May 1985. In this document, agrarian reform appeared as one of the main priorities of the new government. Expropriation for the social interest was seen as the most important means to obtain land. Compensation would be paid on the basis of the value declared for the purposes of the rural land tax. Since this price was known to be below the market price, the Proposal explicitly assumed that expropriation involved the penalization of large landholders who had not used their land for a social purpose. Colonization, land regularization and mechanisms of taxation, which until then had been presented by some of the forces present in the political debate as alternatives to the obtaining of land, now appeared as complementary mechanisms. The Plan proposed to settle, within a period of fifteen years, seven million rural workers with either very little or no land, out of an estimated number of ten and a half million. The remainder would be used in the commercial agricultural sector as employees. Underlying the Proposal was the idea that this shrinkage in the labour market would increase salaries and improve living and working conditions in the commercial agricultural sector. The Proposal also salvaged the idea, first presented in the Land Statutes, of the selection of priority areas for agrarian reform. In other words, it raised the possibility of land transformation in broader areas, rather than just interventions in individual conflicts.

Although it brought the possibilities for the expropriation that existed in the Land Statutes as far as they could go, the Proposal ran into resistance on different fronts. In relation to the representative forces of the rural social movements, it was supported by CONTAG, but opposed by the MST, which considered it timid and based on laws created during the military regime, and by the CUT, which denounced it as being the rural version of the 'social pact' proposed in various circumstances by the Sarney government. In this way, the Proposal ended up rapidly polarizing the main workers' representative organizations, which began to dispute distinct concepts and the priority of interests involved in the struggle for land.

The most vigorous opposition to the Proposal came from the representatives of landowners who, a month after its launch, held a national congress in Brasilia and created a new organization to represent themselves: the UDR (União Democrática Ruralista – Democratic Rural Union), which began to urge its members to use force to combat land occupations. It began to dispute power with the existing employer organizations, especially the CNA (Confederação Nacional da Agricultura – National Confederation of Agriculture) and the SRB (Sociedade Rural Brasileira – Brazilian Rural Society), and in a short space of time the new organization was able to gain space in the means of communication and spokespersons in the National Congress, as well as to polarize the struggle against the Proposal (Bruno, 1997).

The criticisms of the PNRA made by employer/landowner groups emphasized negotiation with landholders as a substitute for expropriation, eliminating the punitive connotation which expropriations had been given in the original Proposal. There was also controversy over the definition of what a 'productive' (and therefore not subject to expropriation) property was, so that in the final version of the PNRA (and subsequent documentation), all rural property, irrespective of whether it was a *latifúndio*, by use or size, once it was 'productive', was to be preserved.[6] Thus, the tendency to reduce social function to productivity indices was established, thereby relegating the importance of the other elements contributing to its definition.[7] The interpretation contained in the Land Statutes in relation to those properties which had high proportions of *arrendatários* or *parceiros* was thus reversed.

Now, once the landholders complied with the legal principles that regulated contracts, no expropriations could occur. Conditions were thereby created for the re-emergence of these forms of land exploitation, which for a long time had shown themselves to create conflict and which were always marked by predatory use and owner absenteeism, traits characteristic of what until then had been considered as *latifúndio*. The future development of this was the attempt during the Collor de Melo government (1990–2) to institutionalize grants for *arrendamento* and *parceria* as an alternative means of access for workers to land. Although this proposal was not implemented, it nevertheless marked the introduction of market mechanisms as a means of access to land. Another aspect was the raising once again of the question of the use of public land, increasing the tendency not to give political weight to expropriations. A large part of this debate took place outside of the Ministry of Agrarian Reform and Development (MIRAD) and the Instituto Nacional de Colonização e Reforma Agrária (INCRA), the institutions responsible for agrarian reform, involving instead the Chief of Staff of the President of the Republic and the military ministers, demonstrating the persistence of the linkage to national security that the agrarian question had gained in the military regime and which it could not shake off during the New Republic.

Following the defeat of the PNRA, the battle to institutionalize channels which would permit the achievement of significant transformations in the landholding structure took place in the National Constituent Assembly. Despite strong popular pressure for the introduction of measures which would allow widescale agrarian reform, the interests linked to landownership closed ranks, expanding their influence in the National Congress through the creation of the 'Rural Bloc', and managed to prevent this.

The results were contradictory. Agrarian reform is one of the subjects of the chapter entitled 'Economic and Social Order'. Here, it was stated that property had to fulfil its social function (art. 5, XXIII), with the definition of social function being inspired by the Land Statutes (rational use, adequate use of the available natural resources and the preservation of the environment, observance of labour relations and exploitation laws which favour the welfare of landholders and workers). Nonetheless, this did not prevent the inclusion in the Constitution of a set of mechanisms blocking the possibility of agrarian reform as defended by the representative organizations of rural workers. These included the disposition that expropriations could only take place after fair compensation had been paid in TDA (Títulos da Dívida Agrária – Agrarian Bonds), with a clause preserving their real value, redeemable in up to twenty years, after the second year, thereby even further consolidating the tendency that had begun in the 1970s of taking market values as the basis for land values.[8] The expropriation of small and medium-sized holdings (less than fifteen fiscal units),[9] as well as productive property, thus became untenable.

The regulations governing the part of the Constitution related to the land question were drawn up almost five years later. Moreover, the raising of the issue led to a new parliamentary battle, resulting in the revival of the 'Rural Bloc', which had initially been formed in the period of the Constituent. The Agrarian Law, as Law no. 8629 of 25/02/93 is better known, allowed for the expropriation of landholdings that did not fulfil their social function. The constitutional criteria for the definition of social function were maintained. In addition, the preferential use of public lands (owned by the Union, states, or municipalities) was now to be included in agrarian reform measures. Several controversial points remained, resulting in expropriations becoming subject to judicial proceedings. The most significant of these was related to the tension that existed between the requirements necessary to fulfil the social function of ownership and the fact that productive land could not be expropriated. Moreover, to the contrary of expropriations for public use, where the owner could only go to court over the value of the compensation, in the case of land expropriated for agrarian reform, the landowner could contest the expropriation itself in court.

With expropriations tending to become more difficult, something which had been emerging since the launch of the PNRA, more systematic alternatives for access to land began to be drawn up. The discussion of the importance of the creation of grants for *arrendamento* and *parceria* and the regulation of land purchases had begun in the Collor de Melo government.[10] On the other hand, the pressure of social movements and the absence of mechanisms for intervening in the agrarian question during the period immediately following the ratification of the Constitution led state governments to intensify their actions in the area, resorting to whatever means were available to obtain land to alleviate spreading conflicts, such as expropriation for public use (therefore, involving a cash payment), the use of state land, the purchase of property and the creation of experimental farms.[11]

In this scenario, the settlement of rural workers and the manner of dealing with land conflicts (negotiations/repression) became important political weapons used by different state government in political disputes. The debate on agrarian reform grew again and, after the approval of the Agrarian Law, a new cycle of demands for land and occupations was unleashed. In the new post-impeachment (of Collor) context, during the short government of Itamar Franco, the federal government recommenced expropriations, in parallel with the opening of dialogue with those demanding land. In addition, individuals with a background in social movements were nominated to the leadership of INCRA.

Agrarian reform through the market: political debates and outcomes

The proposal for market-led agrarian reform emerged in Brazil in the context, from the national point of view, of the intensification of land occupations, but it was also directly linked to the reformulation of the World

Bank's policies, which since the middle of the 1970s had been advocating some general principles, such as the recognition of the importance of family holdings in terms of efficiency and equity; the need to stimulate markets to facilitate the transfer of land to more efficient users; and the importance of an equal distribution of goods and redistributive agrarian reforms (Sauer, undated).

At the beginning of Fernando Henrique Cardoso's first presidential mandate, in 1995, in the face of controversies about the economic stabilization policy and the fight against inflation (the Real Plan), the agrarian question appeared to have lost its place in political debate. The success of the Real Plan led to a wave of popularity for the president and there appeared to be no popular opposition to the government. However, two facts altered this picture. One was extreme police violence against rural workers in events that came to be known as the 'massacres' of Corumbiara (Rondônia) and Eldorado de Carajás (Pará).[12] The second was the recommencing of land occupations, not just by MST, but also by a number of trade unions and worker federations linked to CONTAG, especially in Minas Gerais, Goiás and in the sugarcane region in the northeast, an area where economic crisis and the closure of traditional sugar mills had left thousands of sugarcane harvesters unemployed.

These events once again put the agrarian question into the media headlines and into the centre of the political debate, leading the new government to create the Extraordinary Ministerial Office for Land Policy.[13] With this measure the agrarian question escaped the jurisdiction of the Ministry of Agriculture, an area traditionally controlled by large rural entrepreneurs, and was now directly subordinate to the presidency. The state thus tried to absorb the demands which were emerging with great intensity, redefining them and restructuring them through its own selection mechanisms (Offe, 1984).

Parallel to this, MST intensified mobilizations, looking for a more direct way of expanding the area of debate and of winning the support of public opinion for its cause. The high point of this initiative was the organization of a march from various points in the country arriving in Brasilia, the capital, on the day of the first anniversary of the Eldorado de Carajás massacre. This march lasted around three months and was both peaceful and rich in symbolism for the significance of land (Chaves, 2000). During this period, the demands of the 'landless' appeared on the front pages of newspapers and peak-time television news. The arrival of the march in Brasilia capitalized much discontent and generated the first popular demonstration against the government, which until then had appeared to enjoy an absolute unanimity, due to the economic impact of the Real Plan and the fall in inflation. Since then, agrarian reform has reoccupied an important space in political debate, requiring the actors involved to constantly clarify their positions.

The expansion of mobilization created the challenge for the government of curbing the growing social power and the mobilization capacity of MST in order to reduce its leading role in the struggle for land.[14] The government's initiatives, beginning with the creation of the Ministerial Office, appeared not only to be an attempt to reverse this situation, but also, in doing so, to give a new meaning to agrarian reform, decentralizing it, giving new powers to states and municipalities and trying to adapt it to the logic of the market.

The creation of a series of institutional measures, often without any fanfare, was part of this effort. Most were brought into effect by provisional measures, decrees, or complementary laws, reinforcing Diniz's thesis (1998: 35), that in Brazil 'the Executive has determined the agenda of the Legislature and the content of legal production', as well as highlighting the importance and urgency that the agrarian question had now reassumed in the sphere of state policy. This new institutionalism was inserted in a broader way, coming under the auspices of a reform of the state, centred around the decentralization of action, the reduction of the administrative machine and privatization. Taken as a whole, these measures, on the one hand, made government land action easier, eliminating some sticking points, and on the other, tried to take the initiative away from the movements supporting the struggle for land.

The new legislation created new instruments capable of accelerating the obtaining of land for rural settlements. Among these the following can be highlighted:

- greater speed of the *rito sumário* (summary process), allowing the possession of land within a maximum of forty-eight hours after the granting of legal approval for the expropriation;
- inspection of land together with employers' (CNA) and workers' (CONTAG) trade union organizations, with MST being excluded from this process;
- the prevention of the division of properties, in order to halt the expropriation process, after inspection notice had been received – landholders threatened with expropriation commonly divided their property among various owners (generally family members) in order to make it uneligible for this type of action (according to the Brazilian Constitution, property with an area of less than fifteen fiscal units cannot be expropriated);
- notification of the inspection not just by letter, but also in wide-selling newspapers in the part of the federation where the landholding was located, so as to prevent the landholder from alleging lack of knowledge of the order;
- only technical projects for land use approved by the relevant institution six months before the inspection were recognized, in order to avoid the prevention of expropriation by the last minute formulation of a project for the use of the land;
- a reduction, in the case of expropriations, at the rate of compensation interest incurred on the value of the difference between the evaluated and judicially awarded price from 12 per cent to 6 per cent a year;
- in frontier areas, a period of two years for all landholders concerned to ratify with INCRA all concessions and alienations of land made by the

state. If this was not done within the determined period (which began on 1 January 1999), the Union would declare the alienation or concession null and void, and repossess the property, thus making it available for the purposes of agrarian reform.

This set of measures was aimed, on the one hand, at curbing the high values being paid for expropriations due to frequent legal actions contesting the prices set by INCRA, as well as countering the subterfuges used by landholders to avoid the expropriation of their lands. On the other hand, it sought to speed up the expropriation process, reducing the time it took and the pressure of social movements.

Other resolutions implemented simultaneously to those listed above sought to inhibit the actions of organizations of rural workers, especially MST. These included: the prohibition of inspections in occupied areas, thereby preventing their expropriation; suspension of negotiations in the case of occupations of public buildings, while INCRA employees who negotiated with these occupiers would be penalized; and any organizations suspected, in any way, of encouraging, participating or being co-participants in the occupation of rural or public property, were forbidden access to public resources, in any governmental sphere. These measures were aimed at fighting what had been shown to be the principal form of pressure in the land struggle occupations, which were creators of political facts. In the name of democratizing the agrarian reform process, the new measures not only opened the possibility for landholders to indicate areas to be expropriated, but also localized (on a state basis) the demand for land, trying to isolate the power of national representative organizations. There was always a list of holdings whose expropriation was called for on the agenda of the Gritos da Terra (Cries of the Land) demonstrations.[15] In this context of the exclusion of MST and the consequent privileging of trade union entities, the government sought to drive a wedge between the different currents of workers' organizations, as well as to transfer pressure to the state sphere, a novelty for these groups, which had traditionally presented their demands to the Federal Executive. Thus, the government sought not just to create the conditions whereby it could recover the initiative in the expropriation process, through the restriction of the channels through which the social movements could exert pressure, but also to gain the support of some of them. The development of this proposal could be observed through the successive sparring between the government and those demanding land, especially MST, with dialogue only being restarted when the pressure had become irresistible and politically damaging, due to the growing legitimacy the MST was acquiring in public opinion.

Alongside these legal measures, a process of decentralizing action had begun, as a contrast to the highly centralized model inherited from the military regime. Although this had been rehearsed at previous times (Medeiros, 1997), the first signs of concrete steps in this direction appeared with the changes in INCRA's operational structure, involving an administrative dispersal, the elimination of head-office centralization, and the increase of the powers and roles of the Regional Supervision Bureaux, in order to make the decision-making process faster and more flexible.[16] However, these actions involved the dispersal of functions within INCRA rather than a real decentralization – understood as an action that increases the political participation of other spheres and actors and, at the same time, strengthens the mechanisms of accountability.

It was also sought, through special agreements, to involve states and municipalities. From the government's point of view decentralization was linked to the growing difficulty of institutions in carrying out the tasks related to the settlement process. According to the document 'Directives of the Process of the Decentralization of Agrarian Reform', written in September 1997, decentralization was justified, first, because the national targets for obtaining land were increasingly exceeding the operational capacities of the regional bureaux, and, second, because the complexity of the process was incompatible with the centralization of decisions in Brasilia, since settlements were fundamentally organized at the local and regional level.

From the viewpoint of the decentralization that had been initiated, the state Councils of Agrarian Reform came to be seen as the key element. Among other things, these councils had to: define state agrarian reform policy and identify priority zones for the development of family agriculture and settlements; set the order of priority of landholdings to be inspected; and analyse and give opinions on the acquisition and expropriation processes undertaken by state institutions and/or INCRA. The State Secretariat of Agriculture, INCRA, the state land institution, the federal bank operating in the region, the Federation of Agricultural Workers, the Agricultural Federation (an employer organization), representatives of settled families, the associations of mayors, and other institutions upon the decision of the council, all participated in the monthly meetings of these councils.

These initially scattered governmental initiatives were consolidated in the programme published in 1999, 'Family agriculture, agrarian reform and local development for a new rural world. A rural development policy based on the expansion of family agriculture and its insertion in the market', better known as 'A New Rural World'. Using the motto, 'quality for the settlements', members of settlements were to be treated as family farmers and together with the participation of the State and Municipal Councils of Sustainable Development (an expansion of the initially proposed Agrarian Reform Council), a plan of action was to be drawn up with them. This involved the formation of partnerships with state and municipal governments, in order to define which land would be used and what would be the best way to obtain it, taking into account the cost–benefit relationship, the need for infrastructure, credit demands and technical assistance etc.

Settlements, through their associations, were now given responsibility for various activities that had previously been carried out by INCRA (topography, the demarcation of lots, construction of basic infrastructure, preparation of a development plan for settlements). For this they were given access to grants. The rapid legalization of settlements (two or three years after the demarcation of the land), thereby turning the members of the settlement into proper family farmers, was also part of the proposal. This also meant, though, that within a short period the newly settled farmers would have to begin to pay for the land they had received.[17] On the other hand, members of settlements were now seen as 'entrepreneurs' who would have to adjust to the commercial world and show themselves to be competitive within it. Arguing that the current process of agrarian reform in Brazil had only an 'entrance door' and no 'exit', and that farmers needed to leave the guardianship of the state behind and enter the contractual world fully, the programme pushed, after a short initial consolidation period, the market as the main regulator of the activities of this new contingent of landholders.

The proposal also had a peculiar characteristic: before it was launched the government directly interacted with intellectuals involved with the issue. Many of them were summoned to debates with the minister and to give opinions about various aspects of the proposal. Thus, when the plan was announced, the support of some groups who had played an important role in the creation of the terms of the debate on the agrarian question could be counted on.[18]

Against this general context, marked by actions of the Executive, which aimed at regaining the political initiative in relation to the agrarian question and, at the same time, to change the profile of traditional federal intervention in the area, the proposal to create a Land Bank in Brazil gained credence.

Policies for stimulating market-led agrarian reforms had been implemented during the 1990s in various countries, such as the Philippines, South Africa and Columbia, having emerged from a series of critiques made by World Bank specialists of the classical approach to agrarian reform, in which the state played a central role. This type of reform was considered coercive, directed from above and involving some aspect of confiscation, since land was often paid for at prices considerably inferior to those of the market, partly in money, partly in government bonds. Furthermore, according to this critique, this model also distorted the land market, since it made its proper functioning difficult.

The defenders of market-led agrarian reform proposed a more efficient use of resources and that the transfer of land should have a voluntary nature: in other words, that it should be carried out with the agreement of the landholders, which would make it quicker, more efficient and would not provoke judicial or political disputes. Another characteristic that was emphasized was its decentralized nature, with the substitution of the central bureaucracy by local powers, seen as closer to those involved and, by nature, less subject to corruption (Borras Jr., 2004; Sauer, undated).

Due to the resistance encountered by the implementation of this model, the World Bank opted to carry out two pilot projects to demonstrate the efficiency of this type of land intervention (Sauer, undated). In Brazil, the first concrete experience of this new approach began in the state of Ceará in 1996. In 1995 the Secretary of Agriculture for this state authorized the Agrarian Development Institute of Ceará, 'to carry out studies of the land market and evaluate the performance of the mechanisms historically used for agrarian reform in the state' (Brandão, 2000: 318). In 1996 the Land Rotation Fund was created, establishing a partnership with the World Bank to create a land credit project at the São José Project.[19] In 1997, the federal government implemented a similar programme, called the Land Bill (Cédula da Terra), which was to be developed in the states of Maranhão, Pernambuco, Bahia, Minas Gerais and in Ceará itself, and which had significant international support in the form of a ninety million dollar loan from the World Bank. The equivalent Brazilian investment was sixty million dollars.[20] These resources were meant to obtain land and to allow the beneficiaries access to financing the implementation of the project and to pay for the additional technical assistance offered by the government, or previously given by the federal institution directly responsible for agrarian reform.

The starting point was the creation of an association of small producers or landless workers.[21] This association had to procure a financial agent or state land institute with a proposal for a settlement. Once the request had been analysed, resources would be provided so that it could go to the market and acquire an area, the value of which was to be agreed with the owner. Next, it would return to government institutions for the evaluation of, first, whether the quality of the land was adequate, and, second, if the agreed price was reasonable in relation to the market for that region, and finally, if the land deeds were legally unquestionable. Afterwards, a letter of credit would be given to the association, which, through a state financial agent, would acquire the property under market conditions. From this moment on, the community would be entitled to resources from the Special Programme of Credit for Agrarian Reform (Procera).[22]

In relation to the acquisition of land, the finance provided had to be repaid, with the purchasing association initially having a period of up to ten years to redeem the debt, with a grace period of up to three years.[23] The general criteria for guiding the purchase of land were:

- potential for the sustainable use of natural resources, as well as to generate, with a low level of additional investment, conditions to sustain the beneficiary families;
- prices compatible with those normally practised in the market and with the location, natural fertility and potential economic use of the land;
- compliance with all the legal requirements related to the registration and transfer of the purchase and sale of rural property (legitimate possession,

free of any disputes over ownership, mortgages, obligations or other impediments);
- good access conditions, availability of water and a reasonable infrastructure;
- a size adequate to absorb the number of families who had joined the association – the size of the family property could not be smaller than the minimum land division unit of the region where it was situated, though, in exceptional circumstances, the acquisition of holdings which did not comply with this requirement would be allowed, once the association decided not to carry out the formal division of the property after the liquidation of the debt incurred in its purchase;
- location distant from non-demarcated indigenous lands; and absence of primary forests. (Buainain et al., 1999)

As well as the loan for the purchase of land, resources for community investments were also provided for, in three basic areas – infrastructure, productive and social – as decided by the beneficiaries themselves. These investments could be made by the community itself, including with its own labour, if it so wished. In relation to infrastructure, investments which improved or renewed what already existed were to be given priority. The priority for productive investments was to increase the productive capacity of the property, and to raise productivity, the level of employment and the income of the beneficiaries. Social sub-projects were to be aimed at an immediate improvement of the living conditions of the community.

The limit established for family credit was US$11 200, including expenses with the acquisition and registration of land, mediation, taxes and community investments. The maximum investment subsidy was US$6900 per family, including installation assistance and the land grant of US$1300. In accordance to the logic of the programme, the lower the value of the land credit, the higher the subsidy conceded per family and the amount of resources aimed at community investment (Buainain et al., 1999).

According to Silveira et al. (2000), one of the most important aspects of the project was its 'governing structure', in other words, the rules which avoided 'collusion between buyers and sellers'. The central principles of this structure were based as much on the acquisition of land in a decentralized manner, with the associations choosing the areas they wished to acquire, as on the creation of a commitment on the part of the beneficiaries that the property would be paid for, guaranteeing their investment in it in terms of their labour. In this outline, the supposition is of strategic rationality and is based on the market values of the actors involved, especially those of the workers who have decided to form an association. As the evaluation carried out on behalf of the World Bank itself demonstrated, it was not necessarily this rationality of *homo economicus* which prevailed, but rather more often an affective relationship with the land, the desire not to leave the place where one has always lived, thus indicating the need to introduce other elements into the analysis and operate with a logic of 'moral economy' (Thompson, 1997). This approach, capable of taking into account the cultural elements which underlie the relationship with the land, can help in the understanding of the reasons why associations bought certain areas of land, often without being preoccupied with its price or quality.

In the beginning the programme was implemented without much visibility and without causing any major political debates, despite being widely advertised at a local level, through posters, radio programmes, visits by experts to farmers etc. Even before the evaluation of the experiment had begun, negotiations had started to extend it to other parts of the country, now adopting the name, the Land Bank.

It was legally established by Complementary Law No. 93 on 4 February 1998, with its regulations being issued in 2000. These regulations incorporated some of the criticisms of the Land Bill, while the final version of the project brought together the initiatives of the Executive and the Legislature, shown by the fact that in the Senate, the vote achieved a record difficult to break, with sixty-seven votes in favour, no abstentions and no votes against. Various elements can explain its rapid approval. From the government's perspective the growing pressure of social movements to accelerate expropriations, as well as the high cost of some of these, inflated by legal actions, were the most important. Various internal factors contributed to the visualization of the alternative ways of creating a stock of land, with the main one, according to the minister for land policy, being the supposed reduction in the price of land, provoked by the stabilization of prices brought about by the Real Plan. Starting from the supposition of a fall in prices and that, consequently, this asset would be offered on the market, and that, in addition, 'the spinal column of the large landholders had been broken', the government opted to stimulate the obtaining of land in the market, where, as well as the hypothesis of finding lower prices, there would also be a political gain, since negotiation and not conflict had been privileged. In effect, according to one of the documents announcing it, the Land Bank was described as 'agrarian reform without bureaucracy, conflict or the need to resort to legal actions', and therefore would be much faster.

Despite the recurrent statement in government documents that expropriation would continue to be the fundamental means for access to land, the arguments these documents presented showed the disadvantages of expropriation in relation to negotiated means of obtaining land:

> in its current form the process of acquiring and transferring land supposes the intervention of the state at all phases. The community has no participation, not even in relation to the definition of the price of the land, although by law it will have to pay for it. The fact that the compensation of the expropriated landholder is set by the judicial power implies a transaction cost which increases the price of the land between three to four

times. Another question associated with the expropriation model is that the land always becomes publicly owned and its return to private ownership necessarily involves additional costs. In practical terms this signifies the creation of dependency until definitive title to the land is issued and the payment made in full. (MEPF/MA, 1999: 28)

The government, in the person of the minister for agrarian development, also called attention to the already existing settlements:

they began ... in the absence of sustainability ... in the 34 years that agrarian reform has existed, they have not become 'emancipated', nor become independent, nor have they resulted in a large amount of families entering the programme and leaving from 'the other side'. In other words, until now, agrarian reform has been only 'stock', there has been no flow. The function of agrarian reform is not to create rural clientele, but rather to allow the poor, but productive, man to become a family farmer ... Flux, and not just stock, is one of the central problems and it is strongly linked with the question of quality ... created in the authoritarian period, in the context of ideological polarisation, agrarian reform remained 100% under the wing of the Federal Government. (Economic Affairs Committee of the Federal Senate, 24 March 1999, shorthand notes)

Civil society reaction to the government proposal

Reactions to the proposal of agrarian reform based on market mechanisms were quite varied and divided, whether coming from the different representative entities involved or from the National Forum for Agrarian Reform and Justice in the Countryside. Created in 1995, this Forum created a space for debate and intervention in a variety of areas, congregating a broad range of non-governmental organizations, religious bodies, representative groups and the agrarian secretariat of the Partido dos Trabalhadores (the Workers' Party).[24]

In general, landholders supported the programme, especially since, in addition to trying to eliminate conflicts and disputes over land, it emphasized the right to property and the rules of the market. The Land Bank was considered by CNA as the first step in the direction of democratic access to land. The advantage of the programme lay in the availability of financing

for those people who have a vocation to work the land, whether they are employed rural workers, *parceiros*, *arrendatários*, or small holders, including the children of small farmers and those who have lost their land. It is an important advance in relation to the settlement programme which simply threw people without any familiarity with rural work into landholdings, leaving them eternally dependent on the Government. (www.cna.org.br)

In CNA's opinion, another important advantage of the Land Bank was that the programme could count on the participation of communities, through councils formed in municipalities made up of representatives of local society (www.cna.org.br).

The quotations cited above are quite indicative of how much the proposal for the Land Bank corresponded to the traditional demands of the sector, which had always decisively opposed programmes of agrarian reform based on expropriation, including the constant belittling of members of settlements, accusing them of coming from outside the rural environment and having no agricultural vocation. The arguments used by the leaders of CNA were also constantly used by representatives of the sector in the National Congress, where its representation was very important, frequently blocking proposals which could extend the importance of expropriations.

From the point of view of the rural workers' representative organizations, CONTAG very quickly took a stand against the government's proposal. When the Land Bill was created, the then president of CONTAG, Francisco Urbano de Araújo, said that it was no more than a delay in the agrarian reform process and 'a way for the State to avoid its responsibility by not intervening in the changing of even a part of the Brazilian agrarian structure'. In the 1999 Grito da Terra the main slogan was 'against the privatisation of agrarian reform', with the consequent demand for the extinction of the Land Bill and Land Bank programmes, while at the same time severe criticisms were made of the New Rural World Programme. Expropriation in the social interest was also defended once again, as were the requirement for compliance with the social function of rural holdings, the extinction of compensation interest in legal actions against expropriation and the establishment of a maximum limit for the size of holdings. In addition to expropriation, CONTAG advocated a land restructuring programme as a mechanism of access to land, in which areas subject to expropriation could not be used. There would be widespread worker participation, through their representative organizations, at all levels of this programme, from the project stage to implementation and management. The priorities of the programme were to be family farmers with insufficient land, small rural *parceiros* and *arrendatários*, and young farmers wanting to have holdings of their own, separate from their parents who had not obtained land via expropriation. Landless workers could also benefit from the programme when the property they wanted was not in the legal conditions to be expropriated. Resources for the programme were to be made available at costs and with payment and waiting periods which would make the venture possible.[25] CONTAG's demands decisively influenced the World Bank's approval of the loan, which it granted for Land Credit instead of the Land Bank.

In relation to MST, the initial steps in the implementation of access to land via market mechanisms in Ceará went practically unnoticed by the movement. It was only when the Land Bill programme gained prominence and the government began to raise the possibility of extending it throughout the country as a whole, that MST began to make harsher criticisms, insisting on expropriation as the principal mechanism for agrarian reform and on the fact that it involved

a new strategy to undermine the social movements and trade unions in the countryside, no longer emphasising initiatives in the political, administrative or ideological fields, but rather in the economic, with the Land Bill programme and the creation of the Land Bank, both institutional forms of the proposal for market-led agrarian reform. (www.mst.org.br)

According to Jaime Amorim, an MST director from the northeast,

the large farmers continue to determine agrarian reform. They can stipulate what land they will get rid of, or what part of it. They can also solve two of their own problems: the financial, getting rid of some land of no use to them and getting a nice sum of money in return; and the labour one, since many of them have legal problems in this area. (Interview with João de Barros, *Caros Amigos Especial*, No. 6, October 2000, p. 32)

Due to this posture, MST, despite being invited by the government, refused to participate in the Council of Trustees of the Land Bank. Since 1998, MST, in connection with other groups, nationally, through the Agrarian Reform Forum and internationally, through the Via Campesina (Peasant Way)[26] and the Global Campaign for Agrarian Reform, has intensified its criticism of the programme, both rhetorically and, principally, by insisting on land occupations. On the local level some regions have tried pre-emptive actions, occupying areas destined for the programme (Navarro, 1998).[27]

Another ferocious opponent of the Land Bank was the CPT, which had often restated its theological perspective that land is a 'gift of God' and not just a place of production or a merchandise: 'it is space for living that inspires the dream and the fight for a new society, based on values of different cultures and ethnicities'. Its criticism of the model of market-led agrarian reform was based on this concept.

In its First National Congress, held in Bahia in June 2001, the CPT committed itself to supporting and strengthening the struggles for land, as well as the initiatives that would make the land that had been won 'a good land to live in'. These initiatives involved

necessary and legitimate occupations, and supporting and strengthening the initiatives which make the land that has been won a land which is not only productive and commercially useful, but also a land which can provide the happiness of living, the seed of a new Brazil, a common house for all humans and living beings, the dream of God. (CPT, 2001)

Bearing in mind these general principles, the CPT began to vehemently denounce the government's strategy in relation to land policy and the Land Bank in similar terms to those being used by CONTAG and MST, accusing the government of handing over its responsibility for agrarian reform to large landholders and to state and municipal oligarchies and of condemning family farmers to competing for rural credit in much more difficult market conditions than previously encountered (*Boletim da CPT*, 21 June 2000).

According to this organization, these initiatives assumed a central role in the political and ideological struggle against the social movements:

> ... confuse to reduce mobilisation and divide to manipulate is a tactic that has created preoccupying effects on organisations and popular actions. To co-opt and contain the social struggle, the government has implemented compensation policies such as the distribution of food parcels, Pronaf and land credit programmes such as the Land Bank, which deal with immediate popular demands. This will snowball, since these policies create exclusion and increase misery, accelerating the concentration of income, pushing the poorer classes into making short-term demands aimed at reducing the effects of these actual policies. The results are catastrophic for the social struggle, since organisations no longer consider general political questions, such as the distribution of income and wealth, putting on their agenda instead these short-term demands. (CPT, 2000)

These criticisms were consolidated and gained a wider project through the central position in the struggle against the Land Bank programme the CPT played, which was responsible for the Executive Secretariat of the National Forum for Agrarian Reform and Justice in the Countryside.

The Forum, as has already been indicated, brought together a wide variety of organizations. As the space for the creation of a minimal consensus between groups which had different ways of thinking and acting, some of them disputing between themselves the representation of different groups of rural workers, the Forum engaged in campaigns which, in relation to the question of the Land Bank, were fundamental in calling the attention of social groups to the programme and also in causing some rearrangements of the negotiations between representative agencies, the government and the World Bank.

In a short time, through the Forum, international campaigns were started to debate and react to the proposal, involving Via Campesina and FIAN (Food First Information and Action Network),[28] reinforcing internal resistance to the programme and giving it greater visibility.

The Forum's principal criticisms of the new programme centred on the following points, already mentioned in the individual responses of its member organizations:

- through the system of buying and selling land, agrarian reform was no longer led by the state, it was now under the direct control of the landholders;
- landholders were being rewarded by the new system, since they were paid for land in cash, thereby transforming non-productive land into financial assets;
- the programme implied a substantial increase in the price of land;
- those who had gained access to land through this system, now had not only to pay for the financing of the purchase of the land, but also had to look for financing of production, making its reproduction non-viable;
- the risk of producing 'rotten boroughs' for rural oligarchies was created;
- it would tend to lead to the division of average size holdings, expanding the number of small landholders, the creation of 'ghost associations' etc.

Attention was also called to the uninformed state of beneficiaries and the low quality of land sold (Campaign for Agrarian Reform in Brazil. 'Beware of the Land Bank', www.dataterrra.org.br).[29]

As well as making its criticism of the programme known to the public, the Forum also put pressure on the National Congress, trying to bring the debate into this space. From this point of view, the action of members of the Forum with the parliamentary party of the Workers' Party was fundamental, from the first initiatives and their repercussion onwards, resulting in the calling of a public hearing by the Economic Affairs Commission of the Senate, held on 7 September 1997, to discuss the project. The then president of INCRA and representatives from MST, CONTAG and CNA participated in this hearing. The initiative of the Legislature showed that questions were already being raised in the discussion in the state sphere. Other hearings took place later.

Another step was the demand for a meeting with representatives from the office of the World Bank in Brazil, which took place in October 1998. On that occasion the Bank restated that the programme was inspired by successful experiences in other countries and emphasized:

that the project was in the evaluation phase (the results of which the Bank promised to make public) and only afterwards would the support of the organisation for the expansion of the Land Bill be decided. It was emphasised that the Land Bill and Land Bank projects were complementary actions, qualitatively insignificant in relation to the government's target for expropriations. Furthermore, the fact that the resources of the World Bank were exclusively meant for investment in the area of settlement and not for the purchase of land was highlighted. (Wolff and Sauer, 2001: 176)

Shortly afterwards, in December of the same year, the Forum sent a request, signed by various civic organizations, for the establishment of an Inspection Panel for the Land Bill project to the World Bank.[30] The most immediate reason for this was that the Bank had, in spite of the recurrent criticisms of the ongoing pilot project, approved a new loan to Brazil to extend the experiment to other states in the country. At the same time, the government, through the NEAD (Núcleo de Estudos em Agricultura e Desenvolvimento – Centre of Agricultural and Development Studies), linked to the Ministry of Agrarian Development contracted an independent evaluation of the project.[31]

The demand for inspection was based on multiple arguments. Most emphasized was the suspicion of the progressive substitution of agrarian reform based on expropriation by that of an induced market for land, a procedure which would not allow the state to either control or guarantee the social function of land. Both government and World Bank representatives denied this, arguing instead that the benefits of the new proposal would probably be greater than those of the traditional approach based on expropriation, since there would be fewer setbacks and delays, a better selection of beneficiaries, and sufficient provision of resources for infrastructure. The Forum, though, also drew attention to the choice of states benefiting from the Land Bill, all of which 'had an enormous stock of land which could be expropriated, thus unjustly allowing the possibility of the sale of land which had been kept non-productive as a reserve value' (*Boletim Semanal da Secretaria Agrária Nacional do PT*, 1998).

Another argument used to criticize the programme was that, given the previously mentioned loan conditions, those indebted to the Land Bill and Land Bank would be unable, given the crisis facing Brazilian agriculture, to make their repayments.[32] According to the critics of the proposal, the poverty of the beneficiaries was shown not just in the lack of the material means of subsistence, but also in cultural deprivation and social disorganization. They argued that it would be very difficult for these people to have the initiative to establish an association to carry out a property transaction and even less to deal with the large rural landholders of their region in equal conditions. Examples were provided showing that in Ceará, Maranhão and Bahia many landholders had regimented groups of landless workers, forming associations to carry out property deals with public money.

Based on preliminary evaluation data, the Forum denounced the fact that

in dozens of verified cases, the associations of workers created for the acquisition of land have become politically subordinate to the previous landholders. Furthermore, the lands being sold are those which effectively have the worst soil and climatic conditions for agricultural production. (*Boletim Semanal da Secretaria Agrária Nacional do PT*, 1998)

Attention was also drawn to the fact that 'given the configuration of political power at the local and regional level', the Councils created to manage the programme

> were, in practice, transformed into mere formalities, limited to giving an appearance of popular participation to decisions that in reality were taken by governors, mayors and local political bosses. (*Boletim Semanal da Secretaria Agrária Nacional do PT*, 1998)

Another argument was that the project was heating up the land market, reversing a tendency of decline which had been observed for several years. Finally it was stated that 'the representative organisations of rural workers made an enormous effort to participate in the formulation process of the project and were totally ignored' (*Boletim Semanal da Secretaria Agrária Nacional do PT*, 1998).

In parallel to this, the Forum held a series of other events at a national and international level: demonstrations in front of the office of the World Bank in Brasilia; contacts with state and Church authorities; and the mobilization of international organizations etc. Members of the Forum were also sent to the head office of the World Bank 'to make contact with, inform and put pressure on its directors' (Wolff and Sauer, 2001: 180).

The World Bank finally accepted the request and in April 1999 three representatives of the Panel were sent to Brazil to visit areas connected with the Land Bill Programme and to converse with the parties involved. Parts of Bahia and Pernambuco were visited, with the Bank deciding not to hold the investigation that had been requested, whilst, at the same time, confirming a loan of a billion dollars for the four-year duration of the new project. According to Wolff and Sauer (2001: 181), the visits, especially in Bahia, were marked by actions which biased the evaluation: the interpreter of the group was the actual state coordinator of the Land Bill Programme; the areas had been previously visited by representatives of state governments; meetings were in form of assemblies, allowing a greater control over the group; and the questions were in the sense of whether the workers were better or worse off than before etc.

In refusing the Panel, the Bank alleged that the argumentation of the request had a philosophical character and that those making the request were not the representatives of the beneficiaries. Furthermore, according to one of the members of the Forum, during the process of analysing the request, the World Bank altered two points of the operational rules of inspection panels, due to the intervention of Brazil's Executive Director of the Bank: first, the project was to be analysed not in relation to its objectives, but in relation to the previous situation of the beneficiaries; second, the possibility of an initial provisional investigation was ruled out. The request for inspection ended up being analysed under new rules, distinct from those under which the original inspection request had been drawn up.

The refusal to set up a Panel was flaunted by the Brazilian government as proof, endorsed by the World Bank, of the excellence of the project, and was an important political victory, since one of the justifications for not having an inspection was that the member organizations of the Forum were not representatives of the beneficiaries. In this way, it belittled the request, stating that what was at play was more of a political dispute than a serious evaluation of the results of the initiative.[33]

Despite turning down the request for inspection, the Bank committed itself not to include in the loan in question, or in future ones, areas that could be subject to expropriation. At the same time, the minister of agrarian development altered the conditions of payment, increasing the repayment period from ten to twenty years, with a three-year grace period, favouring future adherents to the fund.

Dissatisfied with the rejection, the members of the Forum managed to achieve the holding of a new public hearing in the Senate (June 1999), when the previous criticisms of the programme were reiterated and the demand for expropriation to be maintained as the central mechanism to ensure that the social function of land was fulfilled was restated.

Shortly afterwards, a new Inspection Panel was requested, this time based on the implementation documents of the project, the recently concluded evaluation of the Land Bill Programme, and technical reports, obtained through a request for information by a deputy and senator from the Workers' Party. This set of documents highlighted a series of problems with the project, giving much more substantial ammunition to the Forum, which also requested the Federal Prosecution Service to investigate the irregularities which had been discovered.[34] After a new visit by representatives of the Panel to Brazil and further discussions with the government and the Forum, inspection was once again not recommended, it being alleged that the Forum had not exhausted all the means of dialogue with the local administration of the World Bank.[35] If this represented an immediate defeat for the Forum, these actions, on the other hand, provoked wide-ranging repercussions, both on the national level, with actors from different parts of the process being forced into taking stances, and the international level.

Parallel to this, the Forum began a national mobilization campaign demanding a constitutional amendment to limit the size of landholdings. Its proposal was to add to the article that defined the social function of property in the Brazilian Constitution, an item which limited the total area of holding that could be owned, in any way, by an individual or corporation anywhere in the country, to a maximum of thirty-five fiscal units. According to the proposal, this requirement would be self-applicable, while the incorporation of those rural holdings which were bigger than the established limit to public ownership would not involve the paying of compensation to the previous owner for the value of the land corresponding to the area exceeding the fixed limit.

This campaign, which did not have the slightest chance of being approved by the National Congress, due to the strong property rights alliance existing there, was defined as

> an action to raise awareness in Brazilian society about the unjust agrarian reality of the country, and the consequent pressurising of parliamentarians to put mechanisms into the Federal Constitution which would limit the size of landholdings in Brazil. (Text from the Campaign launch)[36]

The campaign was carried out, by various groups, via the widespread distribution of posters, explanatory leaflets and a petition, in meetings, over the Internet etc., in order to spread the arguments in favour of the amendment among various publics, not just those closely linked to the agrarian question. Intellectuals, students and trade unions received special attention. In this way, the debate on the question was expected to be updated, absorbing the new terms that the Executive's initiatives were creating.

The Forum, with the support of FIAN and Via Campesina, was also engaged in the Global Campaign for Agrarian Reform in Brazil, launched on 17 April 1998, the second anniversary of the massacre of Eldorado dos Carajás, a date Via Campesina declared the 'International Day of Peasant Struggle'. Its aims included the international distribution of information related to the situation in the Brazilian countryside, in order to raise awareness in other countries. This involved a strategy of systematic action in relation to the means of communications, the organization of international meetings and demonstrations, as well sending delegations from member organizations of the National Forum for Agrarian Reform abroad, and receiving visits from international delegations to Brazil. Other actions that were planned included the sending of protest letters about the consequences of land conflicts in Brazil and exerting pressure and influence on other government and intergovernmental structures, United Nations organizations and multilateral institutions, such as the World Bank, so that decisions favourable to the struggle for agrarian reform in Brazil could be made at an international level. This campaign was the first step of the Global Campaign for Agrarian Reform, created in 1999.

Among the arguments of both campaigns was a critique of the Brazilian government's proposal to create a Land Bank. Its actions, both at the international and national level, were aimed at forcing the Brazilian government, and members of the Forum itself, into clarifying their positions, making it into an arena of political disputes between various social movements, especially CONTAG, MST and the CPT.

In regard to international developments, two angles should be considered: that of relations with multilateral institutions and that of joint actions with social movements. As regards relations with the World Bank, the existence of a resource for official appeals, recognized by everyone, made the Panel a common focus to bring together national and international NGOs in the combined pressurizing of various governments and their representatives in the World Bank, as was acknowledged by some members of the Forum itself (Wolff and Sauer, 2001: 191). Therefore, demands which previously had only a restrictive impact could gain visibility. In the Brazilian case, Wolff and Sauer recognize that the Forum's demands obliged the World Bank and the government to create arguments and to clarify their stance during the drawing up of replies and/or preparations for meetings with the Panel.

According to Jonathan Fox, between 1994 (when the Panel was created) and 1998, fourteen inspection demands were made (of which three came from Brazil), referring mainly to resettlement, the construction of infrastructure and environmental questions. The first request with a different content and aimed at anti-poverty programmes was from Brazil. Moreover, according to Fox, despite the relatively low number of demands, the Panel 'appears to have increased the cost of public relations for the Bank due to the breaching of safeguarding policies, at least for the most obvious ones, such as resettlement and environmental evaluation' (Fox, 2001: 57). In this specific case, the most obvious effect was that the Bank sought to become closer to civic organizations in Brazil, looking for their support, accepting some demands and putting some restrictions on the original project.

In relation to joint actions with social movements, perhaps the most significant was the extension of the Global Campaign for Agrarian Reform (the secretariat of which was held by FIAN), which has been extremely critical of the Bank's anti-poverty policies. According to the Campaign, the principle upon which agrarian reform had previously been based, 'the land is for those who work it', had been converted into the slogan, 'the land is for those who can buy it' (*FIAN Information Bulletin*, May 2000). At the same time as making this criticism, the Campaign raised the thesis that a 'new agrarian reform' was necessary, which would not be just limited to the question of land, but which would

> start with a focus on human rights and seek an agricultural system which would guarantee poor peasants control over the land, seeds and water, so that they could live in dignity; produce healthy foodstuff, free from genetic manipulation, produced in a sustainable manner in order to conserve the means of subsistence for future generations; strengthen the rights of peasant women; guarantee food sovereignty; strengthen local rural communities. (FIAN, 2000)

After this, the First International Meeting of Landless Peasants was held in July 2000 in Honduras, convened by Via Campesina and FIAN, with delegates from twenty-four countries. From the final declaration of this meeting, we would like to highlight, on the one hand, the need to 'globalize struggle and hope' and, on the other, the appeal to international law to justify the demand for a 'new agrarian reform':

> Agrarian Reform is a commitment accepted by States in relation to
> Human Rights, whenever and always a high concentration of agricultural
> land in their these States leaves without land peasants who need this land
> to feed themselves. (FIAN, 2000: 16)

The importance of these moves became clear when the World Bank, according to information from FIAN, put clarifications about the petition into its Internet site, stating that the model being promoted was complementary to other efforts and not a substitution of laws allowing governments to expropriate land; that the model was never purely market-based and, in order to avoid misunderstandings, its focus would now be called 'community based reform', a more exact description of its objectives; and successful introduction of the new concept would be measured by continuous evaluation and constructive dialogue with civil society.

In a continuation of these debates at the beginning of 2001, a seminar entitled 'Innovative Land Reform for Sustainability and the Reduction of Poverty' was held in Bonn, Germany, with the support of the German government and various non-governmental organizations, including FIAN. During the seminar various experiments, including the Brazilian one, were analysed with the result being a declaration (the Bonn Declaration), where the criticisms of the World Bank's agrarian reform policy were reiterated, and the previously mentioned 'new agrarian reform' reaffirmed.[37]

The international seminar, 'The Negative Impacts of the World Bank's Market Based Land Reform', held in Washington in April 2002 in the United States, took place in the same context. This was also supported by various non-governmental organizations, while its final declaration had the subtitle 'land for those who can work it and not for those who can buy it'. Representatives from Colombia, El Salvador, Guatemala, Honduras, Mexico, South Africa, Thailand and Zimbabwe took part, as well as organizations from England, Germany, Switzerland and the United States.[38]

These all pointed to the need to increasingly take into account transnational dimensions, not just to reflect on the nature of public policy in different countries, but also to try to understand the profile of social reactions to certain proposals, and the nature and agility with which new networks come together, within the logic of what Harvey has called the 'shrinking of the world' (Harvey, 1993).

A basic part of the World Bank's anti-poverty policies is the participation of actors from civic society in their implementation. From the very beginning of the discussions about the Land Bank programme, the World Bank's interest in obtaining the support of CONTAG was obvious. According to a statement made by the ex-president of the organization, Francisco Urbano, to the Economic Affairs Commission of the Senate on 4 September 1997:

> the specialists from the World Bank came to CONTAG and told me that the Brazilian government had awful legislation for agrarian reform and did not have the courage nor the political force for it, since the alliance which supports it is very conservative, while misery in the countryside was increasing by the day. They also said that they wanted to offer a programme to help and presented their proposal to me. I told them that it had to be a programme complementary to agrarian reform ... and that if it were destined for areas of smallholdings – which could not be expropriated since they were too small – or in areas not subject to expropriation, we could examine it as a complementary element. I further told them that it could not be in the states of Maranhão, Bahia, or Minas Gerais. Why? In these states an enormous amount of non-productive large properties exist and the corrective mechanism to be used is expropriation. However, it could be used in regions where smallholdings were concentrated, or in other north-eastern states which have large quantities of land which legally cannot be expropriated, such as the Forest Zone, or the lands of the bankrupt sugar cane suppliers, with its various conflicts and fiscal units. (Shorthand notes of session)

The large amount of criticisms the Land Bill programme and its derivative, the Land Bank, received led the World Bank to seek out CONTAG once again, asking the latter to explain its objections to the project. As a result the Bank presented a counter-proposal which was discussed in an event held by CONTAG in the city of Natal in 2000, with delegations from various states, state governors, NEAD and INCRA. Later, another meeting was held with agricultural workers' federations, NEAD and the World Bank, resulting in an agreement concerning the Land Credit Programme, guaranteeing the exclusion of areas that, from the legal point of view, could be expropriated. Under this agreement, the new programme would cover all the northeastern state and the southern region, as well as Minas Gerais and Espírito Santo in the southeast. This proposal allowed individual credit (though in this case there was no right to productive resources), an interest rate lower than inflation, and a 50 per cent rebate of charges, if the instalments were paid on time. During 2001, operational plans were being prepared in various states, most with the participation of agricultural workers' federations.[39]

According to Manoel dos Santos, president of CONTAG in 2001, the advantage of land credit for workers is that expenses with infrastructure (roads, electrification, cooperative buildings etc.) and technical assistance do not have to be paid back and that the payments for land are low (6 per cent a year, while those of the Land Bank were 12 per cent a year plus the long-term interest rate). Even so, paying for the land continued to be untenable. Although the programme was not really a policy that was capable of eradicating poverty, the change in situation had to be considered:

> yesterday he was landless, now he is in debt, but has land to sow ... In the worst hypothesis, you have the possibility to continue struggling afterwards, so he won't leave the land, whether in the case of purchase or of expropriation. (Interview held in November 2001)

The support of CONTAG, an active participant in the Forum, was fundamental for legitimating the project, which had been suffering attacks from various civic organizations, and reopened the old dispute over the right to speak for rural workers. From this viewpoint, the Forum lost its unity, with CONTAG arguing that it had the right to negotiate for what appeared to be best in the interests of its supporters and the other participants in the Forum reiterating their criticisms of the Land Credit Programme, trying to show that it did not at all diverge from the defining principles of the market-led agrarian reform originally presented by the World Bank.[40]

Conclusion

As has been shown throughout the chapter, various needs and preoccupations of rural workers continue to be raised through the demand for agrarian reform, despite the efforts to introduce a new rhetoric through public policies, such as 'rural poverty relief programmes'.

Contrary to the general formulations, which point to the maintenance or increase of rural poverty and imply the preparation of more or less widely focused programmes to combat this, the expression 'agrarian reform' contains actors, political identities and a history of social struggles. If the expression 'poverty relief' appears to diminish the actors, emphasizing the dimension of the profound needs in which significant numbers of the rural population live, the struggle for agrarian reform gives them names (on the one hand, the 'landless workers', who demand land for labour and to socially reproduce themselves, and, on the other, those in whom ownership of the land is concentrated, the large landowners, the *latifundiários*), locates them politically and points to a historically constructed solution: the redistribution of land through the expropriation of non-productive holdings.

The way in which the debate has been evolving is not without consequences. During the last twenty years in Brazil, the defence of agrarian reform has received increasing support, new formats, arguments, meanings and opposition. Until the beginning of the 1990s, what was at stake was the possible expansion of expropriation, with the debate centring on the definition of non-productive land – land that, therefore, could be transformed into rural settlements. In the 1990s though, a tendency which had existed, although only in an embryonic form, since the debate about the Proposal for a National Agrarian Reform Plan in the middle of the 1980s, gained strength: the defence of a negotiated agrarian reform, without conflict, through the parties involved voluntarily adhering to a contract; a programme governed by the rules of the market, where the state would establish some form of regulation (a 'governing structure'), but would forsake the use of its power to intervene, in other words, expropriation; and, more especially, the capacity to use expropriation as an instrument of punishment for, from the legal point of view, the inappropriate use of rural property.

In effect, the debate about agrarian reform in Brazil, as we have highlighted throughout the chapter, now centres on the relative weight of expropriation versus market mechanisms. It was not just by chance that the agreement CONTAG made allowing the effective functioning of the Land Credit and Anti-Poverty Programme was socially justified by emphatically stating that the campaign would not operate in areas subject to expropriation and, therefore, that it would only be of a complementary nature. In the recent Brazilian election campaign in 2002, agrarian reform and support for agriculture appeared in the manifestos of all the candidates, but the Land Bank was only mentioned in the manifesto of the government candidate.

Nevertheless, it is possible that the discussion about the means of obtaining land for agrarian reform, chosen as the central point of the controversy, is obscuring other ongoing processes, including a profound transformation of meaning that 'traditional' agrarian reform appears to be undergoing. In effect, the policy of rapid autonomy for settlements and the conditions in which decentralization is occurring, indicate that the policy of valorizing market mechanisms for agrarian reform goes beyond the question of access to land, profoundly affecting the reproduction of settlements, now condemned to becoming 'competitive in the commercial world', in the context of a deep agrarian crisis and with debts for the land to pay.

Despite the new laws and the consequent restrictions that are being placed on the actions of social movements, land occupations are continuing to happen, bringing together not just rural workers but also people from the peripheries of the large cities who are no longer able to find conditions in which to reproduce themselves there. These actions are being dealt with as threats to the public order, and are seen as being extremely suspicious by the government of Fernando Henrique Cardoso.[41]

However, if there are groups ready to answer the call for occupations, there are also many workers who are politically open and sensitive to the call of programmes which promise to allow access to land without the risk of conflict or violence. Trade unionists and MST activists have, at the same time as making political criticism of the programme, stood in line outside trade union and mayors' offices when it was announced. It is not by chance that CONTAG, defending a land credit mechanism, invoked the interests of 'its support'. The proposals in question, therefore, on the one hand unify organizations in defence of expropriation, and, on the other, show an opening for other alternatives. Without entering the question of the merit of the support for the programme, which is not the objective of the present chapter, attention should be called to the possibility for the making and unmaking of alliances and disputes as a result of a political dynamic created by the state through a set of initiatives which configured a new institutionality for agrarian reform.

Nonetheless, the facts narrated throughout the chapter are also quite suggestive of the social and political processes that need to be investigated in greater depth. These refer to the significance of the networks which are created among social movements, workers' representative organizations, and non-governmental organizations in their relationship with the state and multilateral agencies, both at a national and international level. These networks are acquiring a central role in the discussion of determined questions, taking them out of the local space and projecting them into other spheres which allow the creation not just of new alliances and the visibility of determined actions, but also the rephrasing of certain questions. Above all, they are generators of opportunities for the expansion, strengthening and the pushing to the fore of social movements and the demands society puts on them, thereby moving beyond the specific context in which they emerged.

It is interesting to point out how, as a result of the above, questions taken as national or local, as in the case of agrarian reform, acquire another dimension. The fact that multilateral organizations have turned to agrarian reform as a central component of their 'poverty relief projects' – part of their actions in the 'countries from the South' – has mattered in the revitalization of the debate. Independent of the form that these projects have taken, it is the term 'agrarian reform' that is invoked, a term laden with history and significantly marked by important political disputes. In this way the debate is redirected, causing the opponents in this complex field of political dispute to return to their positions and arguments and, as we have tried to show, to articulate them in plans which go beyond the national context, but which still act on it.

More than the terms under which this debate is conducted, it is important to bear in mind that it projects actors, and in doing so, reactivates itself. MST is emblematic in this sense. Starting as a localized movement, in a short period it nationalized itself and, through its banners and means of action, reinvigorated the debate about agrarian reform, not just at the international but also the national level. Having projected itself far beyond the spaces where it was born, MST is an exemplar case of the effects of globalization on the relational networks between civic organizations. Crossing national frontiers, it was recognized and legitimized by various organizations, leading to the formation of webs of solidarity and cooperation in various countries, allowing it to strengthen itself in the field of internal political disputes. These networks provide financial resources, political support, the possibility of media visibility, greater legitimacy and conditions to maintain their actions, etc. As Scherer-Warren has emphasized, some sort of 'planetary citizenship' is being created by 'possibilities of political interactions between local public and other regional and trans-national spaces, stimulated by social movements and NGOs' (Scherer-Warren, 1999: 82).

These elements allow us to think how agrarian reform became the subject of a global campaign which, despite having a limited scope, reintroduced the theme into political imagination, feeding the various struggles sheltered under this banner, allowing linguistic barriers, as well as those of tradition and custom, to be overcome, though without ignoring them.

On the other hand, the opposition to what is described as 'market-led agrarian reform', has led to the combination of formulations varying from environmental arguments to the right of human beings to food (which signifies not just the right to land, but also the preservation of seeds, natural resources, etc). This wedding gave birth to the possibility of bringing in the human rights banner to guarantee legitimacy. Therefore, it is possible to think that the social movements involved in the struggle for land can surpass the fragmented, dispersed and particular actions which mark their daily existence to longer-term visions and strategies.

Notes

1. Translated from Portuguese to English by Eoin Ó Néill, PhD candidate, Instituto Universitario de Pesquisas do Rio de Janeiro (IUPERJ), Brazil. The present chapter sums up the main ideas developed in the book *Movimentos Sociais, Disputas Políticas e Reforma Agrária de Mercado no Brasil* (*Social Movements, Political Disputes and Market-Led Agrarian Reform in Brazil*) (2002) Rio de Janeiro: UNRISD and Editora da Universidade Federal Rural do Rio de Janeiro (UFRRJ).
2. *Tenentismo* was a movement of young army officers (*tenentes*, i.e., lieutenants) who were particularly critical of the electoral system then in use in Brazil, based on non-secret voting.
3. *Arrendamento* involves the leasing of (normally small) plots of land for which a value in money is paid, agreed in advance at the time of making the rental contract; *parceria*, which is somewhat similar to sharecropping, involves a payment in kind of an agreed part of production (commonly half) for the use of the land. In this latter system, importantly, losses as well as profits are divided. Under the former system the agreed sum of money must be paid, irrespective of other factors.
4. *Moradores* were the workers on sugarcane plantations. At the same time as working in the cane brakes, they had the right to a plot of land where they could carry out subsistence planting and raise small animals. In the areas of coffee plantations, labour relations were similar, but the workers were called *colonos*.
5. The rural land unit, regulated by DL 55891/65, is a measurement unit that expresses the interdependence between the dimensions and geographic situation of rural properties and the form and conditions of their use. The rural land unit corresponds to the area necessary, using the above factors, to provide subsistence for a family.
6. Parallel to this, a critique of property used for merely speculative purposes developed. Obviously, the ambiguity of the definition of 'productive' resulted in speculation, although rhetorically indefensible, functioning, in practice, as the other side of the coin in the debate.
7. According to the Land Statutes, property fulfilled its social function when it simultaneously: '(a) favours the welfare of the owners and the workers who cultivate it, as

well as their families; (b) maintains satisfactory levels of productivity; (c) ensures the conservation of natural resources; (d) observes the legal dispositions which regulate fair labour relations between those who own and those who cultivate' (Land Statutes, article 2°, § 1°).

8. The acceptance of TDAs (until then considered as 'rotten money') in the processes of privatization in the middle of the 1990s reinforced this tendency even further.

9. The fiscal unit is a unit expressed in hectares, set for each municipality taking the following factors into account: predominant type of land use in the municipality; income obtained from the predominant land use; other types of land use existing in the municipality, which, although not predominant, are significant either in terms of income or the area used; and the concept of family property. The fiscal unit serves as the parameter for the classification of rural property in terms of size, with smallholdings being classified as those whose area covers between one and four fiscal units, and medium-sized holdings as those with an area of between four and fifteen fiscal units.

10. One of the aims of the Collor de Melo government was the settlement of 500 000 families, who would be composed of *arrendatários*.

11. This tendency was already visible in the period directly before the New Republic, when the state governments of São Paulo, Paraná and Rio de Janeiro, among others, resorted to different legal means to obtain land and settle rural workers. This was an important element in the political disputes surrounding the leadership of the Diretas Já (Direct Elections Now) Campaign.

12. In the case of Corumbiara, in the state of Rondônia, in 1995, the police acted violently during an eviction resulting in various deaths. The action took place at night, which is illegal. Several months later, in April 1996, in the state of Pará, 'landless' workers who had been blocking a road were surrounded by police. The following confrontation resulted in the death of seventeen of the workers. It was filmed by an amateur cameraman, leaving no doubts about the brutality of the police action. The film was shown throughout the world, provoking protests from several human rights and international organizations.

13. The Extraordinary Ministerial Office for Land Policy was a body with ministerial powers, but without the operational structure corresponding to a ministry. A year later the office was transformed into the Ministry of Agrarian Development with a permanent structure.

14. The term 'social power' is used in the sense attributed to it by Claus Offe (1989), referring to the capacity of workers to organize sanctions against employers. In the case dealt with here, the notion is used to indicate the capacity of a group to create political facts that end up stimulating state action.

15. The Gritos da Terra (Cries of the Land) are large demonstrations led by CONTAG, held annually either in Brasília or in one of the states. The preparation for these events involved the drawing up of a large list of demands to be delivered to the government during the demonstration. The dispute between CONTAG and MST over the banner of agrarian reform was, at this time, intense. CONTAG recognized occupation as a form of the struggle, thus anticipating MST's nationalization movement, which was starting to become visible.

16. According to a document produced by the National Confederation of INCRA Employees (CNASI, 1996: 16), 'the preliminary phase of an expropriation process would last at least 70 days, passing through the Supervisory Bureau and the central institutions of INCRA, sufficient time for the landholder to alter the nature of his holding, dividing it or making it productive'.

17. According to Brazilian law, land which is redistributed through agrarian reform has to be paid for by those who receive it, albeit over a long-term period and only after it is considered to be self-supporting. For this, the law presupposes that the state has created the necessary infrastructure, schools, health, roads, the conditions of production etc.

18. Attention should be drawn to the fact that in Brazil universities, especially public ones, have been used both by governmental organizations (which have used academic researchers to carry out research, evaluate programmes etc.), and by workers' representative organizations (to give educational courses, helping to raise 'current questions'). Therefore, the competition, not just for the appropriation (and the production of different readings) of academic knowledge, but also for the loyalty of these intellectuals, became fierce.

19. An already existing anti-poverty programme, also financed by the World Bank.

20. Of this total, forty-five million came from the federal government, meant exclusively to obtain land; nine million was to be paid directly by the beneficiaries, and six million by the states where the project was to be implemented.

21. According to the Operational Manual of the programme, workers who complied, simultaneously, with the following requirements were eligible: (a) they were landless rural producers, or owners of land classified as smallholdings; (b) they were heads, or the main breadwinners, of families, including women responsible for families; (c) they were of age, or, if minors, had been given full legal responsibility by their parents; (d) they had a tradition of agricultural activity; (e) they had shown the intention of acquiring, by means of purchase through a Producers' Association, rural property which would allow them to undertake sustainable productive activities; (f) they could indicate one or more landholders willing to sell them property, which had been previously agreed in adherence to the conditions specified by the programme; (g) they would agree to commit themselves to repay the sum given to them for the acquisition of the landholding (Buainain et al., 1999). As the evaluation research of the programme showed, those who sought out this alternative had the same characteristics as those who were members of the occupation movements.

22. Procera was created under the ambit of PNRA. It was extinguished as an autonomous programme in 2000 and its target public (settlement members) were incorporated in the National Programme of Assistance for Family Agriculture (PRONAF) as part of the changes proposed by the 'New Rural World'.

23. Later, due to the criticism of, and pressure on, the programme, the period for redemption of the debt was extended to twenty years.

24. Thirty-two groups made up the Forum, including the CPT (which occupied the secretariat of the Forum), CONTAG, MST, the National Conference of Brazilian Bishops (CNBB), the Federation of Educational and Social Welfare Institutions (FASE), the Institute of Socio-economic Studies (INESC), the Brazilian Association for Agrarian Reform (ABRA), the National Confederation of Incra Employees (CNASI), the Brazilian Institute of Socio-economic Analysis (IBASE), the Department of Rural Socioeconomic Studies (DESER), the Central Workers Union (CUT) etc.

25. This proposal was drawn up in 1996.

26. Via Campesina is an international movement created in 1992 and based in Honduras, linking peasant and rural worker organizations and indigenous communities from Asia, Africa, America and Europe. Its priorities are directed to the centres

of power and decision-making of governments and multilateral organizations in order to guide the economic and agricultural policies of these institutions towards the interests of those living in, and making a living from, the countryside, with the slogan 'globalize the struggle, the hope'.

27. Despite the official position of the movement, Navarro (1998) has highlighted situations where local leaders gave aid to associations of the Land Bill programme. On the other hand, some leaders have recognized the difficulty of disputes at a local level, since the possibility of access to land without any conflict has been attracting many of the workers who would otherwise potentially be members of MST. The Brazilian government, through the means of mass communications, especially television, exploited this group immensely. At the beginning of 2001, an official advertisement transmitted at peak time showed a group of workers entering a farm through an open door. The commentator asked something along the lines of 'why force entrance when the door is open?', and displayed an advertisement about the Land Bank. This advertisement had a dual purpose: to turn workers off participating in occupations and to try to show society in general that occupations, thanks to the new government initiatives, were no longer necessary. The advertisement stimulated workers interested in having access to land to subscribe via the post office and to wait for an answer from the government. According to official sources, around 750000 people signed up. The fulfilling of the promise of settlement became another demand of the Gritos da Terra.

28. FIAN, an international human rights organization created in 1986 and based in Germany, acts basically by denouncing violations of the right to feed oneself, as well as spreading information about, and creating pressure for, the guarantee of this right at a world-wide level.

29. One of the representatives of the Forum produced a detailed summary of the evaluation reported ordered by NEAD, which served as the basis for the arguments of this network in the debate about the Land Bill and the prospects for the Land Bank (see Sauer, undated). Before this report was finished, criticism was based on information from local movements and the consultation work the World Bank asked Zander Navarro to carry out at the beginning of the implementation of the Land Bill.

30. The World Bank's Inspection Panel was created in 1993, due to the criticism of environmentalists and activists in the defence of human rights. Citizens of countries affected by the actions of the Bank could, through the Panel, make complaints related to the social and environmental costs of projects. The Panel's function was to investigate accusations that the official policy of the Bank was not being followed in the preparation and implementation of projects. According to Fox (2001), it involved a transnational arena for the administration of conflict. The request for the Panel was signed by member organizations of the Forum, such as ABRA; ANMTR (National Council of Rural Women Workers); Cáritas Brazil; CIMI (the Indigenous Missionary Council); CNASI; CONIC (National Council of Christian Churches in Brazil); CONTAG; CPT; INESC (Institute of Socio-economic Studies); MST; and the Brazilian Network on Multilateral Financial Institutions.

31. The requirement for the evaluation of the projects it finances is part of the regulations of the World Bank. These evaluations are carried out by consultants who are not part of the apparatus of the state. In the case of Brazil, professors from

universities or recognized research institutions are often asked. However, the consultants are indicated by the government, allowing the hypothesis to be raised that the choice of names is often made, although also through academic competence, by taking into account political affinity. The evaluation of the Land Bill was given to a professor from the prestigious State University of Campinas (Unicamp).

32. For this, they disposed of simulations made both by the Agrarian Secretariat of the PT and by the Department of Rural Socioeconomic Studies (DESER), an NGO which provides assistance to rural trade unions in the three states in the south of Brazil.

33. Most of the members of the Forum had links with the Workers' Party, the main and most systematic opposition to the government.

34. The Forum only gained access to this document after a formal request from the office of a Workers' Party senator. Until March 2002, at least, it was not possible to obtain the document from NEAD's site, despite it appearing there as finished. We were informed that it was being revised and edited, but still the new version has not been made available to the public, at least not by the time of the completion of revision of this work for publication. A copy of the original report was received after a formal request was made to NEAD, citing the nature of the research being carried out.

35. In this process, the coordinator of the evaluation research was questioned in writing in May 2000 about the controversial points of the report. All the answers tended to minimize the importance of the criticisms that had been made, restating the success of the project (correspondence between the representative of the World Bank in Brazil, Gobind Nankani, and Steve Schwartzman, an activist from Environment Defense, which lobbies the Bank).

36. Returning to the terms of the 1988 Constitution, the campaign counterpoised paragraph XXII of article 5 ('The right to property is guaranteed') to the content of paragraph III of article 3 (the fundamental objectives of the Federal Republic of Brazil are, 'to eradicate poverty and marginalisation and reduce regional and social inequalities') and to article 5 itself ('everyone is equal before the law'). In the understanding of the leaders of the Campaign, paragraph XXII guaranteed the right to the ownership of land to all who needed it to work and to ensure their sustenance.

37. The Brazilian delegation at this seminar was composed of the national coordinator of CPT, a representative from MST and a university representative. The Brazilian government, despite being invited, did not send a representative, nor did it justify its absence. The importance of Brazilian initiatives in the international arena was evident when the representative from MST was chosen to reply to the presentation about market-led agrarian reforms made by Claus Deninger, the World Bank's representative.

38. MST, CPT and the non-governmental organizations Action Aid, INESC and the Brazilian Network on Multilateral Financial Institutions participated on the Brazilian side.

39. The exception was Bahia (where the federation was politically opposed to CONTAG), which by August 2001 had taken no action.

40. The advisers of the Agrarian Secretariat of the Workers' Party, which also belonged to the Forum, published an article analysing the Land Credit Programme. Suggestively its subtitle was 'Changing six of one for half dozen of another' (Teixeira, 2000).

41. In August 2001, newspapers published numerous denunciations, based on documents from the intelligence services of the Brazilian army, of espionage being carried out on rural social movements, especially MST, designated with the term 'opposing force'. These documents also talked of situations where it would be necessary 'to infringe the rights of citizens', to fight potential actions of these movements.

References

Boletim da CPT (2000) 21 June.

Boletim Semanal da Secretaria Agrária Nacional do PT (1998) Ano II, 86, 12–18 December. www.pt.org.br.

Borras Jr., Saturnino M. (2004) *Rethinking Redistributive Land Reform: Struggles for Land and Power in the Philippines* (thesis). Maastricht: Shaker Publishing BV.

Brandão (2000) 'A reforma agrária solidária no Ceará', in MDA/NEAD, *Reforma Agrária e Desenvolvimento Sustentável*. Brasília: MDA.

Bruno, Regina (1997) *Senhores da Terra, Senhores da Guerra*. Rio de Janeiro: Forense/ Edur.

Buainain, Antonio Márcio et al. (1999) *Relatório Preliminar de Avaliação do Projeto Cédula da Terra* (draft). Brasília.

Caldart, Roseli Salete (2000) *Pedagogia do Movimento sem Terra*. Petrópolis: Vozes.

Caros Amigos Especial (2000) 'Interview with Jaime Amorim of MST', No. 6, October.

Carvalho, Abdias Vilar de (1985) 'A Igreja e a questão agrária', in Vanilda Paiva (ed.), *Igreja e Questão Agrária*. São Paulo: Loyola.

Chaves, Christine Alencar (2000) *A Marcha Nacional dos sem Terra*. Rio de Janeiro: Nuap/Relume-Dumará.

Comissão Pastoral da Terra (CPT) (2000) *Manifesto da CPT*, Goiânia, 28 June. www.cpt.org.br.

Comissão Pastoral da Terra (CPT) (2001) *Declaração do I Congresso Nacional da CPT*, June. www.cpt.org.br.

Congresso Nacional de Auditoria de Sistemas e Segurança (CNASI) (1996) *I Congresso Nacional dos Servidores do Incra. Relatório Final*. Brasília: CNASI.

Delgado, Guilherme (1985) *Capital Financeiro e Agricultura*. São Paulo: Icone/Unicamp.

Diniz, Eli (1998) 'Uma perspectiva analítica para a reforma do Estado', in *Lua Nova*, 45.

FIAN Information Bulletin (2000), May.

FoodFirst Information and Action Network (FIAN) (2000) *Encontro Internacional de Campesinos y Campesinas sin Tierra*. Heidelberg: FIAN/La Via Campesina.

Fox, Jonathan (2001) 'O painel de inspeção do Banco Mundial: lições dos cinco primeiros anos', in Flávia Barros (ed.), *Banco Mundial, Participação, Transparência e Responsabilização. A Experiência Brasileira com o Painel de Inspeção*. Brasília: Rede Brasil.

Grzybowski, Cândido (1987) *Caminhos e Descaminhos dos Movimentos Sociais no Campo*. Petrópolis: Vozes.

Harvey, David (1993) *A Condição Pós-Moderna*. São Paulo: Loyola.

Martins, José de Sousa (1981) *Os Camponeses e a Política no Brasil*. Petrópolis: Vozes.

Medeiros, Leonilde Servolo de (1989) *História dos Movimentos Sociais no Campo*. Rio de Janeiro: Fase.

Medeiros, Leonilde Servolo de (1997) *Reforma do Estado: Instâncias, Conflitos e Atores. O Papel dos Trabalhadores Rurais*, research report. Rio de Janeiro: CPDA/UFRRJ.

Medeiros, Leonilde Servolo de (2002) *Movimentos Sociais, Disputas Políticas e Reforma Agrária de Mercado no Brasil*. Rio de Janeiro: UNRISD and Editora da Universidade Federal Rural do Rio de Janeiro.

Ministério Extraordinário de Política Fundiária/Ministério da Agricultura e do Abastecimento (MEPF/MA) (1999) *Agricultura Familiar, Reforma Agrária e Desenvolvimento Local para um Novo Mundo Rural: Política de Desenvolvimento Rural com Base na Expansão da Agricultura Familiar e sua Inserção no Mercado*. Brasília. www.dataterra.org.br.

Moore Jr., Barrington (1987) *Injustiça: As Bases Sociais da Desobediência e da Revolta*. São Paulo: Brasiliense.

Navarro, Zander (1998) *O Projeto Piloto Cédula da Terra. Comentários sobre as Condições Sociais e Político Institucionais de seu Desenvolvimento Recente*. www.dataterra.org.br.

Novaes, Regina (1997) *De Corpo e Alma. Catolicismo, Classes Sociais e Conflitos no Campo*. Rio de Janeiro: Graphia.

Offe, Claus (1984) *Problemas Estruturais do Estado Capitalista*. Rio de Janeiro: Tempo Brasileiro.

Offe, Claus (1989) *Capitalismo Desorganizado*. São Paulo: Brasiliense.

Paiva, Vanilda (1985) 'Introdução', in Vanilda Paiva (ed.), *Igreja e Questão Agrária*. São Paulo: Loyola.

Palmeira, Moacir (1968) *Latifundium et Capitalisme. Lécture Critique d'un Débat* (unpublished thesis). Paris: Faculté de Lettres et Sciences Humaines de l'Université de Paris.

Palmeira, Moacir (1985) 'A diversidade da luta no campo: luta camponesa e diferenciação do campesinato', in Vanilda Paiva (ed.), *Igreja e Questão Agrária*. São Paulo: Loyola.

Sauer, Sérgio (undated) *Síntese do Relatório de Avaliação Preliminar Programa Cédula da Terra* (mimeo). Brasília.

Scherer-Warren, Ilse (1999) *Cidadania sem Fronteiras. Ações Coletivas na Era da Globalização*. São Paulo: Hucitec.

Silveira, José Maria da et al. (2000) 'Analysis of the sustainability of Cedula da Terra Program – PCT – Projects', in Sober, *Anais do XXXVIII Congresso Brasileiro de Economia e Sociologia Rural* (CDRom). Brasília.

Teixeira, Gerson (2000) *Crédito Fundiário. Trocando o Seis por Meia Dúzia*. www.reformagraria.org.br.

Thompson, Edward P. (1997) *Costumes em Comum*. São Paul: Companhia das Letras.

Wolff, Luciano and Sérgio Sauer (2001) 'O Painel de Inspeção e o caso do Cédula da Terra', in Flávia Barros (ed.), *Banco Mundial, Participação, Transparência e Responsabilização. A Experiência Brasileira com o Painel de Inspeção*. Brasília: Rede Brasil.

Documents

Annals of the National Congresses of Rural Workers

Agendas of the Gritos da Terra

Transcriptions of the Public Hearings of the Economic Affairs Commission of the Senate: 24 June 1997; 4 September 1997; 24 March 1999; 23 June 1999; 3 May 2001

Agrarian Legislation, available at www.incra.gov.br

Webpages

www.mst.org.br
www.contag.org.br
www.cna.org.br
www.dataterra.org.br
www.nead.gov.br
www.incra.gov.br

www.mda.gov.br
www.pt.org.br
www.abrareformagraria.org.br
www.cpt.org.br
www.no.com.br

3
Colombian Countryside between Privileges of *Latifundistas*, Modernizing Authoritarianism and Peasant Repression[1]

Stephan Suhner

Introduction

Colombia has a long tradition of promoting rural development and economic modernization. Historically, after the enactment of several isolated laws in the first half of the twentieth century, in 1961 the country adopted Law 135 of social agrarian reform. This legislation was seen as a model for Latin America, though it was rarely applied. However, in 1994, once more, Colombia set the example by adopting a market-led agrarian reform. Not surprisingly, agrarian issues were of great importance during the 1990s, and they have also been at the centre of debates regarding the resolution of economic, social and armed conflicts. Civil society, academia, peace organizations, trade unions and, most importantly, peasant organizations made key inputs in these debates. Nevertheless, market-led land reform encountered many critics and has shown its limitations in providing a viable solution to the agrarian question. Currently, a national agreement over a democratic and general land reform has been impossible to achieve, while conflicts related to the rural sector have worsened. These conflicts and the reasons that impeded their resolution are the subject of this chapter. Consequently, the study will illustrate the interactions between civil society and the market within the context of rural development. Due to the limited scope of the chapter, the discussion will circumscribe market issues to market-led land reform.

The chapter is organized in three sections. The first section goes back to the creation of the Colombian state in search of the determining factors of the future armed conflicts and constant crisis of its sociopolitical system. Taking a closer view, the historical analysis emphasizes the undulating character of reformism and counter-reformism, and the use of violence at the service of a state whose exclusion mechanisms favour only 'the few'. Furthermore, the concept of *gamonal* (political boss)[2] is introduced as a fundamental element in the social structure of Colombian society. The phenomenon of paramilitarism will be considered as the paradigmatic expression of the use of para-state violence to defend power, privileges and wealth; and the preferred mechanism of the *gamonal* system to undermine any attempt at land reform. In the second section, the emergence of a pronounced process of counter-agrarian reform will be analysed as the product of an alliance between traditional landowners and new social actors that stimulated the tendency to profit through land purchase. More specifically, we will focus our attention on the consequences of the intrusion of the land markets by drug traffickers. Within the background of a vast agrarian crisis that extends to other sectors, the second block of solutions to rural problems are examined in the third section. The critics of the old type of land reform are considered, forming the basis to justify a market-led agrarian reform. While looking into the poor results of Law 160 of 1994, the reasons for its failure are evaluated. We will assess how market mechanisms, and the associated lack of current policies, instead of diminishing negative tendencies in the countryside, nourish them. After exploring the deepening of the state crisis and rural violence, with the consequent counter-agrarian reform, this chapter offers a description of the position of peasant organizations regarding the market-led agrarian reform and the proposed alternative model. In conclusion, it is argued that economic interests, elites' political alliances, 'dirty' warfare and the weakness of peasant organizations have prevented any political alternative promoting social justice and democracy from achieving its objective.

The evolution of the state, *gamonal* system and the role of paramilitary groups

The Colombian state as the source of the crisis

How did Colombia arrive at the multifaceted crisis of the 1990s? The characteristics of the Colombian state are frequently signalled as the causes of the multiple problems the country has been facing. Its main difficulties are described as follows: a tendency towards private and violent conflict resolution, lack of state monopoly over force, scarce or little presence of the state in many regions, the inefficiency of justice and its high level of impunity, and lack of equity due to a concentration of wealth. There are various explanations for these problems, the main issue being an absence of a clear delimitation between the public and private spheres.

The characteristics of the state can be traced back to the indirect way in which Spain dominated its colonies, its process of territory occupation, and formation of the armed forces and the *gamonal* system. First, Spain colonized the country through a structure of local and regional powers centred on town councils of different regions. Each regional authority could deliver justice and in many cases have private militias without the presence of the colonial army. This partially explains Colombia's proclivity towards private resolutions of conflicts and its common recourse to violence (González, 1998). Second, its territorial occupation strategy left big extensions of unoccupied territory with little presence of the empire. These unconquered spaces functioned as a refuge for poor peasants expelled from their land, fugitive slaves, outlawed and indomitable natives. This, in turn, created social groups beyond the control of an incipient state, regulated by initiatives of the population. Moreover, the characteristics of Colombia's economic and political history have not entailed a long-term strategy of territory occupation – as for example the United States had. Private forms of appropriation conditioned space occupation – as a result of colonial administration and the fiscal weakness of the republican government – leading to the alienation of land by the most powerful sectors of society.

Third, in Nueva Granada, the armed forces did not possess a spirit of service to the nation, but to the interests of elite groups. Landed generals reached a determining political influence with high officers, and in alliance with other members of the elite, focused on debilitating the army Bolivar had created, inspired by ideals of emancipation and building a nation-state. The political project of the neo-Granadian elite pointed towards strengthening regional powers, at the expense of a central one.

Finally, the *gamonalismo* as a ruling class is one of the pillars of the Colombian state. Even if its characteristics and roles have varied during the last hundred years, it still represents the ruling sectors of society and is one of the main causes of its crisis. The *gamonal* originated from the colonial functionaries and landowners, becoming the dominant character from 1850. They are linked to the national government mainly through parliament, i.e., the chiefs of the two political parties are *gamonales* that utilize their respective parties as a channel through which to exercise their power.[3] The *gamonal* could be embodied by a rural landowner of an extensive cattle-ranching farm or, more recently, an urban one who exercises departmental power; or a businessman dependent on the state apparatus; a bureaucratic capitalist who accumulates wealth by means of state money and uses his influence to obtain concessions, appropriations or contracts, and interacts with national and/or international commercial networks (petrol concessions, banana plantations or railways) (Mondragón, 2000: 3). The indirect way in which the state was created allowed it to be low-cost and to respond positively to the lack of fiscal resources. The consequence of the almost absolute control that the *gamonalismo* had of the bi-party system is that the state has had to face neither great mobilizations or powerful trade union movements nor an extension of the middle class. That is why there are no popular pressures calling for a higher level of public expenditure, allowing the application of orthodox economic policies without high inflationary pressures. Consequently, other models of the state, such as an interventionist and industrializing state, or a welfare state, are not supported.

According to Daniel Pécaut (González, 1998: 176), Colombian violence is less related to abuses of an omnipotent and omnipresent state than to its lack of regional presence. Colombian violence is embedded within the complexity of integrating and expressing the micro-powers and the micro-societies of the colonized regions with broader spheres of society and state. Francisco Thoumi (1994) – from a critical institutionalist perspective – introduces the concept of a 'web of dishonesty' to account for the increasing gap between legality and normality in Colombian society and economy. He notes that the web of dishonesty is the product of a long historical process. While the country became more urban and modern, growing sectors of society rejected the old vision of the world and realized breaking the law could go unpunished – hence, generating a boost in conflicts between individuals and groups, where segments of the population felt detached from traditional power structures, thereby losing loyalty to national ideals. The web of dishonesty legitimized their rights over the income and resources of other citizens or the state, which, in turn, made business more expensive on account of the need for investment in wealth protection.

The growing illegitimacy of the regime led to the development of private systems of conflict resolution, and an increase in privatization of security services. The rapacious economic behaviour was stimulated by the attitude mentioned above, coupled with the underlying assumption that the state was a loot that could be sacked at will through the clientelist system. The establishment – in order to maintain political and economical control – accepted, and even stimulated, this opening gap between legality and normality, until it extended to all sectors of society (Thuomi, 1994: 103–4).

The particularities of Colombia's state formation dismantled spheres of regional power from the national state project. As the national state was not the sole controller of force and public space, its consolidation as the institution advocating peaceful resolution of conflicts was doomed from the start. In turn, the disarticulation between the local and national produced a gap between legality and normality, thus establishing group conflict as the norm.

The paramilitary as a system of domination of *gamonalismo*

During the 1950s, the civil war called La Violencia[4] started with the objective of impeding the reforms that were threatening oligarchic power, and in the 1960s and 1970s, through state and private violence, social protests were repressed, political alternatives annihilated, and peasant leaders assassinated. The use of violence to maintain authority and privileges has been especially virulent in rural areas, being closely related to power over land. During the 1980s, parallel to the crisis, there was an escalation of violence, even against reform attempts within the state structure itself.

The paramilitaries are the key instrument of this violence. Consequently, in this section we will analyse the origin and development of paramilitaries, their utility for the oligarchy that still today maintains the majority of power.

Following the Chicoral Pact of 1972,[5] the successive governments and landowners were united in a systematic repression of the peasant movement of the Sincelejo faction of the National Association of Usuary Farmers (ANUC-Sincelejo). Armed bands and state security forces demonstrated extreme violence against squatters. Their goal was to impose exemplary punishment to convince peasants that direct action was not a genuine option.

Under martial law, the state militarized whole regions, ordered massive detentions of peasants, and systematized the persecution of ANUC leaders. The goal was obviously to limit the number of protests and squatters. By the end of 1975, more than forty peasants had been killed and hundreds more made prisoners around the country (Zamosc, 1987: 229). The last struggles of the now weakened ANUC-Sincelejo were brutally repressed, and the actions of their members defined as guerrilla activities. The authorities brought in the army and named military mayors in regions of conflict. Landowners organized themselves into 'councils of societal security' and likewise, their first assignment was to fundraise a permanent squadron of *pájaros* (hired gunmen). There was also an attempt to systematically apply the 'Statute of Security 1978'. This statute was related to the context of union mobilization and the activities of the urban guerrillas M-19. The weakness of the peasants' movement in 1978 did not justify such an extreme measure. This statute proved a major blow to the peasants' protest movements (Zamosc, 1987: 330).

The creation of the landowners' private armed groups and their use of the army, combined with exceptional measures designed to repress – among others – the peasants' struggle for land were prominent during the 1980s and 1990s. Likewise, it demonstrated how the vast power of landowners enabled them to utilize repressive instruments of the state to defend their own private interests. During the 1980s and 1990s social cleansing became one of the main activities of the paramilitaries. Since the beginning of the 1970s the first death squadrons had appeared in Medellín, Cali and Pereira, intending to socially cleanse regions by eliminating the *undesirables* or *disposables*: homosexuals, prostitutes, beggars, street children (*gamines*), etc. This recent vocabulary attests the rise of fascist psychology in the middle and high-class sectors of society (Palacios, 1995: 328). It was during the national civic strike (*Paro Cívico Nacional*) in 1977 that the first two disappearances of leaders of MOIR (Independent Revolutionary Workers Movement) took place (Melo, 1991: 489).

Under the mandate of Julio César Turbay Ayala, the police and secret services created the triple A (Anti-communist American Action), a clandestine and parallel structure that avoided judicial processes, increasing the feeling of insecurity and arbitrariness amongst its potential and actual victims. Raul Zelik argued that the creation of these parallel structures was the immediate condition for the rise of paramilitaries. The apparent division between the public force and *obscure forces* permitted carrying out the most brutal repression (Zelik and Azzellini, 1999: 64). In commenting on this point, historian Jorge Orlando Melo noted that it was not clear whether the AAA and death squadrons were independent structures or a simple denomination to cover military operations. Indeed, during Turbay's government, the resort to paramilitary organizations was not needed because public forces felt authorized to perform this type of action. And perhaps more importantly, Melo considers that the *successful* recourse to torture and violence as a substitute for intelligence and police investigation could have prepared the way for the military to develop paramilitary groups (Melo, 1991: 491).

To sustain this warfare, the guerrillas raised their extortion of great landowners and created thorny conditions for them to manage their land while living on it. As a consequence, during the 1980s there was a higher inclination to sell big properties, the main buyers at the time being drug dealers like Pablo Escobar, the Ochoa brothers and Rodríguez Gacha. Drug traffickers paid very good prices in the land market benefiting landowners in crisis. They assumed the security risk as an extension of their own illegal organizations and created private armies for the protection of their acquired territories.

While the selling of land was taking place, the armed forces – based on an old relationship of mutual interest – urged big landowners to encourage setting up militia groups against the guerrillas. Young officers heading local units – particularly after the violence in the 1950s – have been systematically attracted by landowners through companies and facilities to acquire land and cattle, with the principal objective of guaranteeing their military protection. The bond thus created explains the formation of a new layer of 'ex-general landowners', a crucial element of the *latifundist* constellation representing the union between the land and military forces.

The armed forces' cry for 'peasant militia' was welcomed by some political leaders, many landowners, and even peasants tired of the guerrillas' depredations. Along these lines, the call offered the necessary and legitimate framework for the drug dealers to enter an anti-subversive alliance making them worthy of tolerance, even eagerness, on the side of traditional landowners, who in exchange could keep the political control of their regions. Therefore, the drug dealers' position in relation to landowners and armed forces led them to become the main financiers of their self-defence.

Through this alliance, drug traffickers acquired legitimacy for their participation in the dirty war, politics and their massive capital investment in different branches of the economy. This marked the beginning of a new economically and politically powerful social group called the 'narco-bourgeoisie'. The capital accumulated could buy judges, civil servants, politicians, soldiers, intellectuals and marginal sectors of the population, and their bombs and bullets could silence the uncorruptibles. This was the beginning of a bloody period of Colombian violence. The drug dealers' purchase and defence of territories was closely linked to the contra-insurgent strategy of the armed forces and the efforts of traditional parties not to lose their hegemony over the Left (Reyes Posada, 1997a: 281–9). The narrow frames that the country offered in its economy and political representation system were modified, and the rapid and voluminous wealth of drug dealers meant a swift increase of consumption and political power for groups associated with that activity. The tendencies generated by the entry of these resources meant the reinforcement of property concentration and authoritarianism, which are expressions of the imposition of the *latifundia* as a specific form of social relations (Fajardo Montaña, 2002).

During the 1980s, large segments of the elite perceived the apogee of social protests and the peace process as a threat to their privileges. The peace dialogue of Belisario Betancur and the truce with the Revolutionary Armed Forces of Colombia (FARC) found stubborn resistance in the armed forces. One of the objectives of the latter in creating paramilitary groups was to sabotage the peace process and continue undercover actions permitted by the Statute of Security. Betancur made several efforts to control the armed forces, but failed in his attempt to subordinate the military to civilian power, and modify their intransigence in favour of a political management of the 'guerrilla problem'. While the president was looking for peace with subversion, other sectors of the state responded to this 'threatening development' with repression. Many of the guerrilla fighters that were granted amnesty were found murdered soon after, and the recently formed Union Patriótica[6] suffered intense persecution with a high number of casualties (Zelik and Azzellini, 1999: 67). The strategies of private security groups, initially used to prevent kidnappings and payment of revolutionary taxes, were quickly extended when the army realized that extra-legal armed groups could be the key to isolating guerrilla fighters. Through a strategy of 'taking the fish out of the water', they focused their war against the civil populations of conflict zones. Indeed, the paramilitary strategy was quickly modified from a defensive to an offensive one.

In summary, at first, paramilitary tendencies were a phenomenon that provided political, military and socioeconomic benefits to politicians, many economic corporations, landowners and military institutions. However, after their link with drug trafficking, the resulting devastation began to cause immense harm to the state and society (Melo, 1991: 252). Drug trafficking infiltrated many sectors of political and social life in Colombia. When the judiciary started researching the links between the military, politicians and drug traffickers, the paramilitary and groups of private justice directed their efforts not only against the opposition but also against the state itself.[7]

The indiscriminate use of violence and terrorism by the narco-paramilitary in order to defend their interests implied that the state had to assume a new attitude towards them and undertake concrete actions to either dissolve them or to channel them institutionally.

The state created a series of measures against the paramilitary and drug traffickers – the decree that had been the legal base of paramilitaries since 1968 being repealed – and began, at least for a time, a strong fight against these two phenomena. In spite of some important results, paramilitary action and drug trafficking continued to grow rapidly – the former, without any legal framework, becoming a clandestine apparatus and major force since being declared illegal.

When Gaviria declared war against the FARC and the National Liberation Army (ELN), the armed forces renewed the contra-insurgent alliance with these new land buyers and gave the paramilitary an important role. At the beginning of 1995, the creation of the Cooperatives of Rural Security (CONVIVIR) – interpreted by large sectors of public opinion as a way of legalizing self-defence and paramilitary groups, and by others as a legitimate development of the right to defend themselves – was congruent with the real strategy of the armed forces not to abandon their support of paramilitary groups.

Since 1990, the paramilitaries have manifested an intention to broaden their regional support base, particularly in areas affected by armed conflict, and to diversify and project themselves in a wider spectrum. They started to realize the importance of public opinion and aimed to untie themselves from their most brutal actions and cultivate a self-critical tone. Yet, in practice, their methods and actions have not lost their cruelty. The destitution of certain paramilitary commandants because of their excesses is merely a marketing strategy. Additionally, they have shown an unexpected capacity to enter legal politics. Two years after being outlawed, some of the constituencies acted as their intermediaries in assemblies and advocated negotiations. Since then, there has been a constant interaction between members of parliament and paramilitaries. This interrelation recognizes the power paramilitaries have, while officially the possibility of negotiation is excluded and they are treated as common criminals.[8] The tacit signals are more expressive and the respectability that implies their recognition as social actors (armed) is sufficient for their support. If given the choice, paramilitaries prefer power *de facto* instead of *de jure* (Cubides, 1998: 83).

Generally, there is consensus between human rights NGOs and social organizations about the close relationship between paramilitarism and the state. Proof of this relationship is the existence of support, ties and acquiescence of the armed forces to paramilitary projects. The United Nations Human Rights Department in Bogotá and many NGOs have denounced the relationship between public forces and paramilitary groups, and cases of participation of members of the army in paramilitary actions. In contrast to the continuous military offensives against the guerrilla forces, actions against paramilitary groups are punctilious (United Nations, 2001: 31). Peasants in the south of Bolivar denounced the 'Bolivar Operation' at the beginning of 2001, while at the same time public forces used fumigation and fired guns at their houses, and the paramilitary established roadblocks, and murdered and displaced the population. They also protested against official helicopters which evacuated wounded paramilitaries who had been fighting against the guerrillas.

In spite of strong evidence to the contrary, some political analysts and official government sources insisted that the state was autonomous and presented it as 'the third party', a victim of crossfire between the guerrillas and the extreme right-wing groups, and finally adopting the role of observer. However, international pressures and factual evidence forced the government to accept that paramilitarism is a serious threat to institutionalization and the principal cause of the deterioration of the human rights situation. Likewise, according to the government, the growth of paramilitarism responds to the manifestation of drug-dealing criminal bands with networks that provide social, economical and political support, particularly in local or regional contexts. Other sectors of society share similar opinions, viewing armed groups as a product of the vacuum left by the state in the war against the guerrillas. In the last few years, armed forces and the state have made a considerable effort in providing evidence of improvement in human rights issues within the army. A few years ago, the armed forces were responsible for 70 per cent of human rights violations, while today the percentage is 5 per cent. Yet paramilitary participation in human rights violations increased during the same period from 10 per cent to 70 per cent, leaving constant the total number of violations.[9] These data disprove the idea of no linkage between the army and paramilitary, and exemplify the paramilitaries' role of doing the 'dirty work' that the armed forces are not able to do.

Other authors challenge the opinions noted above and suggest that the links go deeper than expected. Fernando Cubides added that even if one could prove the support of the army it is not enough to explain the fast development and diversification of paramilitarism since 1987. He held that it can only be explained if we accept that there are other sources of support than the ones expressed in the open (Cubides, 1998: 81); for example, the executive and judicial powers are also responsible for their lack of political will. These institutions did not take sufficient measures to dismantle illegal groups and structures, and situated the enquiries about paramilitarism in a secondary place, thus reinforcing mechanisms of impunity. The United Nations asserts that legislation and state policies had an important role in the consolidation of paramilitarism (United Nations, 2001: 30).

In addition to support from the armed forces, collaboration of multinational businesses, mainly in the mining, oil and agribusiness sectors should be taken into account. Industry, financial sectors and interests behind privatization of the public sector (telecommunications and other public services), utilize the paramilitary to weaken resistance from unions in cases of enterprise restructuring, privatizations, massive dismissals, salary reductions and social security. Even if broad sectors of the elite are behind the many forms of illegal violence, there is no unified position in the dominant sectors of society, and a minority even opposes paramilitary action. The present model of exclusion and domination in the political and economic sphere could not be sustained without violence and elimination of alternatives. This violence is a central element of the current economic model and in this sense is accepted or tolerated by the majority of economic leaders.

Carlos Alberto Ruiz argues that the paramilitary

> was born inside the state as it is reflected by the dispositions the latter created enabling the paramilitary structure to start developing. The paramilitary developed under state guidance, abiding by national security ideology, receiving arms and help in writing their statutes and mercenary contracts, as well as protection from the armed forces and a large part of civil society organizations to advance through the country, and also guaranteeing political status and impunity. The vitality of these organizations depends on the state; hence they are not merely a 'loose wheel', as has been suggested. (Quoted in Medina Gallego, 1994: 26)

To sum up, today's paramilitarism is a systematic state instrument; well thought through and secured against possible attacks, with mechanisms and legitimating discourses focused on maintaining the status quo. The paramilitary is supposedly a third and independent actor that carries out the dirty work for the armed forces of the state, permitting the latter to preserve the fictitious image of a constitutional state. That is why the paramilitary appears not to contradict the state but to defend its interests. The image of the state as the victim caught in crossfire between the paramilitary and the guerrillas, perceived as weak and fragmented, has been highly effective, because it wipes out responsibilities. An absolute majority of the state and security forces supports and accepts paramilitary groups as long-term associates, though this does not mean that the visible actors of the paramilitary are not dispensable. Even if the state pretends to fight paramilitary groups and captures some of their men,[10] illegal armed groups are still an intrinsic element of state machinery.

The agrarian counter-reform

The main feature of rural areas in Colombia is its organization in *latifundios* with low productivity, monopolizing land as a means of speculation, a source of power or social prestige. Since the 1950s, the *latifundio* has been slowly transformed by policies of production stimulation and the threat of agrarian reform. Large land areas have been divided, partly sold or rented to agribusiness groups and capitalists. However, resistance from large landowners against criteria for minimal production and efficient exploitation, as well as tax on productivity, highlights the lack of uniformity in this process, as a result leaving the inefficiently exploited *latifundio* still partially in place.

In spite of the *latifundist's* resistance, during the 1950s and 1960s commercial agriculture in the plains was mechanized, new technologies were applied, generating an increase in productivity. Import substitution policies attained self-sufficiency on various raw materials like barley, and even cotton export. Yet since 1978, the agricultural sector has entered a crisis, expressed in terms of low productivity and standstill of mechanization, from which it has not yet recovered. The trade unions, led by the farmers' SAC (Sociedad de Agricultores de Colombia) and the National Association of Industry (ANDI), condemned the rural crisis and lack of investment, blaming insecurity and the guerrillas for this. From an economic standpoint (Kalmanovitz, 1991: 288), the agricultural crisis was caused by a general recession of the economy. Globally there was a reduction in the area under crops and many medium-sized farmers faced bankruptcy, while simultaneously, there was more land being used in cattle ranching. Many agribusinessmen and medium-sized farmers facing the combination of the agro crisis and guerrilla violence decided to sell their lands to drug dealers.

Studies show that between 1970 and 1984 the proportion of properties of more than 500 hectares was significantly reduced in favour of estates of between 20 and 200 hectares as a result of modernization and colonization. Consequently, in some aspects the distribution of land improved. Paradoxically, between 1970 and 1984, a process of land consolidation started. The average size of estates bigger than 1000 hectares was transformed from 2674 hectares in 1970 to 3562 hectares in 1984. This process of land concentration can be seen as a counter-agrarian reform that concentrates land in the hands of the biggest producers due to an increase in the land devoted to extensive cattle ranching. Again, one of the main outcomes of the concentration process is purchase of land by drug traffickers.

The drug dealers have strongly influenced land tenancy structures and deeply altered rural society. The investment in land allowed them to launder their illicit profits and acquire social status and even local power, meaning that the profitability criteria of this type of investment were secondary. Drug dealers concentrated their land purchase in the five million hectares of improved pasture and to a lesser extent in regions of natural pastures. The acquisitions are also influenced by strategic search for isolation and territorial control.

The Colombian land market is divided into four productive systems with different characteristics that influenced the drug dealers' transactions. The structure of the land market directs their investments preferably to extensive cattle ranching areas and agrarian expansion zones (Reyes Posada, 1997a: 293). It is estimated that drug dealers and front men actually own between three and six million hectares of land.

Its effects over the socioeconomic structures vary according to the type of purchase. The assets of high-ranking leaders are a typical case of business colonization; hired administrators manage their cattle and do not have many links with local society. It thus produces a split in regional societies because property is now owned by a social group that replaces local elites but who do not take up their leadership functions. Another example is people of a particular region, generally middle-ranking leaders, who, wanting to climb the social ladder, buy land in their region and in the process transform the structure of relationships between owners, businessmen and peasants. The effects in local society are varied. The new owners have leadership over the process of change in the rules of investment, and they include family members, neighbours and friends in the new economic development originating from the accumulation of drug traffic profits. The drug dealers of La Guajira bought big estates in Cesar, Atlántico, Bolívar and Córdoba, but they neglected their cattle ranching business because they were not as interested in supplanting the rural elite as acquiring social prestige. Their fortune was wasted on excesses. They resold their land to the local farmers. In Magdalena the situation was different in that many traditional owners decided to make contact with drug dealers so they could refinance their properties and continue in parallel both their agricultural and cocaine activities. So, drug trafficking did not produce a division in local society, but a symbiotic relationship between them and drug dealing activities. In Antioquia, the drug dealing activity enriched adventurers with a history of illegal activities and families linked to the land (Reyes Posada, 1997a: 298).

The concentration of property, resulting from drug dealers' purchases and reversal from agriculture to cattle ranching, caused many peasant families to be expelled to the cities and agricultural frontiers. When the drug dealers intended to buy disputed land, the groups from the valley found social opposition from peasants and indigenous populations. As a solution, drug dealers resorted to violence. The best lands were cultivated with sugarcane, which permitted relative success in resisting the pressure to sell (Reyes Posada, 1997a: 319). The massacre of Trujillo – in the case of peasants – and of Caloto – in the case of indigenous groups – illustrate this attitude. For the past twenty-five years a strong indigenous movement has existed in Cauca with the aim of recovering land (Reyes Posada, 1997a: 325).

In zones appealing to drug dealers the price of land rose tenfold, while in zones less attractive for investment and with security problems – strong guerrilla presence – the land market was very low and the only buyer was the Colombian Institute of Agrarian Reform (INCORA). Córdoba is one of the centres of paramilitarism and perhaps the region with the highest land and wealth concentration on the Atlantic coast. There is no other place where the polarization between peasants and landowners was more acute during the 1970s, or the substitution of the old cattle ranching sector for drug dealers so swift, on top of having the highest registered private army (the group financed and commanded by Fidel Castaño) in order to fight against the guerrillas and their strongholds. The result of the processes mentioned was the massive displacement of the rural population. Castaño invested part of his drug profits in buying great areas of land in the municipalities of Tierralta, Valencia and Montería, building up a vast cattle ranching empire and then expanding his business to Urabá, and joining the contra-insurgent strategies of the 1980s. He also charged war taxes to other big landowners so they became committed to the war. He also decided to distribute parcels of 10 hectares of land with precarious titles to peasant families and to demobilize the guerrillas, with the aim of creating his own social support. In addition, he financed infrastructure work and social services in his areas of influence.

In the case of Córdoba, drug dealers adopted a business approach in cattle ranching; they developed infrastructure and increased productivity. According to INCORA, 60 per cent of productive land in the region – 80 000 hectares – is in the hands of drug traffickers. The price of land went up to 10 million pesos per hectare, making INCORA's agrarian reform impossible with the modality of voluntary purchases. Furthermore, there is a strong demand for smaller properties by middle-ranking drug dealers and rich Antioquian cattle ranchers, and a strong valorization is predicted with the Urrá dam, that controls the periodic floods of the river Sinú.

In addition, the old *latifundio* expanded, usually associating closely with drug trafficking. As a consequence of economic liberalization during 1990, commercial agriculture was in an even more dire state, using land only for cattle ranching as well as for a few agricultural products in demand by the international market.

Market-led agrarian reform

A new law to solve old problems

In the context of the crisis situation described above, the government of César Gaviria elaborated a new agrarian reform law. From a theoretical standpoint, market-led agrarian reform (MLAR) fits perfectly with the new development paradigm and neoliberal ideology, based on the principles of the market. The different concepts of MLAR are supported in decentralization frameworks, and processes of voluntary negotiations between landowners and the rural poor. The state changes its executor's role to one of facilitating market processes by supporting negotiations and subsidizing the acquisition of land. For complementary services the state looks for support in the private sector and civil society. The models of agrarian reform used until 1994 have been criticized for their excessive centralization, bureaucratization and lengthy procedures, as well as their high costs combined with problems of clientelism and corruption. Previously, agrarian reform was understood as a problem of power relations making state intervention necessary. In the new neo-institutional style, the blame is put on the bureaucratic, clientelistic, inefficient and corrupt institutions; and it is believed that the market is the ideal mechanism to overcome the problems of the old and centralized state institutions. In addition, the government proposes the decentralization of functions and delegation of responsibility for agrarian reform to departmental and regional levels. As such, this new approach does not take into consideration the inhibiting effect of power relations, for instance the influence that landowners have in governmental bodies. If the state delegates the responsibility for the agrarian reform to various private and civil society actors and the market, it runs the risk of diluting responsibilities. Civil society or the imperfections of the market would be held accountable for a new failure of the agrarian reform, and the obvious lack of political will and obstruction of landowners would go unnoticed.

None of the instruments applied in the past has produced real land redistribution with equity and efficiency. Expropriation with compensation has always brought resistance from landowners and it has also been characterized by its slowness and high administrative costs. The different threats of expropriation and the concept of efficiently exploited land did not represent a solution to the problem of rural poverty and violence. On the contrary, they led to a consolidation and modernization of large properties, which benefited from the rent, transferred through subsidies directly by the state, and strengthened landowners politically.

Law 160, reflecting the spirit of neoliberal thinking, was strongly anchored in the land market. But it was impaired by legislative changes in parliament, such as the introduction of regulatory instruments in addition to a strong state role with no coherence or hierarchy. This patchwork-like structure had as a practical outcome the consideration of different modalities of access to land: entitlement of idle land; legalization of land ownership by settlers or occupation through entitlement; acknowledgement of indigenous and black communities' collective property rights; expropriation with compensation for reasons of social demand; direct intervention and purchase of land by INCORA; voluntary negotiations between landowners and landless peasants; cancellation of ownership rights in case of absentee landowners or land that was illegally appropriated by these landowners; and regulation of the use of land in areas of colonization through *zonas de reserva campesina* (land allotted by the state through an agrarian reform programme in order to protect the peasant from the big landowners).

The peasantry has not had any major influence in the approved legislation. On the one hand, peasants continue to assert that the endowment of land is the responsibility of the state through direct purchase and transaction at low or zero cost. Law 160 was not considered by the landless as a mechanism that could accelerate the redistribution process; and the 70 per cent subsidy has not been welcomed by peasants' organizations, as it is very difficult for them to finance the remaining 30 per cent. On the other hand, agribusinesses consented to voluntary negotiations because they could offer their lands at market prices at a time when the sector's activity was collapsing due to measures of structural adjustment. Given that there was no hierarchical order between the different mechanisms prescribed by law, the threat of expropriation began to disappear and landowners could secure payment offered via the national budget and private debts of peasants (Rojas, 1999: 72).

According to this new model, the difficulties of agrarian reform are attributed to the rigidity of land markets. Market imperfections and macro and sector policies inhibit the assignment of resources to the most efficient producers – according to this theory – family producers. The agrarian problem appeared again on the political agenda, but from a very different perspective. Thereupon, agrarian reform is not a problem of political economy with a need for state intervention, but a problem of reduction of distortions and imperfections of policies and markets (Höllinger, 1999: 138).

Market-led agrarian reform has proved to be very inefficient. Since the beginning, the new model of agrarian reform has faced multiple obstacles related to an excessive number of regulations, INCORA's strong centralism, lack of participation of financial intermediaries, misinformation of potential beneficiaries, and the inoperative character of the National System of Agrarian Reform. The first transactions under Law 160 were affected by high prices paid to owners, non-selection of applicants, bureaucratic layout of projects, the excessive cost of each Agricultural Family Unit established, and absence of municipal input in the definition of criteria for purchasing land (Rojas, 1999: 76). The lack of an integrated market at the national level was another big problem, since there are only segmented markets with strong asymmetries and no communication between them. The main division is between markets of small landowners and big properties, with little or no interaction between them. Furthermore, big areas are subject to different forms of territory control and thus are marginalized from typical market behaviour. Law 160 raised too many expectations with respect to the potential role of the land market solving the problem of land inequality in the countryside.

This reform has accentuated even more the bi-modal structure of land tenure: there is a large offer of medium quality land – on average 223 hectares owned by bankrupt business men – and INCORA, in the context of the agro crisis, is the only buyer of land. Meanwhile, large properties of more then 500 hectares are not affected by this agrarian reform, i.e., there are no transactions either with the peasantry or with INCORA, while there is no danger of expropriation or the reduction in the ceiling of estates. On the contrary, big landowners hold the largest concentration of the best lands with high agricultural potential, possibilities of mining and wood exploitation, genetic potential for biotechnology, or possibilities of mega road projects or other infrastructure. There is a negative balance between the lands of large landowners, sold to small and medium-sized landowners, and land bought by large landowners from small or medium-sized landowners. Negotiated land is generally of average or bad quality: only a few parcels sold during agrarian reform are considered to be of quality III, there are practically none of quality II or I, and the majority are quality IV to VI.

Agrarian reform in Colombia was never far-reaching, but under the current model the results are worse than ever. The 1997 census of the National Administrative Department of Statistics (DANE) shows that 1 547 676 families were interested in acquiring land, but only 900 were dealt with using the budget assigned to INCORA for 1999. According to the Four-Year Agrarian Reform Plan, developed in 1994 and based on Law 160 by Samper's government, the agrarian reform should come to an end within sixteen years, with 721 000 families acquiring 4.5 million hectares of land. Clearly, at the pace of the four-year period 1994–8, the sixteen-year plan would take 110 years (CNC, 1999: 4). MLAR is still a micro-programme for some peasant elites, unable to affect or transform deep structural problems, and with the unrealistic possibility of obtaining necessary support, the cost of each Agrarian Family Unit being unreasonably high.

Institutional limitations and problems of participation

Suárez explains the failure of MLAR by the absence of an institutional network where land markets could function. Consequently the law did not set up in practice state agencies with experience in the application of land market programmes. Decentralization of agrarian reform faces resistance from central state institutions like INCORA, that fear losing power and employees, and from landowners and regional politicians who want to maintain their control over land, institutions and agrarian reform processes for their own personal benefit. For many traditional politicians – in many cases, big landowners – INCORA has been one of the main instruments of clientelism through political pay-off and electoral favours. In addition, it was used as an instrument of corruption, as well as social and political control by managing the processes of land transactions and titling of abandoned land.

Since the late 1980s, decentralization and citizens' participation have been on the political agenda. Nevertheless, in practice they suffered many flaws and encountered strong resistance. The cooperation between national (for example, INCORA) and regional or local levels (municipal or departmental councils of agrarian reform) has been very low and the municipalities possess only embryonic planning capacities and mechanisms of participation.

The main political goal of decentralization lies in the existence of diverse preferences, resources, capacities and levels of development in the country. Within this context, new institutions were created – Municipal Councils of Rural Development (MCRD) and Municipal Councils of Agrarian Reform (MCAR) – and municipalities were given new functions and faculties. But in these plans, the themes of property distribution and rural poverty are hardly mentioned, and attention is centred on analysing the agricultural sector in terms of lack of infrastructure, mechanization and technical assistance to small producers. In spite of high concentration and poverty indicators, land distribution is not highlighted as a priority.

Even though Law 160 encourages wide participation of beneficiaries in the process of agrarian reform, there are many obstacles that prevent this from happening. The main factors that limited the participation process are: incomplete decentralization; subordination of the poor to local power structures; their disadvantage at negotiations; and their dependency on the new social actors (NGOs, the private sector and peasant organizations). New organizations like MCRD are still incipient organizations and they generally adopt a passive attitude with little influence to summon mass meetings. Indeed if power relations at a local level are not restructured, decentralization does not automatically mean higher levels of participation. Furthermore, at a cultural level, asymmetries between institutions and political authorities and beneficiaries can restrain the participation of the latter. Violence and insecurity are other elements that can explain low participation of peasants in consultation and planning, as well as in the discussion about the conditions of purchase. Violence directly affects potential beneficiaries;[11] for instance, to access land, peasants have to organize themselves, and this is usually interpreted by paramilitaries as subversive action. The Peasant Association of Beneficiaries of Agrarian Reforms – which encouraged its members to participate in this action – has faced high levels of violence during the process of agrarian reform. Sometimes, merely the announcement that INCORA will buy a *latifundio* for redistribution entails the displacement of the potential beneficiaries by paramilitaries.

The institutions in charge of decentralization and participation, which are part of a policy of democratic consolidation (popular election of mayors, a new constitution in 1991 and so on), have been captured by *gamonales* in order to strengthen their social position. Moreover, territory reorganization reflects the interests of bureaucrats, financiers and landowners, and the electoral pretensions of *gamonales*, and not the geographical, ecological, economical, social and cultural realities of regions. Financial and transnational capital does not find in local contexts agents other than *gamonales* and their paramilitaries. If such outside groups wish to get involved in investment projects in the region, they have to depend on *gamonales* and other dominant forces.

To wrap up this discussion, it can be said that in many municipalities and regions decentralization has in fact increased the power of *gamonales*, and they thus benefited from more independence without a change in social relations. Peasants' organizations have denounced these processes by labelling them 'perverse decentralization'. For decentralization to have a democratizing and modernizing effect, it is necessary to break the oligopoly of land property which is in the hands of *gamonales*.

Guerrilla groups have always wanted to influence the management of municipalities (budgets and setting up local institutions). Decentralization processes and popular elections of mayors facilitated the use of the guerrillas' influence, while simultaneously permitting alternative political movements to run some of the municipalities. This other aspect of decentralization threatened the traditional power of *gamonales* and produced a strong reaction of reconquering power through violence from peasant organizations and alternative movements. Today, *gamonalism* and paramilitarism dominate many municipalities and institutions, and exercise absolute social control. Spaces of debate are monopolized, those voicing a different opinion persecuted, and democratic alternatives and social organizations eradicated. Even the democratically elected mayors who strongly support participation mechanisms became a military target.

In this environment of widespread violence, territorial dispute, and absolute social and territorial control, the consolidation of the institutions in question is practically impossible. Moreover, the state does not have the tools to defend the endangered institutions or does not show interest in protecting the protagonists of participatory processes. Judges or public functionaries in this vulnerable position have to abandon their posts; and peasants' organizations that should be able to participate in MCRD and MCAR are one of the main victims of paramilitary violence. In this adverse context, peasant organizations make great efforts to maintain their organizational structure by forming new leaders, organizing training courses and teaching how to elaborate production and new projects.

The problem of land prices and structures

As mentioned before, market-led land reform needs a relatively perfect land market to succeed, a characteristic that is absent in the Colombian land markets. Land markets possess multiple distortions. Furthermore, there is no national market but multiple regional ones dependent on the use of land (agricultural, speculative, for urbanization, infrastructure or mining projects), the security situation and distance from an urban centre. There are no reliable and up-to-date land registries for all regions and properties, thereby resulting in insecure and often disputable property rights. Tax collection is minimal because land registry values are ridiculously low and only small tariffs apply to property taxes. This situation encourages overvaluation of land, making the development of viable family businesses impossible. Regardless of the sector's crisis and violence, land prices rose from US$811 per hectare in 1991–4 to US$1159 in 1995–7 (Höllinger, 1999: 162). These prices are determined by three factors: expected value, capacity to generate rents, and security. These factors superimpose each other, thereby producing highly distorted markets.

The faults of market-led agrarian reform (MLAR) in relation to land markets and levels of land prices can be summarized as follows (Höllinger, 1999: 137–96). MLAR did not influence the level of land prices, the desired price transparency was not obtained, and the market did not get the dynamics expected, because in the *latifundist* class there is no disposition to sell voluntarily, and even less at prices with respect to the farming profitability of land. There is an intersection of logics in the land market: the logic of production, the speculation, and the extra-economical one encompassing territorial power – factors that reflect in price levels and in the dynamics of land offers. MLAR interprets the gap between market price and price according to productive profitability as a structural phenomenon, the result of distorted policies and transaction costs. It suggests that with policies that will eliminate these distortions the participation of the poor in the market will increase. However, the land's double function as fixed asset as well as a source of cash, and its extra-economical functions cast doubt as to the real scope of these measures. Subsidy seems doubtful and even counter-productive, i.e., if subsidy functions close the price gap, a reduction in price level cannot be expected. For subsidy to act as a compensatory force of the poor's lack of savings, a viable scheme to negotiate land prices is needed, coupled with a correlation of forces that guarantees landowners will accept these prices. Still, the persistency of rent-seeking behaviour creates doubts as to whether voluntary and direct negotiations with subsidy are the adequate scheme. These uncertainties arise because landowners have extra-economical and productive ties with their land that forces them to sell only under extreme circumstances. Before selling, they might opt for calling armed groups to defend it, or have extensive cattle-raising schemes, or wait for better profitability. Voluntary negotiation cannot intervene in this type of situation, and in the context of paramilitary violence, the effect that state measures can have is also quite limited.

Only a small number of landowners sell their land to INCORA or directly to peasants. These are medium-sized owners who have been ruined by the crisis in agriculture or overwhelmed by violence. Hence the agrarian reform helped to wipe out the layer of medium-sized farmers crucial for rural development. The poor peasant who wishes to acquire good land competes in a 'free land market' with agribusiness groups that continue to invest, and a wide spectrum of old and new landowners who buy land for speculation with the aim of attaining social prestige or territorial control. In addition, state subsidies, which in practice cover the breach between the profitability price and the price inflated by the 'market', encourage those landowners willing to sell to adopt a rent-seeking attitude. Indeed, the price per hectare has tended to be considerably lower in the agrarian reform with direct state intervention than with voluntary negotiations. There has been over-expectation of peasants' participation, negotiating capacity and business management within MLAR. Under the scheme of voluntary negotiations peasants pay practically 100 per cent of the initial price suggested. A pilot training programme in negotiations managed, in some cases, to lower the price of purchase down to 50 per cent from the initial price. This shows the need to dismantle dominant power relations and strengthen peasant organizations.

It is also necessary, under a land market scheme with clear redistributive purposes, for the landowners selling land to sacrifice part of their benefits in favour of the less privileged. This could mean negotiating a price below its commercial value, or a change in payment arrangements. Different coercive mechanisms that allow landowners to obtain profits by the state need to be broken, such as privileged access to best land, subsidies and labour. Under the current negotiated land market scheme, many beneficiaries perceive that landowners are the best advantaged, because they can sell parcels affected by conflict and violence at commercial prices.

A new phase of agrarian counter-reform

Since 1984 there has been a real agrarian counter-reform and land consolidation by *latifundistas* due to the armed conflict. Some of the causes of this process have already been mentioned, like purchase of land by drug dealers. In the struggle for territorial domination, we can observe the use of different strategies, including redistributive mechanisms (for example, in Córdoba, where Castaño parcelled some property to create grassroot support and a recruitment base) and other instruments entailing a higher degree of concentration (displacement, massacre of populations viewed as hostile) (Höllinger, 1999: 154).

Behind paramilitary activities there is an economic rationality that enables their consolidation, gaining regional support and social base for military action as the re-establishers of the lost social order. For example, it allows them to buy agricultural products cheaply where the guerrillas are, to provide private security and to gain from high property values. As long as the guerrillas have not been able to gain full control of a territory and consolidate their influence, there is a tendency for a whole region to remain insecure and, in this situation of generalized uncertainty, paramilitary groups prosper as capitalists of insecurity.

There is lack of available data concerning the payment of tributes or collaboration with paramilitaries in the way of a 'vaccine' against the guerrillas. Paramilitaries try to compete with the guerrillas so as not to lose social support, hence they avoid confiscating taxes and assume the function of guarantor of property rights. This frequently served to maintain a precarious equilibrium between demanding voluntary contributions, widening their tributary base and striving to reinvest surplus in land, as the more secure way of retaining, expanding and using political dividends to perpetuate the support gained. Armed groups were rapidly converted into a new type of businessman. Stable security often meant a better quality of life for people in areas that they controlled. Moreover, there were more possibilities for governmental aid for infrastructure.

As previously stated, large segments of the rural elite support paramilitarism. For the agro-industrial sector, the paramilitary project is functional as a violent device to solve labour conflicts with trade union leaders and rural workers. This is the case of the Union of Banana Growers (UNIBAN) responsible for the organization of paramilitary activities in Urabá. Paramilitary terror and the subsequent displacements have led to the seizure of new lands for agro-industrial crops, and overcoming resistance from local communities to these development plans are not in the interests of the rural elite. Furthermore, sectors of the Colombian Agricultural Society (SAC), like the palm tree producers, also support paramilitarism. But its most enthusiastic supporters are the cattle ranching sector and its main organization, the National Federation of Cattle Dealers (FEDEGAN). They are the most affected by subversive violence, yet as political actors they are responsible for the biggest injustices in the countryside (i.e., expulsion of peasants from their lands). Hence, their support of paramilitary operation has two motivations: first as a defence against the guerrillas, and second as an expansionist and offensive strategy. But this model abandoned its defensive character to aggressively take over new regions in order to extend their domination over fertile or strategic land, and thus impose their development model.

Together with paramilitarism, the dominant class pursues projects in the countryside with clear political, economical and social components that Liberdo Sarmiento defines as 'authoritarian rural modernization'. A project is executed in various phases: (a) the incursion stage: the attempt being to 'liberate' vast areas of guerrilla influence and support bases by means of war, implementing a process of land concentration, modernizing road infrastructure and public services, developing cattle-ranching capitalism and a new hierarchical and authoritarian structure of social organization; (b) the consolidation phase: the intention being to 'enrich' the region through subsidizing land, generating employment, concentrating the population in urban areas, building health centres and schools, the 'present' of electricity, etc. The new settlers that inhabit the liberated zones are not those who were displaced by violence, but a new population faithful to the chief of the area rapidly organizing themselves into paramilitary auto-defence groups; (c) the legitimating phase: building up the necessary structure to expand capitalism and 'modernization' of the state with the aid of the private sector (Banco de Datos de CINEP and Justicia y Paz, 1997: 155–8).

Another element to take into account when analysing this new land concentration process is the restructuration imposed by globalization on the Colombian economy, and its rural sector in particular. In a globalized economy, what counts is not a whole agricultural sector devoted to national food security, but also leaving space in rural areas for plans and investment of transnational capital for mega-projects concerning energy, building new roads and exploitation of natural resources, etc. Once the rural sector has adopted this new role, the agrarian counter-reform is initiated. Legal and illegal expropriatory measures are taken against peasants, indigenous or black communities, in part directly as a result of these mega-projects.[12]

This counter-agrarian reform, the new concentration of land in the context of globalization, and the territorial control pursued by armed groups and paramilitary objectives, in general, have given rise to huge displacements. Since colonization, displacement has been a historical phenomenon of land struggle, but in 1985 it increased from 50 000 displaced people per annum to 400 000 in 2002, with a total of 2.8 million in seventeen years. Among these people, 65 per cent were landowners, 7 per cent land tenants, 8 per cent sharecroppers[13] and 6 per cent settlers. Two-thirds of landowners abandoned their land, 12.8 per cent managed to sell it, and 2 per cent to rent it. In this way, displacement has strongly affected reorganization of land tenancy. This reorganization was responsible for many deaths: from 1988 to 1995, an average of 454 peasants were murdered every year, i.e., an average of 1.2 per day. For each person murdered or reported missing in rural areas, between three and seven families were displaced (Salgado and Prada, 2000: 245). Since 1985, displacement has meant that peasants have been leaving behind three million hectares of land (*El Tiempo*, 4 November 2000). According to other sources, in the last ten years, two million hectares have been abandoned because of displacement. The violent recomposition of land tenancy clearly indicates that displacement of peasant landowners is increasing: from 42 per cent in 1997 to 46 per cent in 1998 and 59 per cent in 1999, at the same pace that increases the property of large landowners substantially (*Actualidad Colombiana*, 4 April 2001).

The paramilitary aims to recover or defend the political power of *gamonales*, chiefs and the bi-party system, and globally to avoid any social or economic changes favourable to peasants. The peasant and indigenous movement has been engaged in important protests since 1996, consolidating their internal structure, and allying with other social movements. They have also been elaborating concrete and viable solutions to their problems, in particular, producing a green paper for agrarian reform and focusing their mobilizations on 'a peaceful agrarian reform'. The paramilitary groups have reacted by expanding in the areas where the mobilizations occur, and massacres, the selective assassination of leaders and forced displacements have increased. Through these tactics, at least temporarily, peasants' mobilizations in favour of land reform were halted.

The paramilitary offensive is directed against the populations of regions with strategic interests for the dominant classes, with strong social movements and alternative politics.[14] Since the mid-1980s, there has been an increase in protests against marginalization, culminating in the blocking of the whole department by a multisector social movement in November 1999. Not surprisingly, after that strike, the Bloque Social Alternativo was created, whose candidate Floro Tunubalá – as the first indigenous governor of a Colombian department – won the local elections. As a consequence of these political achievements, the communities that participated in the demonstrations were subjected to a campaign of repression. Since May 2000 the

Autodefensas Unidas de Colombia (AUC) with its western bloc (Frentes Calima, Pacifico, Farallones and Paez) has brought terror to the north and centre of the department, and has highlighted the lack of will in the third brigade to suppress these groups. As a consequence of paramilitary action between May 2000 and February 2001, there were an estimated 200 murders, four disappearances, threats to five mayors, and displacement of 7000 peasants (MINGA et al., 2001). The social organizations of Cauca denounced these actions.[15] It is also worrying that Cauca is one of the departments in the Plan Colombia intending to use massive fumigation of illegal crops. The media markets the idea that all these violent and armed conflicts are only a matter of territorial control between subversives and paramilitaries, without analysing the coincidental presence of national and international economic interests.[16] The territories of illegal crop production are found in strategic developmental zones: mines, natural resources, agro industry. It is thus possible that some industrialists and businessmen are sponsoring paramilitary groups and illegal crops to guarantee private investment and expel poor sectors from the area.

For seven years, the Afro-Colombian communities of the Pacific region have been among the most affected by paramilitary activities, because – as native groups – they oppose the construction of mega-projects in their ancestral territories. There are potentially 4.5 million hectares that, according to the law, should receive collective titles and thus are placed outside the reach of economic interests. The first organization to receive a communal title was the Asociación Campesina Integral del Atrato (ACIA) in 1997, but the title was worthless because the majority of the community were displaced and their lands deforested and used for cattle ranching. The communities of Río Cacarica were displaced after the valorization of their territory with the project of the inter-oceanic canal, while wood has been illegally taken from the region without the community's approval. The Afro-Colombian communities of Alto Baudó in Chocó have been the target of constant violence from armed groups since 1993, causing general displacement and the assassination of various leaders, the aim being to boycott the process of collective titling of their land. On 23 May 2001, they received the last of five titles for 174 000 hectares from a total of 240 000 hectares. Currently, they are facing violent uprooting: from a group of 20 000 in Alto Baudó municipality, almost 4500 have been displaced. With the paramilitary threats and displacement process, the organizational capacity to defend their ancestral territory through peaceful and legal channels is in danger.[17]

Peasant organizations and market-led land reform

From the beginning, peasants' organizations have criticized Law 160 and market-led agrarian reform, as well as predicted many of its negative effects. One of the most negative outcomes is the danger of indebtedness due to the credit at market conditions that peasants have to accept in order to pay the 30 per cent of the value of the Agrarian Family Unit not covered by subsidy. At present, many beneficiaries of this law are in an embargo process or have lost their land (SINTRADIN, 1998: 4; Comisión Campesina de Impulso a la Paz, 1998: 2). In this context, some peasant organizations like the Agricultural and Farm Workers' Union (FENSUAGRO) decided not to enter this scheme, with a high risk of embargo for not being able to repay debt.[18] Other organizations like the Colombian Association of Beneficiaries of the Agrarian Reform (ACBRA) opted for full participation in the scheme, considering it was the only existing mechanism of agrarian reform. Given the peasants' need for access to land, the danger was that, confronted with a negative response by their associations, they would be organized by the same landowners willing to sell, and then left to their own destiny after the transaction. ACBRA considered that while there was danger of falling into the debt trap if thousands of peasants joined the agrarian reform programme and got indebted, it would be very difficult for the government to take away everybody's land for defaulting. Likewise, ACBRA advised its social base to join the programme, trusting that thousands of peasants suffering unpayable debts would suffice to press the government for solutions.[19] And, indeed, that was what happened: after continuous mobilizations and marches the government finally took alleviation measures. The government has not yet come up with a definitive solution to peasants' debts nor is it willing to transform the market-led model, but peasant leaders are confident that small extensions and alleviations gained will promote a better organization of peasants and improve their proposals.

The privatization tendencies of state functions in the acquisition and adjudication of land imposed great challenges to peasant leaders and their organizations. In line with Law 160, peasant organizations are new actors in this process. There are strong stimuli and challenges for peasant organizations to participate as intermediaries in the land reform market. On the one hand, there is the personal interest of the leader, who could personally benefit by acting as a mediator between landowners and peasants. In the light of the continuous threats and precarious economic situation they live in, with this new role peasant leaders might gain political protection and the possibility of improving their quality of life. In addition, in their role as leaders, they face the difficult task of combining their trade union and political functions with their personal interests and need for subsistence, without losing their credibility as leaders. The situation becomes more complex when we consider the competition between the peasant organizations for accessing this role, when the law also opens the possibility for private state agents to act as intermediaries (Höllinger, 1999: 167).

For this reason, peasant organizations had to consolidate in the market to maintain their clientele of peasants and landowners requesting their services to negotiate land. Given that landowners want to sell at high prices and peasants to buy at low ones, leaders face the dilemma of conflicting interests.

Due to their access to information, knowledge of the market, contacts with INCORA functionaries and position as an intermediary between INCORA, peasants and owners, peasant organizations can create the situation that gives them a margin in negotiations. There are ambivalent relations between INCORA and peasant organizations: they need to preserve good relations in order to get subsidies, and at the same time, the law establishes competition between new actors and INCORA for the execution of certain functions. Peasant leaders have a better knowledge of the market than state agents, can charge a lower commission, have good contacts with INCORA, and can use the pressure of their social base, and for all these reasons prove to be the best intermediaries for landowners.

The fact that some peasant organizations participate in market-led agrarian reform does not mean they support it. The majority of organizations oppose the agrarian reform scheme based on Law 160 and the proposals for rural development made by the governments of Misael Pastrana Borrero and Uribe Vélez. They oppose the statement that large properties, international investment and mega-projects nominate themselves as the enclaves of rural activity and pretend that communities can only exist as a satellite of the business sector, in a strategic subordination in their projects. This is also the spirit of the strategic alliances promoted by Pastrana's government as the panacea of the solution to rural problems, where landowners give peasants 20 per cent of their land in exchange for their labour. For peasants to envisage agrarian reform means breaking this historical subordination of their lives, culture and interests and deciding for the first time in Colombia's history their own destiny as citizens and as dignified peasant communities. The opposition of these two types of agrarian reform also imply a contraposition of two models of the economy and society. Therefore, peasants continue to search for a model of development that considers peasant economy as a central element, without denying the use and necessity of agro-industry and large-scale exploitation. The so-called *via de desarrollo campesina* bases its argument on the premise that a peasant is a more efficient producer than a big landowner, but the former has two severe limitations: lack of land and lack of capital, which prevent him from increasing productivity and responding to market incentives (Valderrama and Mondragón, 1998: 2 and 38). All these obstacles can be overcome with necessary assistance, and establishing cooperatives to secure low-cost services.

Nowadays, with the escalation of internal conflict and an unprecedented counter-agrarian reform, peasants fight to negotiate a solution to conflict and enforcement of human rights within a broad civic movement for peace. Against private and violent expropriations from speculators and transnationals, peasants propose the application of an administrative expropriation of land necessary for agrarian reform and the extinction of domination over land suitable for agriculture that is being wasted. As land market prices are higher than their agricultural profitability, generation of small peasant businesses is not viable under the market scheme. Only expropriation and extinction of domination can make agrarian reform affordable and bring productivity to family units. To achieve these ends, concentration of tenure and speculation with land prices should be eliminated, as well as changing the use of the five million hectares owned by drug traffickers, and implementing a property tax that discourages the speculative accumulation of land (CNC, 1999: 6). A system to impede the recomposition of *latifundios* should be put in place when the state invests in an agrarian reform recognizing that landowners tend to sell land to INCORA at high prices. So that reformist efforts are not wasted due to the effects of violent expropriation and landowners' speculation, it is necessary to limit the land market. The *zonas de reserva campesina* (ZRC) are a first step towards the restriction of commerce and land concentration, but to date only six have been approved and only one has actually been implemented.

During recent years, peasant, indigenous and Afro-Colombian organizations have been organizing debates and seminars around the country in order to elaborate the type of agrarian reform to which they aspire. The culmination of this process was the presentation of a peasants' green paper in October 1999. Its objectives are: to redistribute *latifundios*, end agricultural frontiers, initiate scientific land-use policies, relocate settlers from fragile areas, end narco-cultivation, encourage and protect peasant economy and farming according to national interests, and increase the social and entrepreneurial organization of communities to gain real participation. These proposed agrarian reforms would be carefully planned and evaluated by communities and their organizations at the local level. Finally, this green paper advocates the estates' purchase of peasants' debts and the creation of a special line of credit.

Peasant organizations consider agrarian reform to be a public responsibility of the central state; as such they consider that a strengthened INCORA should be responsible for the social relocation of property. But frequently INCORA's budget has been reduced. In the future to avoid this type of millstone, peasants propose to guarantee the financing of the reform with 5 per cent of the annual national budget, and a fixed cut of various taxes. This document also suggests the end of land-use rights in the event of violation of minimal labour laws, or inadequate protection of natural resources. It also argues for a clear limit to the amount of land owned per person in Colombia.

Not surprisingly, until the end of 2002, peasant organizations could not get their project debated in the national congress. To attain this debate or at least improve the current legislation, they had to engage in multiple mobilizations, strikes, roadblocks and occupation of state buildings. They have also had to count on the support of various social sectors like trade unions, democratic opposition in congress, many NGOs and the civic peace movement. Therefore, faced with wide peasant mobilizations, the government promised an increase in subsidies from 70 per cent to 100 per cent as well as other concessions. At the same time, the state also sought to close down INCORA and create a new institution in line with the ideology of neoliberal agrarian reform policies. Peasants aspire to the free handover of *latifundios*, and the establishment of collective titles for rural communities over large areas. However, in Colombia's current political situation these aspirations are impossible to achieve. Without a peace process, and concretization of a humanitarian agreement that prevents uprooting of rural populations, and opens the possibility of safe return to their original land, it is unrealistic to envisage relocation and redistribution of land.

Conclusion

With the present study, we have aimed to explain the persistence of agrarian conflict through a historical analysis of state formation, the Colombian political system and the *gamonal* as its main feature. The continuity and persistency of the bi-party system and *gamonalism* as the nuclear power centres have been emphasized, as well as the recourse to state and para-state violence to defend power and privileges. At the same time, the contraposition of agrarian reform attempts and the increase in agrarian conflicts demonstrate the existing gap between legality, that is, the corpus of norms and laws that govern state and society, and the reality of the countryside, which to a great extent is not guided by these laws but by their own extra-official laws.

It has been shown that agrarian reform has been slow and faulty. In particular, the concept of market-led land reform embedded in Law 160 of 1994 has proven completely inappropriate in the Colombian context. It does not consider the great inequalities existing between landless peasants and landowners, the weaknesses of channels and instruments of participation, nor the particularities of the Colombian land market. The non-existence of an operating land market, in addition to land price distortions linked to potential productivity – a result of the extra-economical functions of land – were two main obstacles to the functioning of market-led agrarian reform. This type of land reform became part of a package of modernizing and democratizing reforms that were only half implemented or that did not have sufficient political support for their implementation. This fact can be explained by the weakness of the reformed sector and reluctance to seek popular support. This sector attempted reforms within the constraints of the old system seeking to adjust social policies to the necessities of new eras, while being confined to the small margins established by traditional power structures. Consequently, the reformed sector was marginalized and the management style of public affairs became repressive.

The image of the *gamonal* is crucial to understanding these processes, given that it embodies territorial, economic, political, as well as military power. We would argue that the crisis of the *gamonal* is identical to the crisis of the sociopolitical system and parts of the economic sectors. Yet, the *gamonal* has successfully remained at the centre of power, hindering national development.

Its attachment to land tenancy, from where it derives most of its power, has not changed. The increase in violence and conflicts is based on the *gamonal*'s urge to maintain power which derives traditionally and currently from monopolizing land. By controlling production, land and territory, the *gamonal* has power over the access to natural and mineral resources, and this is being further reinforced by the construction of roads, energy infrastructure or other mega-projects. By means of uprooting and resettlement of inhabitants, *gamonalism* gains control over these residents and profits politically and economically from their insecurity and economic marginalization.

With an analysis of the historical use of state and para-state violence, we have demonstrated that paramilitarism was consolidated as an institution at the service of the expansion and strengthening of a particular political and socioeconomic project. Hence, this is not only a military phenomenon of the fight against counter-insurgency or an instrument of the landowners' or industrialists' self-defence, but an essential element of maintaining the existing power structures, but with new adaptations and alliances (e.g., links between political elites, paramilitaries and drug dealers). But the *gamonal* is not usually a very efficient producer and capitalist, and by defending its power and privileges it has hindered a more vigorous national development. The *gamonalismo* also impeded the formation of an open political system that can channel aspirations and conflicts of modern society. Through paramilitary groups, unproductive interests of the 'old' *latifundio* are defended as an authoritarian process of modernization in the agricultural, industrial or public sectors, a process that has had as its sole objective to increase productivity and profits for national and international capital.

We have also pointed out that there has never been a long-lasting alliance between the reformist sectors of the elites and popular organizations with the purpose of achieving deep reforms that would break the power of *gamonalism*. Indeed, high land concentration is a fundamental element of Colombian conflict, and dismantling this structure would bring a solution positively affecting economic development, social justice and wider political participation. The proposition advanced by peasants' organizations for agrarian reform and for bringing about an alternative more egalitarian agrarian transformation merits serious consideration. But, partially due to the internal weaknesses of social and peasant organizations and partially due to the strong repression and dirty warfare, these popular efforts have not so far achieved their objectives, although their social and political relevance has far from receded.

Notes

1. Translated from Spanish to English by Constanza Tabbush, Research Assistant, United Nations Research Institute for Social Development (UNRISD), Geneva.
2. See the subsequent section for further discussion on this concept.

3. When the republic was created, two political parties dominated the state: the liberal and the conservative parties. The differences between them can be traced to three basic themes: secular or Catholic state, federal or centralist constitution, protectionism or free exchange. Since the beginning, the bi-party system has been characterized by its hermetical structure. The two parties are power blocs that function as mechanisms of political exclusion of the masses, and as clientelist apparatus that monopolizes access to economic and political power. The liberal party historically achieved a better handling of conflicts, social tensions, and the incorporation of new political and social sectors, though in moments of crisis, the demands for reform and social justice were always subordinated to aspirations of power.

4. *La Violencia* is the civil war that started in 1948. The conservatives launched a ferocious campaign against the liberals, supported by the Catholic Church that justified the murders by declaring them anti-Christian. Through this violence, the conservative party – usually the minority – was going to secure future elections. During this period, the police – controlled by the conservatives – and armed bandits like 'Los Pájaros' committed multiple atrocities, attacking liberal or communist-led towns, displacing populations and assassinating trade union, communist and even liberal leaders.

5. Pact signed during Pastrana's government by the liberal party, trade union of cattle ranchers, rice and banana sectors, and the *latifundio*, in general. This agreement benefited landowners and almost paralysed the activities of INCORA (Colombian Institute of Agrarian Reform).

6. Left-wing movement connected to the communist party that emerged during negotiations between FARC and Betancur's government.

7. In 1984 the Minister of Justice Lara Bonilla was murdered and consequently there was an assassination attempt against General Maza Marques – Director of the Department of Security Administration – an enemy of the paramilitary; and in 1989 the presidential candidate Luis Carlos Galan was murdered, along with many other politicians, militaries and judges.

8. Recently, under Uribe Velez's new government, negotiations with paramilitary groups were underway to achieve quick reinsertion followed by pardon for their crimes. If these negotiations go through, they would produce alarming long-term effects on issues of impunity and would reinforce land and assets concentration.

9. Declaration of Colombian Organizations in the United Nations Human Rights Commission, 55th Period Session.

10. Castaño executed some of his men who committed excesses and the government has suspended some high-ranking military officials involved in supporting paramilitarism.

11. The president of the region of Fuente de Oro was killed by paramilitaries and accused of collaborating with the guerrillas in an attempt to 'clean' the zone of Ariari.

12. Four road infrastructure projects should be mentioned. First, the dry channel Atlantic–Pacific (Atrato and Truandó rivers) and its connections with the railroad Medellín–Buenaventura and the highways from the Pacific to Medellín and Pereira. It is an old project that was given priority because of the transport restrictions through the Panama Canal and because this was no longer controlled by the United States. Faced with the construction of this canal, an expropriation process was initiated. The same scenario occurred in Córdoba and Cesar with the planned Urabá–Maracaibo highway and the road system linking Antioquia and

Venezuela. In relation to the first two projects, an enormous flow of displaced populations was witnessed, caused by paramilitary groups in the Urabá region and the departments of Antioquia and Chocó. Third, the intercommunication project Orinoco river–Meta river–Buenaventura and, fourth, the intercommunication project La Plata river–Amazonas–Napo–Putumayo–Tumaco, with fluvial and dry ports in Asís. In the Meta river region (Puerto López, Puerto Gaitán, Guaroa) there is massive purchase of land and paramilitary presence financed by the buyers. Recently violence has begun in Puerto Asís. The effects of the fluvial projects concerning the rivers Orinoco and Meta in the indigenous and peasant communities were also denounced by the National Indigenous Association of Colombia (ONIC). The river is practically privatized, entitling a multinational company to manage the whole river basin. There has also recently been an increase of paramilitary violence and displacement in the regions of Buenaventura and Tumaco. Similarly, there has been agrarian counter-reform as well as displacements around hydroelectric, oil and mining projects. In the case of hydroelectric projects at the Urrá dam, paramilitaries have played an important role in breaking the resistance from fishermen, peasants and, above all, indigenous groups, by killing, kidnapping or removing various leaders who have demonstrated against the dam. Other types of interventions have occurred directly during the process of obtaining state permits and licences. Indeed, in a letter to the Ministry of Environment and to the Fifth Senate Commission, paramilitaries pressed for rapid approval of the environmental licence in order to begin filling up the dam, arguing that in the negotiations with the Ministry the plight of the indigenous peoples was dictated by the guerrillas, which should not be permitted, and which, in the Colombian context, constitutes a clear threat. Also under the influence of the paramilitaries, the river-beds that dried out after the correction of the river were registered to landowners and not to the fishermen and peasant communities. When the indigenous peoples defend their land, sacred places and fishing rights, they are accused of selfishness and adopting a position against development, while the five politicians and banks that make huge deals with the hydroelectric plant were considered to operate in the interests of the nation. In the case of oil exploitation and carbon and gold mines, there are legal dispositions to expropriate peasants and prohibit the granting of titles within a radius of five kilometres of an oil well. This was applied, for example, against the peasants of Caño Limón. Likewise, the police, army and paramilitary groups vented their anger on the U'wa natives who opposed the presence of the OXY petroleum company on their ancestral lands. OXY eagerly supports the Colombia Plan. The struggles between the guerrillas and the paramilitaries in the mountainous area of San Lucas in the south of Bolívar are related to gold, and in the 1980s the Frontino Gold Mines supported the *autodefensas* (militia) of Magdalena Medio.

13. Small landowners that partly work their own land and partly the landowner's property.
14. Urabá is one of the primary examples, because it is a frontier agricultural area with geostrategic value, natural resources, strong unions as well as the Union Patriotica. On the other side, the Magdalena Medio region – root of paramilitarism with the Puerto Boyacá model – is the centre of important labour struggles; social organizations in Barrancabermeja – the main oil port of the country – have been resisting paramilitary attacks for fifteen years. A recent example is Cauca, a strategic geographical location for drug and arms trafficking, important for many armed groups and vital for projects of economic internationalization. In Cauca an enormous

quantity of agro-business mega-projects have been encouraged (African palms, *Sparragus monocultivos*), thermoenergetic (carbon), hydroelectric and industrial (tax free zones). In the north of Cauca where sugar refineries and cultivation of sugarcane predominate, many hills have been planted with pine trees by the business monopoly called SMURFIT (Cartón de Colombia). However, in spite of these projects there are significant social problems, such as poverty, marginalization, unsatisfied basic needs and lack of intervention by the state, etc.

15. Open letter to the social organizations of Cauca and to the President of the Republic, 19 January 2001.
16. Commission of Communications, Communication No. 2, 'Gran Minga por la Vida', Santander de Quilichao, 15 May 2001.
17. Consejo Comunitario General del Río Baudó y sus afluentes (ACABA), Comunicado a la opinión pública, Quibdó, 8 June 2001; Comisión de Justicia y Paz, Diócesis de Istmina y Quibdó, Comunicado del 7 de junio de 2001.
18. Interview with Gerardo González, Bern, 8 June 2000.
19. Interview with Luis Carlos Acero, Bogotá, 2 December 2000.

References

Actualidad Colombiana (2001) 'Desplazamiento forzado: La realidad invisible', No. 309, 4 April.

Banco de Datos de CINEP y Justicia y Paz, *Noche y Niebla. Panorama de Derechos Humanos y Violencia Política en Colombia* (1997). Enero a Marzo. Bogotá: CINEP and Justicia y Paz.

Comisión Campesina de Impulso a la Paz (1998) *Pliego de Peticiones de los Campesinos del Departamento de Cundinamarca*. Agosto: Fusagasuga.

Consejo Nacional Campesino para la Acción Rural (CNC) (1999) *Paz con los Campesinos. Ponencia ante la Asamblea Permanente por la Paz*. 28 July. Bogotá: CNC.

Cubides, Fernando (1998) 'De lo privado y de lo público en la violencia colombiana: Los paramilitares', in Jaime Arocha, Fernando Cubides and Myriam Jimeno (eds), *Las Violencias, Inclusión Creciente*. Bogotá: Colección CES.

El Tiempo (2000) 'Piden ayuda para millones de desplazados', 4 November.

Fajardo Montaña, Darío (2002) 'Tierra, poder político y reformas agraria y rural', *Cuadernos Tierra y Justicia*, No. 1, Bogotá, August.

González, Fernán E. (1998) 'La violencia política y las dificultades de la construcción de lo público en Colombia. Una mirada de larga duración', in Jaime Arocha, Fernando Cubides and Myriam Jimeno (eds), *Las Violencias, Inclusión Creciente*. Bogotá: Colección CES.

Höllinger, Frank (1999) 'Del mercado de tierras al mercado de reforma agraria', in Absalón Machado and Ruth Suárez (eds), *El mercado de tierras en Colombia: Una alternativa viable?* Bogotá: CEGA.

Kalmanovitz, Salomón (1991) 'Los gremios industriales ante la crisis', in Francisco Leal Buitrago and León Zamosc (eds), *Al Filo del Caos. Crisis Política en la Colombia de los Años 80*. Bogotá: Tercer Mundo Editores.

Medina Gallego, Carlos (1994) *La Violencia Parainstitucional en Colombia*. Bogotá: Rodríguez Quito Ediciones.

Managing Natural Resources, Latin America and the Caribbean (MINGA), Consultoría para los Derechos Humanos y el Desplazamiento (CODHES), Companhia de Desenvolvimento da Paraíba (CINEP), Fundación Comité de Solidaridad con los Presos Políticos, and the Corporación Colectivo de Abogados 'José Alvear Restrepo' (2001) *An SOS. From Cauca and Nariño*. Bogotá, 1 February. http://colhrnet.igc.org/newsletter/y2001/spring01art/soscaucanarino101.htm.

Melo, Jorge Orlando (1991) 'Los paramilitares y su impacto sobre la política', in Francisco Leal Buitrago and León Zamosc (eds), *Al Filo del Caos. Crisis Política en la Colombia de los Años 80*. Bogotá: Tercer Mundo Editores.

Mondragón, Héctor (2000) *Lo que Colombia necesita. Alternativa al Plan Colombia*. 24 April. http://www.derechos.org/nizkor/colombia/doc/mondragon.html#La%20 Colonizaci %F3n:%20De%20Soluci%F3n%20A%20Problema.

Palacios, Marco (1995) *Colombia 1875–1994. Entre la Legalidad y la Violencia*. Bogotá: Norma.

Reyes Posada, Alejandro (1997a) 'La compra de tierras por narcotraficantes', in UNDP, *Drogas Ilícitas en Colombia. Su Impacto Económico, Político y Social*. Bogotá: Ed. Planeta.

Reyes Posada, Alejandro (1997b) 'El problema de la tierra y el dominio del territorio', *El Espectador*, 16 February.

Rojas, Manuel (1999) 'Una mirada institucional de la negociación voluntaria de tierras rurales como estrategia de redistribución y equidad', in Absalón Machado and Ruth Suárez (eds), *El Mercado de Tierras en Colombia: Una Alternativa Viable?* Bogotá: CEGA.

Salgado, Carlos and M. Prada (2000) *Esmeralda. Campesinado y Protesta Social en Colombia 1980–1995*. Bogotá: CINEP.

Sindicato Nacional de Trabajadores de INCORA (SINTRADIN) (1998) *Ponencia: Paz con los campesinos*. August. Bogotá: SINTRADIN.

Thuomi, Francisco (1994) *Economía Política y Narcotráfico*. Bogotá: Tercer Mundo Editores.

United Nations Economic and Social Council (UNESC) (2001) *Informe de la Alta Comisionada de las Naciones Unidas para los Derechos Humanos sobre la situación de los derechos humanos en Colombia en el año 2000*. Report to the Commission for Human Rights. UN Doc. E/CN.4/2001/14, 20 March 2001. New York: United Nations. http://www.hchr.org.co/documentoseinformes/informes/altocomisionado/informes. php3?cod=4&cat=11.

Valderrama, Mario and Héctor Mondragón (1998) 'Desarrollo y equidad con campesinos', *Misión Rural*, Vol. 2. Bogotá: IICA and Tercer Mundo Editores.

Zamosc, León (1987) *La cuestión agraria y el movimiento campesino en Colombia: Luchas de la Asociación Nacional de Usuarios Campesinos (ANUC), 1967–1968*. Bogotá: CINEP and Geneva: UNRISD.

Zelik, Raul and Dario N. Azzellini (1999) *Kolumbien – Grosse Geschäfte – Staatlicher Terror und Aufstandsbekämpfung*. Cologne: Neuer ISP-Verlag.

4
The Dynamics of Market-led Rural Development in Latin America: the Experience of Mexico, Ecuador, Bolivia and Peru

Henry Veltmeyer

This chapter addresses some critical questions about rural development in the current context of 'free market' (neoliberal) capitalist development in Latin America. Development in this form is profoundly exclusionary and rural development has to do with problems such as poverty generated by this exclusion. These problems have been at the centre of a protracted struggle by the poor as well as efforts by outside agents to revert the conditions of this exclusion, to attack poverty in one or more of its conditions or at its roots. At issue in this struggle are diverse efforts to redress the situation of so many people in the rural sectors of developing societies – to bring about an improvement in this situation and the sustainable development of their livelihoods.

The chapter begins with a brief outline of the problems of rural poverty and social exclusion that affect a large part of the rural population in Latin America and a discussion of the basic pillars of the conditions involved. It then brings into focus several case studies of rural development practice in Bolivia and Peru before turning to the dynamics of thought and practice associated with social movements in Latin America. These movements constitute one of several types of political response of people in the popular sector of Latin American 'civil society' to the problems of poverty and social exclusion. As such, these movements have generally rejected the development option in all its forms and are generally oriented in their action and politics towards the project of social transformation. The following section examines the political dynamics of intersectoral linkages and strategic alliances among organizations and movements in the popular sector of civil society, noting a discernible trend towards such linkages.

The chapter concludes with a brief synopsis of the alternative paths towards change in the popular movement. It is argued that the sustainable livelihoods approach has the greatest potential for bringing about an improvement in the quality of life of the rural poor and this approach has been favoured by most social movements. The limitations of the first option are identified while the second option is found to be not viable in the present context and current conditions. The conclusion is that in the current conjuncture the forces of opposition and resistance to government policy vis-à-vis free market capitalism and globalization are not likely to bring about substantive change in the situation experienced by so many in Latin America's rural society. Neither rural development nor social revolution seems to present prospects for a substantial improvement in the lives and livelihoods of the rural poor. For this, a new approach will be needed. What form it might take cannot be said. The section takes a closer look at these questions and proposes further study into the dynamics of political struggle and development efforts, including action by the protagonists of this struggle.

Basic pillars of the conditions of social exclusion and rural poverty in Latin America

The study of development can be traced back to the immediate post-world war context but the need to combat poverty (to alleviate its conditions if not reduce or eradicate it) – identifying poverty as the central issue of the development enterprise – can be traced back to the World Bank's *Development Report* (1973) published under the presidency of Robert McNamara, at that time Secretary of State for External Affairs, in charge of prosecuting the war on Vietnam. Since then the Bank has periodically affirmed the centrality of poverty in the development agenda, particularly rural poverty, given that the problem is most entrenched in rural societies of the developing world, for example, in 1990, after a decade in which other problems came to the fore, and again in 2000.

In any case, the war on poverty and other social conditions of social exclusion over the years has taken on diverse forms, waged though numerous campaigns and in many settings, without, it appears, any appreciable results. Despite six decades of diverse development efforts the problem is as entrenched and widespread as ever, affecting, conservatively estimated, over 40 per cent of the world's population – no less than in 1973 when the problem was first 'discovered' and diagnosed. This raises the question – or rather a number of questions – not only about the root causes of the problem but also about the development effort itself – the forms that it has taken. Why, for example, have these efforts yielded so few results of benefit to the world's poor? Is the problem that intractable? Have these efforts been misguided – based on theoretical models or strategies with misplaced priorities or that fail to identify the critical factors of remedial action? Implementation of the development project over the years could be viewed as ineffectual and inadequate. At worst, the development project was not designed to benefit its stated beneficiaries.

One reason for the general failure of so many, if not all, efforts to bring about either social change or development is that the underlying problem is often misconstrued and its major structural conditions, no matter how well described, are inadequately explained. Academic discourse and explanations of these conditions – of the underlying structure that produced and reproduces them – can be placed into categories: those that relate to the concept of *exploitation* (the extraction of surplus value from the activities of the direct producer or worker) and those that focus on conditions of *marginalization*, or, in more recent parlance, *social exclusion* (Atal and Yen, 1995; Bessis, 1995). At issue in this debate is whether the conditions of rural poverty are connected to the workings of the operating economic system (neoliberal capitalism) or whether, on the contrary, they reflect the relative lack of participation of these social groups in this system – their exclusion.

Without taking a position in this debate, there are several issues on which there is a virtual consensus in the academic literature. One of these is that the neoliberal model is profoundly exclusionary. Analysts of the capitalist development process and the neoliberal model have tended to focus not on this feature but on the exploitative nature of the system and on the social conditions of this exploitation, such as inadequate wages, increased social inequalities in the distribution of income, and poverty. But it is possible to argue that the dominant feature and the greatest social impacts of the capitalist development process in its neoliberal form relate not so much to its exploitative character as to its propensity towards *social exclusion* (Paugam, 1996).[1] For example, the neoliberal model is geared to benefit only a small segment of proprietors and business operators, those few private enterprises – estimated at some 15 per cent of the total – that are able to compete in the world market. Another segment of private sector enterprises, estimated at around 35 per cent, are deemed to have productive capacity but are oriented predominantly towards the domestic market. Under the neoliberal model these enterprises are generally subjected to the 'forces of the free market', with little support and protection from government policies, leading to a process of economic restructuring that, in theory, weeds out the most inefficient. However, at least 50 per cent of all units of economic activity (enterprises, etc.) – primarily those based on the peasant economy in the rural sector and, in the urban environment, owned by operators of micro-enterprises in the informal sector – are left to twist in the winds of change.

The casualties of this process are found everywhere – in the growing mass of producers and workers deprived of their means of production, marginalized in the process of capitalist development and excluded from both the formal political and economic process of this development. Under conditions of this social exclusion a large and growing part of Latin America's rural population is experiencing a social crisis of growing and devastating proportions (Ghai, 1991; IFAD, 2001; Paugam, 1996).[2] The basic pillars, forms and conditions of this exclusion are as follows:

 (i) Dispossession of the means of social production, reflected in the wide-spread condition of landlessness, near-landlessness and a process of rural out-migration;
 (ii) lack of access to urban and rural labour markets and opportunities for wage employment, reflected in the low rate of labour force participation and the high rate of unemployment in the rural sector;
 (iii) lack of access to 'good quality or decent jobs', reflected most clearly in evidence of increased rates of super- and under-employment, and in the growth and prevalence of jobs that are precarious in form (seasonal, involuntary part-time, short-term, etc.) with a high degree of informality and inordinately low wages and other forms of remuneration;
 (iv) reduced access to government social services in areas of social development such as education, health and social security;
 (v) lack of access to stable forms of adequate income, reflected in the incapacity of many households to meet their basic needs and indicators of relative and absolute poverty;[3]
 (vi) and, above all, exclusion from the apparatus of decision-making or 'political power', reflected in the centralized nature of this power structure, elite control of this structure, the prevalence of client–patron relations in the political arena and frequent recourse to political organization and action in the form of anti-systemic social movements.

Neoliberal policy reforms and rural sector

Both the new and the old economic models of (rural) development focus on three critical variables of the production-and-development process: (i) the existing stock (and social distribution) of natural resources such as land (natural capital); (ii) the stock of physical capital, viz. the latest production technologies – and the process of technological conversion and productive transformation; and (iii) the stock, and supply, of financial capital – and the rate of capital formation or productive investment.

Within the framework of the neoliberal economic model (NEM) the facilitating policies are: privatization of the means of production; deregulation of private economic activities and markets; and liberalization of trade and the flow of capital. With regards to agriculture, the dominant locus of economic activity in the rural sector, the critical policy has been the liberalization of trade – eliminating subsidies to the local producers and any tariffs or other protective barriers, including preferential treatment of local producers such as non-commercial sources of credit.

However, to identify the macroeconomic effects of these neoliberal policies on different strata of the rural population is no easy matter, notwithstanding the plethora of studies in this area. One of these macro-effects is suggested by evidence that agriculture is satisfying a decreasing proportion of domestic demand for food, which is, as Crabtree (2003: 144) points out, 'a clearly worrying trend for a country in which a large proportion of the workforce is employed in agricultural activities'. A clear policy objective of trade liberalization was to increase agricultural production and induce greater efficiencies in the process. However, the evidence from Peru, Ecuador, Bolivia, Mexico and elsewhere suggests that his has not occurred. Also, stagnant production and a decreasing domestic demand for food have their social correlates in the large number of rural producers who have been squeezed out of the production process, fuelling the immiseration of a huge and growing landless (and near-landless) rural semi-proletariat, the emigration (to the cities and urban centres) of many of these semi-proletarianized producers and the impoverishment of most of those who remain behind.

Between 1991 and 1994, at the behest of the World Bank and within the framework of an agenda and broad programme of neoliberal policy reforms, the governments of Mexico, Ecuador, Bolivia, Peru and a number of other countries in South and Central America introduced variations of an agricultural modernization law that among other measures included a derogation of constitutional or legal protection of communal property and legal entitlement to land worked by hundreds of thousands of smallholders, increasing their capacity to sell their land and, in the process, building a market in land as well as supposedly increasing the 'efficiency' of production. However, combined with the elimination of subsidies to local producers, the commercialization of credit, the reduction of protective tariffs, and in many cases an overvalued currency, these measures, such as land titling, rather than resolving the agricultural crisis created what analysts have termed a 'difficult environment' for various categories of producers of tradable products, especially 'small scale peasant producers' (Crabtree, 2003: 144). The latter, Crabtree points out with regard to Peru (although the same pattern holds for other countries in the region), have been 'extremely vulnerable to the inflow of cheap agricultural products'. Not only has this increase in agricultural imports and products undermined or destroyed local economies, forcing large numbers of local producers into bankruptcy or poverty, but at the same time, it has brought about or accelerated a fundamental change in production and consumption patterns away from traditional crops, especially grains like quinea, kiwicha, coca, alluco, beans and potatoes. The impact of this change, and its implications, have yet to be evaluated.

In the case of Peru, the abolition of Empresa Comercializadora de Alimento SA (ECASA), one of a number of government market boards and agricultural price support institutions, liberalized the national market in rice, removing an organization which, like its counterparts in other countries in the region, had maintained price stability for the benefit of local producers. Some of the functions of ECASA were taken over by the Programa Nacional de

Asistencia Alimentaria (PRONAA),[4] a government-subsidized food programme for the poor that bought directly from small-scale producers. However, such an institutional change – replicated in the other countries in the region – had relatively little impact on the poorest farmers, many of whom had never benefited from government programmes of any sort (Crabtree, 2003: 147). As for those producers who managed to integrate themselves into the competitive local urban markets, the disappearance of Banco Agrario meant that they were forced to rely on various agro-industrial firms for commercial credit. This credit, when available, was extended to the same producer only under the most onerous terms, with rates that, in the case of Brazil under Cardoso, reached 20 per cent a month, given the enormously 'high risk' taken by the creditors. These creditors are extremely reluctant to lend, even to larger-scale, more prosperous landowners with privileged market access. When they do lend the interest rates charged reflect the perception of the high risk involved in lending to smaller-scale producers. Their appetite for lending is also reduced by the incidence of bankruptcies in sectors such as asparagus that had briefly seemed to offer endless possibilities (Crabtree, 2003: 145, 147).

In many cases, as in Mexico and Peru, the result of these and other such 'institutional changes' and the recourse to the 'market mechanism' has been a drastic deterioration in the market situation of small producers, forced to sell their production at prices below their costs of production, accrue enormous unpayable debts and in many cases pushing them into bankruptcy. In Mexico, this situation has generated one of the largest mass movements in its long history of land struggle – a million-strong organization of highly indebted 'independent' family farmers (El Barzon). As for the peasant economy in Peru, Ecuador and Mexico, in Central America and elsewhere in the region, it was devastated, forcing large numbers to flee the countryside in search of wage employment in the cities and urban centres. The only alternative was – and remains – poverty. Studies that have been undertaken in this area point towards a pattern of increased social inequality and rural poverty – in the not atypical case of Peru from 41.6 per cent of rural households in 1985 to 54.1 per cent in 2000, after a decade of agricultural modernization and capitalist 'free market' development (Crabtree, 2003: 148). The same study shows a pattern of decline in extreme poverty – from 18.4 to 14.8 per cent but without any analysis or explanation – which is probably based on the World Bank's approach, which is to eliminate (or reduce) poverty by statistical fiat (defining it in terms of earnings of less than $1 a day).

Sustainable development and the private sector

In the 1980s, the agenda of organizations in the development enterprise, both bilateral and multilateral, included the aim of bringing about or promoting a participatory form of sustainable development. A key component of this strategy are the non-governmental organizations (NGOs) that were formed in the 1980s under conditions of crisis and the retreat of the state – incorporating these third-sector 'civil society' organizations into the development process as partners, mediating between the donors, who provided development finance or assistance in various forms, and the recipients of this 'aid', the poor and their communities. In the 1990s, however, there occurred a decided shift in this strategy – and in the agenda of official development assistance (ODA) (Mitlin, 1998). Behind this new strategy was the agency of private sector organizations – to incorporate the 'private sector' of civil society into the development process: '[to tap] the considerable resources, technology, competencies, creativity and global reach of the business community and employing these for development ... goals' (Utting, 2000: 1).[5]

Already conceived of as the driving force of the development process, the operators of the economic growth engine, the new 'problem' was how to secure the participation of the global corporations in the sustainable development agenda.[6] The United Nations Development Programme (UNDP) is one of a number of ODAs that have assumed this responsibility, taking the lead in defining and initiating the new strategy, which was laid out in 1989 in a Policy Framework paper on the 'UN–Business Partnership' (Palazzi, 2000; UNDP, 1998; United Nations, 1998; Utting, 2000).

Just as Bolivia took the lead, in 1994, in the implementation of a strategy of local participatory development, the government instituted the sustainable development project of the 'international development community'.[7] In the first administration of Sánchez de Lozada ('Goni'), the government institutionalized the development project in the form of various administrative reforms, setting up ministries of sustainable and participatory development, and introducing enabling legislation – the Law of Popular Participation and the Law of Administrative Centralization. Another initiative in this regard was the setting up of a directorate composed of representatives of the national and provincial governments, 'civil society' and the 'private sector' (chambers of commerce and industry). The mandate of this directorate was to promote environmentally sustainable economic development and to do so on the basis of a 'partnership' with the corporate sector, particularly in relation to the firms that were 'capitalized' (that is, privatized). The workings of this approach can be illustrated by developments in the strategic oil and gas (hydrocarbon) energy sector of the economy, representing as it does a government priority with regard to national economic development.

Within the framework of the government's strategic development plan and the broader agenda of the international development 'community', the key corporations in the hydrocarbons (oil and gas production, electricity generation) industry, according to one of its spokespersons, 'have assumed the environment problematic as a priority' (Arias, 2002: 47ff.).[8] According to the Bolivian Chamber of Hydrocarbon Industry (Arias, 2002: 46), manifestations of this priority include, on the part of the corporations in this sector: (i) respect of international standards guidelines developed for the sector, as well as appropriate government regulations; (ii) implementation of environmental impact assessments (EIA) for all major projects; (iii) environmental damage 'prevention and remediation' measures of waste management, recycling and conservation; (iv) setting up a division dedicated to research and development in the area of renewable (non-traditional) resources ('green technologies'); and (v) concern for the social impacts of corporate activity – for mitigating these impacts.

In addition to these 'principles', according to the Bolivian Oil and Gas Chamber, a critical factor in the implementation of a 'sustainable development' strategy is 'popular participation' – that is, the 'participation of citizens and consumers' as well as 'the growing role of NGOs' (Arias, 2002: 47). Bolivia, the Chamber points out, is not immune from these 'global influences'. Indeed, Arias notes, it exceeds most countries in 'the velocity of these influences [vis-à-vis government reaction to them ... legislation to regulate and institutionalize] these processes'.

This gloss on the approach taken by the government – and the 'industry' – towards the planning for sustainable development is symptomatic of the private sector's understanding of the meaning of the term 'partnership'. The primary role of the government, Arias points out, is to establish a regulatory framework that provides 'legal security' for corporate investors, particularly in regards to 'serious short-term problems that are causing erroneous transaction costs to the companies, delaying projects and placing contractual commitments at risk'. Secondly, the government has the responsibility of protecting private investors (particularly of the capitalized firms) from any liability arising out of the operations of these firms while part of the state. The privatized companies, on the other hand, should assume the responsibility to mitigate where possible the negative environmental and social impacts of these operations. Thirdly, the government should assume the responsibility of mediating relations with the communities involved and perhaps negatively affected by oil and gas development. What this means is clarified by Arias in the following terms: 'We are referring to the social pressures of those communities in areas influenced by oilfield projects.' To wit: 'Many times, the communities use illegal means and *de facto* measures to force the companies to increase damage payments or compensation (which should only be paid when they indeed take place and are proven).' At issue, Arias points out, is the lack of legal security for corporate investors relating to 'the delimitation of native community lands and their ownership'. The problem arises when 'areas of hydrocarbon interest [to the companies] overlaps protected areas', leading local communities to lay claims – and act – against the companies (Arias, 2002: 49). The government in this connection, Arias emphasizes, is responsible for mediating relations with these communities and creating greater legal security for investors.

Although hydrocarbons (oil and gas) exploitation has the 'potential to cause significant environmental damage and harmful social effects', at the same time, Arias notes, 'it contributes in great measure to the country's development through employment, the generation of royalties and foreign currency, and tax payments' (Arias, 2002: 48). The responsibility, and function, of government in this regard, apart from the above, is to 'define development priorities and to implement practices towards achieving these priorities in harmony with the policies [of sustainable development]'. As for the private corporations, they 'will respond to those signals provided they are clear and their application is transparent' (Arias, 2002: 48).

Misguided conception of local participatory development

In 1994, Bolivia placed itself at the forefront of institutional reform in Latin America with the enactment of two laws – the Law of Popular Participation (*Ley de Participación Popular* – 1551, 20 April 1994) and the Administrative Decentralization Law (*Ley de Descentralización Administrativa* – 1654, 20 July 1995). With these laws the regime of Sánchez de Lozada made a conscious break with a political past identified with an over-centralized government and the social exclusion of the vast majority of the rural population, most of which belonged to an indigenous 'nationality'. In this context some observers considered Lozada to be embarking on the most challenging exercise in social reform since 1952, initiating thereby the most significant alternative project of participatory development in all of Latin America (Albó, 1996; Blackburn and Holland, 1998; Booth, Clisby and Widmark, 1995, 1997).

But not everyone agrees with this assessment. Some – for example, Molina (1997), Arrieto and Pinedo (1995), and Medina (1996) – see this legislation as a radical response to social pressures exerted by the popular movement, a pragmatic attempt to respond to the growing demands by peasants and the indigenous population for increased political representation and autonomy. Others, such as McNeish (2003) and Untoja (1992), see in this legislation an effort of the government to secure acceptance for its entire neoliberal agenda, including privatization (capitalization). Others again (for example, Veltmeyer and Tellez, 2001) see in this legislation the influence of the World Bank and the UNDP in the attempts of these and other ODAs to push for a participatory approach towards the planning of a sustainable development process.

The hand of the World Bank and the UNDP in the design of Bolivia's plan for local government reform and municipalization is unmistakable (Bolivia, 1994). In this connection see, for example, the diverse accounts of Molina (1997) and Medina (1996). As these authors see it, the World Bank and the UNDP promoted a model of 'local participatory development' ('municipalization plus popular influence') that combines (i) the effect of decentralizing to local governments ('the municipality') a significant share of government responsibilities/expenditures; (ii) formal recognition of traditional social organizations of indigenous communities (as 'Organizaciones Teritoriales de Base' – OTBs); (iii) creation of an administrative apparatus for rural communities to participate in local development planning (in the form of Popular

Participation Councils – CPP); and (iv) a 'partnership' approach towards planning, bringing together representatives of the central and local governments (sub-prefect, mayor, surveillance committee) and civil society (peasant organizations, unions, association of OTBs and the 'civic committees'). The aim in this process is to bring about 'sustainable local development' in the form of a 'participatory planning' approach and the 'concerted actions' of the 'stakeholders' and partners involved.

In this model, the 'municipality', the legacy of a highly centralized state, is recast into a key role to be played in new programmes for administrative decentralization (Nickson, 1997). This new role for the 'productive municipality' is well illustrated in the government's decade-long efforts to institutionalize a 'local participatory development' in its planning processes (Bolivia, 1994; McNeish, 2003: 232–7; Paas et al., 1991) – to create a complex of productive municipalities; and in its own analysis of these efforts (Delgadillo Terceros and Zambrana Barrios, 2002). In this assessment, the government focuses on the efforts to 'construct a space for concerted action' (chapter 1) and the importance of the CPP in 'the formation of new local elites' (chapter 3). As for 'concerted action' the assessment report focuses on the civil society–state nexus with direct reference to various studies by the UNDP (PNUD, 2000, 2002) that identify the confluence of diverse interests and points of view as the greatest 'bottleneck' in the development planning process. At issue, the Proyecto de Seguridad Alimentaria Nutricional en la Provincia Arque (PROSANA) report (Delgadillo Terceros and Zambrana Barrios, 2002: 1) notes, is how to reconcile interests, which can – and do – come into conflict, and to coordinate decision-making and actions among the key sectors: civil society (citizens, NGOs, OTBs, unions), the local government and 'the institutions' (Provincial Development Councils – CDPs).

The report points to difficulties in this area and a general failure to institutionalize the Provincial Councils of Popular Participation (CPPPs) – to secure this 'concertation' consistently, notwithstanding the efforts to 'construct' the required 'spaces' for it. In other words, and – it has to be said – without any sort of analysis or explanation, the report concludes that efforts to institutionalize the CPPP as a form of popular participation, or concerted actions between civil society and the state, have failed to bring about any concrete results. In this connection, the report for some reason does not attempt to evaluate the outcomes and impacts of any 'projects' decided upon within the institutional framework of municipal development planning – and the government's strategy of Alternative Participatory Development (*Desarrollo Alternativo Participativo*). Rather, its assessment is limited to the level of 'participation' (consistency in attendance) of diverse actors in the planning process, which consists largely of meetings to hear reports prepared by the vice-prefect or bureaucrat. Attendance at these meetings, the report finds, was consistently high – from 78 to 95 per cent – in the case of community organizations and unions, but inconsistently so (46 per cent on average) in the case of representatives of the NGOs.

However, the report adds that this success at the level of participation (securing consistent attendance and popular participation at planning meetings) did not translate into any definable gains – the institution of successful economic development projects. Nor has the government been successful in securing the participation of some highly representative groups in the popular sector of civil society. The *cocaleros*, for example, an organization of some 30 000 coca-producers in the Chapare region and los Yungas, refused the government's overtures to join in the 'participatory planning process'. It opted instead for a strategy of mobilization and direct strike action (*cortas de ruta* – highway blockades) to pressure the government to abandon its 'alternative development plan' (to eradicate the highly marketable coca production).

In December 2002, in the face of this refusal of the *cocaleros* to participate in the government's 'local participatory development planning process' the government proposed the formation of a multisectoral directorate composed of local government officials, representation of the *cocaleros* and private enterprise (*El Deber*, 9 December 2002: A14). The stated aim was to expand the scope for alternative production and a national market 'structured on the basis of popular participation'.

The *cocaleros*, however, the major participant in this struggle, responded that it was not in the least interested in 'participation' as conceived by the government; nor was it prepared to enter into a process of 'negotiation and dialogue, an approach that has been tried before and "utterly failed" ' (*El Deber*, 9 December 2002: A13). As regards the 'private sector', observes Evo Morales, the leader of the *cocaleros* and currently a congressional deputy of the Movement for Socialism (MAS), 'it [the private sector] does not have the slightest interest in participation', and questions the motives of the government in this connection. In opposition to government overtures – to end a confrontational approach as well as further direct actions such as highway blockades, which, the government, stated, would be opposed at whatever political cost – at a popular assembly, the key institution of the new sociopolitical movements that have emerged in the region (see below), the *cocaleros* movement resolved, on the contrary, to continue its strategy of popular mobilizations and direct action, seeking 'strategic alliances' with other sectors to 'massify' them (*El Mundo*, 4 December 2002). On 13 January 2003, this strategy was indeed acted upon, provoking a response from the government in the form of a reprisal that left over a dozen people dead in its wake. The struggle continues. So much for the government's strategy of popular local participation – to create a national complex of 'productive municipalities'.

The sociopolitical dynamics of Latin American social movements

Despite the efforts of governments in the region to incorporate them into the development process, social movements have generally eschewed the development projects approach to change, opting instead for direct collective action, mobilization and struggle – and social transformation. In this regard, social movements can be distinguished from grassroots or community-based social or civil organizations as well as the non-governmental organizations that in partnership with bilateral and multilateral ODAs dominate the development agenda. These NGOs, which in some countries exceed 10000 in number, are the major implementing agents of the development project and the associated process.

The experience of Latin America with social movements, and their history of struggle, can be traced out in the form of distinct waves, each washing ashore in a specific conjuncture of objective (socioeconomic) and subjective (political) conditions. Four such waves can be identified.

The first wave hit Latin America in the 1950s and did not subside until the late 1970s. It took the double form of, on the one hand, a labour movement based on a largely urban struggle for improved wages and working conditions; and, on the other, a land struggle – a struggle for improved access to land and land reform.[9] The context for these movements was complex but it included the Cuban revolution, which gave rise to and strengthened pressures for revolutionary change, and widespread implementation of programmes of state-led liberal reform and diverse strategies to (i) incorporate small-scale or peasant producers, and rural indigenous communities, into the development process – government development programmes; (ii) coopt, where possible, the leadership of indigenous or peasant organizations; and (iii) repress, where and when necessary, any rural or indigenous rebellions or movements for revolutionary change.[10]

The second wave of social movements, roughly coinciding with the late 1970s to the mid-1980s, was composed of what was termed or widely conceived of as 'new social movements' (Alvarez, Diagnino and Escobar, 1999; Brass, 2000; Calderón, 1995; Calderón et al., 1989; Escobar and Alvarez, 1992; Slater, 1994; Veltmeyer, 1997a). These include issue-oriented movements focused on human rights, the ecology, discrimination against or oppression of women and the ethnic struggle for autonomy, dignity of their cultural heritage and identity. In large part these movements were based on grassroots or community-based organizations and supported in their activities by NGOs. The leadership of this form of 'civil society' is largely composed of lower-middle-class professionals (Dominguez, 1994), and their policies and strategies revolved around challenging the military and civilian authoritarian regimes of the time. The context for this wave of social movements was provided by a region-wide debt crisis, widespread implementation of the 'new economic model' and the general retreat of the state from the economy as well as a trend towards redemocratization in the form of decentralization and the return of constitutional regimes installed by recourse to the instrumentation of political parties and the mechanism of elections.

The third wave of social movements developed into a powerful political force as of the mid-to-late 1980s. The context for this 'development' was provided by a process of 'globalization' and the implementation by governments in the region of 'the structural adjustment programme' – a series of measures designed to adjust national and local economies in the region to the requirements of the 'new world economic order' (Veltmeyer and Petras, 1997, 2000). This wave took the form of mass peasant and rural workers organizations engaged in direct action to promote and defend the economic interests of their supporters. The composition, tactics and demands of these movements varied but they were all united in their opposition to 'neoliberalism' (International Monetary Fund [IMF]-mandated policies, etc.) and 'imperialism' (in the form of 'globalization').

The most prominent of these movements include the Zapatistas of Mexico (EZLN), the Rural Landless Workers of Brazil (MST), the coca-producing peasants (*cocaleros*) of Bolivia, the National Peasant Federation in Paraguay, the FARC (Revolutionary Armed Forces of Colombia) in Colombia – a leftover from the social movements formed in the first wave and largely destroyed in the 1970s and 1980s – and the Confederation of Indigenous Nationalities (and peasants) of Ecuador. These movements are led by peasants or rural workers and have struggled for agrarian reforms (redistribution of land) and national 'autonomy' for indigenous communities, and they have struggled against 'globalization' (in the form of ALCA, the Latin America Free Trade Agreement), neoliberalism (in the form of government policy) and United States intervention, including coca eradication programmes, colonization of territory via military bases, penetration of national police/military institutions and militarization of social conflicts, such as Plan Colombia and the Andean Initiative (Petras, 1997; Petras and Veltmeyer, 2003). The basis of these struggles was the neoliberal economic regime, the growing concentration of wealth in the hands of local and foreign elites and the social exclusion of the mass of local producers and their rural communities.

Unlike the third wave of social movements in the region, the fourth wave is centred in the urban areas. It includes the dynamic growth of *barrio*-based mass movements of unemployed workers in Argentina, the unemployed and poor in the Dominican Republic and the shantytown dwellers who have flocked in their hundreds of thousands to the populist banners of Venezuelan President Hugh Chavez. The *piqueteros* of Argentina represent the cutting edge of this new wave (Petras and Veltmeyer, 2003).

In addition to the urban movements, new multisectoral movements, engaged in mass struggles that integrate farm workers, small and medium-sized farmers have emerged in Colombia, Mexico, Brazil and Paraguay as well as Ecuador. The characteristic feature of these movements is an active search for strategic cross-sectoral linkages and alliances (see discussion below), and the concertation of various urban-centred struggles. In many cases these movements are urban-centred but originate in rural struggles – taking them to the cities, resulting in the coalescence of two waves: the integration of movements formed in the third wave with those forming in the fourth.

The nature, mode of operation and style of political action of these movements challenge many of the stereotypes and assumptions of conventional liberal social science thinking and Marxist orthodoxy. For example, the 'new social movement' writers declared the end of 'class politics' and the advent of cultural and 'citizen-based' civic movements concerned with democracy, gender equality and identity politics. However, the subsequent explosion of peasant and urban class movements throughout Latin America in pursuit of land and political power shattered that assumption. The notion that the advent of economic and political liberalism would lead to the end of mass ideological struggles evaporated with the eruption of the Zapatistas in Chiapas (Mexico), the FARC in Colombia, and the Confederation of Indigenous Nationalities of Ecuador (CONAIE) in Ecuador. Each movement in its own way has expanded its territorial influence as well as deepening the level and form of popular participation. Each has become a mass movement. The elite and authoritarian civilian electoral systems (or 'democracies') are challenged by popular assemblies from below, which are in the process of defining a new substantive form of more 'direct democracy'. The defining feature of these 'new' movements is a rejection of all traditional forms of politics (*Que se vayan todos!*), which has led to the speculative notions of 'anti-power' or 'no-power' by some scholars (Holloway, 2001; Negri, 2001) armed with a postmodernist sensibility about popular forms of 'resistance'. In effect, the nature and political dynamics of these popular organizations formed in the fourth wave of social movements are not that well understood. The pattern of their evolution requires close scrutiny and further study. These new actors on the Latin American political stage have no script to direct their actions. Where these actions may lead, even what forms they might take in the immediate and near future, are as yet unclear and certainly not predetermined by the structure of their situation.

The dynamics of cross-sectoral political alliances and urban–rural links

According to the proponents of a Gramscian (as opposed to structural) analysis,[11] the EZLN, and to a lesser extent the MST and CONAIE, have become vital conduits for the development of an effective counter-hegemonic movement vis-à-vis the dominant neoliberal model of capitalist development (Morton, 2001). The outcome has been the articulation not so much of the 'identity politics' associated with 'new social movements' as what could be termed the class politics of societal or social transformation – bringing together broad sectors of the popular movement (and civil society) to devise effective forms of collective action to contest the political, economic and cultural hegemony of the dominant class and political elite. The MST leadership, like that of so many other such peasant-based (and -led) socio-political movements, has had this project in mind, and has taken action, virtually from the beginnings of the movement in the locally based communities and pastoral actions of the Catholic Church.[12] However, the associated politics has undergone a number of shifts over the years. For example, despite the strategic alliances formed over the years with other popular organizations such as the Workers Party (PT), the MST has always insisted on autonomy as a social movement, joining the broader struggle for systemic change and providing or seeking solidarity with other organizations in their struggle in particular situations, while retaining the integrity of their organization and struggle. Since 1995, however, the MST has tacked in a somewhat different direction, pursuing, as a matter of fundamental strategy, a politics of broad intersectoral alliances with non-agricultural and other civil and political organizations in the popular struggle, seeking to concert (but not coordinate) the forces of resistance to government policy while at the same time seeking to advance the struggle for land and land reform, bringing this struggle to the cities, to the streets, government offices and the media. In the process of this struggle, the MST has concerted its actions with a myriad of civil society organizations and movements, including the Central Workers Union (CUT), neighbourhood and civic associations, women's groups, developmental and human rights NGOs, a global advocacy network, and the media – all of the popular organizations that make up 'civil society' broadly defined (but not so broad as to include the business associations and other organizational forms and political expressions of the 'private sector').

Is the political evolution of the MST in connection with this new politics atypical or is it shared with that of other organizations in the popular struggle? If typical, what are the social and political dynamics of the struggles and actions involved? Are these dynamics rooted in conditions that are conjunctural and episodic or are these conditions becoming more widespread and generalized, likely to provoke similar or other forms of organization and further action along the same lines? If so, what manner of forces have been accumulated in the process? Are the forces of resistance and opposition being mobilized in the direction of change and development?

Given the present state of academic study and literature, viz. the relative lack of documentation and comparative analysis of diverse urban and rural social movements,[13] the answers that can be given to these questions have to be tentative at best. At the moment, answers have to be given in terms of the specific contexts that have given rise to them. In these contexts, the most dynamic sociopolitical movements, those that have the capacity to address the central concerns of their members and advance the popular struggle, appear to be the peasant-based (and -led) sociopolitical movements, such as the MST, EZLN, FARC and CONAIE. However, the dynamics of these sociopolitical movements pose more problems and raise more questions than solutions or answers.

First, as regards CONAIE,[14] in the context of conditions found in Ecuador – and similar conditions are found in Bolivia, Peru, and Mexico, to name but a few countries – the critical and at times dominant issue in the orchestration – and, at times, coordination – of collective actions within the popular movement is that of national or ethnic identity and its associated rights.[15] In terms of this issue, which also relates to social movements in Mexico as well as several countries in Central America (Honduras, Guatemala, El Salvador and Nicaragua) and the Andes (Bolivia, Colombia, Ecuador and Peru), the central struggle revolves around issues not of land or land reform but those of ethnic identity, democracy and autonomy, viz. liberation from relations of oppression, respect for indigenous cultures and forms of organization – and, in some contexts, the struggle for a multiethnic or pluri-national state, and in others, for social transformation – a fundamental change in the structure of the national economy and the nation-state.[16] In connection to this struggle, leaders of the indigenous organizations and movements frequently register complaints against other organizations on the social or political Left, their potential allies in the popular struggle for systemic change, that they persist in viewing indigenous peoples as peasants only, seeking to convert them into the same and then to convert them as peasants into a proletariat. By some accounts,[17] this has been a primary obstacle in the formation or endurance of any strategic alliances among indigenous organizations and the civil and political organizations on the Left. It is also likely to be a critical factor in the recent trend within the indigenous movement to ally with a broad network and coalitions of international advocacy or activist organizations and other forms of 'global civil society' (Chalmers, Scott and Piester, 1997; Kleymeyer, 1998; Schittecatte, 1999; Keck and Sikkink, 1998). This type of organization helps create conditions of broad public support and thus political pressures on the government relative to campaigns launched in the struggle.

On the other hand, the Fuerzas Armados Revolucionarios de Colombia (FARC) exemplifies conditions of struggle that were widespread in the 1970s, in a very different regional context, but that for one reason or another, primarily as a result of political reaction and repression by the state, have disappeared or radically changed in the other countries in the region. In the 1970s, in Uruguay, Argentina, Brazil and Chile, and other countries in the throes of a counter-revolution and dirty war prosecuted by the armed forces of the state, the popular struggle was largely located in the urban centres. It was in the more rural societies of Central America and the Andes, particularly those with a significant indigenous population, that the popular struggle was centred in the countryside and took the form of a revolutionary armed struggle and a guerrilla organization, much like that which erupted in Chiapas on 1 January 1994. In the 1970s rural fronts of such organizations and revolutionary movements were formed but with very few exceptions (Colombia, for one) were either destroyed or did not survive the changing conditions. In the 1980s, however, under these changed conditions and thus in a very different context, peasant-based and indigenous organizations and sociopolitical movements were reconstructed and in some cases resurrected. In Central America they engaged in a class and civil war – a confrontation of belligerent social and political forces that was not settled until well into the 1990s, at an unbelievably enormous human and social cost. However, in Brazil, Ecuador, Mexico and elsewhere (Bolivia, Paraguay), these movements took another direction, generating sporadic outbreaks and another wave of 'rural activism' across the region – a wave that also hit the urban centres in the form of a popular movement directed against the neoliberal agenda of governments in the region. These movements were generally oriented towards action on the critical issues of land and democracy, and often they were also constructed to advance the cause of indigenous rights, a cause that led to the growth and proliferation of NGOs with a human rights agenda. In Mexico, for example, by 1990 there were at least thirteen NGOs with a human rights agenda that were active in Chiapas alone.

Collier (1994) argues that market-driven globalization, that is, neoliberal capitalist development, is the primary factor responsible for the activism of social and political movements over the past decade. The EZLN is an excellent case in point. Its eruption in 1994, on the very day that the North American Free Trade Agreement (NAFTA) took effect, was strategically timed to coincide with a development that was regarded as 'the death knell' of the economy on which the households in the Zapatista communities depended for their livelihoods.[18] However, as noted above, there were other conditions that gave rise to the latest wave of rural activism, including, paradoxically, a growing democratization process and increased government repression of the forces mobilized in this process. Under these conditions, the peasant and indigenous organizations in the countryside responded by mounting a resistance movement that has cut across the rural–urban divide, forming an extensive, if shifting, complex of strategic and tactical alliances with other civil and political organizations, mostly urban, involved in the popular struggle. The multitude of intra- and intersectoral linkages formed over the course of the 1980s and 1990s, and the organizations set up to mobilize the forces of resistance and coordinate and concert collective actions within the movement, are clear manifestations of this trend.

These linkages can be put into three categories, each with its own dynamics: (i) horizontal linkages among networks of non-governmental organizations and civic associations and grassroots movements in the urban areas; (ii) intra- and intersectoral linkages among class-based organizations and sociopolitical movements, primarily in a national context; and (iii) regional and international networks of national and sub-national urban and rural organizations.

As for the NGO networks they are generally located within the 'middle strata' of the urban areas, and they are formed, primarily, for the purpose of providing support to, and solidarity with, the struggles and social movements of grassroots organizations within the broader civil society. In this connection these linkages relate to a broad range of concerns, from the protection and enhancement of political and human rights, diverse environmental issues of concern to neighbourhood groups, women or minority groups of various sorts, to shared concern with the impact of government policies in the context of the processes of globalization and structural adjustment. With regards to this latter concern, and in solidarity with the struggle of class-based organizations and movements in relation to shared resistance against government policies or concern with organization-specific issues, these urban-centred civil society organizations (CSOs) also participate in the complex of intra- and intersectoral alliances that characterize the organization and politics of these class-based organizations. In this connection, all of the major sociopolitical movements such as the MST, for the purpose of soliciting support for their campaigns to influence public opinion and pressure governments, have tended to form linkages with international advocacy groups.

Notwithstanding the role of NGOs in the popular struggle, most have positioned themselves as intermediaries, mediating between grassroots or community-based organizations, on the one hand, and governments and international development or donor organizations on the other (Biekart, 1996; Carroll, 1992; Landim, 1988). In this connection, the more development-oriented NGOs generally have entered into partnerships with the ODAs, both bilateral and multilateral, and the local governments or municipalities that have been assigned, or have assumed, the primary responsibility for advancing the development process under the institutionality of the new model (Blair, 1997; Macdonald, 1997). In this process, as executing agents of projects that fall within the development programmes of international donor organizations and central governments, NGOs have tended to play an ambiguous role that has not been exempt from criticisms by both grassroots organizations and certain academics. The thrust of these criticisms is that in many cases the NGOs have wittingly or unwittingly served to advance the interests of external agents – as agents of the forces of 'global domination' or, as some (Petras, for example) would have it, 'imperialism' – at the expense of the communities and grassroots organizations.[19]

It is argued that in conforming to programmatic principles established by the international development agencies and central governments as a funding condition the NGOs have contributed to the disarticulation and disempowerment of many grassroots organizations in terms of their capacity to confront the power structure and the conditions of elite control of the decision-making process with regards to the distribution of society's productive resources.[20] In exchange for giving up their confrontationalist/anti-systemic approach and the search for radical or extensive structural change in the structure of decision-making vis-à-vis macroeconomic policy and other external conditions that impinge on them, the grassroots organizations have been empowered to participate in decisions that are strictly local in their scope and effects (see, for example, Marcos, 1994 in the case of Peru).[21]

To be more precise, in the context of the partnership strategy pursued by international development agencies and central governments, grassroots organizations have been empowered to participate in an identification of their basic needs and decisions as to how, where and on what to spend the poverty alleviation funds provided under the New Social Policy (NSP). From the perspective of a number of grassroots organizations, particularly those concerned with, or oriented towards, more fundamental change, this has been a Faustian bargain. Intersectoral alliances and transnational activist networks are generally formed by federations of peasant producer organizations, producer cooperatives, indigenous organizations and labour unions. In the 1980s a number of such alliances were formed by organizations that were otherwise concerned to retain their autonomy vis-à-vis political parties and their distance vis-à-vis the NGOs that were springing up all over the region.[22]

In the 1990s, however, linkages and strategic alliances between and among these organizations, along sectoral lines, were broadly extended across the region in the form of various regional and international associations of diverse national organizations (Edelman, 1998). In Latin America the Asociación de Organizaciones Campesinas Centroamericanas para la Cooperación y el Desarrollo (ASOCODE), formed in Tegucicalpa in 1991, is an example of this trend. Other examples include Iniciativa Civil para la Integración Centroamericana (ICIC), a lobbying group formed by a network of cooperatives, NGOs, labour organizations, community groups, and diverse organizations of small enterprise operators and agricultural producers; and Via Campesina, formed in 1993 as an transnational network of fifty-five peasant organizations from thirty-six countries in the Americas, Asia and Africa.

Although there are not many studies on the workings and outcomes of these regional associations and transnational networks, there is little question about their critical role in raising awareness of common problems, the establishment of shared principles, and in some contexts the concertation of actions and, in others, the formation of a common front or solidarity actions to improve the capacity to influence the policies of governments in the region. However, the formation of alliances with non-agricultural sector groups, a rejection of political party ties and the building of transnational networks coincided with, or has led to, a more pluralist and less confrontationalist approach to politics – a turning away from the strategy of 'peasant wars' and the tactic of armed struggle. With regard to these shifting dynamics of organized struggle in the case of ASOCODE in Costa Rica and other countries of Central America, see Edelman (1998, 2000). In the case of rural struggles in Chiapas and elsewhere in Mexico diverse studies conducted by Harvey (1994, 1995, 1996, 1998) detail the organizational and political dynamics involved. In the case of CONAIE, the weekly *Boletin ICCI 'RIMAY'* provides a well-documented strategic analysis of the changing dynamics of struggle waged by the indigenous movement in Ecuador and in the region.

As for intersectoral linkages, they have been formed, primarily, between peasant and indigenous organizations, on the one hand, and labour unions, workers' *centrales* or federations on the other. In some cases, political parties of one orientation or another have mediated these linkages, but for the most part they entail organizational links or strategic alliances around critical issues that affect both types of organization. In some contexts (for example, the Central Obrera Boliviana – COB) the interests and actions are concerted and pursued within a common organization, formed with the purpose of broadening the social base for a common struggle against government policies or, more broadly, against the system and process of capitalist development that lies behind these policies. More generally, however, the diverse interests of sectorally driven or class-defined social groups are brought together not organizationally but in the form of a strategic alliance between diverse federations of peasants, indigenous peoples and organized workers. This has been the case, for example, in the struggles waged by MST in one context, the Zapatistas in another, CONAIE in yet another (see the series of attempts, in diverse conjunctures, to form a strategic and tactical alliance with the Frente Unitario de Trabajadores (FUT) and the Coordinadora de Movimientos Sociales (CMS)), and diverse peasant organizations in Costa Rica, El Salvador, Guatemala, Honduras and Nicaragua (Edelman, 2000; Stahler-Sholk, 1990). In this connection, the MST is an organization of landless or near-landless 'workers', while CONAIE and the EZLN are organizations of indigenous communities, the economies of which are based, primarily, on peasant or subsistence forms of agricultural production, as it is generally in Central America. The FARC, in a very different context, and under conditions that are to some extent shared yet unique to Colombia, also has its social basis in the peasantry, broadly defined and located across the country. In each case the noted dynamism of the social movements, in terms of the mobilized forces of popular resistance, can be attributed, to an appreciable extent, to the system of class and intersectoral alliances involved. This is why the political landscape of the Central and South American countryside in the 1990s is littered with so many cross-sectoral organizations.[23] By the same token, the relative failure of these organizations of peasant farmers, indigenous peoples and rural workers to create a sustained popular movement against neoliberalism, and to advance an alternative project, can be similarly explained (Chalmers, Scott and Piester, 1997: 543).

To summarize, it is possible to identify across Latin America a clear and growing trend towards linkages among diverse organizations involved in the popular struggle.[24] The most important of these linkages have been inter- or intrasectoral, sometimes bringing together both peasant farmers, indigenous communities and workers – both urban and rural – within a common organization (for example, Ecuador's CMS – Coordinadora de Movimientos Sociales) but more often bringing them together in the form of a strategic or tactical alliance. Although to date there does not exist any systematic study of these alliances, country by country or for the region as a whole, the importance of their role in the popular struggle cannot be overemphasized. The meso- and macro-dynamics of these alliances are absolutely critical to understanding the nature and scope of political responses to the conditions of neoliberal capitalist development in the region, and to gauging accurately the forces unleashed in the process of popular struggle against these conditions. For one thing, horizontal cross-sectoral links and alliances among organizations involved in the popular movement provide the necessary conditions for coordinating and directing the accumulated and mobilized forces for change – for moving beyond resistance and opposition to constructive change and development. The agency for this cannot be found in the state and certainly not the market, whether regulated or free, or in business associations, but within a burgeoning civil society.[25] To this extent, the shifting focus of most developmental agencies towards civil society, and a shared concern to strengthen it, is not, as suggested earlier, misplaced. It relates to conditions that are real enough, the identification of a possible agency for change, and an assessment of the social forces that can be mobilized in one direction or another – resistance and opposition or development in some form.

However, short of a systematic region-wide comparative study of both the structural conditions that underlie and generate the forces for change and their political dynamics, it is difficult if not impossible to gauge the balance of forces for and against change – for example, in the grossly unequal distribution of society's productive resources such as land and the conditions of social exclusion and poverty associated with the structure of this distribution. In fact, without such an analysis it is not possible to fully understand the issues involved or to prescribe the most appropriate or effective action or policy. This remains a major challenge facing scholars and activists, intellectuals and practitioners, in the field of development.

Conclusion

The past six decades can be divided almost equally into two periods, one characterized by unprecedented system-wide rates of rapid economic growth and significant social advances both in the north and the south of the world economic order, the other by a system-wide propensity towards crisis and diverse efforts to restructure a way out of this crisis. As a condition of this systemic and institutional restructuring, the changes, advances and gains made in the first period were generally – in some cases dramatically – reversed, bringing in their wake a highly polarized form of development, increasing social inequalities in the distribution of wealth and income, and the spread of poverty and other conditions of social exclusion.

Whereas developments in the first period, the era of development, were predicated on state-led reforms to the operating capitalist system of regulated and protected markets, and on the political dynamics of populist or authoritarian (bureaucratic or military) regimes, in the second period, the era of globalization, they were based on the conjunction of economic and political forms of 'liberalization' and 'liberalism' – a marriage (of convenience and convergent interests) between *free markets* and *open elections*.

However, the 'new world economic order' created as a result of this new model provides the policy and institutional framework for advancing the globalization project of the 'transnational capitalist class' (Van der Pijl, 1998). The popular movement, in contrast, has preferred to mobilize the forces of opposition and resistance to this project. As for the projects of social transformation and development, which dominated the first period, in the context of a growing international or global north–south divide, and under conditions of a counter-revolution and a new economic model, they both underwent an involution and a process of convoluted change. In this context, the former have taken the organizational form of sociopolitical movements that continue to challenge 'the system' and the policies that support it. The development project, on the other hand, has been reconstructed in a number of different directions and in different ways on the basis of a new paradigm that emphasizes the need for social inclusion, participation and sustainability (Chopra, Kadekodi and Murty, 1990; Rahman, 1991; Veltmeyer and O'Malley, 2001).

On this basis, the key to substantive change – to move from social exclusion to development – is for its proponents and protagonists to reach beyond both the state and the market into the popular movement and mobilize the forces of resistance in a new direction.

The development project is predicated on state-led structural reform and the reversal of policies designed for the corporate agenda of globalization. That is, capitalism in its neoliberal form is dysfunctional for the development process. To activate this process, governments should re-establish control over the society's strategic resources and industries, regulate markets and private economic activity, and re-establish the public sector vis-à-vis the private sector and the institutions of global capitalism. That is, the state as well the regime or government administration needs to be substantively restructured to serve the public interest – and escape the play, and power, of interests in the private sector of society.[26] This type of change in the structure of political power, and its state apparatus, requires the mobilization of civil society in the organizational and political form of social movements, and the concertation of these forces within a project of social transformation or systemic change.

In effect, we have identified two basic modalities of change and development within the popular movement based on the strengthening of civil society. At this level, there seem to be two fundamental intellectual and political macro-projects at play – *another development* and *social transformation*. Both of these projects are at odds with the 'new economic model' of neoliberal capitalist development and its associated project of 'globalization'. In the current context, there is little to no question about pursuing the path of social transformation in either the mainstream or the margins of development thought and practice. It is possible, nevertheless, to identify a number of permutations in the search for an alternative form of development, including efforts to secure sustainable livelihoods of people in the rural sector. Despite (or perhaps because of) its *reformist* orientation as well as its commitment to allay the negative effects of neoliberalism and the associated project of globalization and structural adjustment the *sustainable livelihoods approach* – SLA (Chambers and Conway, 1998; Helmore and Singh, 2001; Liamzon et al., 1996), arguably, has the potential and some prospects for bringing about an appreciable measure of improvements in the quality of life of the rural poor. The key to the sustainable livelihoods of the rural poor is the accumulation of 'social capital', a resource vested in the capacity to cooperate productively and to form solidarity networks, which the poor have in abundance, thus requiring little to no change in the social organization of production – or, for that matter, in the structure of political power (Coleman, 1988; Knack, 1999; Woolcock, 1998; Woolcock and Narayan, 2000).

The reason that SLA might present a viable option is that the political conditions for a revolutionary path towards development do not exist and are not likely to result from a confrontationalist political approach. Protests against the capitalist system and neoliberal policies in place are one thing, even where there exists the possibility of mobilizing the forces of resistance into a united front. However, to bring about the changes needed to open a revolutionary path towards development is altogether different. In Latin America's countryside today, the repositories of the most dynamic forces of opposition to capitalist development in its neoliberal form – and social change – are associated with a new wave of peasant-based (and -led) socio-political movements that are responsible for an observed resurgence of rural activism in the region. But these movements do not have the organizational capacity or access to the resources needed to mobilize other popular forces of resistance and opposition into a counter-hegemonic bloc – or, for that matter, to mobilize the productive resources (social capital) available to the poor at the grassroots level. A step in this direction, as well as in the direction of substantive social change, is provided by a strategy of horizontal inter-sectoral linkages and strategic alliances among diverse forces of opposition – what Chalmers, Scott and Piester (1997) term 'associative networks'. However, the forces of reaction in Latin America's countryside and urban centres are formidable and likely able to withstand and stave off pressures for systemic or revolutionary change. Depending on one's perspective – or politics – this could be seen as desirable or unfortunate. It is, however, an inescapable fact.

On the one hand, the sustainability of rural livelihoods requires not only the empowerment of the poor and the agency of civil society but a redistributive approach towards the existing structure of productive resources. On the other hand, this approach requires a change in the existing structure of decision-making – a sharing of political power or decision-making power relative to the allocation of these resources.[27]

The problem here, one that has thus far eluded the proponents of SLA, is that such empowerment also requires confrontation of the existing structure of economic and political power.[28] To decentralize responsibilities, policy-making and other forms of governance opens up spaces for popular partici-pation in decision-making. However, it does so only on matters of local import and limited scope such as how (on what projects) to spend the poverty alleviation funds made available from above and the outside. However, the lives and livelihoods of the poor are greatly affected by conditions generated by matters of national policy and related decisions generally made in the interests of those who own and control the major means of social produc-tion, and that as a result dominate the national economy. In this political context, the challenge for the agents of the development project is to face up to this structural fact. In their failure to do so they might very well sow the seeds of further protest and direct action – and reap the bitter fruit therefrom.

Notes

1. At the colloquium organized at the Roskilde University as part of the United Nations World Social Summit in Copenhagen (Atal and Yen, 1995; Bessis, 1995), a number of panelists highlighted the centrality of the notion of 'social exclusion' for understanding the poverty and other conditions lived by a large and growing part of the world population in the new global context of deepening income dis-parities, liberalization and globalization of economic activity, the increased reliance on market forces and the retreat of the nation-state from responsibilities for economic development and social welfare (see Bessis, 1995, for a synthesis of these considerations and conclusions). In an analysis of the social crisis created by these conditions, panelists argued that the conditions of social exclusion and poverty, attributed to 'the mutations of the 1980s' and analysed generally by soci-ologists, have displaced those of exploitation, a concept favoured by economists.
2. In its 1992 report, International Fund for Agricultural Development (IFAD) (Jazeiry et al., 1992) identified up to twenty sources of rural poverty, including the struc-tural sources or pillars. As for the social conditions of this social exclusion and poverty, the associated literature, most of it generated in the past decade, is volu-minous, as reflected in the International Labour Organization's (ILO's) 1994 com-pilation of studies (ILO, 1994). Given the array of international organizations and research institutions, both within the UN system and the international develop-ment community, involved in the war against poverty and the broader conditions of social exclusion, it is clear that the problem has not only reached critical pro-portions but that it is global in scope. One of many organizations set up in the search for solutions to the problem of social exclusion is the Research Centre for Analysis of Social Exclusion (CASE), established in October 1997 at the London School of Economics and Political Science (LSE) with funding from the UK Economic and Social Research Council.
3. A poverty-oriented Basic Needs approach dominated the study of international development in the 1970s. Originating in the 1973 discovery of the World Bank

that upwards of two-fifths of the world's population was in a state of relative deprivation, unable to meet its basic needs. According to Amartya Sen a household without sufficient income to meet the basic needs of its members is poor, a condition that can be measured in terms of a head count, that is, the number and percentage of the population that falls below a defined income poverty line; or, according to Sen, by an index of disparity in income distribution, viz. income gap ratio multiplied by the number of the poor, which provides a coefficient of specific poverty.

 4. Fujimori's poverty relief programme was similar to Salinas' (PRONASOL, 1992) in that it served primarily as a mechanism for securing the rural vote.

 5. In the 'new economic model' of neoliberal capitalist (free market) development, the global corporations in this sector had already been assigned the responsibility for driving forward the growth process – starting and driving the motor of this process (i.e., the world market). In the 1990s, however, further efforts were expended in this direction – in the strategy of expanding the role of these corporations (the 'private sector') in the process of sustainable development (Palazzi, 2000; UNDP, 1998; UN, 1998). The primary consideration here was 'corporate responsibility' in areas of green technology, environmental and social impacts and 'good governance'.

 6. Another problem, Utting (2000) points out, is that 'relatively few companies ... have significantly improved their social and environmental record through a voluntary approach'. Consequently, he concludes, it is important that 'inter-government agreements and regulations remain in force' – as complements to these 'voluntary initiatives' rather than 'replacing them'. This point is made in even stronger terms by Transnational Resource and Action Center (TRAC) which sees the UNDP's 'flirtation with corporate collaboration' as 'perilous' (Karliner, 1999). The only remedy and security in this regard are 'government regulations' imposed and maintained on the basis of an active and alert 'civil society' that provides a close watch on corporate behaviour and public interest institutions.

 7. In its proposals for administrative reform and legislation, the Lozada administration can be viewed as particularly oriented towards 'development'. However, it is just as likely, if not more so, that the government responded positively to the initiative of the World Bank, the UNDP and other institutions of ODA in this regard, taking Bolivia as an ideal locus of experiments with the NEM and associated strategies.

 8. The basic model used to bring about sustainable development includes: (i) a market-friendly reform structural adjustment framework; (ii) the search for new technologies that can extend the limits to economic growth; (iii) appropriate resource conservation measures taken by both industry and the relevant communities (community-based resource management); and (iv) appropriate regulatory frameworks instituted by the government.

 9. For an analysis of, and a series of case studies into, the regional and global dynamics of this struggle see, *inter alia*, Ghimire (2001).

10. In this context the role of the state vis-à-vis the small producers and rural communities of indigenous or peasant producers, includes a number of strategies, implemented as and where possible. On the dynamics of these strategies see Petras and Veltmeyer (2003).

11. In the view articulated and espoused by many critical analysts of the dynamics of the popular movement and a growing global civil society, Subcomandante Marcos and intellectuals engaged in the global struggle against capitalism in its neoliberal

form are much closer to Gramsci than to Marx, that is, this struggle is viewed in terms of the need to build a counter-hegemonic force. Thus Durán de Huerta (1999), in her interviews with Marcos both quotes Marcos and interprets Zapatista discourse in these terms, as does Lynn Stephen (1997).

12. In the well-documented case of Zapatismo in Chiapas, the Church, in the person of Bishop Samuel Ruiz, was a critical factor and played a pivotal role in the mobilization and original organization of the popular forces of resistance not only in terms of a critical insurrectionist ideology (liberation theology) but as the end result of the invitations extended to diverse Marxist and Maoist political organizations to engage in the struggle. On this, see Floyd (1996), MacEoin (1996), Morton (2001: 13–16) and Womack (1999).

13. On this point, see Munck (1997).

14. CONAIE was formed in 1986 as a coordinating network of indigenous organizations such as ECUARUNARI (Confederación de los Pueblos de la Nacionalidad Quichua del Ecuador) and CONFENIAE (Confederación de Nacionalidades Indígenas de la Amazonía Ecuatoriana).

15. On this point see the various monthly issues of the *Boletín ICCI 'RIMAY'* and *Revista Koeyu Latinoamericano*, a news and analysis outlet for the Instituto Científico de Culturas Indígenas.

16. Each of the major rural sociopolitical movements in Latin America – MST, CONAIE, EZLN and FARC – has systemic transformation rather than structural reforms as a broad political objective.

17. This question of social identity (how indigenous peoples see or present themselves) also has a political dimension. Before the current neoliberal era, indigenous groups frequently presented themselves as peasants because many government programmes directed towards the rural areas targeted peasants, not Indians. For example, Mexico's Indian programmes, notably those designed by the National Indigenous Institute (INI) were designed to assimilate indigenous peoples into the peasantry rather than help them as Indians. But with economic restructuring, land became more important to economic planners as marketable commodity and the peasantry as a mobile labour force. The government in Mexico, as elsewhere, eliminated or cut back its programmes that supported peasants. As resources for rural development and support dried up indigenous peoples found little reason for continuing to represent themselves as peasants rather than as distinct societies in their own right. In any case, it is interesting and revealing that the indigenous movement to recover their ethnic or national identity, and to assert their right to autonomous development, coincided with a shift in government policy vis-à-vis the peasantry and a collapse of support for its development.

18. A similar rebellion against the government's neoliberal programme of structural adjustment measures was launched by Ecuador's indigenous organizations in 1994, contemporaneously with the Zapatista rebellion.

19. This view is articulated in very clear terms by Jorge Ulcuango (*Boletín ICCI*, 5 August 1999). In the view of this indigenous intellectual, organically linked to the indigenous movement and CONAIE, its representative body, NGOs, wittingly or otherwise, have been called into arms and used as an 'economic-political weapon' by the organizations of global capital (the World Bank, the IMF, IDB ...) for what in this anti-systemic discourse appears as a struggle for 'global domination'.

20. On this argument see Marcos (1994, 1996) with regards to Peru, and Veltmeyer (1997b) with regards to Bolivia. The regional and global trend towards decentralization and the agency of local governments in the development process

has been viewed in a similar light – as a means of disarticulating traditional forms of social and political organization of the indigenous communities, an opportunity for undermining their traditional authority and consolidating the economic and political power of the elite, viz, its capacity for manipulating the process of local politics with its discourse on 'modernity' (Editorial, *Boletín ICCI 'RIMAY'*, July and September 2000). In all of the countries with a substantial indigenous population – Bolivia, Ecuador, Peru and Guatemala – one of the more critical concerns with neoliberal policies relates to their negative impact on the relative autonomy of indigenous forms of community-based social, economic and political organization. In the case of Ecuador, see Bautista (1999).

21. On this issue, see Veltmeyer (1997b).

22. In the polarized political climate of the mid-1980s in Central America revolutionary movements and activists alike tended to view allies in the region and beyond as crucial for political success and even physical survival. On these early international contacts, see Edelman (1998).

23. See, for example, the struggles of the indigenous movement in Ecuador against the government's various attempts, from 1994 to date, to implement a neoliberal programme of structural adjustment. On the basis of its organizational and mobilizing capacity, and its capacity to concert an alliance of oppositional forces and popular resistance, this movement has been surprisingly successful in preventing the government from implementing its agenda. As noted by Palacios (1999: 1–2), 'as of the promulgation in 1994 of the Modernization law to the crisis of March 1999 the [project to bring about the] neoliberal transformation of [Ecuadorian] society has failed in all respects.' What has been achieved is an extension of a highly speculative structure of economic activity that continues to generate the condition of both an economic and a political crisis.

24. These linkages are horizontal and intersectoral and as such can be contrasted with linkages advocated by the World Bank and the other international financial institutions (IFIs) (IDB, for example) and ODAs, including the UNDP. These organizations, for the most part, advocate the formation of a new form of tripartism – a 'collaborative triangle' between 'the public sector, private business and civil society' (Atal and Yen, 1995; Bessis, 1995; Reilly, 1989). However, as pointed out by some panelists at the Roskilde Colloquium, the 'necessary collaborative triangle' between public, private and 'third sector' organizations 'may build up elements of resistance' within the social movements sector (see Bessis, 1995).

25. On this point note the view expressed by David Rockefeller of the Chase Manhattan Bank, the 174th richest person in the world and one of the architects of the Trilateral Commission, to the effect that 'in recent years there's been a trend toward democracy and market economies [which] has lessened the role of government ... But ... somebody has to take government's place, and business seems to me the logical entity to do it' (quoted by Herman Daly in his address, in 1999, to the International Society for Ecological Economics – http://www.feasta.org/article_daly.htm). This view is entirely consistent with what was termed (Williamson, 1990) the 'Washington Consensus'.

26. In this connection, the project of the World Bank, the UNDP and other ODAs to incorporate the 'private sector' (of global corporations) into the development process is fundamentally flawed or wrongheaded. The private sector is dominated by interests that are committed to the contrary project, and process, of globalization. The drive to accumulate capital on the basis of private property in the means of social production is fundamentally incompatible with the public interest in

economic and social development – substantive improvement in the lives and livelihoods of the mass of independent producers and workers that make up a large part of global civil society.

27. This issue of political power – decision-making capacity vis-à-vis the authoritative allocation of society's productive resources and the institution of relevant policies and changes at the national level – is a blind spot in alternative development approaches towards social change such as SLA. These approaches tend towards a concern for *social* rather than *political* 'empowerment', that is, the building by the poor of their social rather than their political capital. In this connection, the latest (2002) *Human Development Report* of the UNDP, an organization calling for an alternative development approach, presents somewhat of a new departure. For the first time it actually reports on the need for substantive change in the distribution of 'political power', an effective sharing of decision-making capacity not just at the local but at the national level.

28. A review of policy documents prepared by the operational and policy research agencies of the UN, including the Economic Commission for Latin America and the Caribbean (ECLAC), IFAD, the UNDP, the World Bank, as well as UNRISD shows that all of them accept the institutionality of the existing economic system. The issue is the degree and scope of the social reforms that need to be implemented. In no case, however, is the existing power structure confronted in theory or in practice. This could be the Achilles heel of alternative forms of social development. The problem is that unlike social capital, the accumulation of political capital – decision-making power vis-à-vis the allocation of productive resources – requires radical structural change and a direct confrontation with those (the elite) who hold the levers of economic and political power. The rich and powerful, however, will not easily surrender either their wealth or share their political power. Any such 'development' will not result from a process of negotiation and peaceful dialogue. As the social movements have generally demonstrated, it will require direct action and the mobilization of the accumulated forces of resistance.

References

Albó, X. (1996) 'Making the leap from local mobilization to national politics', *NACLA*, Vol. 29, March/April.

Alvarez, S., E. Diagnino and A. Escobar (eds) (1999) *Cultures of Politics and Politics of Cultures: Revisioning Latin American Social Movements*. Boulder, CO: Westview Press.

Arias, Dario (2002) 'Hidrocarburos, protección ambiental y seguridada jurídica en Bolivia', *Petroleo y Gas*, No. 26, July–August.

Arrieto, M. and E. Pinedo (1995) *Hacia una Propuesta Indígina de Descentralización del Estado. Etnias y Participación*. La Paz: PROADE/ILDIS.

Atal, Yogesh and Else Yen (eds) (1995) *Poverty and Participation in Civil Society*, Proceedings of a UNESCO/CROP Round Table, World Summit for Social Development, Copenhagen, March.

Bautista, Carlos (1999) 'Situación de la comunidad de Pijal', *Boletín ICCI*, 1, Issue 7, October.

Bessis, Sophia (1995) *From Social Exclusion to Social Cohesion*, Synthesis of the Roskilde Colloquium, World Social Summit, Roskilde University, Copenhagen, 2–4 March.

Biekart, Kees (1996) 'Strengthening intermediary roles in civil society: Experiences from Central America', in Andrew Clayton (ed.), *NGOs, Civil Society and the State: Building Democracy in Transitional Societies*. Oxford: International NGO Training and Research Centre (INTRAC).

Blackburn, J. and J. Holland (1998) *Who Changes? Institutionalizing Participation in Development*. London: Intermediate Technology Development Group.

Blair, H. (1997) 'Donors, democratisation and civil society: Relating theory to practice', in D. Hulme and M. Edwards (eds), *NGOs, States and Donors: Too Close for Comfort?* London: Macmillan.

Boletín ICCI (1999) 1, 5 August.

Boletín ICCI 'RIMAY' (2000) 2, Issue 16 (July).

Boletín ICCI 'RIMAY' (2000) 2, Issue 18 (September).

Bolivia, Ministerio de Desarrollo Sustenible y Medio Ambiente (1994) *Plan General de Desarrollo Economico y Social: El Cambio para Todos*. La Paz Ed.

Booth, D., S. Clisby and C. Widmark (1995) *Empowering the Poor through Institutional Reform: an Initial Appraisal of the Bolivian Experience*. Working Paper 32, Department of Anthropology. Stockholm: University of Stockholm.

Booth, D., S. Clisby and C. Widmark (1997) *Democratising the State in Rural Bolivia*. Development Studies Unit. Stockholm: University of Stockholm.

Brass, Tom (2000) *Peasants, Populism and Postmodernism: the Return of the Agrarian Myth*. London: Frank Cass.

Calderón, Fernando (1995) *Movimientos sociales y política*, Siglo XX1, Mexico.

Calderón, Fernando G., Jordi Borja, Maria Grossi and Susana Peñalva (eds) (1989) *Descentralización y democracia: Gobiernos locales en America Latina*. Santiago: CLACSO/ SUR/CLUMT.

Carroll, Thomas (1992) *Intermediary NGOs: the Supportive Link in Grassroots Development*. West Hartford, CT: Kumarian Press.

Chalmers, Douglas, Martin Scott and Kerianne Piester (1997) 'Associative networks: New structures of representation for the popular sectors', in Douglas Chalmers, Carlos M. Vilas, Katherine Hite, Scott B. Martin, Kerianne Piester and Monique Segarra (eds), *The New Politics of Inequality in Latin America: Rethinking Participation and Representation*. Oxford: Oxford University Press.

Chambers, Robert and Gordon Conway (1998) 'Sustainable rural livelihoods: Some working definitions', *Development*, Vol. 41, No. 3, September.

Chopra, K., G. Kadekodi and M. Murty (1990) *Participatory Development*. London: Sage.

Coleman, J. S. (1988) 'Social capital in the creation of human capital', *American Journal of Sociology*, Supplement, Vol. 94: S95–S120.

Collier, George (1994) *Structural Adjustment and New Regional Movements: the Zapatista Rebellion in Chiapas*. Working Paper No. 215, The Latin American Program, Conference 'Ethnic Conflict and Governance in Comparative Perspective', Woodrow Wilson Center, 15 November.

Crabtree, John (2003) 'The impact of neo-liberal economics on Peruvian peasant agriculture in the 1990s', in Tom Brass (ed.), *Latin American Peasants*. London: Frank Cass, pp. 131–61.

Delgadillo Terceros, Walter and Jonny Zambrana Barrios (2002) *Experiencias de los Consejos de Participación Popular (CPPs)*. Unidad de fortalecimiento comunitario y transversales. Cochabamba: PROSANA.

Dominguez, Jorge (ed.) (1994) *Social Movements in Latin America: the Experience of Peasants, Workers, the Urban Poor, and the Middle Sectors*. New York: Garland Publishers.

Durán de Huerta, Marta (1999) 'An interview with Subcomandante Insurgente Marcos, spokesperson and military commander of the EZLN', *International Affairs*, Vol. 75, No. 2.

Edelman, Marc (1998) 'Transnational peasant politics in Central America', *Latin American Research Review*, Vol. 33, No. 3.

Edelman, Marc (2000) *Peasants against Globalization: Rural Social Movements in Costa Rica*. Stanford: Stanford University Press.

El Deber, 9 December 2002.

El Mundo, 4 December 2002.

Escobar, Arturo and Sonia Alvarez (eds) (1992) *The Making of Social Movements in Latin America: Identity, Strategy and Democracy*. Boulder, CO: Westview Press.

Floyd, Charlene (1996) 'A theology of insurrection? Religion and politics in Mexico', *Journal of International Affairs*, Vol. 50, No. 1.

Ghai, Dharam (1991) *The IMF and the South: the Social Impact of Crisis and Adjustment*. London: UNRISD and Zed Books.

Ghimire, K. B. (ed.) (2001) *Whose Land? Civil Society Perspectives on Land Reform and Rural Poverty Reduction: Regional Experiences from Africa, Asia and Latin America*. Rome: UNRISD and the International Fund for Agricultural Development (IFAD).

Harvey, Neil (1994) *Rebellion in Chiapas: Rural Reforms, Campesino Radicalism and the Limits to Salinismo*. San Diego: Center for US–Mexican Studies.

Harvey, Neil (1995) 'Rebellion in Chiapas: Rural reforms and popular struggles', *Third World Quarterly*, Vol. 16, No. 1.

Harvey, Neil (1996) 'Rural reforms and the Zapatista rebellion: Chiapas, 1988–1995', in Gerardo Otero (ed.), *Neoliberalisam Revisited: Economic Restructuring and Mexico's Political Future*. Boulder, CO: Westview Press.

Harvey, Neil (1998) *The Chiapas Rebellion: the Struggle for Land and Democracy*. Durham: Duke University Press.

Helmore, Kristen and Naresh Singh (2001) *Sustainable Livelihoods: Building on the Wealth of the Poor*. West Hartford, CT: Kumarian Press.

Holloway, John (2001) *Contrapoder: Una introducción*. Buenos Aires: Ediciones de Mano en Mano.

International Fund for Agricultural Development (IFAD) (2001) *Rural Poverty Report 2001: the Challenge of Ending Rural Poverty*. Rome: IFAD.

International Institute for Labour Studies (ILO) (1994) *Social Exclusion in America Latina: an Annotated Bibliography*. Geneva: ILO.

Jazairy, Idriss, Mohiuddin Alamgir and Theresa Panuccio (1992) *The State of World Rural Poverty*. London: Intermediate Technology Publications (for IFAD).

Karliner, Joshua, with John Cavanagh, Phyllis Bennis and Ward Morehouse (1999) *A Perilous Partnership: the United Nations Development Programme's Flirtation with Corporate Collaboration*. Corpwatch (formerly know as TRAC – Transnational Resource and Action Center), Institute for Policy Studies (IPS) and Council on International and Public Affairs (CIPA), 16 March. http://www.corpwatch.org/campaigns/PCD.jsp?articleid=3388.

Keck, Margaret and Kathryn Sikkink (1998) *Activists beyond Borders: Advocacy Networks in International Politics*. Ithaca, NY: Cornell University Press.

Kleymeyer, Charles (1998) 'Supporting indigenous visions and strategies in Latin America', *Native Americas*, Winter.

Knack, S. (1999) *Social Capital, Growth and Poverty: a Survey of Cross-Country Evidence*. Social Capital Initiative Working Paper 7, Social Development Department. Washington, DC: World Bank.

Landim, Leilah (1988) 'Non-governmental organizations in Latin America', *World Development*, 15 (supplement): 29–38.

Liamzon, Tina et al. (eds) (1996) *Towards Sustainable Livelihoods*. Rome: Society for International Development.

Macdonald, Laura (1997) *Supporting Civil Society: the Political Role of NGOs in Central America*. Basingstoke: Macmillan.

MacEoin, Gary (1996) *The People's Church: Bishop Samuel Ruiz of Mexico and Why He Matters*. New York: Crossroad Publishing Company.

Marcos, Jaime (1994) 'Disolución de comunidades campesinos y dinámica municipio-comunidad', *Debate Agrario*, No. 19. Lima: CEDES.

Marcos, Jaime (1996) 'Las comunidades campesinas en el proceso de regionalización del Peru', *Nueva Sociedad*, 142, April–May.

McNeish, John (2003) 'Globalization and the reinvention of Andean tradition: the politics of community and ethnicity in highland Bolivia', in Tom Brass (ed.), *Latin American Peasants*. London: Frank Cass, pp. 228–69.

Medina, Javier (1996) *La Participación Popular como Fruto de las Luchas Sociales en Bolivia*. La Paz: Ministerio de Desarrollo Humano.

Mitlin, Diana (1998) 'The NGO sector and its role in strengthening civil society and securing good governance', in Armanda Bernard, Henry Helmich and Percy Lehning (eds), *Civil Society and International Development*. Paris: OECD Development Centre.

Molina, M. Fernando (1997) *Historia de la Participación Popular*. La Paz: Ministerio de Desarrollo Humano.

Morton, David (2001) *La Resurección del Maíz: Some Aspects of Globalisation, Resistance and the Zapatista Question*. Paper presented at the 42nd Annual Convention of the International Studies Association, Chicago, 20–24 February.

Munck, Gerardo (1997) *Social Movements and Latin America: Conceptual Issues and Empirical Applications*. Paper presented to the Latin American Studies Association, Guadalajara, 17–19 April.

Negri, Antonio (2001) 'Contrapoder', in Colectivo Situaciones (ed.), *Contrapoder: Una introducción*. Buenos Aires: Ediciones de Mano en Mano, pp. 83–92.

Nickson, R. A. (1997) *Local Government in Latin America*. New York: Lynne Rienner Publications.

Paas, Dieter, Diego Prieto, Julio Moguel and Agustin Sangines (eds) (1991) *Municipio y Democracia: Participación de las Organizaciones de la Sociedad Civil en la Política Municipal*. Mexico: Fundación Friedrich Naumann.

Palacios, Paulino (1999) 'Limites y posibilidades de la acción política: El proyecto neoliberal', *Boletín ICCI*, Vol. 1, No. 1, April.

Palazzi, Marcello (2000) 'Business-municipality partnerships', *Global Futures Bulletin*, No. 120, 15 November.

Paugam, Serge (ed.) (1996) *L'Exclusion. L'Etat des Savoirs*. Paris: Ed. La Découverte.

Petras, James (1997) 'The resurgence of the left', *New Left Review*, No. 223, May–June: 17ff.

Petras, James and Henry Veltmeyer (2003) 'The peasantry and the state in Latin America: a troubled past, an uncertain future', in Tom Brass (ed.), *Latin American Peasants*. London: Frank Cass, pp. 41–82.

Programa de Naciones Unidos de Desarrollo (PNUD) (2000) *Informe de Desarrollo Humano*. La Paz: PNUD.

Programa Nacional de Solidaridad (PRONASOL) Advisory Council (1992) *El Combate a la Pobreza*. Mexico: PRONASOL.

Rahman, Anisur (1991) *Towards an Alternative Development Paradigm*. IFDA Dossier, No. 81, April–June, pp. 17–27.

Reilly, Charles (1989) *The Democratization of Development: Partnership at the Grassroots*. Arlington: Inter-American Foundation Annual Report.

Schittecatte, Catherine (1999) 'The creation of a global public good through transnational coalitions of social movements: the case of the Amazon', *Canadian Journal of Development Studies*, Vol. 20, No. 2.

Slater, David (1994) 'Power and social movements in the other occident: Latin America in an international context', *Latin American Perspectives*, Vol. 21, No. 2: 11–37.

Stahler-Sholk, Richard (1990) 'Mobilization, stabilization and the popular classes in Nicaragua, 1979–1988', *Latin American Research Review*, Vol. 25, No. 3.

Stephen, Lynn (1997) 'Pro-Zapatista and pro-PRI: Resolving the contradictions of Zapatismo in rural Oaxaca', *Latin American Research Review*, Vol. 32, No. 2.

United Nations (1998) *The UN and Business: a Global Partnership*. June. http://www.globalpolicy.org/reform/un-bus.htm.

United Nations Development Programme (UNDP) (1993) *Cooperation for Development. Bolivia Report*. La Paz: UNDP.

United Nations Development Programme (UNDP) (1998) *The Global Development Sustainability Facility: 2B2M* (internal document). New York: UNDP.

United Nations Development Programme (UNDP) (2002) *Human Development Report 2002, Deepening Democracy in a Fragmented World*. Oxford and New York: Oxford University Press.

Untoja, F. (1992) *Re-torno al Aullu*. La Paz: CADFA.

Utting, Peter (2000) *UN–Business Partnerships: Whose Agenda Counts?*, UNRISD News, No. 23, Autumn/Winter.

Van der Pijl, Kees (1998) *Transnational Classes and International Relations*. London: Routledge.

Veltmeyer, Henry (1997a) 'New social movements in Latin America: the dynamics of class and identity', *Journal of Peasant Studies*, Vol. 25, No. 1, October.

Veltmeyer, Henry (1997b) 'Decentralisation as the institutional basis for participatory development: the Latin American perspective', *Canadian Journal of Development Studies*, Vol. 18, No. 2.

Veltmeyer, Henry and Anthony O'Malley (2001) *Transcending Neoliberalism: Community-Based Development*. West Hartford, CT: Kumarian Press.

Veltmeyer, Henry and James Petras (1997) *Neoliberalism and Class Conflict in Latin America*. Basingstoke: Macmillan.

Veltmeyer, Henry and James Petras (2000) *The Dynamics of Social Change in Latin America*. Basingstoke: Macmillan.

Veltmeyer, Henry and Juan Tellez (2001) 'The state and participatory development', in Henry Veltmeyer and Anthony O'Malley (eds), *Transcending Neoliberalism: Community-Based Development*. West Hartford, CT: Kumarian Press.

Williamson, J. (ed.) (1990) *Latin American Adjustment. How Much Has Happened?* Washington, DC: Institute for International Economics.

Womack, John (1999) *Rebellion in Chiapas: an Historical Reader*. New York: New Press.

Woolcock, M. (1998) 'Social capital and economic development: Toward a theoretical synthesis and policy framework', *Theory and Society*, Vol. 27, No. 2, April.

Woolcock, M. and D. Narayan (2000) 'Social capital: Implications for development theory, research and policy', *The World Bank Research Observer*, Vol. 15, No. 2, August.

World Bank (1973) *World Development Report 1973*. New York: Oxford University Press.

5

The Ability of Civil Society Groups to Influence the Debate on the Role of the Market in Rural Asset Building and Redistribution in East Africa

Nyangabyaki Bazaara

Introduction

In the last decade, there has been tremendous growth in civil society organizations in many countries of the Third World. This growth has been stimulated by the belief in many circles that civil society can be an important element in advancing the interests of the poor, especially in this context where economic policies are clearly meant to encourage the market as the principal mechanism through which individuals can access productive resources such as land and implements.[1]

The chapter attempts to explore the character and role of civil society in East Africa in assisting rural people to accumulate rural assets such as land. In particular, it tries to establish whether or not the evolving civil society is able to influence the debate on the role of the market in economic change in ways that assist the poor to access rural assets. It is argued that many (not all) non-state organizations, sometimes loosely called civil society, have emerged to lessen the bad effects of market-based economic policies on the poor by implementing poverty-alleviating programmes such as supplying agricultural inputs like implements and seeds, helping victims of past land policies access to land or advocating for pro-poor land policies (Shivji, 1998; Bazaara, 2000a; MWENGO, 1999). However, the bulk of the non-state organizations are involved in philanthropic activities mainly aimed at alleviating poverty, activities which do not challenge the political power establishment that deprives the poor of, or monopolizes, rural resources. Many of these organizations are dependent on external donors and are yet to beget organizational, financial and ideological autonomy, and cultivate the necessary political alliances in order to dent the power that reproduces poverty conditions.

The first section of the chapter traces the history of rural resource control in East Africa. The second section examines the different types of organizations involved in helping rural people build assets. The third section concludes the study. The analysis in the study is based purely on desk research: an examination of pamphlets and books.

Historical background to rural resource access and control

The one important factor uniting the three countries of Kenya, Tanzania and Uganda is that they were all colonized – Kenya by the British, Tanganyika/Tanzania by the Germans and later the British, and Uganda by the British. The objective of colonization was essentially to have access to natural resources and raw materials (such as cotton, sisal and coffee) in demand in imperial countries. To meet this objective, the colonizers had to wrestle from the 'natives' control over the land as well as natural resources, and institute the technical, infrastructural and administrative base for producing raw materials. The very first step in colonization involved declaration that henceforth land and resources on it were under the control of the colonial state as crown land.[2] The 1901 East African Crown Lands Ordinance vested all rights over land and natural resources in the hands of His Majesty's Commissioner, for example (Mutai, 2000). With the rights of the 'natives' usurped, it was easy for the colonial state to decide how the land and natural resources could be used – for agriculture, forest reserves or game parks. However, the actual evolution of land tenure in the three countries of East Africa depended on many factors such as local political opposition and costs of production. In order to appreciate the history of access to productive resources, particularly the most basic – land – we examine the history of each country.

Kenya: settlers, resettlements and landlessness

In Kenya, fertile lands in the Rift Valley province were alienated to white settlers, who eventually developed plantation agriculture. The development of settler agriculture was, however, preceded by protracted wars to wrestle the control over land from the natives and to create a legal regime. The land regulations of 1897 authorized the Commissioner to issue temporary certificates of short-term occupancy of twenty-one years renewable for another twenty-one years. However, the settlers were not happy with short-term leases. As a result, a Crown Lands Ordinance was enacted in 1915 to provide the colonial Governor powers which he used to alienate huge expanses of land for white settlement. By 1933, argues Tabitha Kanogo, 109.5 square miles of land had been alienated for white settlement and held under long-term leases of 999 years (Kanogo, 1987: 9). Using the same Ordinance, the Governor created native 'reserves' for Africans, located away from white settlements. All the 'native Africans' who lost their land were confined to these reserves, which over years were characterized by fragmentation and overuse which rendered them uneconomic pieces of land.

In the 1920s, the formation of the Kikuyu Central Association marked the beginnings of rural protests (Kanyinga, 2000: 42). Africans agitated for land and equal treatment. In response the colonial state established the Native Lands Trust Board to manage the reserves. The Board had local representation but did not have decision-making powers and its role was advisory as the land was vested in trust and subject to the sovereignty of the crown.

It is important to note that the prosperity of European farmers was based on monopoly tendencies backed by state power. Africans were barred from growing commercially lucrative coffee or, in some instances, rearing cattle, goats and sheep because this would lead to competition with European coffee growers. Colin Leys summarized the situation as follows:

> The settlers had a monopoly of land but little capital and, initially, less know-how. The Africans on the other hand, and especially the Kikuyu, were confined to their traditional areas but were not provided with the techniques, the crops, the capital or the services to farm them intensively for the market. Consequently their own land soon became overcrowded and overworked, using traditional farming methods. (Leys, 1975: 46)

In the 1950s, there emerged an armed land movement – Mau Mau – seeking to regain land that had been alienated to white European settlers. This movement surfaced in the context of increasing population and declining production in the reserves. The Assistant Director of Agriculture, R. J. M. Swynnerton, diagnosed the problems of production in the reserves as emanating from prevailing land tenure system characterized by diffuse rights and collective control. He recommended a land reform of individualization of land tenure as being the best way of providing security of tenure and incentive to invest in land. A land reform followed in which individual rights were adjudicated (ascertained), fragments were consolidated (aggregated), and then a title to that land registered. In the minds of the land reformers, this would lead to a market in land, which would enable efficient farmers to access land and also assist the farmers to acquire loans. The reform had a political dimension as well. It sought to undermine the Mau Mau armed movement by creating a class of people who would collaborate with the whites.

It is important to note that the process of adjudication involved unfair practices. Karuti Kanyinga concludes that the land reform did not solve the land problem. 'The Swynnerton Plan of 1954 did not attempt to address the issue of land alienation, the need for redistribution or even that of inequalities in ownership between the settlers and Africans and inequalities between and within African communities' (Kanyinga, 2000: 44). There were two land-related processes parallel to the land reforms in the reserves.

First, there was the establishment of settlement schemes designed to absorb those who had been displaced by the land reform in the reserves. The second was the programme of 're-Africanization' of the white highlands. A land purchase programme was instituted involving the settlement of Africans on farms formerly occupied by whites. The rationale behind this programme was that it would provide a safety net for landless people in densely populated districts.

> Land transfer schemes, based on 'willing buyer–willing seller' basis, were constructed to promote the gradual purchase of land by Africans. The most important and best known of these was the Million-Acre Settlement Scheme. This settlement programme benefited Africans of all classes, although in later years larger and more fertile tracts were accumulated by rich and prominent, successful Kenyans. (Rutten, 2001: 551)

Both solutions to the problem of landlessness failed. The reform in the reserves involving adjudication and consolidation 'led to skewed distribution of land. The chiefs, loyalists, and the wealthy acquired more land than others while others lost considerable amounts of land, especially if they did not participate in the adjudication of their rights' (Kanyinga, 2000: 44). It is estimated that by the mid-1970s, 'over 70 per cent of the land outside the arid parts of the Coast, Eastern, North-eastern, and Rift Valley provinces had been privatized' (Okoth-Ogendo, n.d.: 1). Most important, the settlers in the settlement schemes acquired the land through a government loan scheme. Many of the beneficiaries could not generate adequate income to repay the loans. In the early 1970s, a good number could not repay the loans, and actually, by 1969 the authorities had evicted ninety settlers (Leys, 1975: 79).

Up to the 1990s, land transfers, whether through the market or state mediation, led to the concentration of land in the hands of the wealthy. With the reintroduction of multiparty politics in the 1990s, the Kenya African Nationalist Union (KANU) government sought to legitimize itself by expelling from their land those who did not support the regime and settling those who supported the regime. Many of the forest reserves were de-gazetted to provide land for supporters of the regime. This process led to ethnic clashes and deaths. In the land reserves, the authority over land was manipulated to privatize land. According to the constitution of Kenya, reserves, or what is known as 'trust lands', are vested in county councils for the benefit of the people who ordinarily reside in the area under what is called customary law of the tribes or families. However, customary tenure lands can be alienated. The county councils are said to lack transparency in their conduct of business. The county councils can compulsorily acquire trust land for public purposes after full compensation. However, the process has historically lent itself to abuse without a possibility of redressing the injustice because once the registration is complete, it cannot be reversed.

In 1999, a Presidential Commission of Inquiry was formed to examine land laws and policy in Kenya (MWENGO, 1999). The Commission of Inquiry came after violent clashes over land had claimed the lives of over 1500 and displaced over 150 000 people from their lands in various parts of Kenya (Maina, n.d.). However, the real impetus for reviewing the land law and policy in Kenya emanated from pressures of the World Bank and International Monetary Fund (IMF) to reform the law in ways that would encourage the market in allocation of resources. In the Kenyan experience, the attempt to encourage a land market began in the 1950s with the Swynnerton plan. However, up to the present time, registration and titling of land have failed to lead to the development of a viable land market. The simple fact is that small farmers view land as a form of security for the future which will not only benefit the present but also future generations.

The privatization of land was supposed to lead to the use of land titles to acquire loans to finance the development of capitalist agriculture. A study conducted in the areas of Kisii and South Nyanza in the early 1970s revealed that land titles were not sufficient conditions for acquiring loans from banks (Okoth-Ogendo, n.d.: 9). In many instances, credit was given after stringent scrutiny, particularly the ability of the applicant to pay loans from off-farm income. In effect, those who received incomes were the narrow group of the rural wealthy. Even more interesting, although loans were given out on the basis of agricultural land, many of these loans were deployed in non-agricultural activities such as commerce. Moreover, loans that were actually used to improve agriculture were channelled through institutional frameworks such as cooperatives and 'group farms'. Here loans were given out on condition that particular crops or techniques had to be adopted. The targets of loan schemes were export crops, such as tea, pyrethrum, coffee and maize, or modern ranches owned by prominent politicians. The problem, however, was that the programmes to which loans were committed were found to be far too expensive to generate profit. Moreover, those who have been benefiting from the loan schemes are the wealthy, with political connections. Credit tended to widen rural inequalities as only a few politically well-connected people accessed these loans. In addition, like many countries of the Third World, the state intervened in the marketing of crops, which tended to reduce incomes of agricultural producers. Kenya in many instances has had to import foodstuffs to feed some of its vulnerable people. It is obvious that there is need to carry out a land reform to ensure that the poor gain access to land and also institute policies that allow the poor access to other productive assets such as seeds, implements and oxen. Like many other countries in Africa, the Kenyan state has increasingly been unable to provide subsidies it used to give to some of the rural producers. In addition, it has had to succumb to programmes of structural adjustment dictated by the IMF and the World Bank to liberalize not only the political landscape but also the economic realm so that the market becomes the mechanism through which rural producers can access assets and resources. However, as is known, the market also has the tendency to marginalize the poor and other under-privileged sections of the population. How non-state organizations and political parties have responded to this will be discussed later in this chapter. We now turn to Tanzania.

Tanzania: freehold, customary tenure, ujaama villagization

German (1885–1916) and British (1918–61) colonialists also carried out a similar process of usurping the land rights of indigenous peoples in the then Tanganyika. During their limited reign, the Germans alienated some land in freehold for plantation agriculture. On losing the First World War, the Germans lost control over land to the British under the mandate of the League of Nations. The 1923 Land Ordinance converted all customary tenure lands into crown land under the control of the Governor. Legally, no one could occupy crown land without the consent of the Governor. The power of allocating land, just like in the case of Uganda, was bestowed on the local chiefs (Kibamba and Miranda, 2001: 4). These chiefs had legislative, executive and judicial powers which they often abused in the allocation of land.

Important changes began to take shape following the Second World War. There was a feeling in colonial circles that one reason why the nationalist movement erupted was because not enough had been done to cultivate a middle class. One way of undermining the nationalist movement was to institute reforms that would lead to the creation of such social groups. One such a move was the encouragement of a market in land. This was well artic-ulated by the 1955 East African Royal Commission that recommended, among other things, the development of a land market. However, when Tanganyika achieved independence, the influential President Mwalimu Nyerere refused policies that would encourage the emergence of a land market. In 1958, in response to calls for individualization of tenure, he wrote:

> The customary system of land tenure has drawbacks which must be removed. It has also advantages which we must preserve. The freehold system, on the other hand, is quite useless … The leasehold system is the best, and even if we must pay a small price for it, we have obligation to do so in order to rid ourselves of the old customary system and to avoid the slavery associated with the freehold system. (Nyerere, 1967: 58)

At independence, freehold lands were converted to leasehold. Customary tenure was vested in the president in trust of the people of Tanzania. Nyerere wanted to transform the rural areas without necessarily encouraging a land market. It was clear that it was difficult to transform peasants in their tradi-tional settings. As Issa G. Shivji observes, the First Five Year Development Plan clearly called for settling peasants and pastoralists in new villages supervised by a government agency – the Rural Settlement Commission (Shivji, 1998: 5).[3] The land tenure in village settlements and range development projects was not based on *customary* but *statutory* law. Statutory law allowed some form of individual tenure but controlled by government in a top-down fashion. After the 1967 Arusha Declaration all land was nationalized and an era of forced settlement of peasants and pastoralists initiated. It is estimated that five million peasants were resettled in villages (Hyden, 1980: 130). The villagization policy was in line with the thinking of the Tanzanian government that production in rural areas had to take two routes, namely 'transformation' and 'improvement' approaches. The transformation approach involved taking people out of their traditional environment and settling them in new areas where they would farm using modern technologies, at the time understood as mechanization, the use of fertilizers and improved varieties of seeds. This approach was attractive to government as it provided it with the ability to control.

> The principal problems of these settlements, however, related to government supervision and aid. Agricultural production in the settlements was carried out with farm machinery of which the settlers themselves had little experience. The machinery was costly to buy and to operate and the settlers were expected eventually to repay the capital costs involved in establishing those farms ... As a result the settlers started off with very heavy debts – 2.5 million Tanzania shillings. Part of the loan was eventually paid by the government but the peasants were still paying it in 1975. (Hyden, 1980: 72–3)

Gradually it was discovered that very few schemes generated sufficient returns to producers. As a result many peasants went bankrupt.

Another plank of the transformation policies of independent Tanzania was the establishment of large-scale agriculture and ranching under parastatals.

> Parastatals took over nationalized assets including land, which they held under rights of occupancy. More land, more often belonging to customary holders in the villages, was alienated to them through allocations justified by the notion of 'public interest' or national project. (Shivji, 1998: 8)

These forced take-overs of land displaced many peasants and pastoralists and led to serious conflict. A case in point is the famous Canadian-supported wheat scheme, which took over land amounting to 100 000 acres, thereby displacing a big number of Barbaig pastoralists (see Lane, 1996). Land available for grazing among the Barbaig was reduced and, therefore, their cattle did not have enough pasture to graze on. Yet the government parastatals were always subject to bureaucratic interference and also were operating inefficiently.

The second approach to agricultural development in the early years of independence was the 'improvement' approach. This approach was based on the belief that what was lacking in rural areas was capital. Once injected from outside, the rural cultivators would modernize techniques of production, increase production and improve their living standards. A lot of subsidies were also injected into the scheme such as subsidized cost of mechanical ploughing. In effect, the 'improvement' approach benefited only the rural wealthy, who in the language of the department of agriculture were termed 'progressive farmers'. The effect of credit and mechanical technology was to create rural social differentiation. This differentiation was accentuated because of regressive tax structures and government-controlled cooperative and produce marketing boards which monopolized the purchase and sale of agricultural produce.

In the 1990s, Tanzania was forced into market-driven economic policies. These policies intensified land disputes and grabbing of land. In response, the Tanzania government established a Commission of Inquiry into land matters in 1991 to collect public views regarding land and make recommendations. However, the push for the government to set in motion a land reform process came from the World Bank and IMF with their market orthodoxy regarding access to land.

Nonetheless, the Commission discovered:

(a) large numbers of people had been displaced by national parks, game reserves and state farms;
(b) claims of people whose land was grabbed to create village settlements;
(c) grabbing of customary tenure by city and town councils through extending boundaries;
(d) corrupt bureaucratic structures that managed land allocations against the poor; and
(e) market-driven economic policies that led to village lands being taken over by foreign companies and speculators.

Despite the recommendations of the Commission of Inquiry, government was not ready to abandon state control over the land and the encouragement of a land market. Moreover, government became secretive, intent on producing a Land Act that clearly reinforced the top-down management of land and facilitation of a land market for outside investors. It is in this context that civil society organizations intervened and in the next section we shall review their strengths and weaknesses in influencing the debate on the role of the market in rural asset distribution. For now, let us turn to the history of land tenure rural asset building in Uganda.

Uganda: mailoland, customary tenure, landlessness

After the wars of conquest, the British were faced with the problem of control and legitimacy in the country that came to be called Uganda. First and foremost, to enlist local collaborators, the British gave square miles of land – the local corruption is *mailoland* – to 1000 Baganda chiefs. In addition, some land was given to planters and religious groups in freehold. The land converted into mailoland was occupied by peasants who were immediately transformed into tenants. As export crop production increased and brought some prosperity to tenants, so did the new landlord class extract the gains in the form of ground (*obusulu*) and commodity (*envujjo*) rents. Their extraction became so oppressive that in the 1920s there emerged a tenant movement – Bataka – protesting against these rents. The colonial government responded by enacting the 1928 Busulu and Envujjo law which basically guaranteed the security of the tenants up to three acres and limited the amount of rents that landlords could extract. This reform led to a tremendous increase in agricultural production/productivity in Buganda.

The rest of Uganda was declared crown land. Authority over crown lands was vested in the hands of the colonial Governor. The Governor had power to decide how the land could be utilized – either as game parks, forest reserves or for peasant agriculture. In the early years of colonialism, there was a view that production in Uganda would be based on plantation agriculture. This would involve alienation of land and disinheritance of peasants – as happened in Kenya. However, progress in that direction was hampered by several factors. First, the powerful textile industrialists were opposed to plantation-based production because the costs of their outputs (cotton) would be extremely high and supply unreliable. These industrialists successfully lobbied the British government to promote peasant agriculture as it involved cheap production costs and hence cheap raw materials.

Second, famines that occurred in the first decade of the twentieth century killed many peasants. This forced the colonial state to import foodstuffs. However, in the early 1920s, the colonial state adopted a policy of 'District Food Self-sufficiency'. The idea behind this policy was that peasants would grow their foodstuffs as a mechanism of obviating the need for importing foodstuffs. This made administrative sense because the Ugandan colony lacked sufficient funds and a developed road network crucial for importing and distributing foodstuffs (see Bazaara, 1995). Economically, this was one way of stabilizing the production and supply of raw materials to industrialists at lower than market prices.

Third, the colonial state realized that the political costs of establishing a plantation economy were extremely high, as this would involve the creation of an army of landless people without alternative sources of income. This army would definitely escalate the costs of administration and security.

The considerations above convinced the colonial state to abandon the idea of plantation agriculture in favour of peasant production. Thus, in the rest of Uganda peasants lived under customary tenure. Under this tenure the ultimate power over land was the Governor but whose local expression was the village chief. The latter had powers of allocation and in effect this power of allocation became one of the pillars of colonial rule. It should be noted, however, that the chief had tremendous powers of legislation, administration and judiciary, all fused in his office. Armed with these powers, chiefs appropriated for their private use the land and labour of peasants (Bazaara, 2001). In some places, such as Bunyoro, chiefs simply began privatizing land and extracting rent from the peasants (Beattie, 1954). Likewise, in Ankole and Toro chiefs extracted rents. In response, the colonial state enacted the 1937 Ankole and Toro Landlord–Tenant laws, and introduced certificates of occupancy in Bunyoro. Behind these legislations was the lesson the colonial state had learnt from giving out mailoland in Bugand – the emergence of landlord–tenant relations and constriction of production. These laws underlined one fundamental fact that the security of tenure of the tenants was to be safeguarded and that rents that landlords could extract had to be regulated by the state. In effect, a market in land under crown control was not allowed. In Buganda, where private property rights developed, a market in land was allowed but natives were legally prohibited from selling to foreigners (Mukwaya, 1953). If a native wanted to sell, he/she would sell to the colonial Governor who would in turn decide whether or not to sell to the foreigner. This control of the market was meant to discourage reckless selling of land, a safeguard that has been eroded by the new market-based land reforms in the 1990s.

The great depression in the 1930s and the Second World War brought tremendous changes not only in metropolitan Britain but also in its colonies. On the one hand, post-war reconstruction of the British economy required increased production. This led to the philosophy of large-scale productive ventures and the encouragement of individualization of land tenure, hence a land market. The idea was that once someone had a title to land he/she could easily sell or mortgage it for a loan to improve agricultural production. On the other hand, there was the rise of the nationalist movement that shook the foundation of colonial power – chiefs – and economic policies of cheap raw material production. The response of the colonial state was the encouragement of individualization of tenure as a mechanism of assisting the emergence of a middle class that was less hostile to colonial rule. However, proposals for individualization of land tenure were rejected in many places except in Kigezi and Ankole. In Lango and Teso districts of Uganda, riots broke out when it was suggested that the process of individualizing tenure be introduced (Bazaara, 1997: 71; see also Bazaara, 1994). People feared that the introduction of private property would lead to the alienation of land as happened in Kenya. Cherry Gertzel records for the Acholi of Northern Uganda:

> The Acholi also suddenly discovered that the Europeans had all along been eyeing the highlands in north-eastern part of Acholi. Opposition was aired in a public meeting in 1954: 'the Acholi people want to have

absolute rights over their land. We will accept advice only from her Majesty's Government on important decisions concerning land. Any power over land should be delegated to the Governor or provincial Commissioner by the Acholi. Any power over land that is now being vested in the Governor or the Provincial Commissioner is regarded with suspicion.' (Gertzel, 1974: 66)

However, the post-colonial government did not cede powers over the former crown lands (now public lands) to the local groups as the Acholi thought. By 1967, that power had been centralized under the Uganda Land Commission. The centralization led to a process where the politically powerful could grab land under customary tenure. A well-known speech by a parliamentarian, Alex Ojera, captured the unfolding process. In his contribution of 26 February 1969, Ojera said:

> I will be speaking at a later date, perhaps this evening, and I will expose that there are land grabbers today in Uganda. We have already seen in some districts where people have misused powers given to them as Land Committees to grant land to individuals such as the one speaking now at the expense of the ordinary man who does not even know the value of land titles. We have seen people in some districts who have actually got as much as ten thousand acres of land. In some of these areas they have included other common men who are supposed to be squatters on their own land, to be tenants. (Republic of Uganda, 1968–9)

In response to this trend the government enacted the 1969 Public Lands Act which basically proclaimed that no one could displace a customary tenant without his/her consent and that no one could acquire land beyond 500 acres without the consent of the minister. However, this protection of the peasants living on the basis of customary tenure was reversed when a military coup occurred in 1971. As the military regime searched for legitimacy, it enacted the 1975 Land Reform Decree which sought to nationalize all land with peasants becoming 'tenants at will'. Freeholds created at the beginning of the twentieth century were transformed into leases and henceforth Buganda tenants, who had been protected by the 1928 busulu and envujjo law, became tenants of the state. The practical consequences of the 1975 Land Reform Decree, however, were that it provided a way for the politically and militarily powerful to grab land under customary tenure without peasant consent and without due compensation. The process of grabbing was slowed down a bit because of the wars – the war to oust Amin (1978–9) and the National Resistance Army (NRA) bush war (1981–6). However, with the restoration of peace in 1986, at least in the southern parts of Uganda, virulent conflicts regarding land resurfaced (see Bikaako, 1994; Ddungu, 1991, 1994; Doornbos, 1975; Kafureeka, 1992; Kaggwa, 1994; Nsibambi, 1981, 1989;

Mugisha, 1992; Muhereza, 1994, 1999; Ssenkumba, 1993; Opyene, 1993; Otim, 1993). It is partly in this context that the World Bank and United States Agency for International Development (USAID) sponsored a study that was undertaken by the Makerere Institute of Social Research (MISR) and the Land Tenure Center of the University of Wisconsin to examine the impact of the 1975 Land Reform Decree on land access. The MISR–Land Tenure Center report called for the development of a market in land (see Makerere Institute of Social Research and Land Tenure Center, 1989; Republic of Uganda, 1990, 1993). It was argued that a market is the best mechanism for transferring land from inefficient to efficient farmers, and in this way development would be achieved. The recommendation of this report became the empirical basis of the formulation of the various land bills and the 1998 Land Act (see Uganda Land Alliance 1997a; *The Uganda Gazette*, 1998a, 1998b).

Like in Tanzania, the government had two approaches to agriculture: the 'transformation' and 'improvement' approaches. The former implied the application of Western capital and technology, and the uprooting of farmers from their traditional social setting and settling them on uninhabited land. In Uganda, this arrangement came to be known as 'group farms'. In order to encourage peasants to join group farms, government provided subsidized tractor hire services and pesticides. However, the farmers had to conform to instructions provided by a group manager, usually an expatriate, as to the timing of ploughing, and what, when and where to plant. Group farms were designed to grow export crops. However, group farms failed for a number of reasons. First, the input costs (tractors, pesticides) were often too high to allow for some profits, especially given the fact that the selling of the agricultural products was handled by government parastatals that gave ridiculously low prices. Second, the settlers lacked a sense of security in terms of land tenure. In fact, while they farmed on these group farms, they maintained their own plots in their traditional social settings. This is because on the traditional plots they were free to plant anything they wanted, including foodstuffs crucial for their subsistence. On group farms they did not have such freedom.

In social terms, group farms created a new social class who benefited from the subsidies while many others remained chained to low production in their tradition areas. It is true that government had a second approach that presumably would cover the rest of the peasants. This 'improvement approach' targeted a few privileged people who were termed 'progressive farmers'. The assumption was that these progressive farmers would through credit and subsidies adopt modern methods of farming and become an example to the rest of the rural people. However, these progressive farmers' schemes ran into problems, first, because of low prices for export crops, arising from the world market prices and/or administratively suppressed prices through the coffee, lint and produce marketing boards. Second, by preventing the emergence of a free wage earning class, a group disinherited from land, settlers perennially faced a labour bottleneck. Previously this problem had been resolved through an immigrant labour system, particularly the Rwandese who came to Buganda to undertake wage labour on the coffee farms. But that system collapsed because the Rwandese preferred to settle as tenants paying rent on Baganda mailoland, as this arrangement was protected by the 1928 busulu and envujjo law.

In the 1970s and 1980s agricultural production declined and the few agricultural production assets acquired in the 1960s became disused because of lack of spare parts. The state could no longer afford resources to subsidize farmers. In 1981, Uganda was compelled to adopt a structural adjustment programme. Under this arrangement the Uganda government was forced to cut back on its expenditure whose practical import was abolition of subsidies to agriculture, health and education; procurement of agricultural inputs at market rates; and a devaluation of peasant products through devaluing the shilling. This was presumed to be a measure that would encourage foreigners to purchase Uganda's agricultural products. It also entailed the abolition of government monopoly in buying and selling of peasants' products and an end to administratively set prices.

The first experiment collapsed in 1984 because of the civil war. However, in 1987 the structural adjustment programme was resumed and pushed to its logical conclusions in the years that followed. Foreign exchange transactions were liberalized in 1992. The lint, coffee and produce marketing boards were dismantled and trade in agricultural products shifted to the private sector – individuals, companies and cooperative societies. Prices were left to market mechanisms. In general terms, this reform was supposed to increase the incomes the peasants used to earn and, therefore, accumulate more assets for production. Moreover, between 1996 and 1998, parliament was involved in a discussion of the kinds of reforms that needed to be introduced in terms of land tenure. The principal thrust of the land bills was clearly the encouragement of a land market.

The question that we now pose is: what was the role of civil society in influencing the debates regarding market-based reform/policies and what are the capacities of these in influencing the policy dialogues in ways that help the rural poor to accumulate assets?

Market reforms: strengths and limitations of civil society in influencing market policy reforms

Civil society has been projected as a third sector that can address social problems when states and markets fail. In the context of East Africa, the presumption is that there is such a sector and it has the ability to influence policy in such a way that at least the poor are not completely marginalized by policies of structural adjustment programmes which put premium on the market as being the best mechanism to allocate factors of production (see, for example, Gibbon, 1995). In the East African context, there is first and foremost a problem of conceptualizing what civil society is, what it can and cannot do, and how it relates to political parties. Some authors have argued that civil society is an imported concept that needs tailoring to local conditions (Oloka-Onyango and Barya, 1997; Bazaara, 2000b). The issue raised is: what is the character of civil society and what does it actually do? Donors have been assuming that the sum and substance of civil society are organizations called NGOs. Researchers at the Centre for Basic Research (CBR) have discovered that many NGOs are involved in poverty alleviating programmes and never interact with the state purposely to influence or change policies. NGOs which do not interact with the state in ways that influence policy do not qualify to be civil society. Such NGOs are created for a variety of reasons. A retiring civil servant or a young graduate can form an NGO purposely to create employment. In the past the state was the major employer of educated people. With a fiscal crisis following the economic crisis that worsened in the 1970s, the state was increasingly unable to employ the ever-increasing number of graduates. With the adoption of structural adjustment programmes in the 1980s, a series of retrenchment exercises followed, including a complete freeze on employment. Those retrenched created NGOs as a mechanism to get income. In addition, some NGOs have been formed by politicians purposely as a mechanism of mobilizing political support and attracting funds from foreign sources. Thus, there are a variety of types of NGOs in the development field whose role is simply fillers of gaps left by the state's inability to provide services – education, health, agricultural extension, etc.

There are, however, a few NGOs involved in advocacy and lobbying that emerged after the end of communism in the late 1980s. Such advocacy and lobbying NGOs focused on human rights issues or specific issues such as women's emancipation; and with the emergence of market-based land (legal) reforms, issues of land and structural adjustment programmes. We shall shortly be analysing their capacity to influence debates related to market policies or reforms.

Suffice, for now, to mention that also prevailing in East Africa as regards the definition of what constitutes civil society are the social movement type of organizations. Examples of these include the rural protests such as those of the tea and rice growers in Kenya presumed to be civil society (see Kanyinga and Torori, 1999). However, in our view, there is a difference between formal organizations and social movements, which are here today and gone tomorrow. NGOs that interact with the state can rightly be characterized as civil society. Civil society involves more organizations than simply NGOs; it involves associational life that can include an array of organizations such as trade unions, women's and professional organizations, human rights NGOs and cooperatives. This associational life can be considered civil society if it is actively interacting with the state with a view to influencing policy-making processes. However, a strict conceptualization of civil society as being organizations that interact with the state and in the process influence policy would actually leave out non-state organizations that are involved in building rural assets for the poor and yet do not seek to influence policy. Moreover, research on the non-profit sector in East Africa has revealed that organizations change roles depending on circumstances. Some organizations may be in advocacy today and yet tomorrow abandon it for purely philanthropic poverty alleviating programmes, thus filling gaps left by the state. For purposes of this chapter, we shall first analyse those non-state organizations that do not fit in our definition of civil society and yet contribute to rural asset building, and then examine advocacy and lobbying organizations and their role in the debate, particularly the role of the market in land redistribution.

NGOs for poverty alleviation

Non-state organizations have been in existence since the pre-colonial period. Subsequent evolution in the colonial period followed the stresses and strains of colonial economy. Many of them considered themselves as non-governmental organizations with philanthropic motives of assisting the poor. These did not seek to challenge state policy but rather filled in gaps left by the state. Such non-state organizations were both secular and church-related and operated in areas of education and health (see articles in Semboja and Therkildsen, 1995).

After independence many of these NGOs survived but were suppressed by the governments of the day, which increasingly provided health and educational services. With the economic crisis that began in the 1980s, the state could not provide those services and many non-governmental organizations emerged as gap-fillers. Their role became even more pronounced as the state was forced to abandon provision of subsidies not only to education and health but also to agriculture. In contemporary East Africa, there are many NGOs involved in a range of activities whose goal is alleviation of poverty. These activities include environmental protection, asset building by the poor (implements, seeds, cattle, irrigation, land, etc.), credit delivery, research and training (skill building) and marketing.

Environmental protection with poverty alleviation

There are NGOs that have taken up issues of environmental protection more particularly in the semi-arid areas of Kenya, Uganda and Tanzania. Pastoral groups such as the Turkana and Samburu in Kenya, Karimojong in Uganda, Masaai in Kenya and Tanzania have been facing a deteriorating environment characterized by overgrazing and desertification. A good chunk of their land was annexed to create game parks or build administrative centres. The effect of this process has been that a large number of cattle have been grazing on dwindling pasture resources, leading to desertification. Some NGOs – for example, Oxfam and the Lutheran World Federation in Kotido and Moroto in Uganda – have been trying to halt this increasing desertification of the otherwise semi-arid areas. Other NGOs have been active in well-watered areas to prevent soil erosion or to preserve water catchment areas. The World Conservation Union (IUCN) around Mount Elgon in Mbale, Action Aid in Mubende, the Kidaago Women's Tree Planting Association in Mbale, and the Tree and Energy Conservation Programme (TRENCOP) in Masindi are NGOs that have been involved in schemes aimed at environmental restoration and conservation, such as aforestation and woodlot management, land conservation, protection of water and other resources (Muhereza et al., 1999; Mamdani, Kasoma and Katende, 1992; Bazaara, 1993). In Tanzania some NGOs 'support soil and conservation through agro-forestry, seeds, nurseries and soil conservation' (Mhina and Meena, 2001: 20).

Poverty alleviation (development) activities

The bulk of NGOs in East Africa are involved in poverty alleviation (development) activities (Kwagala, 1998). This is because of the general decline of East African economies, hence the fiscal crisis of the state, and the demands of structural adjustment programmes that called for cutbacks in subsidies, for instance, to agriculture (Lange, Wallevik and Kiondo, 2000). NGOs and self-help community-based organizations emerged to fill in these gaps. Many of these NGOs began with relief activities in post-famine (for example, the 1980 famine in Karamoja) and post-war (for example, the Luweero triangle in Uganda) rehabilitation efforts. Thereafter, they moved into poverty alleviation or development-related activities. Organizations such as Oxfam, World Vision International, InterAid, Volunteer Efforts for Development, the Lutheran World Federation, Foundation of Netherlands Volunteers (SNV) and District Development Trusts (in Tanzania) have been prominent in activities that alleviate poverty. They have provided seeds, implements, cattle and credit to communities that have suffered from drought, famine or war (Lane, 1996; Nakintu, 1994; Musoke Muyiiya, 1997; Kaija, 1995), as well as implementing development projects aimed at improving crop and livestock production as a mechanism of improving the food security of target communities.

Credit delivery

There are also some NGOs or associations that have specialized in the area of credit delivery. In the days of state dominance, credit delivery was confined to expatriate banks or state-owned or connected banks. These were less inclined to lend to the poor. In recent years, however, there has been a proliferation of associations and NGOs which specifically give out credit to the poor. Instead of asking for land titles as collateral, they use peer pressure as an incentive to pay back. A recent research in Tanzania has revealed that many savings and credit associations and credit cooperatives provide loans for crop production, livestock keeping and petty trading. In addition, there are NGOs seriously involved in micro-finance, namely, Promotion of Rural Initiative and Development Enterprises (PRIDE), Mennonite Economic

Development Associates, Network of Small Farmers Groups, the Traditional Irrigation Improvement Programme, Small Enterprises Development Agency, Credit Scheme for Productive Activities, the Tanzania Women Finance Company, the Tanzania Promotion of Self-employment and Tanzania Micro-entrepreneurs Association and Pride Africa. In Uganda and Kenya, there are many NGOs involved in credit delivery. These include PRIDE, World Vision International, Uganda Women Finance and Credit Trust and numerous Grameen model organizations. The list is not exhaustive and there are no readily available statistics to show the exact numbers of these organizations in East Africa. The point, however, is that there are non-state organizations that are involved in delivering credit to rural people on non-commercial lines. Certainly this credit has an impact on rural production and social structures.

Research and skills formation

There are non-state organizations that are involved in research on issues that affect rural populations such as economic policies and land tenure security. These include the Centre for Basic Research (CBR), a Ugandan non-governmental organization that has for years been researching into land tenure, pastoral crises, appropriate technologies and natural resources management issues. Its research has informed the policy-making processes. In Tanzania, another NGO, Haki Ardhi (Land Rights Research and Resources Institute) advances and supports research 'into land rights of small peasants and pastoralists' (Lange, Wallevik and Kiondo, 2000: 15).

Other NGOs are involved in providing skills to rural populations. Action for Development (ACFODE), Uganda Rural Development and Training (URDT), the Foundation for Rural Development (FORUD), the Development Network of Indigenous Rural Population (DENIVA) and Oxfam, etc., are examples of some non-governmental organizations involved in skills formation in East Africa.

Although these poverty-oriented NGOs contribute a great deal in alleviating poverty, their activities never alter the distribution of political power; power that shapes policies that disadvantage certain social groups. These NGOs do not lobby or advocate for policy alternatives. In a sense, through their philanthropic activities, they could be assisting in buttressing market-based policies in East Africa. Their activities simply soften the impact of neoliberal economic policies. This is not to mention that some of their poverty-alleviating activities are sometimes not sensitive to environmental, cultural and gender factors that shape development processes. Although some organizations emphasize participation of local people, the kind of participation prevalent in East Africa does not empower the poor. In addition, the bulk of rural development projects are supported by foreign funds. This raises questions of sustainability of those projects once the flow of funds dries up.

Civil society and rural change in East Africa

In the 1990s, the World Bank and other Western donors pushed for reforms in the legal framework under which land is (re-)distributed, and extended the life of structural adjustment programmes (SAP) which involve, among other things, abolition of subsidies to agriculture, and rolling back the state in favour of the market as the principal mechanism though which rural people access agricultural inputs and sell agricultural products. SAP advocates argue that the abolition of subsidies and the adoption of free market policies in the purchase of agricultural inputs and the marketing of agricultural products is bound to benefit rural people in terms of increased incomes. However, as experience has demonstrated, market processes have unequal impacts on rural people. Liberalization of trade as it has unfolded in all the East African countries benefit those who have the resources (land, labour, implements, oxen, etc.) to farm economically. Thus, the poor cannot survive in a liberalized economy unless they accumulate rural assets. Given that the three East African countries are clearly locked in a capitalist logic, a reform in that direction requires a strong civil and political society to lobby or advocate successfully for policies that favour accumulation of assets for the poor.

In general terms the liberalization policies have opened space for civil society action – a space that had been closed by the dominance of the state in every aspect of society. In order to understand the limitations and strengths of the current civil society organizations we briefly describe the character of civil society and its historical role in rural asset building in East Africa. In his book, *Citizen and Subject*, Mahmood Mamdani argues that in colonial times civil society was basically a non-indigenous and urban affair (Mamdani, 1996: 13–15). However, this assertion needs modification, as agrarian-based civil society existed in Uganda and Kenya. In Uganda there were many organizations organized by planters, for example Bunyoro Planters Associations, that lobbied the state to create favourable policies for the supply of cheap labour, or monopoly policies in the marketing of crops to enable planters to thrive better. Kenyan settlers had a number of civil society organizations dealing with particular aspects of settler agriculture. Examples of these include: the Kenya National Farmers Union (KNFU), the Kenya Planters Co-operative Union (KPCU), the Kenya Farmers Association (KFA) and the Kenya Coffee Producers Unions (Leys, 1975: 103; Ng'ethe, 1989: 14). Large-scale farmers whose lobbying activities were narrowly aimed at benefiting themselves controlled these organizations. Their lobbying activities were so successful as to force government to legislate policies that allowed them to monopolize the production of all commercially lucrative crops such as coffee and maize. Their lobbying activities also led to the monopolization of agricultural and veterinary extension services and special rail tariffs for settlers. These civil society organizations were against the poor accumulating rural assets because they wanted them as wage labourers and not as independent producers likely to out-compete them, especially in those early years when the settlers lacked agricultural skills. Unlike in Tanzania and Uganda, civil society for the poor did not emerge because of the dictatorial nature of the settler state. This explains why the struggle for rights to resources took a more radical nature in the form of the Mau Mau.

In Uganda, there existed civil society organizations related to agricultural production and marketing such as Planters Associations, Cotton Buying Associations and Ginners Associations (Lury, 1976). Big farmers and traders dominated these civil society organizations and their lobbying activities were narrowly aimed at benefiting the few members. Because these organizations excluded Africans, the latter set up cooperatives or associations to promote or defend their interests. In Uganda, where the burning rural issue was low prices for cotton, cooperatives emerged to advocate for higher prices. Indeed, cooperative societies were effective in peasants' struggles as the colonial state was compelled to increase prices at which it bought agricultural products – coffee and cotton.

In Tanzania, many indigenous associations were involved in preventing draconian coffee inspection rules (for example the Native Growers Association in Bukoba), or dealt with issues of unfair prices (for example, the Kilimanjaro Native Co-operative Union). The activities of these organizations especially after the Second World War led to the increase of peasants' incomes as the colonial states increased prices of agricultural outputs.

It should be noted that the strength of civil society organizations was dependent on the strong nationalist movement and political parties. Thus, in Uganda, the Uganda National Congress (UNC) championed the cause of the downtrodden Africans – low prices, oppressive taxes, land conflicts (Kayunga, 1995). However, those who held privileged positions in the colonial set-up, such as the Buganda landowners, organized to defend their interests in the name of the Kabaka Yekka ('Kabaka Alone') political party. The colonial state responded to radical civil society and political parties by instituting reforms that undermined their social base. For example, African cooperatives were allowed to market agricultural products and to buy ginneries from Europeans. By independence, the Uganda National Congress was no longer one entity but a series of splinter groups. Cooperatives were transformed from organizations of members to those that narrowly served the leadership.

In Kenya, as we have seen, the land problem and the crisis of production in the reserves degenerated into a civil war. However, through programmes of resettlements, the political crisis was averted. It is important to note that the Kenya government borrowed money from the British government which, in turn, lent to landless people to buy land for their settlement. Since the funds were not enough there were also

> Small-scale settlements created by private initiative and self-help (*harambee*).
> Self-help groups of varying sizes, whether companies or co-operatives, were
> formed by people in need of land in order to pool enough money to buy
> the large European-owned farms … In Laikipia 44 self-help groups were
> known to have purchased land in the district by 1981. (Rutten, 2001: 554–5)

Most importantly, political party activities reflected concerns about land. Two
main political parties emerged in post-colonial Kenya – the Kenya African
National Union (KANU) and the Kenya African Democratic Union (KADU). As
is reflected in their names, these parties were for Africans. KANU was a party
that brought together Kikuyu, Embu, Meru, Luo and Kamba. On the other
hand, KADU was a political party of Kalengin, Masaai and Luhya, pastoral ethnic groups that possessed a lot of land, and had less education and exposure
to wage labour. These were concerned that KANU, a party that had within it
ranks of the landless, would nationalize their land. However, within a few
years KADU was absorbed into KANU after the leadership of the two parties
reaffirmed the colonial pattern of land redistribution and capitalist forms
of ownership of property. Large farms remained now run by Africans. The
settlement schemes failed to absorb all the landless. Some forms of agitation
for more redistribution of land continued in post-independence Kenya by
intellectuals, as individuals (for example the novelist Ngugi Wa Thiongo)
or the Nairobi University Academic Staff Union, which was eventually
banned. Within KANU, a radical group standing for the rights of the landless
formed an opposition party. This was later banned and a one-party system
entrenched into the constitution. Under the one-party system, space for civil
society action was circumscribed. As such the real challenge to the dictatorship of the Kenyan state came from the social movements, some of them
clandestine.

Kenya: change or business as usual?

The return of multiparty politics, however, has not brought forth strong civil
society organizations that raise concerns about the likely effects of the market
to the rural poor. Civil society organizations had little say in the economic
liberalization programmes which, in many instances, marginalize the poor
further. For example, the state has had running battles with farmers in the
rice settlement schemes over prices. Only a few, such as the church and the
Kenya Human Rights Commission, are on record for having generally
advocated for reforms in the agrarian sector and in particular 'organized and
mobilized communities to resist illegal evictions and land allocations'
(CODESRIA and UNDP, 1999: 51).

The Presidential Commission on Land Law Systems, led by the famous
Charles Njonjo, was appointed in 1999. In response to the appointment of

this Commission, a number of NGOs formed what is termed as the Kenya Land Alliance (KLA). They defined their objective as being to advocate for the 'formulation and implementation of a national land policy and review of land laws' (Lumumba, 2001). Its emphasis is an 'all-embracing, participatory and thoroughgoing land policy and law reform process'.

The reform process is still ongoing. The KLA is undertaking activities involving sharing of information among members who are supposed to be committed to land reform, and who have never in the past been involved in acts of land grabbing. It has assisted community organizations to present memoranda to the Njonjo Commission. At the moment, KLA's position on the role of the market in land redistribution is not explicit. It appears that the KLA is simply against those who have a reputation of having been involved in land rights abuses, land grabbing, natural resources or other communal property mismanagement. It is not clear as to whether the KLA will advocate for redressing past injustices.

While we wait for this process to unfold, we can discern possible contributions of the KLA. First, through its network activities, it may improve public awareness of the land problems in Kenya. However, just like the Uganda Land Alliance, the KLA is dependent on foreign donors and, in fact, it may be that it was initiated by Oxfam as was the case in Uganda. If the KLA advances a donor agenda, it may fail to contribute to changing land policy in favour of the disadvantaged. Given that it is registered as a trust, KLA may find it difficult to advocate for radical reforms without attracting the wrath of the state. Moreover, as in all networks, it is difficult to enforce discipline, and those who join might not do so because they share the official KLA agenda. While the efforts of the KLA are noble, the framework for changing the land policy and legal framework has limitations. To be effective, KLA needs to entrench itself as an institution, be clear as to its agenda in order to make a niche for itself and make alliances in political society. The political parties formed after the constitutional reform that allowed political pluralism are elitist and are unable to champion an agenda of pro-poor economic policies and land reforms.

Tanzania: civil society still relatively weak

Like Uganda, Tanzania adopted structural adjustment programmes after an initial refusal by the then President Nyerere. However, Tanzanian civil society had little input in the discussions regarding the kinds of economic policies that should be adopted. As such, the abolition of the state's role in the marketing of crops and adoption of the market as a mechanism through which peasants can access instruments or sell their agricultural products was implemented as designed by the World Bank and IMF. A similar attempt was made to ensure that a market-based legal reform in land be adopted with little input by civil society organizations. True, a Presidential Commission of Inquiry into land matters was appointed and it carried out extensive consultations with people. However when it came to drafting the land bill, a foreign consultant was hired who ignored the recommendations of the Presidential Commission of Inquiry. The initial discussions surrounding the bill drafted by the consultant were confined to a narrow circle of government bureaucrats without the participation of the civil society. This is understandable because the bill reinforced state control over public land where the majority of the Tanzanians lived. The bill allowed for the alienation of village land, thereby opening the way for the rich to buy the lands of the poor. It did so by ensuring that power of allocation of land was vested in the hierarchy of central government commissioners. As in the Ugandan case, the bill refused to redress injustices perpetrated in the past. For example, the problem of the Barbaig pastoralists who lost their land to the Canadian wheat scheme was not redressed by way of restoring it to them. The bill provided for the formation of land associations that can be titled. But, as the experience of the group ranches in Kenya revealed, this could become one way of further privatization of land.

In 1996 church organizations and land NGOs became concerned at the top-down approach to land reform and the absence of public debate on the land reform bill. They formed a Gender Land Task Force (GLTF) to advocate for gender-related issues, such as women's ownership of the land, equal representation of women and men in land administration and dispute settlement committees, customs related to gender discrimination, joint titling and youth rights (Kibamba and Miranda, 2001: 9). In 1997, several gender, pastoral and media NGOs formed an alliance called the National Land Forum (NLF). The NLF led a campaign against the secretive government approach to the reform. It also advanced an alternative view of what the reform should look like.

The NLF argued that the radical title be vested in representative bodies at the grassroots instead of the president as one way of ensuring that the poor cannot lose land very easily to the politically and economically powerful. It observed that the bill gave too much administrative control over land to the executive and that this power could very easily be abused to deprive the poor of their land. This was particularly so because the existing laws favoured foreigners in acquisition and ownership of land. The NLF also called for a dispute settlement machinery that was representative and transparent in its operation and was accessible. The NLF and Gender Land Task Force (GLTF), just like the Uganda Land Alliance described below, raised awareness and consciousness of the public through its lobbying, theatrical plays, media campaigns, seminar/workshop and publicity activities.

However, the Tanzanian civil society had several limitations. First, it had not planned for the task; it was merely reacting to a process. As such, it was ill-equipped in terms of knowledge and advocacy skills. This problem was worsened by the fact that the coalition was not agreed on many issues and therefore could not make a united stand on very critical matters. This enabled the state to play divide and rule by, for example, giving concessions to gender concerns, which made the gender NGOs abandon the alliance. Sometimes, there were disagreements on the approach to certain issues. In general terms,

> Civil society pressure on parliament was ultimately successful in making the parliament create space for public hearing on land and delaying the passage of the act for some time. Despite these efforts, much of the platform of the civil society was not integrated in the final act. A notable exception was some important changes made in terms of representation of women in land governance and women's rights to land ownership. In addition, the debate and NGO activism served great value in bringing land issues and the rights of women to the public agenda. (Kibamba and Miranda, 2001: 11)

It remains to be seen whether or not civil society can again organize for yet another round of reforms that may favour Tanzania's poor.

Uganda: limited achievements by civil society

Uganda is now well known for implementing furthest structural adjustment programmes. Particularly after 1986, the National Resistance Movement (NRM) government implemented most of the elements of structural adjustment programmes. Government abandoned the setting of prices for agricultural products to the market process. In early 1990s, it liberalized trading in agricultural products, effectively ending the monopoly of parastatal organizations such as coffee, lint and produce marketing boards. Transactions in foreign exchange were liberalized and subsidies to agriculture abolished. The reintroduction of SAPs after their initial failure was not accompanied by a serious debate. Apart from critical commentaries by a few academics, no civil society organization was involved in advocacy so that the market reforms do not disadvantage the poor.

The area where civil society organizations played a visible role was land reform. This was perhaps so because land is a sensitive resource upon which the majority of the people derive their livelihood. To appreciate the capacity of civil society to influence the debate on land we briefly sketch out the process from its inception.

The reform process surrounding land began in the late 1980s when the government, with funding from the World Bank and USAID, commissioned a study to establish the effects of the 1975 Land Reform Decree on access to land. The research was completed in 1989 and a report issued (Makerere Institute of Social Research and Land Tenure Center, 1989). On the basis of the report, the first Land Tenure Bill was proposed (Republic of Uganda, 1990).

Some NGOs were alarmed at the designs of the research and its conclusions. As it is known today the terms of reference were narrow and the geographical coverage (mainly around Buganda) also extremely narrow for confident conclusions to be derived for the whole country. The conclusion, for example, that a land market leads to investment was not derived from the findings/ analysis. The Centre for Basic Research (CBR), a non-governmental research organization, criticized the report and instituted its own research in thirteen districts.[4] The findings of CBR revealed that many peasants had been unjustly displaced by state projects (e.g. ranches, parks, forests) and the politically and militarily powerful. Secondly, peasants lived under tenure insecurity and evidence revealed that the market did not lead to better agriculture through mortgages and acquisitions of loans. The implications of these findings were that the new land reform would have had to redistribute land to address past injustices, guarantee the security of tenure of actual cultivators by abolishing landlordism and safeguarding the land of pastoralists and, obviously, reviewing the land management systems so that all social categories, including women, were represented in those systems. The CBR sent a memorandum to the Technical Committee on land and also published a version of its findings in the press (CBR, 1993a, 1993b).

Despite this intervention, the Technical Committee was still bent on ignoring the findings of the CBR. In 1995, some of the CBR's concerns were picked by what later became the Uganda Land Alliance (ULA) (Uganda Land Alliance, 1996, 1997a, 1997b, 1997c). The ULA put up spirited campaigns advocating for the poor. It pointed out the injustice suffered by the people of Kibaale district who had been living under land tenure insecurity on account that they were tenants of Baganda landlords. It went to elaborate length to explode the myth that the market is critical for growth. It pointed out that the mindless encouragement of the market was bound to lead to marginalization of the vulnerable, such as the women, children and the disabled.

The Uganda Land Alliance had achievements. First, it helped raise the consciousness of the public about the negative implications of the land bills and the plight of the Kibaale tenants who have been suffering land tenure insecurity. The ULA can claim to have contributed to the articles in the Land Act that safeguarded the rights of women and children by entrenching provisions such as obtaining the consent of women and children prior to the sale of land. The ULA also contributed to the idea that customary tenure be retained as one mechanism of shielding the poor against landlessness and the institution of a Land Bank so that the poor could borrow loans to purchase land.

However, the achievements of the ULA cannot be construed as having been fundamental or extremely original. There are many reasons why this was the case. First, the Uganda Land Alliance was initiated by foreign NGOs such as Oxfam and World Vision. In the early years of existence, government simply shrugged them off by claiming that, being foreign, these NGOs were peddling foreign agendas. In response, these NGOs desperately tried to recruit local

NGOs. However, many local NGOs joined not because land was at the heart of their programmes but rather they hoped to access donor funds by having greater visibility through the Alliance. Moreover, until 1999, the ULA had no legal existence and was vulnerable to state threats, and donors could not contribute funds to it unless it had a legal existence. When it got registered in 1999, as it was unable to continue lobbying for land laws favouring the poor, its focus shifted to the implementation of the Land Act.

Since many of the NGOs in the Alliance joined in reaction to the unfolding process, they had limited knowledge about the subject and often found themselves challenged by the bureaucrats involved in drafting the land bill. In some instances, they ended up embracing donor agendas simply because they were universal but not burning social issues. A case in point is the co-ownership clause that was approved by the parliament but mysteriously disappeared from the Land Act.

The disappearance of the co-ownership clause from the Land Act brings us to another serious weakness of civil society organizations in Uganda. First, their dependence on foreign donors makes them vulnerable to state threats. It is enough for the state to point out that a particular civil society organization is dependent on foreign funds and hence is pushing a foreign agenda for that organization to retract. Second, this vulnerability becomes more pronounced because what the ULA advocated was not what the poor had put forward as their need. Rural women and children, for example, did not meet to make a demand of co-ownership. Civil society took it upon itself to advocate for co-ownership but when the male-dominated parliament cleverly omitted the co-ownership clause, civil society did not have a constituency to fall back to. Even threats by the women advocacy civil society organizations that they would not vote for the current president, Y. K. Museveni, came to nothing because the struggles of women civil society organizations were not anchored in real life needs of the peasant women. This is not to forget that some of the middle-class women were opposed to the co-ownership clause because they had earned their income and had bought land and other properties and were not ready to share it with their spouses upon separation.

Civil society advocacy groups avoided politically sensitive land matters, such as the Buganda land question, where the problem of landlord–tenant relations had led to increased poverty and whose resolution was important in once again increasing production. They avoided the controversial displacement of pastoralists in the government ranches of Masaka and Ankole. The ULA could not advocate for land redistribution, as this was politically sensitive and instead jumped on the bandwagon of those who called for a Land Bank for the poor to borrow money to buy land for themselves. In a way, it entrenched the market as the mechanism for land redistribution and inequalities in access to land as the market favours the rich and powerful as opposed to the poor and vulnerable.

Conclusion

This chapter set out to explore the character and role of civil society in East Africa in assisting rural people to accumulate rural assets such as land. More particularly, the chapter has tried to establish whether or not the evolving civil society is able to influence the debate on the role of the market in economic change in ways that assist the poor to accumulate rural assets. We have noted that in the 1990s all the three countries of East Africa were compelled to adopt structural adjustment programmes and to carry out reforms aimed at encouraging a land market. During the same period we see a proliferation of civil society organizations, especially NGOs. Some of these civil society organizations have lessened the bad effects of market-based economic policies on the poor by implementing poverty alleviating programmes (supply of agricultural inputs such as implements and seeds), helping victims of past land policies gain access to land or advocating for pro-poor land policies. However, the bulk of the non-state organizations are involved in philanthropic activities such as poverty alleviation, which do not challenge the political power establishment that deprives the poor of, or monopolizes, rural resources. Many of these organizations are dependent on external donors. This undermines their organizational, financial and ideological autonomy, so crucial for reconfiguring power that reproduces poverty conditions.

Notes

1. Many of the Third World countries have been forced to implement structural adjustment programmes characterized by the 'rolling back of the state' and to adopt the market as the main mechanism through which individuals can access resources. In practice, this policy has meant the abolition of subsidies, the end of monopoly of parastatal organizations through which the state depressed prices for agricultural crops, and a floating exchange rate assumed to encourage exports. In the 1990s, many countries have been forced to carry out land reforms that are based on the assumption that the market is the best mechanism through which people can access productive resources such as land; that it allocates factors from inefficient to efficient ones.
2. For example, in the case of Uganda the Commissioner proclaimed as follows in 1900: 'I, Henry Hamilton Johnston, Knight of the most Honourable Order of Bath, Her Majesty's Special Commissioner and Commander in Chief for the Protectorate of Uganda, concluded with the Kings and chiefs of the aforesaid Protectorate and its adjoining Territories H.M. Government has *acquired the sole right of disposal over waste and uncultivated lands of the protectorate* and adjoining Territories; that in addition it is forbidden to any person not native of the Uganda protectorate to acquire land either purchased from natives, by deed of gift, or by occupation, without prior consent of the principal representative of her majesty's Government administering Uganda Protectorate' [emphasis added] (*The Official Gazette of the East Africa and Uganda Protectorates*, 1900). See also Okoth Owiro (2000).
3. For an elaborate treatment of the settlement schemes, see Hyden (1980).
4. See CBR working paper series in the references. For the critique, see Ddungu (1991).

References

Bazaara, Nyangabyaki (1993) 'Food crises and transformation in East Africa: (re)searching for viable food security alternatives', in Ronnie Vernooy and Katherine M. Kealy (eds), *Food Systems Under Stress in Africa African-Canadian Research Co-operation.* Proceedings of a Workshop (Ottawa, 7–8 November).

Bazaara, Nyangabyaki (1994) 'Land policy and the evolving forms of land tenure in Masindi District', in Mahmood Mamdani and Joe Oloka-Onyango (eds), *Uganda: Studies in Living Conditions, Popular Movements and Constitutionalism.* Kampala: Centre for Basic Research.

Bazaara, Nyangabyaki (1995) *Rethinking Food Security in Uganda.* Department of Political Studies. Kingston, Ontario: Queen's University.

Bazaara, Nyangabyaki (1997) *Agrarian Politics, Crisis and Reformism in Uganda, 1962–1996* (PhD Thesis). Kingston, Ontario: Queen's University.

Bazaara, Nyangabyaki (2000a) *Civil Society and the Struggle for Land Rights of the Marginalised Groups: the Contribution of the Uganda Land Alliance to the Land Act 1998.* Paper presented at the Sub-Regional Reflection Forum for NGOs Working on Land Issues in East Africa, Ms-TCDC, Arusha, Tanzania, 29 November–1 December 1999.

Bazaara, Nyangabyaki (2000b) *Contemporary Civil Society and Prospects for Democracy in Uganda: a Preliminary Exploration.* Working Paper No. 54. Kampala: Centre for Basic Research.

Bazaara, Nyangabyaki (2001) *From Despotic to Democratic Decentralisation in Uganda: a History of Accountability and Control over Nature.* A research paper arising out of a collaborative research project between the Centre for Basic Research (CBR), Kampala and the World Resources Institute (WRI), Washington, on the theme 'Environmental Accountability in Decentralised Contexts', September.

Beattie J. H. M. (1954) 'The Kibanja system of land tenure in Bunyoro, Uganda', *Journal of African Administration*, Vol. 6, Nos. 1–4.

Bikaako, Winnie (1994) *Land to the Tillers or Tillers to Land: the Existing Forms of Land Tenure Systems in Mpigi District.* CBR Working Paper No. 44. Kampala: Centre for Basic Research.

Centre for Basic Research (CBR) (1993a) *Memorandum on the Proposed Land Tenure and Control Bill.* CBR Working Paper No. 33. Kampala: Centre for Basic Research.

Centre for Basic Research (CBR) (1993b) 'Land tenure: search for social justice', *The New Vision*, 10 February.

Council for the Development of Social Science Research in Africa (CODESRIA) and the United Nations Development Programme (UNDP) (1999) *Civil Society Empowerment for Poverty Reduction in Sub-Saharan Africa.* Paper presented at a regional meeting (Dakar, 14–15 April).

Ddungu, Expedit (1991) *A Review of the MISR–Wisconsin Land Tenure Center Study on Land Tenure and Development in Uganda.* CBR Working Paper No. 11, June. Kampala: Centre for Basic Research.

Ddungu, Expedit (1994) *The Other Side of Land Issues in Buganda: Pastoral Crisis and the Squatter Movement in Sembabule Sub-district.* CBR Working Paper No. 43. Kampala: Centre for Basic Research.

Doornbos, Martin (1975) 'Land tenure and political conflict in Ankole, Uganda', *Journal of Development Studies*, Vol. 12, No. 1.

Gertzel, Cherry (1974) *Party and Locality in Northern Uganda, 1945–1962.* London: Athlone Press.

Gibbon, Peter (ed.) (1995) *Markets, Civil Society and Democracy in Kenya.* Uppsala: Nordic African Institute.

Hyden, Goran (1980) *Beyond Ujamaa in Tanzania: Underdevelopment and an Uncaptured Peasantry*. Berkeley: University of California Press.

Kafureeka, Lawyer (1992) *The Dynamics of Land Question and its Impact on Agriculture Productivity in Mbarara District, Uganda*. CBR Working Paper No. 25. Kampala: Centre for Basic Research.

Kaggwa, B. Jennifer (1994) *Land Tenure and Land Use in Kampala District*. CBR Working Paper No. 45. Kampala: Centre for Basic Research.

Kaija, Darlison (1995) *The Role of NGOs in Poverty Alleviation in Uganda: a Case Study of Nakanyonyi World Vision Project in Mukono District* (MA Thesis). Kampala: Makerere University.

Kanogo, Tabitha (1987) *Squatters and the Roots of Mau Mau 1905–63*. Nairobi: Heinemann Kenya.

Kanyinga, Karuti (2000) *Re-distribution from Above: the Politics of Land Rights and Squatting in Coastal Kenya*. Research Report No. 115. Uppsala: Nordic African Institute.

Kanyinga, Karuti and Cleophas Torori (1999) *Into the Mew Millennium in Kenya: Reconstructing Civil Society from Below*. Nairobi: Kenya National Council of NGOs.

Kayunga, Sallie Simba (1995) *Uganda National Congress and the Struggle for Democracy: 1952–1962*. CBR Working Paper No. 14. Kampala: Centre for Basic Research.

Kibamba, Deus and Johnson Miranda (2001) *Governance and Civil Society Interventions in Land Reform Processes in Tanzania*. A research paper prepared as a contribution to MWENGO's Research Paper Series.

Kwagala, Betty (1998) 'The role of NGOs in the delivery of health and water services', in Apolo Nsibambi (ed.), *Decentralisation and Civil Society in Uganda: the Quest for Good Governance*. Kampala: Fountain Publishers.

Lane, Charles (1996) *Pastures Lost, Barabaig Economy, Resource Tenure, and the Alienation of their Land in Tanzania*. Nairobi: Initiatives Publishers.

Lange, Siri, Hege Wallevik and Andrew Kiondo (2000) *Civil Society in Tanzania*. Bergen: Chr. Michelsen Institute.

Leys, Colin (1975) *Underdevelopment in Kenya: the Political Economy of Neo-Colonialism 1964–1971*. Berkeley: University of California Press.

Lumumba, Odenda (2001) *Towards an Institutional Framework for Land Laws and Policy Advocacy in Kenya*. Nakuru: Kenya Land Alliance.

Lury, Dennis (1976) 'Dayspring mishandled? The Uganda economy 1945–1960', in D. A. Low and Alison Smith (eds), *History of East Africa*, Vol. III. Oxford: Clarendon Press.

Maina, Wachira (n.d.) *Untying the Gordian Knot: an Inquiry into the Political Economy of Agrarian and Land Reform Under Structural Adjustment Programme in Kenya* (mimeo). A concept paper.

Makerere Institute of Social Research and Land Tenure Center (1989) *Land Tenure and Agricultural Development in Uganda*. January. Kampala: Makerere Institute of Social Research.

Mamdani, Mahmood (1996) *Citizen and Subject: Contemporary Africa and the Legacy of late Colonialism*. Princeton: Princeton University Press.

Mamdani, Mahmood, P. M. B. Kasoma and A. B. Katende (1992) *Karamoja: Ecology and History*. CBR Working Paper No. 22. Kampala: Centre for Basic Research.

Mhina, Amos and Ruth Meena (2001) *Non-profit Impact in Key Fields: Health, Economic Improvement and Human Rights Advocacy*. Paper prepared for the Johns Hopkins Comparative Non-Profit Sector Project (Bagamoyo, Tanzania, 30 November–1 December).

Mugisha, Robert (1992) *Emergent Changes and Trends in Land Tenure and Use in Kabale and Kisoro District*. CBR Working Paper No. 26. Kampala: Centre for Basic Research.

Muhereza, Frank Emmanuel (1994) 'Land tenure and peasant adaptations: some reflections on agricultural production in Luweero District', in Mahmood Mamdani and Joe Oloka-Onyango (eds), *Uganda: Studies in Living Conditions, Popular Movements and Constitutionalism*. Kampala: Centre for Basic Research.

Muhereza, Frank Emmanuel (1999) *Ranching, Common Property Relations and the Alienation of Pastoral Lands in Uganda: a Study of the Buruli Ranching Scheme*. Alarm Working Paper No. 10, September. Kampala: Centre for Basic Research.

Muhereza, Frank, Josephine Ahikire, Zie Gariyo, Lawyer Kafureka, Winnie Bikaako and Peter Otim (1999) *Uganda's Renewable Natural Resources (RNR): a Background Paper Report Prepared for the British Overseas Development Administration (ODA) – Uganda Sector Review Mission*. CBR Consultancy Report No. 4, August. Kampala: Centre for Basic Research.

Mukwaya, A. B. (1953) *Land Tenure in Buganda*. Kampala: Eagle Press.

Musoke Muyiiya, Emmanuel (1997) *The Role of Indigenous Non-Governmental Organisations in Poverty Alleviation: a Case Study of Orphans Community Based Organisation (OCBO) Rakai District* (MA Thesis). Kampala: Makerere University.

Mutai, J. K. (2000) 'Management of public land in Kenya', in the Catholic University of Eastern Africa, *Alienation of Public Land in Kenya*. Nairobi: Catholic University of Eastern Africa.

MWENGO (1999) *Report on the Workshop on Sub-Regional Reflection Forum: NGO Action on Land in East Africa* (Arusha, Tanzania, 29 November–1 December).

Nakintu, Jane (1994) *The Contribution of Non-governmental Organisations to Economic Growth Strategies for Poverty Alleviation* (mimeo). Kampala: DENIVA/URDT/ACFODE Training Unit.

Ng'ethe, Njuguna (1989) *In Search of NGOs: Toward a Funding Strategy to Create NGO Research Capacity in Eastern and Southern Africa*. Occasional Paper No. 58, Institute of Development Studies. Nairobi: University of Nairobi.

Nsibambi, Apolo (1981) 'From symbiosis to antagonism: the case of the relationship between the landlord and the tenant in the rural development of Uganda', in Apolo Nsibambi and James Katorobo (eds), *Rural Rehabilitation and Development*. Proceedings of the Conference on Rural Rehabilitation and Development, 14–18 September.

Nsibambi, Apolo (1989) 'The land question and conflict', in Kumar Rupesinge (ed.), *Conflict Resolution in Uganda*. London: James Currey.

Nyerere, K. Julius (1967) *Freedom and Unity: a Selection from Writings and Speeches, 1952–1965*. Dar-es-Saalam: Oxford University Press.

Official Gazette of the East Africa and Uganda Protectorates (1900) Circular No. 11 of 1900 by H. M. Johnston, HM Special Commissioner and Commander-in-Chief, Entebbe (9 April 1900), Vol. 11, No. 15, Uganda National Archives, Entebbe, 15 June.

Okoth-Ogendo, H. W. O. (n.d.) *The Perils of Land Tenure Reform: the Case of Kenya*. http://www.unu.edu/unupress/unupbooks/80604e/80604E0c.htm.

Okoth Owiro, Arthur (2000) 'The state and public land: an analysis', in the Catholic University of Eastern Africa, *Alienation of Public Land in Kenya*. Nairobi: Catholic University of Eastern Africa.

Oloka-Onyango Joe and J. J. Barya (1997) 'Civil society and the political economy of foreign aid in Uganda', *Democratization*, Vol. 4, No. 2.

Opyene, James, E. (1993) *Recent Trends in the Lango Land Tenure System*. CBR Working Paper No. 36. Kampala: Centre for Basic Research.

Otim, Peter (1993) *Aspects of the Land Question in Mbale District*. CBR Working Paper No. 35. Kampala: Centre for Basic Research.

Republic of Uganda (1968–9) *Parliamentary Debates*, Vol. 88. Kampala: Hansard.

Republic of Uganda (1990) *The Report of the Technical Committee on the Recommendations Relating to Land Tenure Reform Policy*. October. Kampala: Agricultural Secretariat (Bank of Uganda).

Republic of Uganda (1993) *Report of the Technical Committee on Land Tenure Law Reform*. April. Kampala: Agricultural Secretariat (Bank of Uganda).

Rutten, Marcel (2001) ' "Fresh killings": the Njoro and Laikipia violence in the 1997 Kenyan election aftermath', in Marcell Rutten, Alamin Mzrui and François Grignon (eds), *Out of the Count: the 1997 General Elections and Prospects for Democracy in Kenya*. Kampala: Fountain Publishers.

Semboja, Joseph and Ole Therkildsen (1995) *Service Provision under Stress in East Africa: the State, NGOs and People's Organisations in Kenya, Tanzania and Uganda*. Kampala: Fountain Publishers.

Shivji, G. Issa (1998) *Not Yet Democracy: Reforming Land Tenure in Tanzania*. Dar es Salaam: HAKIARDHI.

Ssenkumba, John (1993) *The Land Question and the Agrarian Crisis: the Case of Kalangala District, Uganda*. CBR Working Paper No. 34. Kampala: Centre for Basic Research.

The Uganda Gazette (1998a) 'The Land Act, 1998', No. 41, 2 July.

The Uganda Gazette (1998b) 'The Land Bill, 1998', No. 12, March.

Uganda Land Alliance (1996) *Position Statement of the Uganda Land Alliance on the Proposed Land Bill of 1996 to the Technical Committee and Agricultural Policy Committee*. Uganda Land Alliance Publication, Kampala, December.

Uganda Land Alliance (1997a) *Open Letter to the Minister of Lands Housing and Physical Planning on the Proposed Land Bill of 1997*. Uganda Land Alliance Publication No. 3, Kampala.

Uganda Land Alliance (1997b) *Customary Land Holding in Uganda: a Case Study of Lira and Apac Districts*. Uganda Land Alliance, Kampala.

Uganda Land Alliance (1997c) *Growth and Equity: Are We Growing at the Expense of 65% of Ugandans?* Uganda Land Alliance Publication, Kampala.

6
Crisis of Rural Livelihoods, Economic Reforms and Civil Society in Egypt

Ray Bush

Introduction

This chapter examines the impact of recent changes in the relationship between landowners and tenants in Egypt.[1] It does so by looking at the implications of Law 96 of 1992 for improved opportunities for rural civil society and rural livelihoods. One key question is whether there has been any link between economic liberalization on the one hand and political liberalization on the other, specifically related to Egypt's countryside. Have the possibilities for political expression by farmers and rural dwellers through local organizations and associations expanded, as the opportunities for entry into a land market are supposed to have also increased?

These questions raise issues that are at the heart of rural livelihoods, asset redistribution and especially land. The chapter will examine the declared intentions relating to political liberalization and expansion of rural civil society, of the Government of Egypt (GoE) and donors, notably the United States Agency for International Development (USAID) and the World Bank. These intentions will be set against actual recent outcomes for political representation, participation in local institutions and the rule of law and the improvement of rural well-being and protection of rural livelihoods.

This is not always easy work in the Egyptian context. Egypt's ruling elite views the control of access to information and the debate of policy issues as central to its maintenance of political and economic power. Egypt has at different times been characterized as 'a democracy of newspapers', as the centre of Middle Eastern media and cultural liberalism. This view has always been questionable and it is especially so at the start of the twenty-first century.[2]

While there have been many GoE announcements of the importance of a widening of political participation, and by donors of the need particularly for an expansion of what they call 'civil society', neither has taken place. This failure raises two immediate questions related to Egypt's countryside that the GoE is reluctant to address. The first of these is what the likely outcome of the state's withdrawal from the provision of agricultural inputs and marketing will be for the *fellahin*'s (peasant's) ability to continue agricultural production. How have the *fellahin* managed to cope with the reduction of GoE support for agricultural services as rural poverty increases? Second, has there been an increase in the number and variety of civil society organizations to substitute for state withdrawal from agricultural provision and has this ushered in a new era for political liberalization and democratization?

The study will indicate that in recent years there has been a political deliberalization (Kienle, 2001). There has been a narrowing of the possibility for political action independent of the state. This narrowing authoritarianism challenges the view that a civil society exists other than as a slogan used by the GoE to curry favour from the donor community. This is not surprising. While there was a degree of political reform following the death of President Nasser in 1970, with his successor, Anwar Sadat's provision for political parties in 1977, Egyptian politics has been unable to break from the fact that the main political parties were created by the state. Any new political party still has to be approved by a committee on the formation of political parties. The state continues to determine what constitutes formal political practice – the extent to which a political party can politicize, organize and recruit new members as well as hold meetings and organize democratic opposition to the regime.

Nasser depended upon limited and restricted political participation from the social and class forces the revolution used to fight the injustice of the previous regime. Yet the social contract that was imposed to protect the revolution coerced the *fellahin* and working class to accept political quietude for limited land reform and improved living and working conditions. That compact limited political participation during the Nasser years and inhibited reform to widen the scope for decision-making and formulation of policy beyond the armed forces and crony political and economic elites.

Hosni Mubarak's Egypt of the twenty-first century has failed to move away from the authoritarian corporatism and nationalist populism that characterized previous regimes. He has concentrated efforts to sustain his political power that at the time of Sadat's assassination was without much legitimacy. The 1960s and 1970s were marked by severe limitations on political participation as the regimes tried to quell unrest with moderate improvements to service provision. That limited improvement to health and education was only possible while the regime could finance it. Egypt's economic crisis intensified, however, as it proved difficult for it to generate growth that was not dependent upon its traditional rentier sectors of the Suez Canal, migrant labour remittances and oil. Economic crisis and recession deepened with a fiscal crisis of the state (Frischtak and Atiyas, 1996; Waterbury, 1983; Richards and Waterbury, 1990). The record of the 1980s and 1990s has been a story largely of the Egyptian regime equipping itself with the ability to continue to manage dissent, while also promoting a muddled message of the need for economic reform, market liberalization and financial austerity, for farmers and workers.

This chapter examines opportunities that have arisen for tenant farmers, and those dispossessed since 1997, to mobilize and promote their interests within the context of Egypt's uncivil state. It will also raise the issues discussed by several tenants who lost land after 1997 and the consequences of that land loss for their asset base, their level of poverty, the social exclusion that they have endured and assault on their rights to land. It will examine the level of violence that took place in Egypt's countryside, especially after 1997, and assess the extent to which that might be seen as indicative of protest within the realm of civil society, or if it can be understood instead as a new form of political mobilization. It will become clear that while the declared rationale for donors and the GoE at different times has been that the 1992 reform of tenancy was intended to promote improvements in Egypt's land market, with the parallel development of improved opportunities for rural political expression, this has certainly not taken place. The focus will not be on issues of a land market, which has been looked at elsewhere (Bush, 2002). Instead, what will be highlighted is that civil society groups have not emerged as a result of market reform. Where opportunities of local speaking out have taken place, or for organizing against impoverishment that has resulted from market liberalization, they have tended to emerge around family and kinship structures. Market liberalization has generated greater rural poverty and unemployment that has been managed by the *fellahin* in terms of a greater dependence upon family resources. Yet this has also become jeopardized as economic hardship has intensified.

Improving opportunities for civil society representation has never been on the Egyptian policy-makers' agendas. It has at different times, as will be shown, been part of the pretence of political liberalization that commentators have assumed will *ipso facto* emerge alongside market reform but the GoE has no intention, or need, to liberalize politically. Moreover, if it did, it certainly would not focus on rural political empowerment that might jeopardize the wealth and status of landed interests.

The first section will begin with a brief review of whether the concept of civil society is an appropriate one to use and whether it has any usefulness in understanding rural Egypt. It will also trace the recent process of deliberalization and then provide the context for examining agriculture and rural livelihoods by looking at what the characterization of Egypt's persistent agricultural crisis has been. It will then be possible to look at the debate about tenure and markets and the impact recent government policy has had on rural livelihoods and assets.

Deliberalization and politics: whither civil society?

The role of civil society in keeping rulers and politicians in check, in the promotion of democratic transition and consolidation, is dominant throughout the donor community and the rhetoric of many Third World governments (Keane, 1988; Clark, 1991). Political conditionality has been written into most aid and donor relations with developing countries. The need for civil society has been taken for granted (DFID, 2000; USAID, 2000; World Bank, 2000a). Egypt is no exception in receiving that policy advice, although what is meant by civil society at a time of deliberalization and assertiveness of the authoritarian regime is unclear (Kandil, 1994; Ibrahim, 1995).

Civil society

Since the mid-1980s the term 'civil society' has been used to 'suit a variety of ideological, intellectual and practical needs' (White, 1996: 178; see also Keane, 1988). In its broadest definition, civil society refers to *public space* independent of the state where many different forms of associational life exist. But it also refers to associations between firms, families and the state used to refer to the presence of voluntary organizations. These two views have left a lot of room for confusion and they do not adequately address the need to see what it is that associations actually do to determine whether they can be called 'civil' or not. Farmers in Egypt adopted a range of strategies to cope with economic liberalization. These involved aspects of using formal protest through existing state orchestrated avenues as well as elements of what Bayat has called 'quiet encroachment' (1997; 1998; 2002). They have most obviously been characterized by farmer adoption of coping strategies to reduce economic stress and they have failed to impact positively on the creation of rural civil society defined as the presence of associations.

The organized routinized character of associations is often seen to characterize civil society organization (Stewart, 1997, citing Hadenious and Uggla, 1996). But this view does not capture the forms of protest and opposition that have arisen in Egypt since 1990 or elsewhere in the Western liberal democratic world. This is because of the difficulty of knowing what to include in the list of 'non-state' actors – those that operate outside the sphere of the state. It is clear, for instance, that many civic institutions like academic unions, public sector interest groups and those citizens who derive core income from the state are firmly embedded in the state system itself (Bangura, 1999: 1). This raises issues related to the boundaries of civil society when discussing associational groups. Are all groups and associations, irrespective of membership and the groups' aims and objectives, to be included as part of civil society? If civil society is to be linked with political liberalization, do all groups within it contribute to that process or is it more appropriate, for example, to look at not only the aims and objectives of different groups, the types of recruitment mechanisms and social base that they have but also the precise relationship they may have with the state?

Theoretical slippage in the civil society debate is exacerbated by limitations related to its automatic linkage with democratization. Civil society and NGOs are seen as the necessary ingredients for promoting and consolidating democracy; empowering people in their struggles against states and increasing political participation. Chris Allen, among others, has questioned, however, the simple linkage between civil society and democratization. This questioning is partly driven by the terms of close association with 'neo-liberal ideological campaigning' and the assertions of its neoliberal origins (Allen, 1997: 330). These include preoccupation with associational life asserting civil society is the source for liberal democratic values, like openness, transparency, accountability and the rule of law. Civil society is also seen as the motor for democracy and is posed in opposition to the state. Crucially, a flourishing civil society requires a non-interventionist state – one that furthers the interests of market-oriented individual freedoms (Allen, 1997: 335).

A consequence of this view is a development agenda since the early 1980s that has made donor funds conditional on policies to facilitate a strong civil society in recipient countries (Fowler, 1991; Powell and Seddon, 1997). Donors have been careful to channel funds to NGOs that broadly agree with donor policies for development, economic liberalization and political reform that does not challenge the interests of foreign capital. But there are many different types of NGOs with different agendas that might complement, or oppose the state (Marcussen, 1996: 418). And of course there are NGOs that are undemocratic in their internal organization and in their ultimate aims and objectives.

NGOs do not necessarily oppose the state. The NGO sector is subject to divisions between them, in relation to what their aims and objectives might be and what position they might adopt, or be encouraged to adopt vis-à-vis the state. It is more likely that some business NGOs, although clearly not all in the Egyptian case, will be more sympathetic to the state than, say, a human rights organization. And while NGOs are divided horizontally, they are also divided vertically, internally in terms of their class membership, organization, recruitment and activist base.

It is more fruitful in understanding civil society to take the focus away from a preoccupation with NGOs and associational activity *per se* and instead to use the term to describe the *processes* by which states configure relations of consent and coercion. Gramsci's concern in the spiralling fascist Italy of the 1930s was to grapple with a topsy-turvy world where life outside or beyond the state at different times and often in quick succession became enmeshed with the state, separate or subordinate to it (Gramsci, 1976; Showstack Sassoon, 1978).[3] For Gramsci, the essential way in which dominant classes maintained authority was to present themselves as legitimate rulers. This was done, most of the time, by convincing subordinate classes of the hegemonic dominance and legitimacy of ruling (governing) class actions. The constant creation and recreation of hegemony, rule by consent, but when necessary by force, was for Gramsci the crucial factor characterizing the exercise of political power in the interests of the dominant economic classes. For Gramsci, civil society was only meaningful as a political concept or political reality if it was part of a relationship with the state. Thus while contemporary donors, and mainstream academic commentators, have tended to talk about civil society in opposition to the state, or as a substitute for it, for Gramsci, civil society could not exist without the state.

This leads us to the paradox that a strong civil society needs a strong state (Marcussen, 1996: 421). It is thus mistaken to counterpoise civil society to the state. This dichotomous view is guided by the ideological premise that states are necessarily bad and civil society good. While this neoliberal concern was founded on the importance of securing individual rights, it has been harnessed since the 1980s in an ideological battle by donors against perceived corrupt and inefficient states. The policy formula that has resulted has been a view to downsize state activity and improve opportunities for individuals to organize collectively in civil society. While the need for much state reform in the south is beyond question, to open up the arena of decision-making, improve transparency and opportunities for political expression, and especially to promote and uphold the rule of law, donors have tended to insist on a crude formulation that has seen the state as a homogeneous inefficient unit in contrast with the need to empower individuals through NGOs or the market (Stewart, 1997: 12). Strong states are necessary for a vibrant civil society as the state helps facilitate the arenas in which NGOs and other bodies can operate. States provide the rules for the game, for participation and opportunities to express dissent. In short, states deliver the different political, social, economic and cultural processes whereby hegemonic classes remain dominant. States provide the framework, therefore, and are also subject to contradictions and oppositional forces that emerge resulting from conflicts that states can never fully contain. There is a further contradiction. Strong states are required for strong civil societies but can jeopardize the possibilities for NGOs to be independent and vigorous in their defence of their own agendas. In Egypt the relationship between the state and civil society is harnessed around NGOs, syndicates and 'partnerships' between government and associations that reinforce rather than radically question the relationship between the GoE and civil society.

One conclusion from this analysis would be for donors to no longer undermine already fragmented states by bolstering civil society seen in opposition to the state but to enhance state capacity. Where this has been adopted, however, it has tended to promote management reforms, including privatization that has lessened rather than promoted state effectiveness and enabled the continuation of spoils politics (Bangura, 1999: 5). Donors have prioritized the political liberalization of the state with the intention of assisting economic liberalization under the pressure for globalization. Yet because of the Egyptian state's persistent rentier character, the GoE remains insulated from the pressures of local political forces. This has been aided by a corrupt electoral process, severe limitations on political organizations and censored media. While donors have been fixated with encouraging the GoE to withdraw from economic activity, to shed its 'socialist' inheritance, they have effectively promoted a wish list for NGOs to replace government service and other provision. Yet that fails to understand that the state's withdrawal cannot be adequately picked up by the new donor funded entrants – even if that was the policy intent – and such intervention would be divisive and would fragment opposition political forces. In other words, while it is useful to view the relationship between the state and NGOs as one of a struggle for ideas, policy and active legitimacy, it would be wrong to invest in NGOs as the force for democratization simply because they may emanate from beyond the state.

Deliberalization in Egypt

The idea of *rural* civil society is usually excluded from any debate about political liberalization. Whether donor- or government-led, debate normally focuses on urban society. Egypt is no exception to this.

It is difficult to estimate accurately the number of NGOs in Egypt. A World Bank study in 1998 suggested there were 28 000, while the ministry responsible for registering NGOs, the Ministry for Insurance and Social Affairs (MISA) (prior to 2000 this ministry was the Ministry for Social Affairs) indicates that there were far less than this: 14 600. MISA has the responsibility to effectively regulate NGOs under Law 32 of 1964. While that law was revised in 2000 it was deemed unconstitutional and a new law to replace Law 32 was redrafted in 2001 (effective from the middle of 2003). This legislation intensifies the policing and marshalling of NGOs. Effectively that policing role is managed by internal security and the previous Minister of Social Affairs, it seems, was removed partly because of the challenge to subordinate her ministry to intervention from the security agencies. Among other things, the legal restraints on NGOs ensure that no foreign funding finds its way to the organizations unless it has been channelled through and agreed with MISA. The registration of NGOs characterizes them into welfare or development agencies, the latter more commonly known as community development associations or CDAs.

Welfare organizations, or *Gamiyat Reiaia*, are required to focus on a specific activity, such as delivery of health services, welfare or literacy. CDAs may have a range of activities as long as they are approved by MISA and based in a single location. This classification is restrictive, fails to capture the complexity of different NGO activities and hides many different political and religious actions (Abdel Rahman, 2001).

Superficially, the numbers of NGOs indicate a certain vibrancy in Egypt's civil society, but the measures of state control and the limitations imposed on NGOs constrain effective independent action. USAID note that less than one-third of MISA's figure of 14 600 Egyptian NGOs work in the countryside and only about 3000 actively play a part in 'developing and representing their communities' (USAID, 2001: 1). This is despite the fact that 50 per cent of Egypt's population are rural. And for USAID, the importance of NGOs for rural governance is significant. Before Egypt's structural adjustment programme (SAP) in 1991, the GoE controlled agricultural input and output markets and the major vehicle for driving agricultural growth was the cooperative. These were located in every village. Nasser's vision had been that they would provide part of the social contract with the *fellahin* substituting the power of merchants and feudal landlords.

There were effectively two kinds of cooperative. The multi-purpose cooperative handled issues of credit, agrarian reform and land reclamation. They provided production and marketing services to a membership that was compulsory where individuals had benefited from Nasser's agricultural reform. The cooperative was the sole vehicle for access to farming inputs. The second type of cooperative was specialized in areas like livestock, poultry and agricultural machinery. In 1998 there were 6604 agricultural cooperatives including 776 agrarian reform cooperatives and 596 land reclamation cooperatives.[4]

These figures are misleading, however. They suggest a lively cooperative structure, yet with the implementation of economic reform they have collapsed. Their demise has led to much unrest among poor landowners and tenants who were previously dependent upon subsidized inputs and guaranteed marketing structures. They have been deprived of subsidized inputs and controlled markets. While there had been considerable and widespread dissatisfaction with the old cooperative system, it was little compared with the unrest expressed by villagers with the new control by merchants and large landowners that emerged with market liberalization. These groups now fix prices of inputs much higher than with the old system and control markets in less flexible ways than the old cooperatives.

There is a clear tension between the erosion of old rural structures and institutions for the maintenance of agricultural productivity and the rhetoric that market reform will empower the rural individual to make decisions that will enhance agricultural productivity. On the one hand the rhetoric of both USAID and GoE has repeatedly paid lip service to rural governance issues and political liberalization alongside economic reform. On the other hand there has been the dissolution of Nasserist agricultural institutions (albeit many of these had served to depoliticize farmers), the erosion of the legal rights of tenants and increases in costs of production that have led to higher levels of rural poverty and unemployment (USAID, 2000, 2001; Fergany, 2002).

USAID has noted, for instance, that there is an important role for NGOs in developing Egyptian society. They are keen to promote 'participatory, accountable governance and a strong non-governmental organization (NGO) community' because they are 'also important for supporting economic growth' (USAID, 2000: 1). USAID also recognizes that:

> Most Egyptian PVOs [private and voluntary organizations]/NGOs are not meeting the needs of their communities due to lack of autonomy, institutional capacity, and resources ... Overall, few PVOs/NGOs in Egypt

are effectively engaged in making contributions to Egypt's development. (USAID, 2001: 1)

There are two reasons why USAID is unlikely to see any improvement in the role that NGOs might have in developing Egypt's political economy including its organization of governance. The first is simply that too much is invested in the idea that NGOs will transform Egypt's political structures. We have rehearsed this argument in relation to donor optimism regarding the importance of NGOs in struggles for development. There is little point in promoting NGOs as a vehicle for democratic governance (meant here to go beyond formal democratic practices of regular free and fair elections). They seem unable, without other political and social pressures, to encompass issues like the possibility for agenda setting, popular mobilization, and citizenship with social and economic rights defendable in an independent judiciary. In other words, while NGOs may be important as conduits for expressing particular interests, they will not add much to the processes of democratization unless and until institutional reform recognizing the right of democratic participation and expression is actively promoted. And this needs to be promoted by non-NGO forces too. There needs to be an arena in which citizens can dissent without fear of reprisal, torture or ridicule. And this broader and deeper view of democracy extends to the issue of human rights. These latter can only be effective if obligations of people are felt and acknowledged by everyone in society, and political institutions need to effectively deliver the normative basis of the way people recognize and respond to attacks on people's rights (Beetham, 2000). This is far from being achieved in Egypt.

This leads to the second reason why it is inappropriate to invest in the idea that civil society promotion through NGOs in Egypt is a vehicle for democratization. The GoE in the 1990s has promoted a strategy of deliberalization. Eberhard Kienle (2001) has detailed the processes whereby the GoE has restricted positive liberties in the central institutions of the state by, among other things, restricting participation in government, political parties and in the 'election' of the president in a referendum where for four terms he has been unopposed. Kienle has also examined the ways in which the GoE has restricted participation in municipal and local government arenas. What Kienle has euphemistically called 'streamlining the state apparatus' included preventing participation from below in elections for *umdas*, or village headmen, and deans of university faculties. During Mubarak's presidency, these officeholders have become state appointments rather than electoral positions (Kienle, 2001: 164).

There are many reasons for Egypt's deliberalization and, among these, the idea of a conflict between the regime and radical Islamic groups has been central. So too has the impact of economic reform that has generated greater inequality and the threat of greater political dissent. The GoE has tightened press laws preventing criticism that is seen as unsubstantiated. The evidence of deliberalization is substantial. It was much debated in Egypt during the referendum campaign that confirmed Mubarak for an unprecedented fourth term on 26 September 1999. The state-controlled media pulled out all the stops in the referendum campaign. Many street banners and news headlines read, 'God gave three gifts to Egypt; the pyramids, the Nile and Mubarak'. Mubarak himself declared a new dawn for the country after gaining a declared 93.79 per cent of the vote. The president called for greater political participation to accompany economic liberalization. Yet in the cabinet 'reshuffle', he retained nineteen of the old guard and the ageing technocrat Atif Abeid was named prime minister. The thirteen new appointments, moreover, were greeted with derision by commentators in private and as the government progressed, especially after the 2000 parliamentary general election, it became clear that the government of Atif Abeid was the most criticized for many decades (*Cairo Times*, 19–25 July 2001).

Agricultural neglect and economic reform

There have been two major themes of continuity and discontinuity in the history of land and agriculture in Egypt. The first is the depoliticization of Egypt's farmers, the felt need to reduce opportunities for farmers to organize independently of the state; and the second is the politicization of land. This politicization was first promoted by Nasser as a vehicle to marginalize feudal royalist landowners who were opposed to Egypt's 1952 revolution in his attempt to redraw rural political boundaries, to secure small farmer legal rights in land and to stabilize prices and security of tenure. The politicization of land, however, continued after Nasser's death, in the struggle for de-Nasserization, to reverse the revolutionary changes of land tenure and security that Nasser had put in place and to replace them with increased strength of the social and economic forces of the previous regime. Initiated by Sadat and continued by Mubarak de-Nasserization has taken the form of market liberalization in agriculture driven by deputy prime minister and minister of agriculture Yussef Wali. It culminated in Law 96 of 1992. This law revoked rights of tenure for tenants that had been a hallmark of Nasser's social revolution.

Egypt's land reform in 1952 was the first large-scale reform in the Middle East.[5] Although the sanctity of private property was retained, the land reforms in 1952 and 1961 redistributed about one-seventh of the country's cultivable land from large landowners to middle peasants and the landless. Before the reforms, about 0.1 per cent of total landowners owned 20 per cent of the cultivated land. Three million *fellahin* owned less than 1 feddan. The near landless represented about 75 per cent of landowners but only held 13 per cent of the total cultivable land.

The reforms gave the state the authority to seize privately held land over 200 feddan, a ceiling reduced to 100 feddan in 1961, although families could still hold up to 300 feddan. Seized land was distributed to agricultural labourers and tenant farmers with holdings of less than 5 feddan. The recipients on average received 2.4 feddan and paid for the land in instalments over a forty-year period. There were almost two million beneficiaries of the reforms and smallholders also benefited from an increase in land sales as landowners feared expropriation or sequestration of their estates. The biggest impact of the reforms was felt by the largest and the smallest landholders. Those with less than 5 feddan increased by 13 per cent and the land they owned by 74 per cent. The biggest estates of more than 200 feddan disappeared. The reforms helped to improve income distribution and rural diets and levels of productivity.

According to El-Ghonemy (1993, 1999), the land reforms between 1952 and 1975 helped reduce poverty and promoted growth. One estimate is that rural poverty fell from a level of 56.1 per cent in 1950 to 23.8 per cent in 1965 (El-Ghonemy, 1999: 11). This reduction was not solely due to agrarian reform. The rural poor benefited from extensive government food and agricultural input subsidies, improved health and education provision. Yet the reforms might also have been more effective. Ceilings on land holdings remained high so they did not substantially undermine the interests of big landlords. When challenged regarding their continued large holdings, the landowners simply signed land ownership to family members, or used local or national patron–client links to influence policy implementation and keep the state off their backs.

Sadat began reversing Nasser's legacy in the 1970s by reducing the gains made by smallholders and tenants. He reinforced the economic and political strength of large landholders, removed elected farmers from representation in cooperatives and other rural institutions, and in this he paved the way for the eventual passing of Law 96 of 1992.

Exit Left, enter Right – economic reform in agriculture

Agricultural reform intended to redress the record of poor growth. Between 1981 and 1992 the average rate of real growth in the agricultural sector was about 2 per cent per annum. This was 2 per cent less than was thought to be necessary to sustain economic growth and far short of the GoE target of 5 per cent. Agricultural growth of 1.9 per cent 1980–5, down from 2.8 per cent 1965–80, was less than the estimated population growth of 2.7 per cent per annum, and government policies that had favoured food imports led to an estimated annual net deficit of $3 billion in agricultural trade by the mid-1980s (Khedr, Ehrich and Fletcher, 1996: 53).

Egypt's Ministry of Agriculture and Land Reclamation (MALR) blamed the history of government intervention as the cause for the agricultural crisis. Price and marketing controls, state ownership of major agricultural industries and an overvalued exchange rate were all seen as the reason for a decline in agricultural productivity. In the early 1980s the GoE began working with USAID to liberalize agricultural markets.

USAID estimate that agriculture accounts for about 19 per cent of Egypt's GDP, at least 36 per cent of employment and an estimated 22 per cent of commodity exports. According to USAID, half of Egypt's population of approximately 65 million live in rural areas. Industrial activity linked to agriculture, like the processing and marketing of commodities, provision of agricultural inputs like water, fertilizer, pesticides and seeds account for another 20 per cent of GDP and 'a substantial portion of the work force' (www.usaid. gov/eg/proj-agr.htm).

Egypt's agricultural sector reform predated the Economic Reform and Structural Adjustment Programme (ERSAP) agreed in 1991. Its two main elements have been to liberalize markets and input provision. The second has been to promote the production for export of high value, low nutrition foodstuffs (and cut flowers) for Europe (for the programme, see USAID, 1998b; USAID and GoE, 1995; http://www.usaid.gov/eg/proj-agr.htm; and, for a detailed critique, Bush, 1999).

USAID has been a major driving force in Egypt's strategy for liberalization and land tenure reform. It has initiated two major programmes: the Agricultural Production and Credit Project between 1986 and 1996 at a cost of $289 million and the Agricultural Policy and Reform Programme. The emphasis between 1986 and 1996 was market-led growth, liberalization of inputs and prices and reducing the role of the state agricultural credit bank, the Principal Bank for Development and Agricultural Credit (PBDAC). After 1996 USAID focused on export-led growth, encouraging Egypt to emulate a United States farm type model of extensive capital-intensive agriculture.

The aid community and many academics have declared the agricultural reform process a success. The success lies, advocates argue, in an increase in the real value of crop production for the twenty-three major crops between 1980 and 1990; an increase in farm incomes; and a doubling of wheat production between 1986 and 1992 because of improved yields and area planted. There has also been a decline in food subsidies and the deregulation of controls on cropping patterns (Faris and Khan, 1993; Fletcher, 1996).

Despite the rhetoric of reform success, there are a number of persistent concerns[6] that help provide the context for understanding the implications of Law 96 and possibilities for local political actions against reform. These concerns are, first, the flimsy *evidential base* used by reformers to indicate aggregate production and growth figures. Second, it continues to be the case more than fifteen years after reforms in the agricultural sector began that defenders of reform continue to rely on the *early evidence* of increases in output and changes in cropping patterns, particularly for the period 1986–92. Yet there is little evidence that early improvements in productivity have been sustained or that early increases were due to price reform *per se* (Mitchell, 1998: 23).[7] Indeed, the World Bank suggests that the rate of growth in agriculture since 1990 has been less than for 1980–7, apart from 1996/7 (World Bank, 2000b). Third, any increase in agricultural exports has been surpassed by increases in major agricultural *imports*. Agriculture contributes more than 33 per cent of Egypt's trade deficit. Fourth, economic reform has had a disastrous impact on employment. Job losses in agriculture for 1990/5 alone were at least 700 000 (Fergany, 2002). Finally, poverty levels have dramatically increased. This is evidenced by the GoE Household Income and Expenditure Survey (HIES), which indicates the level of poverty more than doubling between 1990/1 and 1995/6 – from 21 per cent to 44 per cent. The poverty line is defined here by the cost of a minimum basket of nutrition, yet if the criterion is used of $1 per person per day, and we assume that LE 500 is necessary for a family of five per month, the extent of poverty is far worse. By this measure more than 80 per cent of Egyptians are poor.

There is very little debate about Egypt's agricultural future apart from the notion that it lies with export of high-value horticultural products. The MALR and US Embassy have indicated the need to press forward with the agricultural reforms, it seems, precisely because the recent record has been less good than when the reforms began. The institutional response in other words has failed to address the character of the strategy itself – its appropriateness in the teeth of mounting poverty, persistent marginalization of the poor, the landless and near landless, and particularly women and women-headed households.

The failure of USAID to promote a policy of greater transparency and of greater sympathy with the majority of Egypt's farmers has played into the hands of Egypt's landed elite. That elite has taken advantage of the veil that market reform offers to repoliticize land as a significant policy issue but not one that should be openly debated. It was very evident from the 'debate' about Law 96 of 1992 that farmers were regarded as lazy and as charlatans who had benefited after Nasser's reforms, while landowners had lost status, wealth and political influence. Yet the way the legislative proceedings for Law 96 were affirmed and the way in which the media were unwilling to debate the impact of tenure reform on tenants demonstrated precisely the power and influence that landowners had to marginalize the interests of the rural poor. There was certainly an absence of any discussion for improved rural civil society or political and institution building for local governance.[8]

Land tenure reform and political violence

Law 96 of 1992 revoked Nasser's Agrarian Reform Law of 1952 that had given tenants security of tenure and rights of inheritance in perpetuity. Law 96 was not fully implemented until October 1997. In the transitional period land could still be inherited but the rent was increased from seven to at least twenty-two times the land tax. The land tax is revised every ten years and is based on the fertility and geographical location of the land. After 1 October 1997 all landowners could retake their land. Tenants were charged market-based rent which, in some cases, rose to between LE 1200 and LE 1800 per feddan – LE 2500 by 1997. Tenancies became annual contracts renewed at the landowners' discretion, but it is rare for an actual contract to exist.

Tenants were shocked at the implementation of the Act. They either naively thought their president would not allow it or they were misinformed about what Law 96 entailed. Perhaps as much as 15 per cent of Egypt's agricultural land is tenanted and tenants may often access their own family land as well as rent land in – some may also rent out land. No allowance was made in the Act for the complexity of tenancy.

Opposition to the implementation of the Land Act was downplayed by the GoE. It characterized opposition to the act as terrorism and as being un-Islamic as the Act was seen as a legitimate restoration of property rights defended by Koranic teaching.[9]

While restoring property rights to landowners, Law 96 did not promote a more open and comprehensive land market. And neither did it lead to the emergence of a rural civil society in the form of organized NGO or other formal activity. Opposition to the Land Act was largely uncoordinated and it was dealt with harshly by security forces. Instead of the emergence of NGOs or associational groups to protect and further peasant interests, there seems to have been a greater reliance upon family and kinship for coping with the rural disruption and increased poverty that followed tenure reform.

Table 6.1 indicates the extent and geographical spread of violence linked to the implementation of Law 96. The figures for fatalities, injuries and arrests

Table 6.1 Recorded deaths, injuries and arrests in rural Egypt relating to Law 96 and related land conflict, January 1998–December 2000

Governorate	Deaths	Injuries	Arrests
Giza	12	116	169
Assuit	24	92	157
Sharkia	10	122	243
Minya	8	69	61
Dakhalia	6	21	36
Sohag	15	70	79
Damietta	–	–	42
Fayyum	6	44	103
Suez	–	–	7
Minoufia	1	35	84
Kalubia	4	34	46
Gharbia	5	58	123
Qena	13	53	66
Beheira	4	39	74
Aswan	1	8	3
Beni Suef	9	27	46
Port Said	–	25	30
Kafr El Sheikh	1	27	31
Ismailia	0	6	9
Total	119	846	1409

Source: Land Centre for Human Rights, Cairo, 2002.

are indicative rather than comprehensive.[10] The figures reflect the growth in the politicization of land-related violence. This can be violence linked to dispossession of tenants by the forces of law and disorder – the security forces, landowners and thugs. It also relates to the increase in conflict between farmers over disputed boundaries, irrigation and other issues. All these disputes seem to have increased following October 1997. The new legislation allowed former owners to try and reclaim land that had been appropriated by the state as land reform land not included as part of Law 96.[11]

For USAID, Law 96 was a vehicle to promote further economic liberalization of economic relations in the countryside and to establish a clear market in land (USAID, 1999a: 2, 9). But USAID's focus on establishing a land market was misplaced and ahistorical. It was also out of kilter with the revised positions on tenure expressed by the international financial institutions (IFIs) themselves elsewhere on the continent (see Adams, 2000; Deininger and Binswanger, 1999; Toulmin and Quan, 2000). USAID certainly slurred over any notion of conflict and upheaval and failed to ask questions about governance and rural institution building. They instead pushed the mantra that legislative change was necessary to remove obstacles for rural organizations.

Formal and informal rural resistance and livelihoods

The GoE seems nowhere to have indicated what role it would like for rural civil society during a time of immense change and flux. Its position on urban-based NGOs is draconian. The regime does not encourage civil society activity and what exists is heavily policed. The more effective agencies have usually been those registered under civil law as private non-profit companies which also act effectively as NGOs. The Ibn Khaldun Centre was one of these until its director Saadeddin Ibrahim and associates were incarcerated by the GoE in 2001 and again in 2002 for, among other things, being found guilty by a military court of receiving foreign funds without declaring them and bringing Egypt into disrepute. Ibrahim was finally released in March 2003 after two state security court trials that had sentenced him each time to seven years in prison. His release followed an appeal to the Court of Cassation that acquitted all defendants in the case except one.[12] The GoE does not encourage any political or associational group activity because it fears that it will generate opposition to the regime even if the activity is around issues which might be seen as marginal to local political reform.[13] Donors refuse to live up to their own rhetoric of the importance of civil society for political liberalization because they are driven by the importance of Egyptian political stability and regional influence – although this latter has diminished significantly.

The only formal policy instrument that is in place by the GoE is *Sharouk*. This was an initiative for integrated rural development driven by the United Nations Development Programme (UNDP) and early donor interest regarding rural representation. Sharouk was intended to reduce the development divide between town and country. Launched in 1994, its aims and objectives were to incorporate service provision for all Egyptian villages by 2002. It was to function until 2017 and promote infrastructural development, human resource development, economic and institutional development. The programme's greatest achievements have been limited improvements in rural services like roads and drainage but the programme has also called for 'popular participation' and 'providing democratic channels for the participation of the rural population in the decision making process' (Institute of National Planning, 1996: 85). These are nowhere evident. Moreover the programme relies heavily on GoE financial support which is not forthcoming as rural development is not a policy commitment.[14]

In addition to Sharouk as a vehicle for improving local governance, USAID has identified another formal activity, namely water-user associations (WUAs) for enhancing local decision-making structures. WUAs began in the mid-1990s. They were formed to improve water delivery into *mesqas*; to operate and maintain improved *mesqas* and improve on farm water-user efficiency. USAID estimate that by 1999 there were 2900 registered WUAs (USAID, 1999c: 5).

USAID is very optimistic about the role of WUAs. It has been argued that they have achieved greater 'equity in the distribution of irrigation water while reducing the cost of irrigation' and these improvements have extended to increasing crop productivity. USAID note that 'the establishment of water-user associations offer a success story for an institutional arrangement that can contend with the problem of using common property: irrigation water' (USAID, 1999c: 5). Yet the optimistic write-up about WUAs skates over many issues. It skates over the mechanisms that ensure local dignitaries maintain a presence in determining WUA policies and strategies for irrigation, and it certainly skates over a gender bias against women whose irrigation needs are often subordinated to male interests. The way in which gender issues are obscured by institutional structures has been highlighted in several recent reports (Ibrahim, 1998).

In appraising several irrigation and WUA schemes Somaya Ibrahim has noted the ways in which gender issues have been ignored and the way in which WUAs operate to sustain the marginalization of women in rural decision-making structures. This is not to downplay women's struggles to maintain a voice within WUAs and in household structures across a range of activities including, but also going beyond, irrigation matters. It is instead to note that 'All members of the water associations are men. This male domination reflects the assumption that irrigation tasks in general and water management specifically is a male affair' (Ibrahim, 1998: 4).

Ibrahim found that stereotypes regarding so-called women's work and status informed the ways in which WUAs operated. For example, despite the fact that she examined many de facto and de jure women-headed households, it was assumed women did not irrigate. There was thus little communication between women and men over issues of irrigation. Women were not, in her Minia case study, consulted by WUAs regarding the selection of WUA board members; they did not know what the terms of reference were of office holders, and did not have a voice in policy relating to the distribution of water. All board members were men and this division over the administration of irrigation was mirrored in the distinction made by men and women in terms of the problems that they identified for agriculture. Men identified problems of the efficiency of machinery, and prices of irrigation, while women noted issues of water shortage because of competition with male users and night irrigation slots. As Ibrahim (1998: 4) notes, 'Needless to say it is the male farmers who can better defend their interests and get their turns at appropriate times during the day.' It seems that, while WUAs have been an initiative that has accompanied rural market liberalization, they have acted to promote the interests of many existing village officeholders, dignitaries and landowners. Opportunities for voicing out concerns of a broader range of rural social and class forces, women and near landless have not improved.

Community Development Associations (CDAs)

There is one other recent development where an existing formal structure has been used to try and promote improved rural governance. This has been with the development agency CARE – Egypt's work with CDAs. CDAs are one of two types of NGO that the GoE allows to register with MISA. There has been much debate about these organizations, their effectiveness, independence and outreach (Abdel Rahman, 2001; Saad, n.d.). The criticism of CDAs is that they lack autonomy and serve only the interests of the state. CDAs often deliver welfare benefits that the state should be delivering and thus they subsidize government expenditure and generate little improved governance because of tight MISA control. A recent example, however, of an attempt to empower CDAs with opportunity to deliver resources *and* improve governance is highlighted in a development initiative.

CARE Egypt, together with the Swiss Development Fund, initiated in 2000 a project for the Capability Enhancement through Citizen Action (CAP) (CARE, 2000). This project is intended to 'improve the quality of life including participation in civic affairs of 32,500 vulnerable households in rural communities of seven governorates of middle and Upper Egypt by 2003' (CARE, 2000: 2). While the strategy of a donor to improve local livelihoods is not new, CARE's project concern with enhancing community participation does seem important. CARE's work is not directly related to changes in land tenure and market liberalization, although clearly the burden of helping to improve rural livelihoods during economic reform has become a greater challenge: they report an increase in the needs of respondents who recently lost land. CARE's aim is to ensure 130 community-based NGOs in seven governorates 'will be better able to represent and involve their constituencies in community affairs and decision making processes' (CARE, 2000: 3).

The innovation in CARE's work seems to be the recognition that there might be some space for CDAs, often where they have lain dormant, to become vehicles for greater rural decision-making. While CDAs may have been 'on the books' since the 1960s, they often have been empty shells. Alternatively they may have had their local administration dominated by landowners, rural elites and village sheikhs, who act as local policemen and informers to government of any potential local unrest. CARE has tried to combine an improved efficiency of CDAs, a reorganization of administration and decision-making, with the involvement of the CDA in promoting a household livelihood/security framework for allocating donor resources.

One of the first questions aimed at the CDAs by CARE has been: 'If you want to help the poor are you willing to pay for change?' CARE has promoted, in effect, a rights-based approach to their work, seeking to move away from simple philanthropy. The problem that CARE admits to with this approach, however, is that for the livelihoods strategy to be effective it is necessary for issues of local social differentiation and conflict to be recognized by CDAs (interview, July 2001). Ultimately, moreover, the CDAs must admit members of the disadvantaged groups in society to become officeholders in the CDA. This involves the rich and powerful relinquishing authority and control of the CDAs, including headmen or *umdas*, who were appointed by the government to keep control and act as local intelligence for possible sources of village conflict.

CARE's work is still in its early stages. It highlights the possibility of concentrating on existing structures within civil society and the need to revitalize them. Working with local and central government personnel and institutions, CARE has operated fully within the restrictive practices of the Egyptian state and persuaded bureaucrats and villages alike of the benefits that might accrue from more open and accessible rural decision-making structures of the CDA. Reinvigorating CDAs is intended to initiate a round of debate about local democracy and greater participation for landless and smallholders. The intention is to help the reactivation of CDAs by marginalizing the older generation of officeholders, facilitating greater opportunity for younger elements and the poor. It seems that CARE is more optimistic about the outcome of this work in the newer CDAs and where landless and day labourers can more effectively express their concerns. It seems, too, that returning unemployed university graduates or technical graduates to the countryside from their studies in urban areas might add to the development of a movement that demands local change, greater representation and the marginalization of an older generation of officeholders. It is too soon to see how sustainable this strategy will be and, while individual CARE workers and others linked to the attempt to empower CDAs may be optimistic about their liberalizing potential, it is important to note that CARE works fully with central and local government agencies. This ensures CARE's opportunity to deliver its declared aims and it legitimates the donors' strategy. In so doing, it might also, therefore, be a way for the strategy itself to be used by the Egyptian state to promote a new regulation of hegemony. Yet as in most of these processes of negotiation between donors, states and social forces, there is a dialectic of struggle at work. This means that there is always a possibility that while the forces of the state are dominant they are not immune from social and class pressure to change or develop conditions for rural civil society. At the turn of the twenty-first century, however, there is little indication that the struggles between these competing forces are being resolved in favour of smallholders or the rural poor.

Informal rural civil society

Egypt does not have a rural civil society in the sense of one that is autonomous and active, free and able to organize and publicize, as well as politicize, agendas for action to redress grievances, government neglect and facilitate associational life. What has taken place since 1997, when the Land Act was fully implemented and the consequences of economic reform for increasing rural poverty intensified, is more active use of informal, usually family support mechanisms, to provide a safety net against market failure. There was a tendency in 1997 to see the absence of mass rural revolt against landlords as another example of farmer quietude. Yet there were bloody confrontations, usually in the governorates like Daqahliya where there were large landholdings, and landowners were impatient to test the legality of Law 96. In el Zeni in Dekerniss in Daqahliya, a landlord sold 82 feddans that had been rented to 126 tenants and he needed the help of security forces to ensure new landowners could take possession of the tenants' land. Protesting villagers were tear-gassed, 90 arrested and seven imprisoned for 45 days more than 120 kilometres from their village.

It seemed inevitable that a government that had used the threat from Islamists as a reason to maintain the state of emergency and deploy the military now blamed outside forces for the dissent that emerged (*Al Ahram Weekly*, 10–16 July 1997). Yet the favoured view of authoritarian regimes (and liberal democratic ones too) of blaming dissent with unpopular legislation on terrorist activity rather than a legitimate criticism of government policy does not withstand scrutiny. The extent of continued rural unrest caused by disputes over land is indicated in Table 6.1 above. It is now important to try and indicate a way of understanding it.

One fruitful attempt to understand opposition to state and dominant class action in Egypt and elsewhere in the Middle East has been offered by Asef Bayet. He has used a notion of 'quiet encroachment of the ordinary'.

> This refers to non-collective direct actions of individuals and families to acquire basic necessities (land, shelter, urban collective consumption, informal jobs, business opportunities) in a quiet, unassuming fashion. (Bayat, 2000: iv)

Bayat formulated the idea of quiet encroachment (1997, 1998, 2002) while discussing essentially urban unrest. For him, it is:

> qualitatively different from defensive measures or coping mechanisms ... It represents a silent, protracted, pervasive advancement of ordinary people – through open-ended and fleeting struggles without clear leaderships, ideology or structured organisation – on the propertied and powerful in order to survive. (Bayat, 1997: 5)

One of the reasons Bayat gives for this type of struggle is the outcome of the Nasserist social contract with the working class and peasantry. Effectively, as I indicated earlier, the relationship Nasser established in the 1950s, and which has had the most serious consequences for Egypt's political history since, was the social contract: the state provided basic services while the subordinate classes agreed to political passivity. The peasantry certainly did not agree to passivity, however. There are many cases of political opposition and violent antagonism being expressed by the *fellahin* to landlords and the state.[15] Yet the legacy for Bayat is that political struggles have often taken the form of individualistic solutions to problems instead of class or group solidarities being the major vehicle for opposition.

Bayat has also noted that in the 1990s, while there has been opposition to the austerity packages of the IFIs, and these have been often opposed by trade unions, these bodies represent only a small proportion of the workforce. The majority of workers toil in small-scale informal locations in the urban economy and it is therefore in these areas, among neighbourhoods and within communities, that Bayat has argued collective action might find support and opportunities for success. This may well be a useful model to examine in relation to recent rural struggles over land access, access more generally to resources as well as outputs and market power. Yet more research is needed to demonstrate that farmers are doing anything more than adopting coping strategies in the face of worsening hardship rather than taking initiative to recover lost ground.

Since October 1997 tenants have experienced a dramatic increase in the level of poverty resulting from changed lifestyles accompanying expulsion from the land. There has been an increase in rural debt, dispossession and enforced proletarianization – the search for wage employment often in harsh labour regimes that are reminiscent of indentured and contract labour. This has had a particular impact on child labour. Children have been removed from school as families recently dispossessed try and compensate for loss of agricultural income by reducing costs of schooling.

Significantly there has been an increase in rural *insecurity*. Evidence suggests at best a very uneven level of information reached tenant farmers regarding implementation of Law 96. Many respondents in Giza and Daqahliya either simply did not know about Law 96, or had not been informed regarding the content of the new legislation and how it would impact on tenants. There had been scant regard paid by government to farmer access to information, and formal networks like cooperatives, local and village councils were unclear both about the law and its consequences especially about the legal rights of tenants to appeal non-renewal of contracts. Tenants had not been informed about the legislation in a systematic way. There had not been the provision of information either by central government or governorate authorities regarding Law 96 and many tenants only knew about the dramatic implication of the law on 1 October 1997 when landlords refused to renew rental contracts.

One group of tenants that have especially suffered from a decline in their livelihoods are women who headed households and worked the tenancies registered in their late husbands' names. These women were very commonly expelled from the land in October 1997. They could either not pay the new higher rents or suffered the prejudice of landlords who did not want to renew to women. Respondents in this category visited over a twenty-month period, 1999–2001, confirm a pattern of greater reliance upon family and neighbours for accessing resources and defending livelihoods. While they reported many tensions within the village from Law 96 in villages in Giza and Daqahliya, it also seems that the lines of cleavage within the community may have reinforced family and kinship bonds while also stretching these to the limit in their uneven delivery of material assistance.

While respondents had not engaged in direct opposition to the Land Act or in trying to establish a formal organization to oppose the Act's implementation, they had promoted a range of actions to defend their original position. Many women had tried to use networks of family and kin to put pressure on landlords not to dispossess them, although this did not appear successful. The women had experienced a dramatic loss of income after 1997. One respondent who previously had a net income of LE 6965 was reduced to accepting infrequent loans from relatives of LE 25–50, handouts from an Islamic charity and the removal of her children from school to work in neighbouring fields. Another respondent, who had in 1999 managed to keep her son in school, had by autumn 2000 removed him to work as a carpenter. He regularly reminded her of the difficult and hard life that at fourteen he was forced to begin and he blamed her for it. And while she had dreams that one day he would have a workshop of his own to sustain the family, she had herself become a seasonal agricultural labourer, picking vegetables when there was enough demand. Other respondents became dependent upon charity, help from family and child labour.

Respondents had also sold jewellery to raise cash for daily living expenses; one to also pay for the costs of her daughter's wedding and two had managed to eke out a living based on savings from livestock sales in October 1997, when they lost land. Yet, by 2001, these savings were exhausted.

For women respondents in Giza and Daqahliya, the dependence upon family for loans, and opportunity to visit for weekend respite, thereby lessening weekly expenditure, were central to coping with economic difficulty. It nevertheless remained extremely difficult for respondents to transform increased reliance upon family and friends into a strategy to oppose the reasons for their new poverty. It was also not always possible to see that elements of a strategy for 'quiet encroachment of the ordinary', conflicts over land and access to rural resources, were transforming coping mechanisms into a pro-active strategy against those that were responsible for accelerated rural poverty.

Conclusion

Egypt does not have a healthy civil society. Attempts to enliven it beyond the watchful eyes of the state and its cronies spread throughout the country in the governorates have not been successful. This is not surprising, given the historical past. It is also the case that because associational life itself can so easily be hijacked by both governments and donors, perhaps the absence of civil society in the way it is most talked about should not be too loudly lamented. But civil society is more than just associational life. It involves the struggles within the state and beyond it that embody the many ways in which the dominant bloc of classes try to ensure the reproduction of its dominance. In this, the GoE has been very successful. For while there might occasionally be signs of dissatisfaction with economic reform, market liberalization and broader regional issues, demonstrations, wildcat strikes and even the quiet encroachment of the ordinary, nowhere have these been able to come close to a counter-hegemonic political movement.

It remains remarkable that criticism of Egypt's agricultural strategy including Law 96 has been limp, ineffectual and unfocused. Some university academics and departments have reported on the devastating impact of increased poverty linked with economic reform, but internal security pounces on any attempt to hold meetings with affected farmers or the mobilization of peaceful dissent. The agricultural cooperatives have been devastated, rural trade unions are non-existent and agricultural research centres keen to accrue donor resources have complied readily with the message of market prudence and economic liberalization.

One difficulty in mobilizing an academic and intellectual opposition to agricultural reforms has been the problem of making a case for the necessity of reform while not capitulating to the international financial bodies and GoE agenda. The 'debate' about market liberalization has crudely and naively parroted the mantra that the Nasserist 'socialist' period was the cause of Egypt's economic crisis of the 1970s and 1980s and the only alternative was state retrenchment and economic liberalization. This dominant discourse is a disservice to the credibility of Egyptian intellectual life and it has promoted a neglect of debating the crises of rural livelihoods. For where academics and party political leaders have sought to use the parliament or newspapers to criticize the GoE, it has invariably been a critique of the impact of reform on Egypt's macro economy, or on its urban landscape and social forces. Egypt's *fellahin* remain the government's forgotten souls. They do speak out, however, even if it tends mostly to be to each other with little impact on aloof urban elites. There is little evidence that Egypt's market reforms are promoting new configurations in rural civil society that will in the short term generate political mobilization capable of shaking government from its complacency.

Notes

1. I am grateful to Sarah Bracking, Asef Bayat and Kléber Ghimire for comments on an earlier draft of this paper. I gratefully acknowledge research support from the Nuffield Foundation that helped facilitate some of the data collection. I am, however, alone responsible for the contents of what follows.
2. Extensive media censorship seems at odds with President Mubarak's repeated observation that he is concerned to protect the 'freedom of the press', although these comments are usually hedged by his view that 'such freedom is governed by national conscience' – whatever that is. See *Cairo Press Review*, 17 July 2001: 15.
3. This formulation of 'processes' is not meant to relegate any concrete 'spatial location' for civil society. Gramsci was clear, using the evocative language of trenches, ditches and fortifications around the state, that consent was manufactured defusing any raw class relations of exploitation within and beyond the institutions of the state. Civil society thus becomes, among other things, the arena(s) in which culture, structures of power and creation of social order are reproduced and any possible class-based identity is undermined. We will see below how, on the one hand, the development of a more robust structure for CDAs is a tremendous achievement to help promote greater democratization and openness for rural decision-making. Yet CDAs also potentially serve to continue to fragment class-based opposition to government-imposed actions.
4. USAID and MALR, 1999c.
5. The following section draws on Ray Bush, 'Land reform and counter revolution', in Bush (2002).
6. The detailed critique of the strategy has been dealt with elsewhere (Bush, 1999; Mitchell, 1998, 1999).
7. Mitchell is led to the conclusion that 'the impact of the free-market reforms may have been greater on the statistics published by the state than on what farmers actually grow' (Mitchell, 1998: 23).
8. See Saad (1999, 2002) for detailed discussions of the way in which the tenancy bill became law and the way in which farmers, in general, and tenant farmers, in particular, were depicted by the state-controlled media.
9. This was not universally accepted, however. While the Grand Sheikh of Al Azhar supported the restoration of full property rights to the landed class, the radical Gamaa al Islamia criticized any legislation that further impoverished the poor.
10. Data for January to May 1997 indicates 5 deaths, 86 injuries and 167 arrests. Private communication with the Land Center for Human Rights, Cairo.

11. For example, descendants of Amin Wali in Fayoum tried to regain land that had been confiscated from the family during Nasser's land reforms.
12. A six-month suspended sentence was imposed on a defendant for forging an official stamp.
13. This is why the GoE is reluctant to support Egyptian Palestinian solidarity groups that were frustrated from transporting aid to Gaza in 2001 and which led to disturbances en route in el Arish. Such repression backfires on the regime but the strength of security forces seems immeasurable. Hence, Islamist students at Al Azhar, protesting in 2000 about Ministry of Culture-supported publications that were deemed by the students rhetorically to bring Islam into disrepute, might be more accurately seen to have been demonstrations about the absence of opportunities to legitimately promote student concerns with youth unemployment and to have organizations that could promote student politics.
14. While the erstwhile Prime Minister Kamal Al-Ganzouri did seem sensitive to the need for rural development, renaming the Ministry of Local Administration in 1997 the Ministry of Rural Development, noting 'The new ministry aims to develop the rural areas which constitute a major and important sector in the structure of the Egyptian society', there was no accompanying indication of the strategy or extra resources that would be used to promote effective rural development. See *Al Ahram Weekly*, 10–16 July 1997.
15. The bloody episode at Khamsheesh is one illustration. See Brown (1990).

References

Abdel Rahman, M. (2001) *State Civil Society Relations: the Politics of Egyptian NGOs* (unpublished PhD Thesis). The Hague: Institute of Social Studies.

Adams, Martin (2000) *Breaking Ground: Development Aid for Land Reform*. London: Overseas Development Institute.

Allen, Chris (1997) 'Who needs civil society', *Review of African Political Economy*, Vol. 24, No. 73, pp. 329–37.

Bangura, Yusuf (1999) *New Direction in State Reform: Implications for Civil Society in Africa*. UNRISD Discussion Paper No. 113, September. Geneva: United Nations Research Institute for Social Development.

Bayat, Asef (1997) 'Cairo's poor: dilemmas of survival and solidarity', *Middle East Report*, No. 202, Spring.

Bayat, Asef (1998) *Street Politics: Poor People's Movements in Iran*. Cairo: American University Press.

Bayat, Asef (2000) *Social Movements, Activism and Social Development in the Middle East*. UNRISD Programme Paper on Civil Society and Social Movements, PP CSSM 3. Geneva: United Nations Research Institute for Social Development.

Bayat, Asef (2002) 'Activism and social development in the Middle East', *International Journal of Middle East Studies*, No. 1, Winter, pp. 1–28.

Beetham, David (2000) *Debating the Universality of Human Rights*. Seminar Presentation to the Centre for Development Studies and Centre for Democratization, University of Leeds.

Brown, Nathan (1990) *Peasant Politics in Modern Egypt: the Struggle against the State*. New Haven and London: Yale University Press.

Bush, Ray (1999) *Economic Crisis and the Politics of Reform in Egypt*. Boulder, CO and Oxford: Westview Press.

Bush, Ray (ed.) (2002) *Counter Revolution in Egypt's Countryside: Land and Farmers in the Era of Economic Reform*. London: Zed Books.

Cairo Press Review, 17 July 2001.

Cairo Times, 19–25 July 2001.

CARE Egypt (2000) *Capability Enhancement through Citizen Action (CAP) Project, Amendment of CAP Project Grant Agreement (ESDF 015) in View of Results of Pilot Phase Assessment (July 1999–June 2000)* (mimeo). Final Draft, 25 October. Cairo.

Clark, J. (1991) *Democratizing Development: the Role of the Voluntary Organizations*. London: Earthscan.

Deininger, K. and H. Binswanger (1999) 'The evolution of the World Bank's land policy: principles, experience, and future challenges', *The World Bank Research Observer*, Vol. 14, No. 2, August, pp. 247–76.

Department for International Development (DFID) (2000) *Eliminating World Poverty: Making Globalisation Work for the Poor*. London: HMSO.

El-Ghonemy, M. R. (1993) 'Food security and rural development in North Africa', *Middle Eastern Studies*, Vol. 29, No. 3, July, pp. 445–66.

El-Ghonemy, M. R. (1999) 'Recent changes in agrarian reform and rural development strategies in the Near East', *Land Reform*, Vols 1–2, pp. 9–20.

Faris, M. A. and M. H. Khan (eds) (1993) *Sustainable Agriculture in Egypt*. Boulder, CO and London: Lynne Rienner.

Fergany, Nader (2002) 'Poverty and unemployment in rural Egypt', in Ray Bush (ed.), *Counter Revolution in Egypt's Countryside: Land and Farmers in the Era of Economic Reform*. London: Zed Press.

Fletcher, Lehmann B. (ed.) (1996) *Egypt's Agriculture in a Reform Era*. Ames: Iowa State University Press.

Fowler, A. (1991) 'The role of NGOs in changing state–society relations: perspectives from Eastern and Southern Africa', *Development Policy Review*, Vol. 9, No. 1, pp. 53–84.

Frischtak, Leila and Izak Atiyas (eds) (1996) *Governance, Leadership, and Communication: Building Constituencies for Economic Reform*. Private Sector Development Department. Washington, DC: World Bank.

Gramsci, Antonio (1976) *Selections from the Prison Notebooks*. Quinton Hoare and Geoffrey Nowell Smith (eds). London: Lawrence and Wishart.

Hadenius, A. and F. Uggla (1996) 'Making civil society work, promoting democratic development: what can states and donors do?', *World Development*, Vol. 24, No. 10.

Ibrahim, Saad Eddin (1995) 'Civil society and prospects for democratisation in the Arab world', in A. R. Norton (ed.), *Civil Society in the Middle East*. Leiden: E. J. Brill.

Ibrahim, Soumaya (1998) *Discussion and Reflections about Gender Roles and Responsibilities in Irrigation Activities and Water Resource Management* (mimeo). Cairo: Three Parts.

Institute of National Planning (1996) *Egypt: Human Development Report*. Cairo: Institute of National Planning, Government of Egypt.

Kandil, Amani (1994) 'Socioeconomic policies and interest groups in Egypt', in A. Öncü, Ç. Keyder, K. Çaglas and S. E. Ibrahim (eds), *Developmentalism and Beyond: Society and Politics in Egypt and Turkey*. Cairo: American University in Cairo Press.

Keane, J. (1988) *Civil Society and the State: New European Perspectives*. London: Verso.

Khedr, H., R. Ehrich and L. B. Fletcher (1996) 'Nature, rationale and accomplishments of the agricultural policy reforms, 1987–1994', in L. B. Fletcher (ed.), *Egypt's Agriculture in a Reform Era*. Ames: Iowa State University Press.

Kienle, Eberhard (2001) *A Grand Delusion: Democracy and Economic Reform in Egypt*. London: I. B. Tauris.

Land Centre for Human Rights, Cairo (2002) 'Farmer struggles against Law 96 of 1992', in Ray Bush (ed.), *Counter Revolution in Egypt's Countryside: Land and Farmers in the Era of Economic Reform*. London: Zed Books.

Marcussen, H. S. (1996) 'NGOs, the state and civil society', *Review of African Political Economy*, Vol. 23, No. 69, September, pp. 405–23.

Mitchell, T. (1998) 'The market's place', in Nicholas Hopkins and Kirsten Westergaard (eds), *Directions of Change in Rural Egypt*. Cairo: American University in Cairo Press.

Mitchell, T. (1999) 'No factories, no problems: the logic of neo-liberalism in Egypt', *Review of African Political Economy*, Vol. 26, No. 82, December, pp. 455–68.

Powell, Mike and David Seddon (1997) 'NGOs and the development industry', *Review of African Political Economy*, Vol. 24, No. 71, pp. 3–10.

Richards, Alan and John Waterbury (1990) *A Political Economy of the Middle East: State, Class and Economic Development*. Boulder, CO: Westview Press.

Saad, R. (n.d.) *Community and Community Development in Egypt* (mimeo). Social Research Center. Cairo: American University in Cairo.

Saad, R. (1999) 'State, landlord, parliament and peasant: the story of the 1992 tenancy law in Egypt', in Alan Bowman and Eugene Rogan (eds), *Agriculture in Egypt from Pharaonic to Modern Times*. Oxford: Oxford University Press.

Saad, R. (2002) 'Egyptian politics and the tenancy law', in Ray Bush (ed.), *Counter Revolution in Egypt's Countryside: Land and Farmers in the Era of Economic Reform*. London: Zed Press.

Showstack Sassoon, Anne (1978) 'Hegemony and political intervention', in Sally Hibbin (ed.), *Politics, Ideology and the State*. London: Lawrence and Wishart.

Stewart, Sheelagh (1997) 'Happy ever after in the marketplace: non-government organizations and uncivil society', *Review of African Political Economy*, Vol. 24, No. 71, March.

Toulmin, Camilla and Julian Quan (eds) (2000) *Evolving Land Rights, Policy and Tenure in Africa*. London: Department for International Development, IIED and Natural Resources Institute.

United States Agency for International Development (USAID) and Government of Egypt (1995) *The Egyptian Agricultural Policy Reforms: an Overview* (mimeo). Paper presented at the Agricultural Policy Conference, Taking Stock, Eight Years of Egyptian Agricultural Policy Reforms, 26–28 March.

United States Agency for International Development (USAID) and Ministry of Agriculture and Land Reclamation (MALR) (1998a) *Horticultural Sub-Sector Map*, Report No. 39, USAID Agricultural Policy Reform Program, Reform Design and Implementation, Cairo, June.

United States Agency for International Development (USAID) and Ministry of Agriculture and Land Reclamation (MALR) (1998b) *USAID/Egypt Agriculture*. http://www.info.usaid.gov/eg/econ.htm.

United States Agency for International Development (USAID) (1999a) *Agriculture – Vision for 2003*, RDI Policy Brief, No. 12, November.

United States Agency for International Development (USAID) and Ministry of Agriculture and Land Reclamation (MALR) (1999b) *Land Tenure Study Phase II*, APRP/RDI Unit, Cairo, March.

United States Agency for International Development (USAID) and Ministry of Agriculture and Land Reclamation (MALR) (1999c) *The Impact of Liberalization and Role of Rural Organizations: Policy Issues*, APRP/RDI Report No. 78, October.

United States Agency for International Development (USAID) (2000) *Congressional Presentation, Financial Year 2000*. http://www.usaid.gov/pubs/cp2000/ane/egypt. html, accessed on 6 June 2001.

United States Agency for International Development (USAID) (2001) *PVO Development in Egypt*. http://www.usaid.gov/regions/ane/newpages/perspectives/egypt/egpvo. htm, accessed on 14 June 2001.

Waterbury, John (1983) *The Egypt of Nasser and Sadat: the Political Economy of Two Regimes*. Princeton: Princeton University Press.

White, Gordon (1996) 'Civil society, democratization and development', in Robin Luckham and Gordon White (eds), *Democratization in the South: the Jagged Wave*. Manchester and New York: Manchester University Press.

World Bank (2000a) *Can Africa Claim the 21st Century?* Washington, DC: World Bank.

World Bank (2000b) *Towards Agricultural Competitiveness in the 21st Century, Egypt Agricultural Export-Oriented Strategy* (mimeo). Cairo, July.

7

The Farmers' Movement and the Market Question in Senegal[1]

Nora McKeon

> We grow lots of groundnuts, but little millet, niebe and manioc, which used to nourish us better. We sell groundnuts to have money, but we never have enough. We are slaves of money and the outside world. Everyone fends for themselves. The head of the family doesn't dare open his mouth. (ENDA, 1985: 50)

The impact of the introduction of monetarized markets on West African societies in the nineteenth and twentieth centuries was inestimable, and the relation of small farmers to markets has remained an important factor in the political economy of these still dominantly rural countries. It has also continued to be a sizeable bone of contention in the revindications of rural protest movements, although the 'market question' cannot be examined in isolation from other aspects of agricultural and economic policy.

This chapter will examine the case of Senegal, the West African country in which the farmers' movement has made the most progress in constructing an articulate and effective platform bringing the concerns of rural people to bear on policy decisions. The first section will briefly review the history of the movement in Senegal and the policy context within which it has operated. It will trace the evolution of farmer organizations' engagement with the state and with the process of liberalization of the economy. The second section will focus more closely on how the movement has dealt with the market question and what results it has obtained. The final section will attempt an assessment of the platform's achievements and identify some open questions and challenges facing the farmers' movement today.

Peasants, state and economy in Senegal

The silent majority takes the floor

From dusk to dawn of a night in January 1993 just a few weeks before vociferously contested national elections were to take place, towns and villages throughout Senegal were papered with posters announcing a national forum on 'What Future for Senegal's Peasants?' (*Quel avenir pour les paysans du Sénégal?*), a politically delicate topic since 70 per cent of the electorate were rural dwellers drawing their livelihoods from agriculture. Much to the surprise of the president's office, which had ignored the organizers' invitations for weeks, the poster asserted that the president himself would open the forum. When the farmers' federation responsible for the event was queried on the phone, they replied by taking rhetoric at face value and turning it to their advantage, a twist that has come to characterize them: 'We represent the majority of the Senegalese people. It would be inappropriate for us to meet in the absence of the Father of the Republic.'

The forum was opened by the prime minister on 18 January 1993, at the president's instructions. It sparked the creation of a unified platform of rural federations that came to impose itself, in the space of a few years, as an unavoidable interlocutor of government and a major donor in policy and programme negotiations. In the ten years since its establishment the Comité national de concertation des ruraux (CNCR) had accumulated a remarkable list of accomplishments. It had bound a disparate series of rural people's federations into a national platform. It had overcome a century of oblivion and won recognition for peasant farmers by the government and development partners, and a place at the negotiating table. It had used this position to achieve a significant impact on policies and programmes affecting rural development. In a political context marked by the rule of a single party, it had weathered the 'alternance'[2] and demonstrated that its role was an institutional one, not dependent on party relations. It had spearheaded the construction of a regional peasant movement and made its presence felt in key global forums. This is not to say, of course, that the record was unmitigatedly positive, as the CNCR itself pointed out in an evaluation it commissioned in 2000 (see CNCR, 2000). But it was an impressive record and possibly unique in sub-Saharan Africa. How had it come about?

Colonial and post-colonial roots

Any understanding of peasant associations in Senegal must start from the broader colonial and post-colonial political economy. This is not the place to rehearse the pre-capitalist character of pre-colonial Senegal, but a brief account of the transformative effect of the French colonial project is indispensable to situate the emergence of peasant associations in the late twentieth century. The impact of colonialism on West African peasant societies, in its simplest terms, was to usurp these societies' control of their environment and their economy and, more intimately, to transform the very sense of their own identity (see, for example, Copans, 1975; Dupriez, 1980; Franke and Chasin, 1980; Watts, 1983). Unlike the transition from an agrarian to an industrial society in the West, the deep changes which took place in Africa were not the product of an internal dynamic of capitalist accumulation. The colonial state and merchants' capital combined to expand the class prerogatives of some local ruling elites, and to deepen commodification in a way that extracted peasant surplus through complex mercantile systems, often imbricated with religious networks.

Cash cropping of groundnuts was introduced into Senegal in 1841. Groundnut production rose from 45 000 tons in 1884–5 to 600 000 tons in 1936–7 (Franke and Chasin, 1980: 76). The advent of cash cropping disrupted both the ecological and the socioeconomic equilibrium of West Africa. Monoculture consumed soil fertility and provoked erosion of the fields, previously protected by traditional practices like inter-cropping and minimum tillage, which European agronomists condemned at the time as messy, lazy and primitive. The pressure of cash cropping, coupled with population increase, provoked a curtailing of fallow periods and subverted the complementarity of cultivation and livestock.

Monetarized markets were at the very heart of the dispossession operated by the colonial experience. In fact, the major inducement brandished by colonial administrations to convince or coerce farmers to grow cash crops was the introduction of taxation and monetarization. The monetary demand exercised on peasant producers in the form of taxes and the prices charged for manufactured goods and staples outweighed the monetary value of their agricultural produce,[3] and the prices they received were subject to unpredictable fluctuations. Precariousness had previously been a function of natural hazards which farmers could foresee to a large degree, and against which they had developed an arsenal of defence. Now it depended on the interests of the mother countries and on market mechanisms which totally escaped their ability to strategize.

The unequal exchange and the advance credit system practised by merchants and moneylenders provoked a no-exit spiral of debt in rural areas, prevented farmers from accumulating capital to invest in increasing productivity and exploded the extended family unit. The family head found it increasingly difficult to fulfil his responsibilities towards the members of his entourage and the depleted collective grain reserves no longer sufficed to meet collective needs. The position of women deteriorated. Their workload was intensified, while the cash revenues passed into the hands of the men, introducing a dualism between 'modern' cash and 'invisible' domestic subsistence sectors that persists today. Colonialism and the cash nexus also generated new socioeconomic inequalities that were no longer subject to control by stable norms and values, and a class of administrators who owed their position to the favour they culled with foreigners rather than the consensus of their people. Even when colonial administrators were obliged to recognize the multiplication of food shortages and famines, their reaction was not to buttress local coping mechanisms but to introduce 'effective modern' grain stores (Copans, 1975: 12–13) and to organize the rural population into 'Sociétés indigènes de prévoyance' highly dependent on the administrative authorities.

In a very pervasive way, the colonial experience discredited African peoples' knowledge, skill, culture and values, particularly insofar as economic development was concerned. As a workshop on 'Tradition and Modernism' which brought together some of the most prestigious West African intellectuals shortly after independence concluded: 'We have tried objectively to see what our traditional values, as we call them, could contribute to our economic advancement. Not much, to tell the truth. It is from Europe that we have borrowed those values that can lead to progress' (Rencontres internationales de Bouaké, 1965).

The wave of independence that swept across the African continent in the early 1960s brought hope that the end of colonialism would signal significant changes in the conditions of Africans. In practice, however, the Senegalese state – like others on the continent – was weak and more attentive to the threat of uprisings by discontented urban dwellers than to the interests of a dispersed rural population. Producer prices were kept low to hold food costs down in the cities, while the state continued to siphon off profits from the rural sector through mechanisms such as marketing boards. The towering Marketing Board building in Abidjan, whose elevators shoot officials up to their comfortable twentieth floor offices – when the electricity is functioning – is a symbolic monument to the way in which West African peasants have funded a style of development whose fruits they are the last to taste. The new states' margin of manoeuvre to create a policy environment conducive to healthy rural development was limited, in any event, by their dependence on the former mother countries for investments and subsidies to their running budget, their rapidly growing foreign debts, and the unfavourable and fluctuating terms of trade they encountered on the international market. The pressure to organize the rural world – in function of export crops – was strong.

The history of agricultural and rural development policy in Senegal since independence can be divided into two major blocks: two decades of determined but increasingly vacillating state interventionism followed by two decades of initially reluctant but increasingly thorough liberalization under the guidance of the International Monetary Fund (IMF) and the World Bank.[4] One of the first issues to which the newly independent government turned its attention was the organization of rural producers. Behind the agricultural cooperatives' decree of 1959 was the vision of a prosperous mechanized agriculture which would 'raise the productivity of the African peasant, liberating him from the bondage which is so out of place in the twentieth century' (Mamadou Dia, 1957, quoted in Lecomte, 2001). The 800 cooperatives established with the flourish of a pen – which the farmers were totally unprepared to manage – assumed responsibility for marketing the country's major cash crop. They were intended to replace one of the most visible signs of the colonial economy: the foreign traders who circulated throughout the countryside purchasing groundnuts and selling their merchandise to the villagers in return. The cooperatives were to be flanked by the Animation rurale service of the Promotion humaine, established at the same time, which was expected to promote 'the growth of an entire network of development cells destined to become the cadre of the local population's economic, social, cultural and political activity' (Ben Mady Cisse, quoted in Lecomte, 2001: 13). The Promotion humaine, however, was phased out following Prime Minister Mamadou Dia's ousting in 1962. Standing alone, the cooperatives functioned as a system imposed on rural producers rather than as an instrument of their self-expression. Managed by government technicians and largely controlled by local elites affiliated with the ruling party, they were hardly designed to foster participation and oversight by the rural producers who were obliged to be their members.[5]

In 1961 a comprehensive four-year development plan was presented for negotiation to Senegal's major partners – France and the European Union (EU) at the time. The donors, however, preferred to fund programmes aimed at promoting the production and marketing of single export crops through the establishment of specialized parastatal regional development structures: the Société nationale d'aménagement et d'exploitation des terres du delta du fleuve Sénégal et des vallées du fleuve Sénégal et de la Falème (SAED) for rice production in the Senegal River valley in the north, the Société d'aide technique et de coopération (SATEC), and then the Société du développement et de la vulgarisation agricole (SODEVA) in the 'groundnut basin' in the centre, the Société de développement des fibres textiles (SODEFITEX) for cotton in the east, the Société pour la mise en valeur de la Casamance (SOMIVAC) for the rice of the south. Whatever the crop, these societies shared a disregard for the polyvalent nature of peasant agriculture, for the socioeconomic logic of the extended family unit, for the knowledge and skills of the farmers, and for the impact of monoculture on the environment. They also shared an extension approach based on armies of *encadreurs* hired to convince or oblige farmers to adopt the 'modern' technical packages they recommended. The system was undergirded by the Office national de la commercialisation et de l'assistance au développement (ONCAD), which supervised the cooperatives, marketed the crops, and provided farmers with inputs and equipment on a credit basis (with subventions for fertilizer use in the groundnut basin): the Agricultural Programme (Programme agricole) on which Senegalese farmers came to depend.

The impact of the development approach that characterized this period has been described by the farmers' movement in the following terms: 'All told, the peasant didn't even need to think any more. The state took care of everything, convinced as it was that only a centralized state planning system could ensure the rapid development of the country' (FONGS, 1991: 2).

State-directed intervention did, indeed, succeed in disseminating the use of animal traction, and improved seed and fertilizers, resulting in gains in production and productivity. As elsewhere in sub-Saharan Africa, however, the underlying goal was the extraction of financial surplus through the pricing policy of the state marketing boards. The system was directed essentially to export crops. So far as the production and marketing of food crops was concerned, sectoral policies were designed not primarily to expand local coarse grain production but to capture a portion of it to meet urban consumption needs (Jayne et al., 1997: 3). The tendency of state food marketing structures in the Sahel to fix farmgate prices at a low level discouraged farmers from producing surpluses (Terpend, 1993: 45). Keeping the food prices low in urban areas was also behind the recourse to imported commodities (Bates, 1981), putting a spin on the vicious circle whereby African farmers have lost their natural markets to artificially cheap surplus production in the north.

The genesis of autonomous peasant associations

By the early 1970s the system was in crisis, provoked by a decline in export commodity prices on the world market, the weight of the state structures, the increasing indebtedness of the farmers, and the severe droughts that ravaged the Sahel in 1973–4. A quantitative drop in marketed production combined with a reduction in producer prices drove farmers' revenues down dramatically. The fall in prices of groundnuts, the primary source of agricultural monetary revenue, was caused by the termination of French subventions to groundnut prices following France's entry into the European Common Market, the general drop in oil prices on the international market due to the increased productivity of competing products like soja, and the escalating costs of intermediaries along the commodity chain (Duruflé, 1995: 77–8).

In this context autonomous peasant associations began to spring up in various regions of the country, as rural people broke with a habit of fatality to seek solutions to problems with which the all-provident state was impotent or unwilling to deal.[6] In some cases the initiative came from young people who had travelled outside of the village and returned home with ideas and energy. The membership was dominantly women and young men, the 'powerless' in the traditional structures, and the associations had to negotiate their space with the elders of the village, on the margins of the main agricultural activities of the family units. They also had to strike an uneasy peace with the local administrators, who saw them as subversive antagonists of the official cooperative structures. In some cases, the leaders of the associations could call on the support of political parties,[7] but such relations were not without their problematic aspects.

By 1974 the associations were exchanging visits and meeting among themselves. In 1976, at the initiative of a Senegalese NGO whose president, Diedhiou Famara, had been an official in the extension service, twelve associations formed a national federation, which obtained legal status in 1978 as the Fédération des ONG Sénégalaises (FONGS), a title imposed by the government to distinguish them from the official cooperatives.[8] Famara has described what laid behind this initiative in the following terms: 'I felt there was a threat to the peasant associations which were springing up throughout the rural areas.

The state could perfectly well play them off against each other, in the context of its policy of domestication of the rural world. So we engaged in a process of reflection to counteract these tendencies of the state' (Diedhiou, 1998: 64).[9] The federation's objectives were to reinforce solidarity among peasant associations; meet its members' training and communication needs; support their development initiatives; and serve as a facilitator between its members and the outside world (FONGS, 1991: 4–5). Support for productive and economic activities was not high on their agenda at that stage.

Where did the fledgling peasant movement obtain support in these early years? In most cases the individual groups received small amounts of assistance from European non-governmental and Church-linked organizations, whose presence in the Sahel was stimulated by the drought of 1973–4.[10] The most original and significant support mechanism was, without any doubt, the international NGO Six S,[11] established in 1977 with funding from several European NGOs and the Swiss Development Cooperation, which was designed specifically to support emerging village-based groups in West Africa and encourage them to federate.

Structural adjustment and the evolution of the FONGS

For practically a decade the FONGS limited itself to operating training and exchange programmes for its members. The onset of structural adjustment and state retrenchment, coupled with the drought of 1984–5, opened a new phase in its history.[12] By the end of the 1970s the government had been driven close to bankruptcy by the declining income from groundnut exports, the high costs of the agricultural support policy and the growing external debt burden. In 1979 the bankrupt ONCAD was abolished,[13] and in 1983 the government signed an adjustment credit with the IMF. The New Agricultural Policy (Nouvelle politique agricole – NPA) of 1984 obliged the state to withdraw from the interventionist role it had played heretofore. The parastatal regional development societies were to be dismantled, extension and other services reduced, prices liberalized, subsidies for input purchase reduced or eliminated, and credit reorganized and downscaled. Finally, peasant farmers were to be 'responsibilized' and their organizations – along with the private sector – were expected to take over the functions and services which the state was abandoning. One of the measures taken in the context of liberalization was the establishment of a new category of legally recognized organizations, the 'economic interest groups' (GIE) whereby as few as two individuals could obtain credit for a profit-making activity.[14] The stated objectives of the NPA were laudable: remunerative producer prices, reinforced producers' organizations, liberalization and rationalization of the commodity chains, and natural resource protection (Duruflé, 1995: 79). Prospects for their attainment, however, were less rosy, and in the meantime this profound change was experienced as a dramatic abandonment by the farmers, who had come to depend on the omnipresent state and the omni-comprehensive Agriculture Programme.

Market liberalization was at the heart of the Structural Adjustment Programmes (SAPs) promoted by the IMF, the World Bank and other major donors throughout sub-Saharan Africa from the mid-1980s on. The potential implications of major changes to marketing systems, however, were generally not considered in advance. Priority was given to 'getting the prices right' on the assumption that the private sector would have little difficulty in taking over crop marketing operations. Insufficient consideration was given to the fact that the parastatal marketing structures had also provided inputs and performed a quality control function. Reforms ignored the fact that the private sector in most countries was weak, poorly articulated, operating under a series of handicaps, and hardly likely to venture into remote areas of the country. Producers' organizations were vaguely expected to gear up to take on new responsibilities, but no accompanying measures were foreseen to facilitate this process.[15]

In reaction to this profoundly changed situation, the FONGS began to undertake more ambitious national activities that ventured into the economic domain, such as cereal banks, 'triangular' exchanges between village associations in areas of surplus and deficit production, and support to members to establish savings and credit programmes. In 1988, drawing on members' savings and support from northern partners,[16] it became a shareholder of the Caisse National de Crédit Agricole du Sénégal (CNCAS) which had been created under the New Agricultural Policy. In retrospect, the FONGS has attributed this intensification of initiatives to a series of factors. State retrenchment had created problems that no single association could handle on its own. The drought of 1984–5 had stimulated increased solidarity between associations in better- and worse-off areas. Northern NGOs were pressuring the FONGS to operate as an intermediary structure, processing the thousands of individual micro projects that were landing on donors' desks (FONGS, 1991: 5–6). The result was a rapid period of growth as the FONGS took on a series of functions for which it was not necessarily prepared and which escaped the control of its member associations. A 'crisis of confidence' broke out in 1989. It led the FONGS to engage in a self-evaluation which paid off in a strengthened and refocused organization. In 1991, at a 'Round Table between the FONGS and its Partners', key challenges facing the movement in a rapidly evolving environment were identified: mastering the economic sphere; access to land and protection of natural resources; the issue of power, both internal leadership and participation in the political life of the country; maintaining social and cultural values and developing new forms of solidarity; building partnerships with outside actors; and developing capacity to formulate and defend proposals (FONGS, 1991: 37–41). The importance of mastering the economic sphere and of gaining access to the resources of national rural development programmes of which peasants were the intended beneficiaries was highlighted for the first time in a FONGS forum (FONGS, 1991: 48–9). These points, as we will see, lay behind the creation of the CNCR two years later and helped to determine its agenda for action. A consortium of donors agreed to provide support for a programme to address these challenges.[17]

The National Committee for Rural People's Dialogue and Cooperation (CNCR)

The timing was opportune. The World Bank/IMF-promoted Agricultural Structural Adjustment Programme (ASAP) was in the offing in Senegal, as it was in countries throughout the region, and farmers were nowhere near the negotiating table. The FONGS had expanded by then to include twenty-four regionally based associations throughout the country, totalling over 2000 village groups with an active membership of about 400 000. But the government rejected its requests to take part in the ASAP discussions on the grounds that it was not the only national federation representing rural people.

In any event, the FONGS and its members realized that they needed to develop their own understanding of the crisis of Senegalese agriculture and alternative proposals to advance. Playing the card of alliances and complicities that has been a mainstay of their strategy from the outset, they approached the NGO desk of the Food and Agriculture Organization of the United Nations (FAO) to request that it extend to the farmers' movement the kind of technical assistance normally reserved for member states. Support was forthcoming (McKeon et al., 1993) and the FONGS was helped to translate the language of structural adjustment into terms comprehensible to farmers and to carry out a capillary reflection on peasant reactions to the New Agricultural Policy (Von der Weid, 1992).

The results of this process were served up at the National Forum with which this study opened, the first time that the peasant movement had called representatives of government services and donors to a public debate.[18] In the farmers' analysis, the NPA and the drought had simply exposed the failure of the agricultural development model applied in Senegal since independence, which had been maintained under artificial conditions of state services and subsidies that were now being withdrawn. Although the FONGS did not have a fully-fledged substitute proposal, its member groups were experimenting with elements of an alternative involving diversification of crops and greater integration between agriculture, forestry and animal husbandry. They were aiming at an integrated approach that would make economic, social and environmental sense at the level of the household, the village and the agro-ecological zone, in contrast to the prevailing tendency to think in terms of commodities. The membership of the FONGS did not oppose the state retrenchment that accompanied structural adjustment. But they claimed the right to participate in the redefinition of policies and programmes, and the support they needed to take on new functions (FONGS, 1993).

The farmers were justified in accusing the New Agricultural Policy of not fulfilling its promises. Rural revenues had continued to drop, from a base of 22 000 FCFA in 1960 to 10 000 FCFA in 1985 and further still to 8000 FCFA in 1990 (Kasse, 1996: 31). The rates and procedures of the Caisse nationale de crédit agricole were out of phase with the realities of small producers. The state's overly abrupt retrenchment had resulted in a dramatic decline in the use of inputs, fertilizer in particular. Above all, the political and economic interests which benefited from the status quo opposed extremely powerful resistance to any real change in the control of the revenues generated by the commodity chains.

In political and institutional terms, the forum's main agenda was to promote the establishment of a platform of national rural peoples' federations. Over the following weeks assemblies were held in all regions and intensive negotiations took place between the FONGS' leaders and the other federations. On 17 March 1993 the National Committee for Rural Peoples' Dialogue (CNCR) was established at Thiès by seven national federations of farmers, pastoralists, fishworkers, horticulturists and rural women. They were joined in 1995 by two federations of forestry workers bringing total membership up to an estimated three million.[19] The CNCR's stated aims at the outset were to promote dialogue and exchange of experience among its members, encourage the pooling of resources and skills, and to act as a spokesperson for the peasant movement vis-à-vis the state and its donor partners.

The CNCR membership was a very mixed bag, including state-established cooperatives now left to fend for themselves, national federations of GIEs, and the autonomous associations of the FONGS. Among them, the FONGS was the organization with the vision and the village-level roots required to play a federating role at national level. The decision to establish a platform including all national federations which could claim to represent some portion of the rural population – irrespective of their organizational legitimacy and the nature and interests of their leadership – was certainly in part a tactical one, aimed at overcoming government resistance to allowing peasants to be represented in the ASAP negotiations. But it was very likely a strategic choice as well. It took into account the fact that the membership of the various national federations was overlapping and that there were different interests at play even on the part of the same farmers.[20] It recognized that – in the view of those leaders who championed the establishment of the CNCR – the stakes could not be higher. The future of Senegal's agriculture, its villages, its rural society and culture, risked being irremediably compromised by what they considered to be a short-sighted policy of agricultural 'modernization' and 'professionalization'.

The strategic choice, in this perspective, was to privilege obtaining a place at the negotiating table in order to influence policy decisions and gain access to national programmes. The expectation was that the nascent platform's advocacy action could generate sufficient recognition by government and development partners and sufficient awareness and mobilization at the base to enable Senegal's farmers themselves to play a major role in progressively renovating their representational and support structures – and Senegalese society – from the local level up. This strategy was not universally accepted even among the leadership of the FONGS, some of whom felt that the UNCAS[21] was unredeemable and that the new platform would be better off without it. As for the other member federations of the CNCR, the unifying factors were universal respect for the FONGS' president, Mamadou Cissokho, and the hope that an alliance with the FONGS would open up channels of funding. The only exception was the Union nationale des coopératives agricoles du Sénégal (UNCAS), whose management was able to perpetuate itself thanks to the cut-off it received on the groundnut crop, which was destined to disappear sooner or later with privatization. They tagged along, hugging the past and their privileges to their chest, out of fear of isolation.

Almost three years elapsed from the Declaration of Thiès to the constituent assembly of the CNCR in December 1995. A slow, methodological approach was necessary in order to build a basis of consensus among the disparate members of the Council, to demonstrate that membership brought benefits and to budge the more recalcitrant along in the direction of renewal and democratization of their organizations. It was also needed to build a solid negotiation agenda, to construct alliances with other sociopolitical actors, and to avoid antagonizing a suspicious state.[22]

From the outset, a strong accent was placed on a self-critical reappropriation of the peasant farmers' identity and responsibilities, rebuilding their self-confidence and self-esteem for their role in society, their culture, traditions and religion, and their work. This was the first, most basic, building block of the CNCR's project. At the same time, the Council commissioned studies and organized fora on issues of concern to rural producers: credit and savings; training, research and extension; subsidies and the constitution of a fund to provide for calamities affecting production. Increasingly, the focus was on the basic production unit in Senegal, the family farm, and the logic of its socioeconomy, ignored for decades both by the commodity-oriented official agricultural services and programmes and by the autonomous associations of the FONGS, which had grown up on the margins of mainstream agricultural production (see CNCR, 1994). The vision of a family-based agriculture able to hold its own in a context of liberalization was the CNCR's second building block. Gradually the Council built consensus among its members around a lobbying platform aimed at creating a favourable policy environment for family farming and directing resources and appropriate services to small producers.[23] This vision also facilitated the establishment of alliances with other national institutions and with an important political category, the local elected representatives.[24] A meeting held in Kaolack in December 1995 brought the elected presidents of the rural communities together with representatives of the CNCR federations and government services to agree on a basic philosophy of local development and define modalities of dialogue and partnership among local actors.

Negotiating with the state

At the same time, the CNCR was thrown into an extenuating series of negotiations on policies and programmes, stretching its extremely limited human resources to keep up with the rapid pace of change.[25] The agricultural structural adjustment programme negotiations, in which the CNCR was invited to participate, led to the publication of the *Lettre de politique de développement agricole* in 1994[26] and a multiplication of technical committees and policy fora in which the CNCR was called upon to voice the rural producers' views or to backstop member federations in their lobbying efforts. The establishment in 1995 of the Senegalese Association for the Promotion of Small Grassroots Development Projects (ASPRODEB), from which the grassroots member groups of practically all of the CNCR federations have benefited, was another important achievement. For the first time, the government agreed to retrocede public funds to a mechanism in which the decision-making authority on how to allocate them was vested with the representatives of the intended beneficiaries, the CNCR and the Association of Presidents of Rural Communities (APCR). The CNCR's Constituent Assembly in December 1995 consolidated the results of this activity and adopted a four-pronged action programme aimed at achieving 25 per cent self-funding by 1998, institutional strengthening of the CNCR and its member federations, an effective communications programme linking the apex and the base, and support to investment and agricultural development.[27]

By 1996, the CNCR was deeply engaged in the negotiation of the World Bank-promoted Agricultural Structural Investment Programme (ASIP), which was intended to provide support for the implementation of the ASAP and to guide investment in the agricultural sector generally. Despite the rhetoric of stakeholder participation which accompanied the liberalization process, Senegal was one of the very few sub-Saharan African countries in which farmers' organizations were seriously involved in determining the content of the ASIP.[28] The negotiation process was interrupted in June 1996, however, when the CNCR announced a boycott of all official negotiations. The walkout was prompted by the government's failure to respect its commitment to take timely action to equip farmers with the tools, inputs and credit they needed to block the continued deterioration of production. The Bank refrained from continuing negotiations in the absence of the CNCR. The stalemate lasted for four months, until the situation was brought to the attention of the president of the Republic. A meeting held on 27 February 1997 between 150 CNCR representatives and the president, surrounded by all of his ministers, resulted in important gains in the form of a Programme to Relaunch Agriculture: agricultural credit interest rates were reduced from

12.5 per cent to 7.5 per cent per annum, agricultural inputs and equipment were exonerated from import taxes, a five-year moratorium on farmers' debts was declared, and regular meetings between the farmers' organizations and the minister of agriculture, the prime minister and the president were instituted.

ASIP negotiations started up again, focusing on the 'Programme of Agricultural Services and Producers Organizations' (PSAOP), intended to redesign the entire institutional map of the rural sector. The CNCR invested a great deal of its efforts and human resources into ensuring that this programme reflected the farmers' interests, with considerable success. The PSAOP vision reads as though it emerged from a CNCR pen: strong and effective producer organizations; extension services accountable to producers and responsive to their demands through a new agency[29] in which their organizations are destined to become majority shareholders and decision-makers; and a separation of research funding from research execution with final decisions regarding allocations to be taken by a management committee with a majority representation of research users.[30] For the Support to Producers' Organizations (PO) component of the PSAOP – $20 million over ten years – the CNCR won acceptance of the idea that it was up to the producers themselves to identify their capacity-building needs and to select the forms and the service providers whereby these needs would be met, with emphasis on farmer-to-farmer exchange. Committees were set up at local and regional levels, bringing together representatives from local and regional POs (irrespective of whether or not they are members of a CNCR federation), to agree on common priorities. The initial phase of execution of the programme, however, highlighted the problems that emerge when an externally funded development programme interfaces with local processes of civil society self-structuring. The procedures and the rhythm of planning and execution militated against 'losing time' to make sure that the local community had actually developed ownership of the structures and initiatives proposed by the programme. We will return to these problems and the challenges they pose in the concluding section of this chapter.

The PSAOP and the Programme to Relaunch Agriculture may have been the most visible negotiations in which the CNCR took part during its first years of life, but they were by no means the only dossiers with which it had to deal (see McKeon et al., 2002). Others included the delicate interface with the evolving process of decentralization;[31] negotiating the inclusion of a strong rural infrastructure component in the ASIP; influencing the orientation of the Special Programme for Food Security initiated by FAO in 1995;[32] participating in the formulation of the National Programme of Environmental Action[33] and in discussions on the World Bank-promoted Poverty Reduction Strategy Paper;[34] making input into the government's Operational Strategy and Action Plan for the Agricultural Sector, and the current reform of the land tenure system.[35] In most cases the CNCR has succeeded in making its mark on the final product in defence of the interests of peasant producers and family-based farming. The finalized version of the Operational Strategy and Action Plan for the Agricultural Sector, adopted in January 2002, incorporates the essential aspects of the CNCR policy proposals. It recognizes that Senegalese agriculture is dominated by family farming, which provides sustenance for 60 per cent of the population and occupies 95 per cent of the land devoted to agriculture. It criticizes the concentration of public investment on capital-intensive irrigation adopting technology which excludes the vast majority of small farmers. It posits, as the basic strategic objective of agricultural development, the promotion of the progressive evolution of family farming towards a more competitive, entrepreneurial form while maintaining the specificities and the richness of the family model so that this evolution can profit the greatest possible number of rural people.

The farmers' movement and the market question

An alternative platform

As we have seen, support for family-based farming is at the heart of the Senegalese farmer movement's approach to market issues in an epoch of liberalization.

> The family farm is the dominant unit of production, consumption and natural resource management in West Africa. It is the basis for our economies, our societies and our environment. The web of solidarity which constitute our system of 'social security' are woven within the family farm. The family farm not only guarantees our countries' food security and natural resource management, but also generates most of the employment possibilities, income, savings, and investment. There cannot be a prosperous agricultural economy in our countries if the family farms are engulfed in a process of pauperization. The economic good health of our family farms is thus the key to all processes of development. (ROPPA, 2001: 4)

The vision is not one of romantic autarchy but of a determined policy orientation in favour of the modernization of peasant agriculture. The 1999 CNCR platform 'For a productive and sustainable family-based agriculture in a liberalized economy' traced the process of decapitalization and impoverishment that the family unit in Senegal has undergone in preceding decades. In most areas agricultural production covers the family food needs for no more than three to six months of the year and productivity has declined dramatically due to indebtedness and lack of access to credit, inputs and equipment (CNCR, 1999).[36] The CNCR's reasoning is impeccable. In Senegal, as in Africa generally, poverty and malnutrition are predominantly rural phenomena. Encouraging the rural poor to move to cities is hardly a solution due to the paucity of employment opportunities in the increasingly ungovernable urban centres. Nor is the promotion of a 'modern' industrialized approach to enhanced agricultural productivity, potentially attractive to government in terms of its high-tech quick fix glitter, its export orientation and links to multinational commodity chains, and its capacity to cater to elite economic interests. In terms of reducing hunger and poverty, however, the resource-poor producers who constitute the problem would not be in a position either to engage in such a model of production or to purchase its products.

The key question facing agriculture and the rural milieu in Senegal, the CNCR platform underscores, is what to do for the vast majority of peasant farmers who live from rain-fed agriculture without access to the irrigation systems which received 70 per cent of public investments between 1980 and 1995 to the benefit of less than 10 per cent of the rural population (CNCR, 1999: 27–8). The modernization of agriculture in Western countries was accomplished in a situation of burgeoning industry and state budgets, mastery of population growth, and a political orientation that permitted protection and subvention of agriculture. Senegal, and West Africa generally, is obliged to transform its agriculture in a context of liberalization and globalization, of demographic growth, and of resource-poor states. The approach has to be different.

The CNCR's reading of the situation is corroborated by that of other authoritative observers. A 1997 Michigan State University study of the impact of market reform on agricultural productivity in Senegal and six other African countries did not find evidence that food marketing reform had promoted intensification of the key African food crops. The challenge, it states, 'is to design input and output marketing systems for the millions of low-input semi-subsistence rural households that can't move and have limited capacity to change their crop mix' (Jayne et al., 1997: 13). At meso level, an FAO study conducted in 1998 in the region of Tambacounda suggested that the potential for the healthy development of rural economies was strongly linked to creation of upstream and downstream off-farm employment opportunities which, however, was blocked by the persistence of parastatal monopolies and other constraints such as insufficient transport and difficulties in obtaining access to credit (Sall, 1998: 12).

The farmers' movement's alternative platform is oriented towards providing family units with the policy environment, infrastructure and support services they need to be able to produce for and sell on their 'natural' national and regional markets in the first instance. At the same time, it advocates diversifying the rural economy by promoting off-farm employment and retaining more value added in rural areas through locally controlled processing and marketing of agricultural products. The CNCR notes that the government's declared option in favour of family-based agriculture has not been translated into action and invites those who feel peasant agriculture is incapable of modernization to debate in public rather than drag their feet behind the scenes. The CNCR's platform accents the need for a broad-reaching land tenure reform targeted principally to small-scale farmers. It calls for determined investment in the rural economy and rural societies, reversing the practice of draining resources from the countryside to feed the cities. It advocates an agricultural policy with the political courage to restructure the parastatal agro-industrial enterprises, promote real competitiveness in input supply, and reinforce dialogue and cooperation among the actors of the commodity chains in order to improve overall performance and ensure a fairer division of value added. In global terms, the movement has adopted the concept of food sovereignty as defined by the NGO/civil society organizations – CSO Forum held in Rome in June 2002 in parallel to the World Food Summit: Five Years Later (NGO/CSO Forum for Food Sovereignty, 2002). The final declaration of the Forum – 'Food Sovereignty: A Right for All' – underscores 'the right of peoples, communities and countries to define their own agricultural, labour, fishing, food and land policies which are ecologically, socially, economically and culturally appropriate to their unique circumstances'.

Initiatives at national level

Promoting the implementation of its platform has led the CNCR and the more active of its member federations to engage in a series of initiatives over the past years. Chief among these, as the previous section has shown, has been strong engagement with government in policy and programme negotiations, advocacy and mobilization on a wide range of issues related to agricultural, food and rural development.

The advent of the Wade administration in March 2000, however, interrupted the process of building an institutional basis for ongoing dialogue and negotiation which the CNCR had initiated with the previous government, and brought a new set of people to key positions in the ministries. President Wade's initial declarations seemed to indicate an orientation towards a productivist, capital and technology-intensive future for Senegal's agriculture, although he has recognized on many occasions the centrality of family farming in the country's economy. Reaching an understanding with him is all the more important given the dynamic role he has assumed on the African scene.[37] Given the apparent failure of less demonstrative forms of dialogue, the CNCR organized a mass demonstration on 26 January 2003, following the president's announcement that an agricultural policy document would be soon be debated and adopted in parliament without prior stakeholder consultation. The demonstration, held exactly ten years after the Forum which had led to the creation of the CNCR, brought 35 000 farmers from all regions of the country to the Leopold Senghor stadium in Dakar to defend a 'Peasant Manifesto' denouncing the crisis of Senegalese agriculture. The Manifesto calls on government to formulate a long-term strategy to reduce rural policy by developing smallholder agriculture and off-farm employment and to take a series of steps to deal with immediate problems. In terms of political method, the CNCR continues – as it did already ten years ago – to battle for meaningful involvement of stakeholders in defining the country's vision of and strategy for rural development and agrarian reform and for the institutionalization of periodic consultations between farmers' organizations and the state. Following the demonstration, widely reported in the press, the government has submitted the draft bill to the CNCR and other civil society organizations for comment. The CNCR then conducted a process of consultation at rural community and regional levels and within each commodity chain, leading to a national seminar which formulated the farmers' proposals for amendment of the draft law (CNCR, 2003).

Alongside policy dialogue and advocacy, the CNCR has sought to develop a certain number of concrete farmer-controlled instruments and programmes to support the modernization of family-based agriculture. ASPRODEB, referred to above, is one of these. The Second Congress of the CNCR, held in June 2001, adopted a resolution which defined the role of the CNCR as the farmers' movement's spokesperson in policy and programme negotiations and that of ASPRODEB as a support service to assist farmers' organizations in programme implementation and provide them with capacity building, financial management and technical advice. The sense of this resolution was to distinguish between the political and economic realms of action and to ensure that the movement was well equipped in both. The support that ASPRODEB has been able to channel to the base, thanks to its management of the Special Programme for Food Security (SPFS) and the Support to Producers' Organizations component of the ASIP, has had an undoubtedly positive impact.[38] The SPFS alone had covered 318 villages and 43 urban sites by early 2002, increasing the revenues of some 10 000–15 000 families and helping to develop local capacity for multiplication of quality seeds, farmer-controlled marketing of horticultural products, and improved water control through simple and low-cost techniques. Decentralized savings and credit programmes are another essential tool for small, family-based units which a number of the CNCR member federations have developed. The Fédération nationale des groupements d'intérêt économique de pêcheurs (FENAGIE)-Peche's network of savings and credit mutually benefits both the fishermen and the processing and marketing operations of the women. Under the FONGS programme of support to village-based savings and credit initiatives the number of groups grew from 370 with 17 489 members in 2000 to 617 with 34 037 members in 2001. The volume of credit rose from 208 million FCFA in 2002 to 753 million in 2001, with a reimbursement rate of close to 100 per cent in most zones (FONGS, 2002: 17–18).

Another instrument targeting the market question developed by the CNCR and ASPRODEB is the International Fair of Agriculture and Animal Resources (FIARA), the 'rendezvous of the rural world', now at its fourth annual edition. Opened by the president of the Republic, the FIARA is populated by stands advertising the produce of CNCR and other West African farmers' federations, as well as the services offered by agricultural organizations and enterprises. It provides an occasion for the development of commercial exchanges within Senegal, in the region, and at European agricultural fairs, where FIARA represents the farmers' movement.

Providing effective support for the modernization of the family farm presupposes having access to solid information about the situation of the family unit in the different agro-ecological areas of the country, how their survival strategies are evolving under stress, the constraints they are facing and the opportunities that they could exploit given the necessary support. The CNCR and some of its member federations have been taking action over the past few years to collect this kind of information, filling in a vacuum created by decades of data collection which artificially sliced the economy of the family farm into commodity chains rather than looking at it as a whole. The CNCR is working to develop 'rural identity cards' for the different agro-ecological zones. The FONGS is promoting a programme of support to family units whereby the family itself is helped to analyse its situation using simple audit tools. The results are discussed in 'family assemblies' in which inter-generational and gender tensions are aired and recomposed around an agreed strategy which takes account both of the common good and of the interests of each component of the family. This approach underscores the farmers' movement's conviction that the family farm is a way of life and not just an enterprise, and that the economic realm cannot be dealt with in isolation from the social and the cultural.

The process of privatization of the commodity chains, foreseen in the *Lettre de politique de développement agricole* of 1994, is an important market-related issue for the CNCR member federations (see McKeon et al., 2002)[39] which has run parallel to the formulation of national investment programmes and sectoral strategies described in the previous section. It is at the very heart of one of the biggest challenges facing the CNCR: that of helping family farms to harness the economic energy of commodity production, processing and marketing in order to generate and retain resources they can reinvest in agricultural modernization.

The National Interprofessional Committee on Groundnuts, intended to bring together the various actors involved in the commodity chain, was established in 1994 with EU backing. Similar committees for other commodities joined it on the national scene over the following years with strong support from development partners who favoured the option of privatization, the French cooperation programme in particular. The CNCR was less visible at the outset in this process, in which the individual member federations concerned with specific commodities are expected to play the leading role, than in that of national policy negotiations. Various factors may have contributed to this stance. On the one hand, the state constituted a far more familiar interlocutor for the farmers' organizations than the private sector that, in the Senegalese context, appeared to be poorly structured and not terribly efficient or far-sighted. It has taken the CNCR some time to size up this emerging actor. At the same time, the pace and scenario of structural adjustment pushed the producers' federations into a negotiating relation with the private sector without adequate preparation and accompanying measures on the part of the government. The Council's reticence was further increased by the fact that the interprofessional committees were seen and used by some as a means to divide and rule the CNCR.

Nonetheless, the CNCR has been able to help its members situate themselves in the context of privatization. The FENAGIE-Peche is a good example. In 1995 the CNCR provided it with an expert in savings and credit to help formulate a programme for the women involved in fish processing and marketing and to find an NGO willing to fund the programme – Association pour une dynamique du progrès économique et social (ADPES). The CNCR also supported the FENAGIE-Peche's efforts to participate in the negotiation of the fishing agreement with the European Union in 1995 and 1996/7 and to benefit from the counterpart fund. Most recently, it has backed the federation's successful efforts to purchase and manage the fish storage and marketing centre at Rufisque, one of those privatized by the government.

The ten new members admitted to the CNCR at its second General Assembly in June 2001 include several which are strongly engaged in restructuring their commodity chains. The Senegal River valley, with its market-oriented irrigated system, has been the locus of some of the most interesting processes of this nature. The tomato chain illustrates what can happen when a dynamic producers' organization, the Fédération des producteurs de tomates industrielles in this case, is helped to negotiate a mutually beneficial agreement with a processing plant and is facilitated to access the necessary support in terms of credit, inputs and adaptive research. Tomato production in the area is reported to have jumped from 3000 to 60 000 tons in the past few years.

The eternal problem of the Senegal River valley rice, the victim of competition from cut-rate imported Thai 'broken' rice, is being tackled energetically by the Fédération des perimètres autogérés. This is an organization of relatively young, well-educated heads of family who have taken over the privatized rice fields previously run by the parastatal regional development agency, SAED. They are bringing a logic of professionalization and rigour to a highly competitive field. Their goal is the development of a modern family farm that respects the regulations of the credit system and product quality norms and takes into account market perspectives and opportunities for cost reduction. The CNCR has helped them to negotiate their members' debts with the Caisse nationale de crédit agricole and to establish a system of grouped input purchase. The CNCR has also supported their advocacy work on the issue of unfair competition from imports and has promoted a not totally successful experiment in solidarity among CNCR members involving marketing of the rice by the Fédération des groupements de promotion féminine du Sénégal.

The cotton chain is another in which things are on the move. Here a new member of the CNCR, the Fédération nationale des producteurs de coton du

Sénégal, is playing a central role alongside of the SODEFITEX, whose management seems open to innovation and partnership with the producers. The enterprise has withdrawn from input provision, now handled by the producers, and the French cooperation programme is supporting the establishment of a mechanism grouping all of the actors of the chain. Production is said to have risen from 15 to 36 tons per year over the past few years.

But the toughest nut to crack is the groundnut, the perpetual invalid of Senegal's rural economy. As we have seen, privatization of the groundnut chain, breaking the stronghold of the economically and productively unviable parastatal Société nationale de commercialisation des oléagineux (SONACOS), has been one of the CNCR's agenda points since its birth. But the political and economic interests involved and the unsatisfactory state of health of the UNCAS, the CNCR's representative in the National Interprofessional Committee on Groundnuts (Comité national interprofessionnel de l'arachide – CNIA), have made it a difficult objective to attain.

The volume of marketed groundnuts dropped from 1 200 000 tons in 1975 to less than 200 000 in 1996. In 1997 the government decided to transfer a series of functions related to the management of the commodity chain to the CNIA and introduced a mechanism for producer price-fixing which was intended to take world prices more strictly into account. The 2000 harvest was an excellent one, thanks to favourable rains and improved access to inputs. The producer price was maintained at the level of previous years, however, despite a drastic drop in world prices. The heavily indebted SONACOS was unable to market the crop, leaving thousands of small producers in a crisis situation. In January 2001 the CNCR urged the government to organize a stakeholder forum to discuss and resolve the situation before the agricultural season opened, but without success. In November 2001, following closed-door discussions in September with the World Bank and the IMF, without any previous consultation with the national actors of the commodity chain, the government signed a new convention disbanding the SONAGRAINES, the marketing branch of the SONACOS. A forum was finally held in Louga in October 2001 to discuss the strategy and procedures for a takeover of groundnut marketing by private operators and producers' organizations. A system was established whereby the SONACOS would approve applications by prospective marketers and assign them collection points. In theory the marketers were to pay cash for the groundnuts and be reimbursed only at the factory (the *carreau usine* system), but in fact they did not have the necessary liquidity to apply this practice and the government opened credit lines for a few of the larger operators.

As always, the producers have suffered most from the dysfunctions of this hastily concocted handover. UNCAS, the major producers' federation involved in the marketing operation, was accused by some of having used the credit the government put at its disposal to build up its infrastructure rather than to remunerate the producers rapidly and fully. The FONGS, in contrast, was assigned eleven collection points but no credit line. It operated a pilot marketing operation drawing on the network of confidence and mobilization existing among its member associations. Based on the results of the 2002 operation, it was gearing up to undertake a broader programme in 2003 reaching out to promotion of quality seed multiplication by farmer associations and local semi-industrial processing. The FONGS *Vision of the Crisis of the Groundnut Chain*, published in March 2002, is a lucid analysis of the causes of the crisis, accompanied by recommendations for its solution at various levels: institutional and juridical, marketing and finance, and strategic and technical. As for the SONACOS itself, it was scheduled to be privatized in 2003 under strong donor pressure. Among the CNCR revindications at the 26 January 2003 demonstration was an evaluation and improvement of the *carreau usine* marketing system and the full involvement of peasant organizations in the privatization of the SONACOS. The CNCR has placed on the negotiating table the results of a study it has conducted which formulates a series for recommendations for the restructuring of the commodity chain in the short and the long term.

The regional dimension[40]

At the same time as it was building its presence on the national scene, the CNCR was playing a leadership role at regional level. The West African states began to take regional integration more seriously during the 1990s under the stimulus of globalization. As compared with the more politically motivated first-generation wave of African regionalism in the years immediately following independence, the 'new regionalism' stresses the potential economic gains to be achieved from reducing administrative and transaction costs and other barriers to intercountry trade. Assessments of the degree to which these benefits can be realized in the West African context vary, but the consensus seems to point in the direction of cautious optimism. A 1999 study documented prospects for intra-regional commerce in West Africa in positive terms following the 1994 devaluation of the CFA franc (Yade et al., 1999).[41] Regional trade in cattle, under strong competition from EU dumping to coastal markets, increased considerably following the devaluation. Regarding cereals, widely traded among West African countries but poorly documented, expanded exchange seemed possible, given the existence of complementary surpluses and deficits, although the high cost of transport remained a problem. The African regional market could prove to be a more effective motor of development for the dynamic horticultural sector than the European niche markets. The African demand for onions, tomatoes and garlic is substantial and these products are less demanding in terms of storage and quality controls than some of the perishable export crops. At the same time, however, experts have warned that larger commercial farms are likely to benefit more from regional market opportunities than semi-subsistence smallholders and have stressed the need for accompanying measures to assist low-income farm households to increase the volume and the quality of their output (Matthews, 2002).

The impetus towards West African regionalism is also fired by the reorientation of cooperation between the EU and the African, Caribbean and Pacific Group of states (ACP) countries. Under pressure to comply with WTO regulations, the Cotonou Agreement foresees that the support which had been granted previously to ACP countries in the form of non-reciprocal trade preferences will be transformed in the future into Economic Partnership Agreements with regional economic entities. Negotiation of these agreements is now underway and they are expected to become operational by 2008.

On the farmers' side, relations among West Africans and the flow of products on informal markets had never been interrupted by artificial national frontiers. Seasonal or more permanent immigration has remained a fact of life in the sub-region. Initiatives like the Six-S, referred to above, had helped to put exchanges among farmers' organizations on a more structured basis already in the late 1970s. In 1991 five farmers' organizations in Senegal, Gambia and Mali had joined to form a far-sighted commercial venture, 'Exchange Crossroads Ltd.', aimed at promoting exchange of agricultural products among the three countries and with Europe.[42]

As the 1990s advanced, the farmers' movement noted an increasing tendency for decisions that strongly conditioned national agricultural and rural development options to be taken at super-national levels. Responsibility and accountability remained unclear and changeable. Also, it was important to seek institutional interfaces with the various intergovernmental forums in which important negotiations were taking place. In 1996, acting on a proposal by the Coordinator of the Senegalese CNCR and building on existing relations, a Platform of Sahelian Peasant Organizations was established with support from the Comité permanent inter-états de lutte contre la sécheresse au Sahel (CILSS). At the same time, the Economic and Monetary Union of West African States (UEMOA) was emerging as a strategic interface. Created in 1994 by eight states with a common currency administered by the Central Bank of the States of West Africa, the UEMOA was moving ahead towards the establishment of a common external tariff in 2000 and the negotiation of a common agricultural policy. The promoters of the Platform of Sahelian Peasant Organizations began to reach out to farmers' organizations in non-Sahelian UEMOA countries like Côte d'Ivoire, Benin and Togo. The first major activity of this larger grouping was a workshop in September 1999 aimed at enhancing farmers' involvement in the formulation of ASIPs and of the common agricultural policy (Organisations paysannes de l'Afrique de l'Ouest, 1999). The process of exchange and reflection that began with the preparation of this workshop culminated in an assembly in Benin in July 2000, which saw the creation of a ten-country[43] Network of West African Peasant and Producers Organizations (Réseau des organisations paysannes et de producteurs agricoles de l'Afrique de l'Ouest – ROPPA).[44]

The ROPPA's immediate target was the UEMOA common agricultural policy, due to be signed by the end of 2001. Seeking to bring peasant farmer concerns to bear on the negotiation process, the ROPPA organized a series of national seminars culminating in a regional workshop in October 2001 on 'Common Agricultural Policy and Family Farms within the UEMOA Area'. The memorandum adopted at this workshop (ROPPA, 2001) is a lucid denunciation of the unequal competition to which African agriculture is subjected by exports from industrialized countries that benefit from subventions denied to African farmers. Two months later it was presented to the Summit of UEMOA heads of state by a ROPPA delegation backed up by 500 farmers from all countries in the sub-region. Taken by surprise, the heads of state received the delegation and incorporated the measures advocated by the ROPPA, including that of placing family-based agriculture at the heart of the policy, in the agricultural policy document they signed on 19 December 2001.[45]

As in the case of national agricultural policy, however, the next step is to move from the declaration of principles to the formulation and implementation of the entire series of interconnected measures required to put them into practice. The ROPPA has succeeded in gaining governments' in-principle agreement that promoting family-based agriculture will require commitment to policies which protect local production from unfair competition, develop local and regional markets, defend family farmers' access to land and other productive resources and help them to secure added value from their production. As a first step, the ROPPA is advocating an increase in common external tariffs to provide greater protection for West African agricultural production against cheap imports and ensure remunerative prices for producers. At the same time, it is seeking to ensure that small producers' interests are reflected in the agricultural component of the New Economic Partnership for African Development (NEPAD) and the trade agreement which the European Union is gearing up to negotiate with the Economic Community of West African States (ECOWAS) which englobes the UEMOA countries. The challenges here for the ROPPA include building up relations with farmers' organizations in the non-UEMOA members of the larger grouping, Nigeria in particular, gaining recognition by the ECOWAS secretariat and governance, and mastering the dynamics of this more complex interstate grouping.

The global scene

Some leaders of the Senegalese farmers' movement woke up early to the significance of the Uruguay Round of the General Agreement on Tariffs and Trade (GATT). Already in 1993 the FONGS published a paper which analysed the mechanism of northern subventions and dumping practices and their impact on food markets and peasant agriculture in the south (Seck, 1993). In 1997–9, at the request of the CNCR/FONGS, FAO organized a training course for farmer leaders on the implications of WTO negotiations for Senegalese agriculture (FONGS/FAO, 1999). Given the paucity of data and analysis available to southern negotiators at that time, the members of the government delegation trekked out to the FONGS' headquarters in Thiès for an amicable briefing before departing for Seattle.

In fact, there could be room for ample areas of potential consensus between the farmers' movement and government regarding the Agreement on Agriculture (AoA), if the government were less subject to internal and external conflicts of economic and political interest. As an FAO study of fourteen developing countries – including Senegal – noted in 2000 (FAO, 2000), these countries had already eliminated their non-tariff barriers under the SAPs. They had obtained high bound tariffs under the AoA, but their applied tariffs were much lower due to pressure from the international financial institutions, the fear of ruining trade relationships with the big exporters who provide preferential market access, and the political necessity of maintaining low consumer prices. The study demonstrated that the countries concerned had shown no improvement in agricultural exports, with the partial exception of fruits and vegetable, while their food imports were rising rapidly. It also documented a process of increasing concentration of farms and marginalization of small producers. At the same time, an overall review of export crop liberalization in Africa (FAO, 1999) pointed to a rapid vertical integration of export crop marketing such that overseas buyers – the real winners in a regime of low liberalized commodity prices – were financing exporters who financed processors who, in turn, financed traders. The general trend observed was towards concentration of trading in the hands of a limited number of companies and increased uncertainty for farmers, particularly those in remote areas.

The position of the Senegalese government, and that of the WTO African Group of which it is a member (WTO, 2001a, 2001b), stresses the need to allow African countries the right to protect their domestic markets through special safeguard measures designed to curb anti-competitive practices which jeopardize domestic agricultural production. It also advocates 'progressive substantial reduction' in export subsidies by rich countries, and the introduction of flexible measures to allow developing countries to support their domestic agricultural sector in order to ensure food security, preserve jobs in rural areas, and reduce poverty. There is nothing in this published position with which the farmers' movement would take issue, although they would fault the government for over-accenting access to northern markets and for a lack of coherence between its stance in WTO negotiations and the national and regional agricultural policies it applies.

On global trade negotiation issues the West African farmers' movement has directed considerable attention to international networking aimed at building understanding and alliances between farmers' organizations in the north and the south and contributing to effective lobbying of northern governments. Two related processes, in particular, have provided forums for global civil society dialogue in this domain. The ROPPA participated actively in the preparations for the World Food Summit: Five Years Later, held in Rome in June 2002, and the parallel NGO/CSO Forum, which targeted food sovereignty as one of its four priority issues.[46] The ROPPA is one of the African regional members of the international civil society committee which is carrying forward the action plan adopted by the Forum. This includes ongoing exchange on trade issues among farmers' organizations and NGOs/CSOs in different regions and debate with FAO officials and government delegations on the implications of the concept of food sovereignty for international commodity markets and the WTO Agreement on Agriculture. The effort was to go beyond principles to formulate cogent proposals for their application.

A related arena for debate and alliance building has been a series of workshops bringing together southern and northern farmers' organizations to discuss international agricultural trade issues, identify common concerns and work through questions where there could seem to be conflicts of interest. The second workshop in this series, held in Brussels in October 2002, with participation by over thirty farmers' organizations from Europe, Africa and North America, approved a common declaration denouncing the imperfection of international markets in agricultural products – particularly when they involve only a small proportion of total production – and, as such, their unsuitability to ensure proper remuneration of producers and to set appropriate price levels on domestic markets. The declaration identified promotion of family-based farming and food sovereignty as the principles on which rules governing international agricultural trade should be based. It advocated supply management instruments such as production quotas at national level to improve farmers' position on the market. It called for a ban on trade flows in forms which destabilize the internal markets of other countries and agreement on the right for developing countries to use customs tariffs to protect national markets. Finally, it advocated negotiating international product agreements particularly for tropical products, and establishing preferential import quotas for products from the south on the regulated markets of the north. One offshoot of this dialogue was a Declaration for Fair and Equitable Agricultural Trade Rules at the WTO signed by the ROPPA and eight other national and regional farmers' organizations in Europe, North America and Asia, posted on the WTO website on 25 October 2002. Another was coordination between ROPPA members and NGOs in denouncing the United States government's subsidies to, and dumping of, US cotton on the world market which have caused a drop in prices and a direct loss of $191 million to cotton producers in West Africa (see Oxfam, 2002; ROPPA, 2002).

The ROPPA hosted a third workshop in this series in Senegal on 18–21 May 2003 in the run-up to the WTO Ministerial Session in Cancun in September 2003 and the negotiation of the EU–ACP economic partnership agreements. This time the participants, representing farmers' organizations from Africa, Asia, Europe, Latin America and North America, focused on issues which had created greatest difficulty in earlier discussions, such as the relationship between subventions and dumping. The resulting Dakar Declaration, 'For Mutually-supportive Agricultural and Trade Policies', makes it clear that the dominant conflict of interests is not between northern and southern farmers, but between different models of agriculture. The positions formulated by the West African farmers' platforms are thus feeding, directly and indirectly, into global advocacy campaigns targeting the WTO and European Union and US agricultural and trade policies.

Looking forward

That the CNCR would achieve the results it has in the space of a decade was by no means self-evident. As the CNCR's first president, Mamadou Cissokho, recalled in his opening speech to the Second CNCR Congress in June 2001, 'in 1993 we were menaced, discouraged, divided, awaiting miraculous solutions from outside our families and our organizations. The CNCR was our only chance, our project based on our ideas, our experiences, our strengths and our weaknesses. We had no other option: our backs were to the wall.' The ability of the Senegalese farmers' movement to make its mark has been the result of a carefully crafted strategy, taking advantage of the new spaces and political opportunities opened up by retrenchment of the omnipresent state. This strategy has included unambiguous recognition of the state's sovereignty,[47] maintenance of a unified platform despite the diverse nature of its membership,[48] construction of alliances with a range of actors at different levels,[49] and disciplined use of protest and social mobilization on key occasions.[50] The movement owes a great deal to the vision and political acumen of its leadership.

A vision that embraces more than purely economic and productive goals is clearly needed. A leader of the movement has recounted that, when he started his mobilizing activity, people who stated their occupation as 'peasant farmer' on official forms were told that this reply was inadmissible. The CNCR has worked to make it an object of pride. And since the Senegalese citizens who recognize themselves as falling within this category constitute a good proportion of the population, the political clout of this reinvention is evident. As for the focus on family-based agriculture, it amounts to a rediscovery of the basic unit of Senegalese society, still alive although stressed to its limits by the economic, political and social changes of the past century. The ROPPA Memorandum quoted above recalled that the family farm is the locus of production, consumption and natural resource management, as well as of the links of solidarity which constitute the West African system of social security (ROPPA, 2001: 4). The CNCR's project, in the final analysis, is about helping to reweave the torn texture of Senegalese society and renegotiate a social compact from the smallest unit on up. A recent study of democracy in Senegal (Schaffer, 1998: 75–6 and 95–6)[51] suggests that 'the notions of *demokaraasi* held by many non-French-speaking Wolofones appear to be largely conditioned by the repertoire of normative and institutional strategies used by this largely poor and vulnerable population to respond to their precarious life conditions. ... In an electoral system shot through with clientelism ... no clear distinction is made between the public good and private benefit or between corrupt and legitimate mechanisms of distribution of the material wealth of the *buur*.'[52] The farmers' movement is working against this kind of perception through its efforts to render the attribution of national resources transparent and accountable, to demonstrate that the CNCR can function as an effective instrument of claims making for rural people, that the local and national arenas can be linked in meaningful ways, and that values like solidarity, self-respect and responsibility can be painted on a broad social canvas.

The principal challenge facing the CNCR and the ROPPA, in order to consolidate and build on their gains in both the political and the economic realms, is that of promoting the emergence of effective and credible peasant organizations in communication with, and accountable to, their base. Linked to this central challenge are three related issues: translating the policy gains of the past few years into concrete economic benefits and activities which local farmers perceive and appreciate; overcoming the present dependence of the movement on outside support; and broadening the network of committed and informed leaders.

To discuss the representativeness of the CNCR it is necessary to differentiate between its formal base, constituted by its member federations, and its social or ideal base, the rural people of Senegal who make up the majority of the country's population and are largely dependent on small-scale agriculture and related activities. As we have seen, the relationship between the social base and the formal base is far from neat. Many rural people are formally members of more than one CNCR federation, many others are not members of any, and the meaning of membership itself is elusive.

Two important factors which attest to the CNCR's legitimacy are its capacity for social mobilization and its success in creating a single platform recognized by all national farmers' organizations and by the state and development partners. An authoritative government spokesperson has stated the case in these terms: 'The CNCR includes many different federations. There are conflicts within the CNCR and even within a single commodity chain. But what is important for the state is that the CNCR constitutes an organization with which we can dialogue because it is recognized by all of the farmers' organizations. When the CNCR commits itself it sticks to its commitment' (interview conducted in January 2002). Another legitimizing factor is the fact that the CNCR has, by all accounts, acted in the interests of peasant farmers even though it has not systematically consulted them and explicitly received its mandate from them. On other common criteria of legitimacy, however, the CNCR and its member federations score less well. Only a very few of the federations can claim documented, dues-paying membership, periodic re-election of governing bodies, and regular means of communication with them. Both a cause and a result of this situation is the fact that these federations do not now provide services that could induce resource-poor farmers to invest time and money in membership. The CNCR has had difficulties in accessing resources from development partners to support the restructuring and strengthening of the federations and building up two-way communications with the base.

However well the CNCR has interpreted the interests of Senegal's family farmer, the fact remains that the majority of rural producers are unaware of, and unconcerned by, these negotiations. Most of the battles that the CNCR has waged thus far have tended to appear far-off and abstract to farmers – with a few exceptions which responded to immediate interests, like that of the reduction of interest rates for agricultural credit, or to deeply felt concerns, like the reform of the land tenure system currently under review. 'Achievements at the national level are not communicated to the base. People at local level most often don't even know what is being negotiated and why' (group interview of CNCR members, January 2002). Thanks, at least in part, to the CNCR's lobbying action, a policy consensus has been formed around the centrality of family-based farming for the future of Senegalese agriculture and rural society. The challenge is to formulate and implement concrete proposals that translate this option into action by supporting the modernization of family farms and the creation of a rich texture of rural activities, both agricultural and non-agricultural. This requires recognizing that family farming is destined to become increasingly diversified as modernization moves ahead and that it will be necessary to go beyond generic discussions to formulate a more modulated approach that takes this diversity into account. This is the most effective route to building accountability to, and control by, rural people from the base up. The more policies are translated into concrete stakes, activities and services which are of direct concern to farming families, the more rural people will insist on playing a role, and the more the idea of membership in farmers' organizations will take on meaning.

Shaping alternative approaches to agricultural and rural development implies demonstrating that economic growth and the modernization of agricultural need not be inimical to the social and cultural values of family-based farming. A major challenge in this connection is that of making the link between the economic and the social spheres, between the resource-generation capacity of the commodity chains, the global strategies of family farms, revitalized rural economics, and the social values like solidarity which the movement champions.

The CNCR leadership has a vision of where it wants to head. It has identified some of the instruments needed: a strengthened and decentralized economic arm in the form of ASPRODEB providing effective services to family farms and local associations; democratized and renovated member federations dealing with the various commodity chains and transversal issues nationally; inclusive peasant association structures at the level of rural communities and regions acting as the socioeconomic interlocutor of the elected local authorities; effective two-way communications with the base; institutionalized dialogue with government at all levels. It is working in these directions, but it is overly dependent on the government and development partners for the resources to make it happen. The CNCR itself has operated on a skeleton budget since its establishment, relying on the commitment of its staff and cadres and the input of convinced external allies. Equally pernicious in terms of its capacity to implement a long-term strategy is the fact that the CNCR has found it difficult to access the external funds required to finance some key elements of its action plan, in particular its communication programme, the promotion of dialogue among farmers' organizations at the level of the country's regions, and the democratization and 'redynamization' of its member federations. There is an element of fragility inherent in the fact that the CNCR is dependent on external sources to implement a strategy which aims, in the long term, at rendering it self-sufficient. According to the CNCR's financial report for 2000, only five of the Council's member federations, nine at that time, paid their annual dues and the amount received, 520 000 FCFA, covered only about 10 per cent of the running costs.[53] Yet the federations' contributions cannot be expected to increase unless they are helped to develop services which induce producers to become dues-paying members in their turn.

This situation raises the issue of the interface between social movements and development cooperation.[54] Up until the 1990s the worlds of social movements and mainstream development programmes were practically non-communicating. Over the past decade the development agenda has been fundamentally recast in terms of structural adjustment, liberalization, privatization, institutional development, decentralization, good governance, and now poverty reduction, with an accent on civil society actors. In this context there is a general consensus within the development community regarding the necessity of building legitimate, well-structured producers' movements capable of representing the interests of rural people and providing them with the agricultural services they need. Nudging this process along has become an object of great interest to development partners. Views of what form a structured farmers' movement should take and what functions it should perform, however, vary from donor to donor, and the agricultural and rural development programmes they fund tend to become instruments whereby each donor promotes the implementation of its vision. At the same time, the political implications of a strong organization representing the interests of the rural population are not lost on governments. Donor conditionality intervenes to complicate positioning between governments and farmers' movements.

A related issue is the need to address the incongruities between the logic, the rhythm, and the methodology of building a social movement and those governing the formulation and implementation of development strategies and programmes. As the account of the first ten years of the CNCR's life has demonstrated, the overall social and political vision which animates a budding social movement tends to become disarticulated by the project logic, chopped up into pieces, and forced into a mould which is not congenial to it. The pace and the way in which national negotiation forums operate are inimical to consultation with the base. The methods and rhythm of project planning and execution do not allow for appropriation by local actors. A long-term process is telescoped into a time-bound logical framework.

Central to the movement's ability to deal with the entire range of challenges it faces is the question of leadership: How do peasant leaders attain power in their organizations? How are they perceived by the base? How to handle the tendency of many leaders to seek to maintain their positions and accumulate responsibilities rather than sharing them out? And what is the relation of leaders to political parties and to donors?[55]

In the course of a particularly rich group interview that took place in the context of this study, one of the participants reflected with a sigh on the difficulty of situating oneself in a constantly evolving context. His federation, he noted, had been one step ahead of the decentralization game in setting up regional coordinations in 1995. But the levels of decision-making seem to be jumping around like frogs, from the national, where the CNCR is in place, to the UEMOA, where the ROPPA has managed to mobilize itself. But tomorrow it will be the ECOWAS, with the new challenge of relating to a mammoth like Nigeria, and the day after the NEPAD, the ACP, the WTO... How to decide which end of the stick to grab in order to make progress quickly? The temptation of just huckling down to work in one's corner, he noted, is strong. But it is no longer an option. Perhaps the most important challenge facing the CNCR is that of cultivating a capacity for multi-tiered strategic thinking and propagating it among a whole new generation of leaders – men and women of vision, integrity and tenacity operating at all levels, from the local on up, able to situate specific issues in a more global context. Here the CNCR returns to the most basic objective: that of helping the rural people of Senegal reconstruct their sense of pride and, along with it, the capacity to weigh decisively and responsibly in decisions which affect them and the society in which they live.

Notes

1. This chapter is based on over two decades of familiarity with the rural areas and peasant associations of Senegal, a close reading of the literature (above all, documents produced by the farmers' organizations themselves over the past decade) and a series of individual and group interviews conducted during January 2002 with CNCR members and respondents from other categories of organizations with which the Council interacts at national level: government, private sector, local authorities, NGOs, development partners. This chapter incorporates some material published in McKeon et al. (2003).

2. The elections of May 2000, in which the current President Abdoulaye Wade ousted Abdou Diouf of the Parti socialiste which had governed Senegal since independence.

3. See Dupriez (1980) for extremely interesting calculations in this regard.

4. On the evolution of official policies and the farmers' movement in Senegal see, among others, Lecomte (2001); Barbadette (2001); McKeon et al. (1999); Jacob and Lavigne Delville (1994).

5. In fact, a combination of under-remuneration of producers, questionable management and clientelism provoked a major agricultural crisis at the end of the 1960s, known as the 'peasant malaise', and engendered a period of decadence and lethargy of the cooperatives up to the mid-1980s when the government tried – unsuccessfully – to reform the system with the creation of the Union nationale des coopératives agricoles du Sénégal (UNCAS). See Ba et al. (2002: 260).

6. The names these groups were given by their organizers were often expressive of their determination to overcome a difficult situation: for example, 'Hope is for Tomorrow' or 'Together we will grow'.

7. A multiparty system was introduced in Senegal in 1974.

8. Famara's organization, the Maisons familiales rurales (MFR) – the Senegalese version of a French association – was a contact point for advice to new groups and also helped direct the first European NGOs which began to arrive on the scene for initiatives they might support. ENDA Tiers Monde, headquartered in Dakar, was another early adviser. The Centre d'études économiques et sociales de l'Afrique de l'Ouest (CESAO), a sub-regional training centre in Burkina Faso founded by the White Fathers, provided training for a whole generation of association leaders.

9. At the same time, it should be emphasized that Senegal's relatively good record of guaranteeing civic liberties has a lot to do with the fact that the peasant movement has developed earlier and more strongly here than in other West African countries.

10. See Soumaré (2001) for a detailed autobiographical description of a group of young Malians and Senegalese workers in France on the Malian bank of the Senegal River, with support from a French association that was among the earliest sources of small amounts of funding for endogenous initiatives, the Association champenoise de coopération inter-regionale (ACCIR). Other early donor partners included the World Council of Churches and Agriculteurs français et développement international (AFDI).

11. Se Servir de la Saison Sèche en Savane et au Sahel (Taking advantage of the dry season in the savana and the Sahel), co-founded by Bernard Lecomte and the Burkinabe farmer leader, Bernard Ledea Ouedraogo. The decision to focus activities on the long dry season was dictated in part by a desire to take advantage of an unexploited opportunity and to fight against rural exodus, but also to avoid conflict with the dominant agricultural calendar and, in consequence, the village and administrative authorities (interview with B. Lecomte, 6 April 2001). See also Gueneau and Lecomte (1998: 75).

12. For an account of the dynamics of peasant action in the words of village associations belonging to four of the FONGS regional members, see ENDA (1985). See also ENDA (1988); Descendre (1990); CIRAD (1993).

13. Leaving behind it a debt of some 100 billion FFCA. See Utting and Jaubert (1998: 33).

14. The GIE began to federate nationally in the late 1980s along commodity lines, adding another component to the national panorama of rural producers' organizations.

15. On SAPs and agricultural markets in Africa, see FAO (1990); FAO (1994); Padilla (1997); FAO (1999); Dione (2000).

16. The Canadian and Swiss government cooperation programme, the Ford Foundation, Oxfam – Netherlands (NOVIB), SOS-Faim and Recherches et applications de financements alternatifs au développement (RAFAD).
17. The members of the consortium were SOS-Faim (Belgium), CIPSI (Italy), EZE (Germany), NOVIB (Netherlands), the Swiss Development Cooperation, and the European Commission through its NGO co-funding window.
18. The FONGS was the convener, but they invited all of the other national federations that could claim to represent a portion of the rural population.
19. Out of a total population of about 8 million. Estimating membership, however, is a difficult exercise since very few of the federations have a documented dues-paying membership.
20. A farmer might well belong to a cooperative to obtain credit and inputs, to a member association of the FONGS to seek a community space relatively autonomous of traditional hierarchies and state control, and to a GIE to promote a small-scale enterprise of some kind.
21. The state-established Union of Agricultural Cooperatives of Senegal, which had not held an electoral assembly since its establishment in 1983.
22. From the outset the CNCR has emphasized recognition of the state as 'the only institution authorized to draw up a development policy for the agricultural sector' (Declaration of Thiès).
23. An FAO capacity-building programme helped the CNCR to develop its first comprehensive agricultural policy proposal in a document entitled *For a Productive and Sustainable Family-based Agriculture in a Liberalized Economy*, which was debated at a national seminar in October 1999. These proposals have served as a platform for CNCR input into subsequent policy and programme negotiations both nationally and sub-regionally.
24. Senegal was undergoing a rapid and thoroughgoing process of decentralization in this period. In 1990 important management authority was transferred to the Rural Communities (which had existed since 1972). A revision of the Constitution had been voted in 1994 creating local collectivities, followed by a law in 1996 detailing their attributions and regional, municipal and local elections.
25. For a detailed account of the negotiation processes in which the CNCR has been involved and an assessment of its impact, see McKeon et al. (2002).
26. The CNCR's negotiating platform included the privatization of the groundnut and other commodity chains in the interest of improving their productivity and to the profit of the producers. Although its mastery of the art of negotiating agricultural policy was still limited in 1994–5, it successfully advocated recognition of peasants as actors and indispensable participants in all negotiations regarding the rural milieu and commitment to reinforcing their capacity.
27. Through the ASPRODEB, the promotion of alternative approaches to credit and the establishment of a calamity fund. See CNCR (1995).
28. As noted at the Second International Workshop on ASIPs, held in Malawi in November 1997.
29. The 'Agence national de conseil agricole et rurale' (ANCAR), in which the FONGS has invested, becoming a shareholder on behalf of the CNCR.
30. The 'Fonds national de recherches agricoles et agro-alimentaires' (FNRAA), whose president is a farmer leader.
31. The first regional, municipal and local elections were held in 1996. The relationship between the farmers' movement and political processes was clearly a significant question. The CNCR itself has carefully avoided identification with any political

party. Many farmer leaders, however, are involved individually in regional and local politics. The local authorities wield decision-making power in a number of domains of importance to the farmers' movement, from natural resource management to the preparation of local development plans. The CNCR has been concerned from the outset to increase the weight of the 'development' agendas of the local authorities relative to the purely 'political' agendas and to avoid manipulation of the farmers' movement.

32. Senegal is the only country in which a national farmers' platform is a full partner of the Special Programme for Food Security, along with the government and FAO, and the CNCR has had a strong influence on the shape of the programme, for which the farmer organization-controlled ASPRODEB is the executing agency.

33. In the context of the UN Convention to Combat Desertification. The Plan, an outcome of the follow-up to the 1992 United Nations Conference on Environment and Development, has not been implemented due to lack of funding.

34. Less participatory in reality than in rhetoric. See Phillips (2002).

35. In 1964 Senegal adopted a law regarding the national domain which abrogated traditional family and lineage rights to land and invested ownership in the nation. The modalities for the application of this law, however, were never clearly defined and the rural councils charged with administering it have not been provided with the necessary human and financial resources. This situation has resulted in a climate of uncertainty regarding tenure that has blocked investment, accelerated depletion of natural resources, and exacerbated conflicts linked to access to land. In 1996 the government commissioned a paper that was intended to serve as a basis for a reform of the land tenure system. The paper was transmitted to the CNCR and the APCR for their comments before proceeding with finalization of the proposed reform. With support from the French cooperation programme, the CNCR has initiated a thorough process of consultation with its members at local, regional and national levels, whose results should be made available over the next few months. The delicacy of this issue, and the economic interests at play, are evident.

36. See also CNCR (2001) for a more detailed analysis.

37. Wade is one of the African political leaders at the origin of NEPAD and a strong player in the sub-regional economic organizations of which Senegal is a member.

38. Problems have arisen, however, due to the under-resourcing and weaknesses of ASPRODEB and, as indicated above, to the procedures and the rhythms of planning and execution of national programmes, which militate against 'losing time' to make sure that local communities develop the kind of ownership of, and responsibility for, the initiatives which, for the CNCR, is the major goal.

39. See McKeon et al. (2002). On the particularly complex question of the groundnut chain, see Freund et al. (1997) and Sy (2002).

40. On regionalization and regional markets in West Africa, see Lavergen (1997); Padilla (1997); Yade et al. (1999); Matthews (2002); Soderbaum (2001).

41. In Senegal, however, the positive impact of the devaluation for small farmers was minimal due to the fact that the increase in the cost of imported inputs was borne entirely by the producers.

42. Two of the factors which contributed to the failure of this operation are worth citing since they illustrate the difficulties of successfully evolving alternative market approaches. One was the complexities of penetrating the European niche

market for anacardia nuts, which the Exchange Crossroads Ltd. attempted as its first activity in order to build liquidity to underwrite regional exchanges. Another was the difficulty of maintaining control of the operations by the farmers' associations, the 'owners' of Carrefour, without undermining the economic management of affairs.

43. Benin, Burkina Faso, Côte d'Ivoire, Gambia, Guinea Bissau, Guinea-Conakry, Mali, Niger, Senegal and Togo. Membership in the Network is reserved for a single platform per country, which is expected to group all of the existing national federations into a forum in which they can dialogue on common problems and agree on positions that can be negotiated in a unitary fashion with the state and other interlocutors.

44. Its declared objectives are to promote the development of productive and sustainable peasant family-based agriculture, organize training and information programmes and exchange of experience among network members, support the growth of strong peasant/producer organization structures in each country, promote solidarity among member organizations, represent its members at regional and international levels, and promote dialogue with similar networks in other parts of the world. See Réseau des organisations paysannes de l'Afrique de l'Ouest (2000).

45. Acte additionnel No. 03/2001 portant adoption de la politique agricole de l'UEMOA.

46. See Suppan (2001) and the Forum's final statement on 'Food Sovereignty: A Right for All'.

47. 'The CNCR's principle of recognizing the political mission of the State has enabled the State to develop a positive complicity with it', stated a representative of the prime minister's office in an interview in January 2002.

48. 'The CNCR has managed to keep us together, and when we are together we intimidate the authorities', as a leader of a member federation put it.

49. The CNCR's efforts to build alliances beyond national boundaries, as well as in-country, have been important to the movement, first and foremost the construction of a West African peasant farmers' network. Internationally, the CNCR and the ROPPA have built up an informal network of 'accomplices' in international organizations, donor agencies and NGOs throughout Europe and North America, which has had a significant impact in terms of furthering the movement's objectives and constructing more formal, institutional partnerships.

50. The 1993 Forum, the boycott in 1996, the demonstrations at the UEMOA Summit in 2001 and in Dakar in January 2003 are prime examples.

51. See also the classic Jean-François Bayart (1993).

52. Woloof word roughly equivalent to 'king' or 'ruler'.

53. The sources other than members' dues from which the CNCR has drawn support for its core costs and programme activities are primarily the Government of Senegal, the World Bank, the cooperation programmes of the Swiss and the French governments and the Walloon region of Belgium, the 'Agence internationale de la francophonie', the West African Rural Foundation, the SAED, and the Panos Institute, for a total of 102 045 807 FCFA in 2000.

54. For a more detailed discussion of the impact of aid on the farmers' movement in Senegal, see McKeon et al. (2003).

55. See Ba et al. (2002: 275–6) for a thoughtful analysis of these issues by three members of the CNCR's technical support unit.

References

Ba, Cheikh Oumar, Ousmane Ndiaye and Mamdou Lamine Sanko (2002) 'Le mouvement paysan (1960–2000)', in Momar-Coumba Diop (ed.), *La société sénégalaise entre le local et le global*. Paris: Karthala.

Barbadette, Loic (2001) *Le rôle des organisations professionnelles paysannes face aux autres acteurs dans la négociation des politiques agricoles et la gestion des filières agro-alimentaires* (mimeo).

Bates, R. H. (1981) *Markets and States in Tropical Africa: the Political Basis of Agricultural Policies*. Berkeley, CA: University of California Press.

Bayart, Jean-François (1993) *The State in Africa: the Politics of the Belly*. New York: Longman.

Centre de coopération internationale en recherche agronomique pour le développement (CIRAD) (1993) *Etats désengagés, paysans engagés. Perspectives et nouveaux rôles des organisations paysannes en Afrique et en Amérique latine*. Paris: Le librairie FPH.

Conseil national de concertation et de coopération des ruraux (CNCR) (1994) *Exploitations familiales et développement durable: atelier de réflexion*. Dakar: CNCR.

Conseil national de concertation et de coopération des ruraux (CNCR) (1995) *Rapport du Congrès constitutif*. Dakar, 2–3 December. Dakar: CNCR.

Conseil national de concertation et de coopération des ruraux (CNCR) (1999) *Pour une agriculture familiale productive et durable dans une economie libéralisée. Les propositions d'orientations et de stratégies des organisations paysannes sénégalaises*. Dakar: CNCR.

Conseil national de concertation et de coopération des ruraux (CNCR) (2000) *Diagnostic institutionnel du CNCR*. Dakar: CNCR.

Conseil national de concertation et de coopération des ruraux (CNCR) (2001) *Rapport portant propositions paysannes pour la politique agricole de l'Union économique et monétaire de l'Afrique de l'Ouest*. Dakar: CNCR.

Conseil national de concertation et de coopération des ruraux (CNCR) (2003) *Projet de loi d'orientation agricole. Compte-rendu de l'Atelier d'information et de formation des responsables de cadres locaux et régionaux de concertation et des animateurs*. Dakar: CNCR.

Copans, Jean (ed.) (1975) *Sécheresses et famines au sahel*. Paris: Maspéro.

Descendre, Daniel (1990) *L'Autodétermination paysanne*. Paris: L'Harmattan.

Diedhiou, Famara (1998) *Mouvement paysan sénégalais: les sentiers du future*. Dakar: FRAO.

Dione, Josue (2000) 'Food security policy reform in Mali and the Sahel', in R. James Bingen, David Robinson and John M. Staatz (eds), *Democracy and Development in Mali*. East Lansing: Michigan State University.

Dupriez, Huges (1980) *Paysans de l'Afrique noire: quels savoirs pour quelle révolution agraire?* Nivelles: Terres et Vie.

Duruflé, Gilles (1995) 'Bilan de la nouvelle politique agricole au Sénégal', *Review of African Political Economy*, No. 63, pp. 73–84.

Environnement et développement du tiers-monde (ENDA) (1985) *Initiatives paysannes au Sahel. Environnement africain*. Dakar.

Environnement et développement du tiers-monde (ENDA) (1988) 'Report from Senegal', in *The Image of Africa: International Exchange on Communication and Development*. Rome: FAO.

Food and Agriculture Organization of the United Nations (FAO) (1990) *Selected Papers on Structural Adjustment and Agricultural Marketing*. Rome: FAO.

Food and Agriculture Organization of the United Nations (FAO) (1994) *Structural Adjustment and the Provision of Agricultural Services in Sub-Saharan Africa*. Rome: FAO.

Food and Agriculture Organization of the United Nations (FAO) (1999) *Export Crop Liberalization in Africa: A Review*. Rome: FAO.

Food and Agriculture Organization of the United Nations (FAO) (2000) *Agriculture, Trade and Food Security: Issues and Options in the WTO Negotiations from the Perspective of Developing Countries*. Vols I and II. Rome: FAO.

Fédération des ONG sénégalaises (FONGS) (1991) *Document de synthèse des restitutions des auto-évaluations et des conclusions de l'Assemblée générale*. Thiès: FONGS.

Fédération des ONG sénégalaises (FONGS) (1993) *Processus d'analyse et de réflexions paysannes face aux politiques agricoles au Sénégal. Rapport du Forum 'Quel avenir pour le paysan sénégalais?'*. Thiès: FONGS.

Fédération des ONG sénégalaises (FONGS) (2002) *Fonds d'appui aux initiatives rurales*. Thiès: FONGS.

Fédération des ONG sénégalaises (FONGS) and Food and Agriculture Organization of the United Nations (FAO) (1999) *L'Organisation mondiale du commerce (OMC): contraintes et opportunités pour l'agriculture sénégalaise*. Thiès and Rome: FONGS and FAO.

Franke, Richard W. and Barbara H. Chasin (1980) *Seeds of Famine*. Totowa, NJ: Rowman and Allanheld Publishers.

Freund, Claude, Ellen Hank Freund, Jacques Richard and Pierre Thénevin (1997) *L'Arachide au Sénégal. Un moteur en panne*. Paris: Karthala.

Gueneau, Marie-Christine and Bernard Lecomte (1998) *Sahel: les paysans dans les marigots de l'aide*. Paris: L'Harmattan.

Jacob, J.-P. and Ph. Lavigne Delville (1994) *Les associations paysannes en Afrique. Organisations et dynamiques*. Paris: Karthala.

Jayne, T.-S., James D. Shaffer, John M. Staatz and Thomas Reardon (1997) *Improving the Impact of Market Reform on Agricultural Productivity in Africa: How Institutional Design Makes a Difference*. East Lansing: Michigan State University.

Kasse, Moustapha (1996) *L'Etat, le technicien et le banquier face aux défis du monde rural sénégalais*. Dakar: Nouvelles éditions africaines du Sénégal.

Lavergen, Réal (ed.) (1997) *Regional Integration and Cooperation in West Africa*. Trenton, NJ: Africa World Press and IDRC.

Lecomte, Bernard (2001) *Une fresque esquissant les stratégies des acteurs de l'aide internationale dans le domaine de l'organisation des paysans en Afrique de l'Ouest (1958–2000)* (draft).

Matthews, Alan (2002) *Regional Integration and Food Security in ACP Countries*. Rome: FAO.

McKeon, Nora, Wendy Wolford and Michael Watts (1993) *National Forum: 'What Future for the Peasants of Senegal': a Case Study in FAO/NGO Cooperation*. Rome: FAO.

McKeon, Nora, Wendy Wolford and Michael Watts (1999) 'Grassroots development and participation in policy negotiations: bridging the micro-macro gap in Senegal', in Hans Homén and Enrico Luzzati (eds), *Grassroots' Organizations, Decentralization and Rural Development: African Experiences in the 1990s*. Proceedings from a workshop, International Training Centre of the ILO, Turin.

McKeon, Nora, Wendy Wolford and Michael Watts (2002) *Farmers' Organizations and National Development: the Experience of the National Council for Rural Peoples' Dialogue and Cooperation in Senegal* (mimeo).

McKeon, Nora, Wendy Wolford and Michael Watts (2003) *Peasant Associations in Theory and Practice*. Geneva: UNRISD.

NGO/CSO Forum for Food Sovereignty (2002) *Final Statement*. Rome: International NGO/CSO Planning Committee for the World Food Summit: Five Years Later.

Organisations paysannes de l'Afrique de l'Ouest (1999) *Atelier sur les programmes d'investissement du secteur agricole (Ouagadougou, Burkina Faso, 1–3 September 1999). Rapport final des travaux.*

Oxfam (2002) *Cultivating Poverty: the Impact of US Cotton Subsidies on Africa.* Oxfam Briefing Paper 30. Washington, DC: Oxfam International.

Padilla, Martine (1997) *Food Security in African Cities: the Role of Food Supply and Distribution Systems.* Rome: FAO.

Phillips, Wendy (2002) 'All for naught? An analysis of Senegal's PRSP process', in Alan Whaites (ed.), *Masters of their own Development? PRSSPs and the Prospects for the Poor.* Monrovia, CA: World Vision International.

Rencontres internationales de Bouaké (1965) *Tradition et modernisme en Afrique noire.* Paris: Editions du Seuil.

Réseau des organisations paysannes de l'Afrique de l'Ouest (2000) *Rapport final: Atelier de Cotonou, 4–6 July 2000.* Dakar: ROPPA.

Réseau des organisations paysannes de l'Afrique de l'Ouest (2001) *Conclusions de l'atelier régional sur la politique agricole de l'UEMOA (Ouagadougou, Burkina Faso, 2–4 October 2001).* Dakar: ROPPA.

Réseau des organisations paysannes de l'Afrique de l'Ouest (2002) *Le coton ouest africaine et la plainte brésilienne auprès de l'OMC contre le dumping américain: Papier de position paysanne.* Dakar: ROPPA.

Sall, Samba (1998) *Approvisionnement en intrants et commercialisations des produits dans la région de Tambacounda.* Rome: FAO.

Schaffer, Frederic C. (1998) *Democracy in Translation. Understanding Politics in an Unfamiliar Culture.* Ithaca, NY: Cornell University Press.

Seck, Ibrahima (1993) *Impact des accords du GATT sur les pays en voie de développement.* Thiès: FONGS.

Soderbaum, Frederik (2001) 'Turbulent regionalization in West Africa', in Michael Schulz, Frederik Soderbaum and Joakim Ojendal (eds), *Regionalization in a Globalizing World.* London: Zed Books.

Soumaré, Siré (2001) *Après l'émigration le retour à la terre.* Bamako: Jamana.

Suppan, Steve (2001) *Food Sovereignty in the Era of Trade Liberalization: Are Multilateral Means Feasible?* A preparatory paper for the NGO/CSO Forum on Food Sovereignty, International NGO/CSO Planning Committee for the World Food Summit: Five Years Later, Rome.

Sy, Racine (2002) 'Au coeur de la filière arachide', *Défis Sud*, No. 53, 2002/2003. Brussels: SOS Faim.

Terpend, Noelle (1993) 'Private sector marketing of agricultural products in Africa: a decade of development experience', in FAO, *Promoting Private Sector Involvement in Agricultural Marketing in Africa.* Rome: FAO.

Utting, Peter and Ronald Jaubert (eds) (1998) *Discours et réalités des politiques participatives de gestion de l'environnement. Le cas du Sénégal.* Geneva: UNRISD and IUED.

Von der Weid, Jean Marc (1992) *Rapport de la mission FAO/FONGS sur l'impact de la politique d'ajustement structurel en milieu rural sénégalais.* Rome: FAO.

Watts, M. (1983) *Silent Violence.* Berkeley: University of California Press.

World Trade Organization (WTO) (2001a) *Agricultural Trade Negotiations in the WTO – Preliminary Positions of Senegal.* G/AG/NG/W/137, 19 March. Geneva: WTO.

World Trade Organization (WTO) (2001b) *WTO African Group: Joint Proposal on the Negotiations on Agriculture.* G/AG/NG/W/142, 23 March. Geneva: WTO.

Yade, Mbaye, Anne Chonin-Kuper, Valerie Kelly, John Staatz and James Tefft (1999) *The Role of Regional Trade in Agricultural Transformation: the Case of West Africa Following the Devaluation of the CFA Franc.* Paper presented at the Workshop on Agricultural Transformation (Nairobi, 27–30 June 1999). East Lansing: Michigan State University.

8
Markets, Land Redistribution and Rural Social Movements in the Philippines[1]

Saturnino M. Borras Jr.

Introduction

Despite the series of land reform initiatives that have occurred over the past century, effective access to land by the rural poor remains a serious problem in most developing countries today (see Kay, 1998; Ghimire, 2001a). A combination of factors, such as the debt crises in the 1980s, has contributed towards the dropping of agrarian reform from policy agendas. While the land-based political conflicts in the 1990s have partly helped the renewal of interest on the issue (see Rosset, 2001; Petras, 1997, 1998), arguably, it has been the initiative by the pro-market policy circle that provided the most important push towards the resurrection of agrarian reform into the policy agendas. But this time, the national development policy contexts have been changed – from inward- to outward-oriented – and so, for pro-market scholars a more 'appropriate' agrarian reform model is necessary – thus, the market-led agrarian reform (MLAR). The mainstream push for market-led type of agrarian 'reform' has gained strong currency among international financial institutions and initial implementation has been underway (Borras, 2003, 2002a; see also Ghimire, 2001d; Bernstein, 2002).

Proponents of MLAR explain that it is a 'mechanism to provide an *efficiency- and equity*-enhancing *redistribution* of assets' (Deininger, 1999: 651; emphasis added), as it aspires to overcome the long-standing problem of 'social exclusion' of the rural poor (Deininger and Binswanger, 1999: 249). MLAR is a voluntary land reform, and it aims to replace the coercive, confrontational state-led approach (ibid.: 267). Under this model, landlords are paid 100 per cent cash based on 100 per cent market value of the land (Deininger, 1999: 663). The MLAR model adopts a demand-driven approach: only poor families who explicitly demand land and only the lands being demanded are negotiated for the reform programme. In order to find the 'fittest' beneficiaries, a 'self-selection' process among the prospective buyers is undertaken in order to avoid taking in 'unfit' beneficiaries. Moreover, the model adopts a decentralized method of implementation for speedy transaction and for transparency and accountability. 'It privatizes and thereby decentralizes the essential process [of land reform]', explains Binswanger (1996: 155). Moreover, the model would stimulate, rather than undermine, land markets (Deininger and Binswanger, 1999: 267). MLAR proponents also explain that 'closing the gap between agricultural land values and market values of the land makes land more affordable and enhances repayment ability because buyers of land will now find it easier to repay a loan from the productive capacity of the land itself' (van Schalkwyk and van Zyl, 1996: 333). This can be done partly through subsidy withdrawal (from large farmers), progressive land taxation, systematic land titling (Bryant, 1996), land sales and rental liberalization (Banerjee, 1999), and better market information systems. This market reform measure is anticipated to increase the amount of land available for purchase by different strata of producers. The MLAR model has been pilot-tested in Brazil since 1998, while it has been implemented on a national scale in Colombia and South Africa. Proponents of MLAR claim that the initial implementation in these countries has been generally successful (Deininger and Binswanger, 1999: 268). However, closer examination of the initial outcomes of MLAR implementation in these countries shows that the model is not working the way its inventors have expected and claimed. The World Bank officials also claim that MLAR has been underway in the Philippines as early as 1999 (ibid.: 267), which, as will be demonstrated later, is not correct.

But land reforms in the past that have achieved significant degrees of success in terms of land redistribution have been 'state-led' (Barraclough, 2001; El-Ghonemy, 2001; Herring, 1983; see Ghimire, 2001c). In this approach, the central state played a key role in redistributing lands to peasants. These state-led approaches can be broadly categorized either as revolutionary, conservative or liberal types. The first is basically guided by the principle of 'confiscation without landlord compensation and free land redistribution to peasants'; the second is a limited reform focused on resettlement programmes in unoccupied public land frontiers and some very partial coverage of private lands purchased at full market price; the third type is generally premised on the principle of 'expropriation with landlord compensation and land redistribution to peasants at subsidized land prices'. These are the three broad ideal types. In reality, the more common type of land reform policies that actually existed and have been implemented with varying degrees of success have combined features of the three types; and regardless of the type of policy, land redistribution outcomes have almost always been partial (see Borras, 2003).

The general setting of such national initiatives was the pre-neoliberal period when many countries that carried out land reform have, in varying degrees, been into national development campaigns within 'inward-looking' nationalist strategies, such as the import-substitution-industrialization (ISI). However, with the demise of most of the inward-looking, nationalist development campaigns by the late 1970s, amid the rise of market-based neoliberal policies, land reform was dropped from national policy agendas (Kay, 1993). Only a few countries have attempted major land reforms since the 1980s, such as El Salvador, Zimbabwe, Brazil and the Philippines. But land reform initiatives in these countries, while still well within the state-led tradition, have been enshrined with market-friendly land redistribution mechanisms and have been embedded in national and international political and economic conditions generally ruled by the forces of the 'free market'.

Among the countries that attempted large-scale land reforms during the neoliberal era, the Philippines has emerged to be among the top performers – achieving modest, but significant, accomplishments in terms of land redistribution (as percentage to the total agricultural lands and peasant households) – as compared to its contemporaries like El Salvador and Zimbabwe.

The Philippines' Comprehensive Agrarian Reform Programme (CARP) is a generally state-led agrarian reform initiative but has several pro-market land redistribution mechanisms. Moreover, such a reformist project is being implemented in the context of national and international political and economic conditions that are market-friendly.

The ideologically diverse rural social movement groups in the Philippines at first rejected CARP on the basis of its less revolutionary character (see Putzel, 1992). A few years later, however, most of the progressive rural social movement groups changed their position, and started to launch widespread claim-making initiatives within the CARP framework. Such change in position by most rural social movement organizations has been instigated by various factors – both internal and external to these groups. After a lacklustre start, CARP began to gain momentum after 1992 when the majority of the progressive rural social movement groups started to actively engage CARP amid the rise of a reformist leadership within the Department of Agrarian Reform (DAR). Since 1992, there has been a higher degree of unity in understanding and realization among most of the rural social movement organizations that CARP, in fact, has vast potential to effect a significant degree of land redistribution, and that these potentials can be best harnessed through the positive interaction between initiatives by state reformists 'from above' and mobilizations by autonomous rural social movements 'from below' (see Borras, 1999, 2001; Franco, 1999c).

Nevertheless, there are serious divisions within and between rural social movements with regard to CARP – careful examination of which can lead to a better understanding of the whole agrarian reform process and outcomes in the Philippines. These divisions can be seen – and explained – in a number of ways. *First*, divisions within and between rural social movement groups with regard to CARP are principally rooted on ideological differences between them rather than on the basis of differences of analyses on the actual and potential pro- and anti-reform features of the programme. For example, only the communist- (CPP-) controlled and influenced national peasant organizations are outrightly opposed to CARP on the basis that to them 'genuine agrarian reform' must be based on 'land confiscation without landlord compensation, and free land redistribution to peasants'. This type of land reform obviously can only be implemented by a revolutionary government. To these groups, e.g. KMP (*Kilusang Magbubukid ng Pilipinas*, or Peasant Movement of the Philippines), CARP is 'pro-landlord and anti-peasant'. KMP's positions on other specific issues related to CARP, such as CARP's processes and outcomes, are secondary and tactical, meant merely to strengthen its main framework: i.e. CARP is a 'fake land reform' programme. Meanwhile, the remaining national rural social movement organizations have – in varying degrees and forms – supported CARP and believe that it has vast reformist potential.

Second, at the national level, there are no major – apparent or real – divisions among rural social movement organizations with regard to their rejection of the World Bank's MLAR, or their rejection of market-friendly land redistribution mechanisms within CARP. Perhaps some minor differences between these groups may lie in how to actually make their opposition to such a scheme more effective. The controversial issues of market-friendly land redistribution mechanisms within CARP and the MLAR – and the rural social movement groups' rejection of them – have, to some extent, even contributed to the unity among ideologically diverse rural social movement organizations.

Third, the level at which serious divisive impact of market-friendly land redistribution mechanisms on rural social movement organizations is most real is at the level of local communities – or more specifically, at the level of estate or landholding. The various local case studies presented in this chapter demonstrate this most concretely.

Fourth, it is most likely that the officially reported accomplishments by CARP through market-friendly land redistribution schemes are devoid of any fundamental elements of 'redistribution' and 'reform'. This is especially so with voluntary land transfers (VLT), stock distribution options (SDO) and leaseback arrangements.

The four interrelated analytic insights presented above constitute the main arguments put forward in this chapter. They warrant further explanation. National rural social movement organizations are more coherent ideologically and politically compared to their local counterpart organizations. Most of the former reject market-based solutions to the problem of landlessness. And while the mass bases of these national organizations are in fact highly differentiated (from landless poor to rich farmers), the more ideological and political leaderships of national progressive organizations tend to be controlled and/or influenced by activists who reject market-friendly approaches to land redistribution. It is at the estate level that divisions among the peasants brought about by market-friendly land redistribution mechanisms are real and operative. It is at the estate/local level where landlords and other anti-reform focus are strongest, and where peasant organizations are localized and relatively isolated, and thus easily divided and defeated. And because the local estate-based peasant organizations are the most basic organizational building blocks of national or federal peasant coalitions or federations, divided and weakened local peasant organizations due to market friendly mechanisms can (and do) have profound weakening, divisive and debilitating impact on national or federal peasant movements. Weak 'institutional bridges' that connect national leaderships of peasant movements and other external ally organizations such as NGOs (see e.g. Fox, 1992; Ghimire, 2001b) with the local grassroots associations (partly due to lack of logistical resources to create, maintain and consolidate such institutional bridges) aggravate further the already hostile conditions for peasant movements. This is an even more serious concern when viewed from the perspective of the need for horizontally and vertically integrated and consolidated social movements, such as peasant movements, in the era of globalization (see Fox, 2001; Chalmers et al., 1997; Franco, 2001b).

The current literature correctly argues that market-friendly mechanisms divide and weaken rural social movements – groups that are essential in the successful implementation of reformist programmes such as land reform (see e.g. Dorner, 2001; El-Ghonemy, 2001). However, empirical evidence to demonstrate how actually this happens remains limited. In this chapter, it will be argued and demonstrated how market-friendly mechanisms in land redistribution actually cause divisions among rural social movement groups, leading to their weakening, and so adversely affecting the chances of redistributive reforms from being implemented fully. First, some market-friendly mechanisms in land redistribution favour those who are relatively better off among the peasantry, namely, tenant-farmers and regular farmworkers, at the expense of the poorest of the rural poor (semi-proletariat), e.g. seasonal farmworkers and women. This is premised on the pro-market agenda of effecting the most economically efficient and competitive use of land resources – an agenda that favours the better-off sections of the peasantry. This type of division is 'horizontal' – that is, cutting along social classes.

Additionally, some market-friendly land transfer mechanisms tend to consolidate pre-existing patron–client relationships between peasants and elites, or tend to create new lines of patronage based on market relations. This is especially because one principle of market-friendly schemes is the 'voluntary nature' of transactions – and so, landlords will choose peasant-beneficiaries whom they do and can co-opt. This type of division is more of a 'vertical' one – cutting across social classes. Third, some market-friendly land transfer mechanisms tend to exclude women from the benefits of land reform. Fourth, some market mechanisms in land redistribution tend altogether to exclude the landless rural poor from the benefits of land market transactions, such as conversion of land uses to non-agricultural purposes where landlords and real estate developers are the biggest beneficiaries. Finally, some market-friendly mechanisms tend to exclude some modern productive farms. It is important to note, however, that some ostensibly market-friendly mechanisms are in fact not really market-friendly but more of a 'rent-seeking' type of landlord manipulation cloaked in pro-market discourses. In short, this chapter argues that in the current context of the Philippines, market-friendly land redistribution mechanisms have, in general, no divisive impact on rural social movement organizations at the national level. In fact, the effect seems to be the reverse – ideologically diverse groups have been united on the issue of rejection against market-led agrarian reform (MLAR). The level where the exclusionary, divisive and debilitating impacts of market friendly mechanisms are most real is at the local level – 'local' meaning 'estate level'.

The Philippine agrarian transformation[2]

The Philippines has an important agricultural sector: in 1999 it contributed a 19 per cent share to the gross domestic product (GDP), and directly employed some 40 per cent of the country's total active labour force (see Putzel, 1992; Peralta, 2001). The agrarian transformation which has occurred during the twentieth century, however, has been less than dynamic. It has taken place against the backdrop of highly skewed land ownership distribution and widespread rural poverty. The Gini-coefficient on land distribution was 0.64 in 1988 (Putzel, 1992); in 1999, the rural poor accounted for two-thirds of the total poor in the Philippines. After the politically and economically chaotic years of the Aquino administration (1986–92), a significant degree of political stability and economic revival was achieved by its successor. The Ramos administration (1992–8) tried to squeeze the agriculture sector of surplus factors of production for industrial development, while maintaining and consolidating productive farms that generate export earnings. While agriculture continues to be important in financing the industrial project of the elite, two other key sources have emerged over time, namely, foreign direct investments, and remittances from overseas Filipinos. Like the Ramos administration, the Estrada administration (1998–2001) tied its hopes for development to the three main pillars of the national economy. The new president, Gloria Arroyo, seems likely to continue or even deepen the same policies, given that she was the chief architect of neoliberal reforms in agriculture when she was still a senator.

Philippine agriculture is diverse in terms of products and production systems but can be broadly differentiated into two types. The traditional sector (rice, corn, coconut and sugarcane) is characterized by obsolete production and exchange relations, but continues to be the major sector in terms of nationally aggregated monetary value and land use. With high-volume, low-value crops and antiquated production technology, this sector is dominated by traditional landed elites whose provenance dates back to colonial times.[3] In contrast, the non-traditional sector produces low-volume, high-value crops and products such as banana, pineapple and fish products, and has seen expansion, albeit less than expected, since the neoliberal resurgence. With different production and exchange relations, such as contract growing schemes and wage relations, this is the sector in which non-traditional landed elites, including urban-based entrepreneurs and multinational corporations, have gained the most ground. Modern technology and equipment, as well as a capitalist management system, also characterize these modern farm enclaves (see Hawes, 1987; Ofreneo, 1980; Tadem et al., 1984).

This traditional–modern dichotomy is not static and the line between the two broad types of farming system is in reality quite blurred: most farms exhibit some features of both types. Two important factors to note are that the process of rural capital accumulation is set against a background of inequitable distribution of productive resources, and that the Philippine agricultural sector seems ill-prepared for global neoliberal competition. Since the mid-1990s, the Philippines has been transformed into a net agricultural importing country, as its non-competitive farm sector struggles amidst cheap imports.

The structure of the country's economy, particularly its skewed landownership distribution, has had a profound impact on the structure of power relations and political institutions. Rural politics is dominated by local political bosses (*caciques*) who lord it over the countryside through a complex network of patronage (Anderson, 1988; Kerkvliet, 1990) that combines socioeconomic benefits for the rural poor with the threat and/or actual use of violence.[4] The rise in economic significance of the non-traditional export crops sector has entailed a relative rise in the political influence of landlord-entrepreneurs, challenging the historical political influence of traditional landlords. This process is best illustrated by the fact that during CARP policy-making, the concession that the rice and corn landlords received was a modest adjustment of the compensation package for their lands (Riedinger, 1995: 201) while, in contrast, owners of commercial farms were able to force through coverage deferment (Borras and Quiambao, 1998). Still, some traditional landlords have shown resilience over time and diversified their political and economic investments (Angeles, 1999).

Against this political background, cycles of violent peasant-based upheavals in the Philippines have been able to gain only intermittent concessions from the state. The elite response to peasant unrest has traditionally been a combination of repression, resettlement and limited reform. The Marcos land reform in 1972, for example, targeted close to a million hectares of tenanted rice and corn lands for redistribution, but was mainly directed against Marcos' political enemies and the nascent communist insurgency. While the Marcos land reform helped instil the concept of land reform, and install the necessary administrative machinery, after more than a decade of implementation, the programme's output in terms of land redistribution was far below the official claims (see Wurfel, 1988). It did, however, achieve significant output in leasehold (that is, reform from share tenancy to lease arrangement) of 500000 hectares. Since none of the pre-CARP tenancy and land reform programmes seriously addressed the underlying causes of peasant unrest – the widespread lack of access to land for the rural poor – peasant unrest remained an important part of rural politics throughout the twentieth century. The most important post-war peasant-based revolution was the insurgency led by the Communist Party of the Philippines together with its armed wing, the New People's Army (NPA).

The transition from an authoritarian to a national electoral regime in 1986 did not lead to complete democratization of the countryside: even now, entrenched political elites continue to dominate the rural polity (Franco, 2001a; Putzel, 1999). These local elites use extensive patronage networks that combine (partial) provision of daily subsistence needs of rural poor households with the threat and/or use of violence. However, in recent years there has been some erosion of these rural authoritarian enclaves, in a political process which can be traced back partly to the series of highly constrained elections held during and immediately after the period of authoritarian rule, and to sustained social mobilizations from below (Franco, 1998b). The transition period opened new political opportunities for democratization which led to a heated policy debate on agrarian reform.[5] After initially dragging its feet on the issue, the Aquino administration was forced to act after thirteen peasants were gunned down by government troops near the presidential palace. Subsequent actions by the government eventually led to the legislation of a new land reform policy: CARP.

CARP: a state-led land reform within a market-friendly policy environment

CARP targets and implementing mechanisms[6]

CARP is a public policy that does not fit with the typical kinds of revolutionary or conservative or market-led agrarian reform policies. Here, 'conservative land reform programme' is defined as a policy that is generally characterized by selective and limited reforms, focusing mainly on resettlement, and usually excludes productive farms. Revolutionary land reform is broadly defined as a policy that expropriates all private estates without landlord compensation and redistributes land for free. CARP, while having some degree of expropriationary power, has incorporated major elements that are less revolutionary and are market-friendly, for example, paying landlords based on the 'just compensation principle'. In addition, and in theory,

CARP covers all agricultural lands in the Philippines, private and public, regardless of tenurial relations. Based on the original 1987 scope, CARP was intended to reform tenure relations in all 10.3 million hectares of the country's farmland. The programme was intended to redistribute these to around 4 million landless and land-poor households, comprising close to 80 per cent of the agricultural population. It should be noted that the average farm size in the country is about 2 hectares, while the land reform award ceiling is fixed at 3 hectares.

In addition, tenancy reform, through leasehold, is to be implemented in farms of 5 hectares or less. Moreover, private lands and some government-owned lands are to be redistributed by the Department of Agrarian Reform (DAR), while redistribution of public alienable and disposable (A&D) lands is to be implemented by the Department of Environment and Natural Resources (DENR). Finally, there are more than twenty state agencies, big and small, that are directly involved in land redistribution processes. The Land Bank of the Philippines (LBP) handles the land valuation process, landlord compensation and beneficiary payment. There are a number of exclusions guaranteed by CARP: among them are military reservations, penal colonies, educational and research fields, 'timberlands' and some church areas. Undeveloped hills with 18 degrees slope are also excluded. In the mid-1990s, further exemptions were introduced, namely, agricultural sectors that are 'less dependent on land', e.g. poultry, livestock, salt beds and fishponds. The CARP scope, however, was revised in January 1996 by the Presidential Agrarian Reform Council, the inter-agency and multisectoral body in charge of the overall implementation of CARP. This is part of what the DAR under Ernesto Garilao called 'data clean-up'.

Providing flexibility in the process, CARP has adopted various acquisition modes for private lands. First, Operation Land Transfer, or OLT, is the mechanism used for rice and corn lands under the Marcos-era land reform programme, or Presidential Decree No. 27 which was later integrated within CARP. Second, devised to lessen landlord resistance to reform, the Voluntary-Offer-to-Sell, or VOS, increases the cash portion in landlords' compensation by 5 per cent with a corresponding 5 per cent decrease in the bonds portion. A third mode that aspires to court landlord cooperation to the programme is the market-friendly Voluntary Land Transfer or VLT. It provides for the direct transfer of land to peasants under mutually agreed terms between peasants and landlords. The government's role is reduced to information provision and contract enforcement. Both VOS and VLT operate in the context of expropriation, i.e. if landlords refuse VOS or VLT, their estates will nonetheless be acquired by the state. This brings us to the last acquisition mode, i.e. Compulsory Acquisition, or CA, through which land is expropriated whether or not the landlord cooperates. OLT is akin to CA. Furthermore, there are some related acquisition and distribution policies that are important to note. For one, the Stock Distribution Option, or SDO, is a distinct mode designed for corporate farms. SDO exempts such lands from redistribution if the owner opts for corporate stock sharing with peasant beneficiaries. Moreover, the acquisition of some 50 000 hectares of highly productive commercial farms, e.g. banana plantations, was deferred in 1988 for a ten-year period, ostensibly to allow plantation owners to recoup their investments and to prepare farmworkers for eventual takeover. In addition, under certain conditions, CARP allows for peasant beneficiaries to lease out awarded lands to an investor. Finally, acquired lands can be transferred to individuals or cooperatives, although the general bias is towards the former.

Land redistribution outcomes: unexpected, uneven and varied – a national view

By the end of 2001, contrary to earlier pessimistic predictions, CARP has been able to achieve significant output in land redistribution – although it is far below the optimistic claims of government. James Putzel, a notable scholar on Philippine agrarian reform, has recently admitted that: '[CARP] has certainly touched a far greater proportion of the country's land and rural population than its early critics predicted' (2002: 219). Table 8.1 shows CARP land redistribution accomplishment over time. A number of initial observations can be made. First, by the end of 2001, CARP has been able to redistribute close to 5 million hectares of land that account for roughly two-fifths of the total farmland. Second, this accomplishment represents more or less two-thirds of the total CARP adjusted scope. Third, 2.1 million rural poor households, who constitute about two-fifths of the total agricultural population, have directly benefited from the land redistribution.

Further scrutiny of Table 8.1 reveals a number of important insights. First, almost two-thirds of the total CARP accomplishment was delivered by the DAR, as compared to the DENR. Second, by administration, the biggest accomplishment under the DAR was achieved under the Ramos administration (1992–8), accounting for close to two-thirds of the department's total output. Third, the land acquisition mode of VLT cornered a little more than one-fourth of the DAR output in private agricultural land. Finally, government-owned and public lands cornered a little more than two-thirds of the total CARP accomplishment. Most CARP critics take this data as evidence to suggest that CARP has focused mainly on the 'less contentious' components. Further explanation is necessary.

Carrying out analysis based solely on the technical property classifications of lands between private and government-owned to assess the depth and breadth of CARP achievements may be misleading, at least in the Philippine context. This can be explained in a number of ways. For one, most public lands in the Philippines are in fact under widespread agricultural cultivation, unlike in other less populated countries in the past. Hence, the concept of 'colonization' or resettlement in ('unoccupied') public lands as a form of

Table 8.1 Land acquisition and distribution output (1972/88–2001)

Average annual output by administration, under the Department of Agrarian Reform (DAR)

Type of land acquisition and distribution	Output (hectares)	Marcos 1972–86	Aquino 1987–June 1992	Ramos July 1992–June 1998	Estrada July 1998–December 2000	Arroyo January–December 2001
National total	*3,209,637 (total)*	*67,124 (total)*	*135,420 (annual average)*	*314,896 (annual average)*	*133,355 (annual average)*	*105,224 (annual average)*
OLT	521,326	15,061	56,674	23,603	7,483	5,892
CA	197,553		2,247	20,138	19,106	15,476
VOS	416,283		9,001	42,556	30,758	30,034
VLT	443,110		3,456	54,775	29,338	20,374
GFI	143,394		3,823	17,583	4,762	3,052
KKK	775,328		23,720	90,623	27,408	20,749
Landed estate	79,168	11,041	4,296	6,866,83	388	174
Settlement	633,475	41,022	32,201	58,749	14,110	11,473

Total output by administration, under the Department of Agrarian Reform (DAR)

National total	*3,209,637*	*67,124*	*812,522*	*1,889,377*	*333,389*	*107,224*
OLT	521,326	15,061	340,045	141,620	18,708	5,892
CA	197,553		13,482	120,828	47,767	15,476
VOS	416,283		54,011	255,341	76,896	30,034
VLT	443,110		20,737	328,654	73,345	20,374
GFI	143,394		22,938	105,498	11,906	3,052
KKK	775,328		142,321	543,738	68,520	20,749
LES	79,168	11,041	25,781	41,201	971	174
Settlement	633,475	41,022	193,207	352,497	35,276	11,473

Total output under the Department of Environment and Natural Resources (DENR)

National total (approximate)	*1,800,000 hectares*

Notes: OLT started in 1972 under the Marcos dictatorship; land distribution in landed estates and settlement areas was also begun during the Marcos era. These land distribution mechanisms were later subsumed within the CARP law in 1988. Technically, the Macapagal–Arroyo administration started in February 2001, and not in January. Hence, a minor error due to the one-month difference has to be noted because, to simplify periodization, this administration's record in this chapter starts in January 2001. The data in many of the columns are my own computation based on: (a) Land Acquisition and Distribution Status Report, or Table 4, dated as of 31 December 2001, Management Information Service, Department of Agrarian Reform, and (b) Land Distribution Accomplishment: area in hectares, by administration, year, region and province, 1972 to December 2000, Management Information Service, Department of Agrarian Reform.

land reform adopted in some Latin American countries does not apply, to a large extent, in the contemporary Philippine context; it was relevant between the 1950s and 1960s during the campaign to open up new land frontiers. The latter reached exhaustion by the 1970s. Moreover, many public lands in the Philippines have in fact been under the *effective control* of private elites despite absence of formal, legal ownership titles. Here, the concept of redistribution goes beyond the technical issue of legal property rights; it runs right through the question of political power, of control. It follows that the degree of 'contentiousness' in expropriating land is not necessarily restricted within the types of property regime (private or otherwise). This explains why acquisitions of government-owned lands in the country have proven highly contentious on many occasions. Furthermore, tenurial relations actually exist in public lands that are under elite control. Peasants, who may not even be aware of the exact property question of the land, have been paying land rents to the elites who maintained control over the public lands (see Franco, forthcoming).

For reasons cited above, this chapter argues that CARP's accomplishment in public lands cannot be dismissed as some activists tend to do, nor can it be compared to some 'colonization' projects elsewhere. Even if all the lands 'redistributed' under the dubious method of VLT – at a total of close to 400 000 hectares – were to be struck out of the land redistribution accomplishment data, the national aggregate of land redistribution output will still be substantial, at more than 4 million hectares, benefiting around 2 million poor peasants.

As said earlier, the land redistribution outcomes are varied and uneven across land and crop types, geographic locations, policy components, and over time. It is relevant to look into the accomplishment data more closely: While the general pattern follows the skewed concentration of land distribution based on crops towards the traditional, low-value crops like rice, corn, coconut and sugarcane, land redistribution has also gained ground in the highly productive, modern farms planted to crops like pineapple, banana, palm oil, rubber and vegetables. To date, the remaining balance in land redistribution under DAR had the following crop distribution estimates: 75 per cent coconut, 15 per cent sugarcane, 5 per cent remaining rice and corn lands, as well as 5 per cent commercial plantations whose redistribution was deferred from 1988 until 1998. Sugarcane haciendas have been largely untouched by land reform despite incessant attempts of past DAR administrations mainly because of the strong resistance of landlords and the continued state subsidies the sugarcane barons enjoy. But coconut farms that were originally thought as croplands that would be relatively easy to expropriate proved to have been left behind in the implementation. Two possible explanations are relevant: the dominance of small coconut owners who are resistant to reform, and the relatively weaker reformist rural social movement in the coconut lands that have been and remain a bastion of the armed insurgency that is opposed to 'reformist' agrarian reform. Finally, some portions of highly modern plantations have been redistributed to farmworkers over time, despite the previous belief that redistribution was unlikely to occur in these areas (see Lara, 2001; Feranil, 2001; Cuarteros, 2001; Rodriguez, 2000; Franco, 1999b; Franco and Acosta, 1999; Borras and Quiambao, 1998). One explanation is that most multinational companies (MNCs) abandoned their alliance with local landed elites and manoeuvred to implement land reform in these areas. The motivation rests on MNCs' belief that CARP offers better opportunities for more profits. This can be done via different joint venture arrangements like contract growing schemes and lease arrangements (see Vellema, 2002). Again, this issue will prove strategic in relation to post-land transfer development. It is important to note, however, that during the past two years, despite the cleavage between MNCs and the local landed elite that is favourable for land redistribution, the anti-reform landlords made important anti-reform manoeuvres and victories – largely because of the major swing of the current Arroyo administration towards more market-based mechanisms in land reform (see e.g. Borras, 2002b). On another plane, the uneven and varied outcomes of land redistribution can be viewed based on geographic locations. A number of issues are important. First, the current DAR land redistribution is highly concentrated in six (out of the total of fourteen) regions; these six regions account for more than three-fourths of the total current land redistribution balance. Second, observers would quickly note that these are the same regions where coconut and sugarcane farms are important, if not dominant. This corresponds to the cropland breakdown cited earlier. Finally, it is important to note that in these regions autonomous peasant movements and NGOs have highly uneven, relatively thin, presence.

Meanwhile, it is also important to look into the varied and uneven outcomes of land redistribution based on policy components, specifically based on land acquisition modes. A few observations are relevant. First, Operation Land Transfer and Compulsory Acquisition have a combined percentage share of close to half of the total redistribution output in private lands. OLT and CA have been lumped together because in essence they are the same – expropriationary in nature. The other half has been more or less split between the market-friendly voluntary-offer-to-sell and voluntary land transfer. Here, it is important to note that VOS in practice is not exactly and automatically 'voluntary'. Most landlords who resisted expropriation, but later realized the overwhelming force of redistribution, negotiated instead for better compensation terms. Under VOS the cash portion in landlord compensation is increased by 5 per cent, with corresponding decrease of the same percentage from the bonds portion (see Borras, 2001, 2002b).

However, what is alarming is the extent to which VLT has been employed, cornering one-fourth of the total redistributed private estates under the DAR. An outrightly pro-market, pro-landlord measure, VLT is a 'land transfer' process directly negotiated between landlords and peasants, with the government as mediator (it is not exactly the same as the MLAR model, but has some core components that overlap with the former). There is sufficient empirical evidence demonstrating that most likely all the VLT-facilitated 'land transfers' are completely devoid of any fundamental elements of 'redistribution' and 'reform'. The annual internal programme audit of the Presidential Agrarian Reform Council (PARC) has discovered, documented and presented numerous cases of VLT transactions across geographic locations showing that it is either 'faked' land redistribution with fake beneficiaries (intra-family transfers and/or dummy beneficiaries), or straightforward cases of corruption (with government officials or their family members becoming beneficiaries of this market-based scheme). It is important to note that the regions and provinces where the VLT cases did occur in larger scales are the regions and provinces where the organizational presence and political influence have been quite thin and weak as, for example, Regions 1 and 12 and the provinces therein.

Finally, land redistribution outcomes have been varied and uneven over time, across different regimes. The Aquino regime had a yearly average output of 135 420 hectares. This was almost doubled by the Ramos administration's yearly redistribution achievement, at 314 896 hectares. The Estrada administration had an annual average of almost the same as Aquino's record, at 133 355 hectares. The current Macapagal–Arroyo administration (and its DAR Secretary Hernani Braganza) has targeted only 100 000 hectares output per year under the DAR, and another 100 000 hectares per year under the DENR – the lowest in CARP history – and has delivered the least quantity of redistributed land in CARP history: 107 324 hectares.

In sum, the partial outcome of land redistribution has been unexpected from two perspectives. It is more than the earlier pessimistic predictions by CARP critics, but it is far below the earlier optimistic claims of its proponents. The outcomes are also uneven and varied across farm, land and crop types, geographic locations, policy components, and over time. These variegated outputs are largely influenced by the political dynamics in general and political strategies employed by key actors in particular in the process of CARP implementation as well as the role of market-friendly state policies. These political dynamics sometimes upset the structural obstacles to reform, and offset the limitations of state policy elites. Meanwhile, it is relevant to briefly look into some other CARP policy components.

Some specific policy questions

(i) Land reform reversals

Some critics argue that the land redistribution accomplishment is not accurate because there are reversals that occurred in the process. These reversals happened primarily in the form of land award cancellation and non-installation beneficiaries on to the awarded lands. It is necessary to elaborate. Many Certificates of Land Ownership Awards (CLOAs), have been cancelled by government. Different reasons have been offered to explain the cancellations, like 'erroneous' government decisions and the 'sudden appearance' of original land claimants. It is to be noted that these reversals have occurred mainly in areas of the urban sprawl. To date, there are about 90 000 hectares of land affected by these decisions involving more or less 35 000 households. The exchanges between the DAR and civil society organizations on this issue have since then been highly polemical. What is thus important is to carry out a serious audit to determine the extent of these reversals. A related issue is the non-installation of some beneficiaries on to the awarded lands. Meaning, some peasants were already given the land award certificates but could not take over the awarded estate due to landlord opposition (see e.g. Feranil, 2003). To date, there are about 75 000 hectares affected by this problem involving more or less 30 000 households. Using these cases, most critics have accused government of lacking political will despite a few successful (and even dramatic) reinstallations of beneficiaries onto the land backed up by the military and police (see e.g. Franco, 1998a, 1998b). In short, the area affected by land reform reversals and 'uninstalled' beneficiaries is an important issue and must be addressed. However, in terms of volume, it is unlikely to upset the overall output and pattern of land redistribution outcomes. Moreover, converting farm use into non-agricultural land uses can facilitate evasion from expropriation and at the same time allow landlords to cash in handsomely from land sales. Land use conversions have occurred legally and illegally, although the latter, which are more difficult to monitor, are believed to have been more widespread than the former. However, the 1990s witnessed the surge of urbanization that spurred widespread land use conversions. Between 1992 and 1997, there was a total of 12 541 hectares (875 case applications) approved by DAR for conversion. But this figure is quite low compared to illegal land use conversions. There is a popular belief outside and even inside government that land use conversions have occurred amidst widespread corruption within the DAR bureaucracy and other state agencies, from national to local offices.

(ii) Leasehold

Leasehold reform has to be implemented in farms below 5 hectares (under the retention rights of landlords). In this regard, leasehold has great potential in recasting social relations in more than 2 million hectares of farmland (mainly coconut), involving more or less 2 million rural poor households. For example, many tenants in coconut farms are under *tersyuhan* arrangement (two-thirds share to landlord; one-third to peasant). Meanwhile, leasehold requires an arrangement based on the principle that peasants should pay lease rents to landlords at not more than 25 per cent of the land's net produce, thereby significantly increasing the income of poor peasants without much public spending, and guaranteeing the security of tenure of the peasants. Yet, the implementation of this policy has been slow and limited over time, benefiting a few hundred thousands of poor tenant households between 1972 and 2001.

(iii) Deferred commercial farms and joint venture arrangements

Here, joint venture arrangement is taken in its most general sense to include stock distribution schemes, but all of them are pro-market policies and mechanisms. There are four related issues, namely, stock distribution option (SDO), deferred commercial farms, leaseback option, and joint venture agreements. The best known, SDO (where distribution of corporate stocks to farmworkers is deemed in compliance with the land reform law), is the one applied to the 6400-hectare Hacienda Luisita sugarcane plantation owned by ex-President Corazón Cojuangco-Aquino's family. The Hacienda Luisita SDO depressed the value of land, and overpriced non-land assets. In the end, a small percentage of the corporation was awarded to farm workers (Putzel, 1992: 332–8). The living conditions of the farmworkers have not significantly improved since then. Meanwhile, unlike most agrarian reforms elsewhere that excluded highly productive and modern farms, CARP is formally mandated to expropriate the lucrative plantations in the country. The ten-year grace period for acquiring commercial farms lapsed in June 1998. It involves roughly 50000 hectares planted mainly to bananas. As expected, the acquisition process has been highly contentious. There are a number of interrelated issues in this regard. For one, during the deferment period companies were obligated to pay farmworkers production and profit shares, that is, 5 per cent of annual gross sales and 10 per cent of annual net income. For some 30000 hectares of banana plantations alone, this means several hundred millions of dollars due to farmworkers. However, while most companies complied with the mandatory scheme, most of them have cheated the farmworkers by giving only a small fraction of what was due. Proper accounting of unpaid production and profit shares may render these plantations fully paid by farmworkers. Moreover, during the deferment period, plantation owners waged a campaign to purge their plantations of claim makers and so launched widespread retrenchment of workers. Between 1988 and 1998, it is estimated that about 20000 farmworkers were put out of employment. The first ones to go were leaders and members of militant farmworkers' unions. Today, retrenched farmworkers are in the forefront of the struggle for land redistribution. Finally, several elites who failed to evade redistribution via conversions to non-agricultural land uses have been coercing farmworkers to agree to post-land transfer leaseback arrangements or joint venture engagements with lopsided contract terms (see Franco, 1999b; Franco and Acosta, 1999; Feranil, 2001). Furthermore, MNCs have even earlier worked for land redistribution in some plantations.[7] The main agenda was to forge a new partnership with what they should have perceived as a 'weaker' partner – the agrarian reform beneficiaries. Subsequent leaseback arrangements entered into between the beneficiaries, on the one hand,

and MNCs like Dole and Del Monte and other local landed elites, on the other hand, proved to be favourable only to the latter, although non-leaseback arrangements like contract growing schemes are emerging to be better alternatives (and these are primarily endorsed by MNCs against local landed elites' preference for leaseback). In many cases, effective control of the plantations remains in the hands of the MNCs and local landed elites. Today, most agrarian reform beneficiaries have become hostile to such terms of contracts and have been mobilizing to recast the terms of relationships (see Lara, 2001; Franco, 1999b; Feranil, 2001).

Finally, the manoeuvres by elites in commercial plantations have seen parallel initiatives by other landlords elsewhere. Between the unacceptable outright expropriation and the near impossibility of complete redistribution evasion, more landlords are manoeuvring in between, that is, exploring and gambling on the possibility of some forms of joint venture arrangements where they can still maintain control of their lands. Instead of focusing on rapid land redistribution, national administrations in recent years have been interested in exploring market-induced redistribution schemes, and as evidenced by the dramatic rise of transactions under the VLT scheme in recent years. The usual reason being cited by the DAR is the lack of funding to acquire lands, especially the high-value orchards and fruit plantations. The DAR under the leadership of Horacio Morales (Estrada administration, July 1998–January 2001) has attempted to institutionalize further the pro-market provisions within the CARP law. It must be noted that the CARP law has ample pro-market provisions, such as the stock distribution option, leaseback, voluntary land transfer, and the like. The Morales DAR attempted to package such market-friendly CARP components into a more 'catchy' pro-gramme called 'corporative' aimed at attracting foreign and domestic capi-tal to invest into agriculture, specifically the agrarian reform sector. According to DAR, the corporative scheme attempts to mobilize the so-called best features of a cooperative (equity) and a corporation (efficiency). While in this scheme there was really nothing new as far as the CARP law is con-cerned, the Morales DAR was severely criticized by rural social movement groups as promoting a 'market-led agrarian reform' in the Philippines. In fact, most rural social movement groups have erroneously equated the cor-porative scheme to MLAR.

The exchanges between the DAR and NGOs on this particular issue have missed the essential issues. For example, while the Morales DAR issued DAR Administrative Order No. 2 series of 2000 ostensibly to promote joint ven-ture arrangements within the framework of a 'corporative scheme', the same official guideline also explicitly prohibited any certificate of land ownership awards or titles of farmer-beneficiaries from being used as equity in these joint ventures – and that only the 'land use' can be put up as equity. Depending on the length of a joint venture, this guideline should at least protect the beneficiaries from losing their effective control and ownership over their land. But beyond the details of complex specific cases, the crucial issue that is not highlighted so often is the fact that the central government under various administrations, including the current one, has chosen to automatically allot billions of dollars from the annual national budget to pay off external debts rather than ensure the budget and annual funding of land acquisition and agrarian reform support services. Instead, all national administrations, past and present, have banked on the strategy of promoting and encouraging transnational and domestic capital to invest into Philippine agriculture – ostensibly to make the sector more globally competitive.

(iv) Policy reforms

CARP is not static. It has been transformed over time. Many of its policy components and implementation designs have been altered due to the political dynamics that went through with programme implementation. Agrarian reform, especially in settings where there are more landless rural poor than the available lands for redistribution, is potentially exclusionary. Experiences in various countries, including the Philippines, show that land reform programmes tend to benefit the not-so-poor rural poor because the priority beneficiaries have been almost always those who have prior access to land through various tenancy arrangements. Land reform programmes tend to exclude the poorer section of seasonal farmworkers. Thus, among the losers in the land reform process, at least in the plantation setting in the Philippines, has been the sector of seasonal plantation workers. While it may be understandable that prioritization has to be made, the government has failed to provide alternative sources of employment and livelihood to these seasonal farmworkers. And many of these seasonal farmworkers are women. CARP started with vague policies regarding women. After the controversial case of a plantation in Mindanao where all the 482 beneficiaries were men, in 1996–7, the DAR came out with a policy reform more favourable to women (see Rimban, 1997a). Again, while the new policy does not guarantee automatic recognition of the distinct right of women to become beneficiaries separate from their spouses' claims over the land, the reform has given women better room for political manoeuvre. Again, the pro-market bias of agricultural development strategy of the government (and even some NGOs) has somehow driven CARP away from a primarily anti-poverty measure towards an 'economic efficiency enhancing public policy' that has strong exclusionary and differentiating currents.

Moreover, less known to most people, CARP could have been legally ended in 1998 despite incomplete implementation if not for the passage of a new law, the Republic Act 8532 in February 1998 (see Borras, 1999: 80–4). This law mandates the extension of CARP implementation for another ten years, or until 2008, with the same budget allocation as during the 1988–98 period, or PhP 50 billion, roughly $1 billion (late 2002 exchange rate) – but it is a budget cap. But while it is laudable that, under rare political circumstances, the Philippine Congress passed a new law on agrarian reform, the budget allocation is only about 40 per cent of what is needed to at least complete the land redistribution component of CARP. Again, the preference of the state to toe the line of international financial institutions to allocate automatically billions of dollars annually for debt servicing has taken away a significant degree of the financial capacity of the Philippine government to finance social justice and pro-poor programmes like agrarian reform.

The contemporary peasant movements in a changed and changing context

Since the early 1970s until the late 1980s, the rural polity of the country was marked by the rapid growth of the communist insurgency led by the Maoist Communist Party of the Philippines (CPP) and its army, the New People's Army (NPA).[8] This CPP-led movement became known as the National-Democratic Movement, or 'Nat-Dem' or 'ND', because of its programme of a two-stage revolution, i.e. first to achieve 'national democracy' by over-throwing imperialism, feudalism and bureaucratic-capitalism, before going to the second stage, the socialist revolution. In this context, the principal form of struggle is armed, patterned after the Maoist dictum of 'wave by wave, surround the cities from the countryside'. The ND movement subor-dinated all other forms of struggle to the principal armed form. Finally, it identified the 'proletariats' as the 'leading force', while the peasantry was considered the 'main force' (see Guerrero, 1970; but see Putzel, 1995 and Franco, 2001b). The subsequent ideological, political and organizational make-up of the ND peasant organizations, led by the Peasant Movement of the Philippines (KMP) was framed mainly from this general orientation set out by the CPP. Two aspects of this orientation have to be reiterated. First, 'genuine agrarian reform' can be achieved only after victory of the revolution; and second, while the revolution is being waged, partial and selective implementation of revolutionary agrarian reform may be carried out. This orientation accounted for the phenomenal growth of the ND movement, especially in the countryside, during the 1970s and the early 1980s under the authoritarian regime. However, the same ideological and political fram-ing became the source of the movement's weakening since the early 1990s amidst significant political-economic changes in the global, national and local settings. The intensification of internal conflicts within the CPP lead-ership, which occurred amidst the movement's isolation during and after the EDSA people's uprising in February 1986 that overthrew the Marcos govern-ment, led many of the movement's key leaders to question the basic princi-ples of the revolution. This in-fighting led to the movement's split in 1993.

The KMP was formally launched in July 1985 and immediately became the main open-legal peasant movement opposed to the authoritarian regime (see Putzel, 1995). The KMP's biggest contribution during the remaining months of the Marcos regime was to overtly expose the failure of the land reform programme, the deteriorating economic condition of the peasants, and the widespread violations of human rights in the countryside. The KMP remained the most vocal and active peasant organization even during the early years of the Aquino administration. It was able to play a significant role in the subsequent policy debate about agrarian reform. It was also the KMP that led a march of some 20000 peasants to Malacañang Palace on 22 January 1987 to press for land reform, but they were fired upon by the police and military forces, killing thirteen marchers and wounding dozens more. During the subsequent legislative debate about land reform, however, the KMP was no longer the only organization publicly projected and popularly recognized. Other progressive peasant organizations developed, such as the highly differentiated social-democratic group, during the political opening in 1986. This social-democratic bloc pushed for the formation of a broad national coalition of peasants, the Congress for a People's Agrarian Reform (CPAR) launched in mid-1987. The KMP and other ND rural people's organizations joined the coalition. They did so with extreme reservations, however, principally rooted in ideological differences with the moderate social democrats.

The CPAR was at the forefront of the peasants' lobby for a more progressive land reform policy, often receiving more publicity than the KMP. The KMP never believed that a meaningful land reform policy could be enacted by a national legislative body overwhelmingly dominated by big landlords. Its scepticism was not without basis. Thus the stress of the KMP was to expose the 'anti-land reform character' of the Aquino regime and at the same time to put forward the alternative of a radical version of land reform. The KMP intensified its national campaign for widespread peasant occupation of idle and abandoned lands and Marcos crony-owned lands in order to project the land reform issue politically, more than to secure and consolidate actual lands to address the peasants' pressing needs.

When CARP was enacted into law in June 1988, it was rejected by almost all peasant organizations across the political spectrum. The CPAR formulated its alternative policy proposal of land reform called the 'People's Agrarian Reform Code' or PARCode, and vowed to amend CARP through a nationwide signature campaign, invoking the 'people's initiative' clause enshrined in the Constitution. The KMP advanced the most radical critique of CARP, totally rejecting the policy as 'pro-landlord' and 'anti-peasant'. Ignoring the CPAR signature campaign, it instead intensified its land occupation campaign, a strategy it deemed to be more effective to polarize the political situation and thus put the ND radical form of struggle (i.e. armed struggle), which was then beginning to lose vigour, back on the agenda as the most viable option for a radical transformation of the society. In many cases, the KMP conducted its land occupations with the direct participation of the

NPA. In other cases, areas that were projected as KMP-occupied lands were the same communities that had in fact earlier been subjected to the CPP's 'agrarian revolution' programme. In still other cases, local peasants had occupied lands and later sought assistance from the KMP. But most, if not all, of these land occupations were not sustained (see Putzel, 1995; Kerkvliet, 1993; Canlas, 1992, 1994; Franco, 2001b). In a major summing-up activity made by the KMP in early 1992, the organization's secretary general, who comes from Negros Island in the Visayas where the KMP had occupied about 45 000 hectares, admitted two crucial points about land occupation. On the one hand, the majority of invaded lands were later recovered by the land-lords with the aid of private armies and the military, and relatedly, on the other, those lands which were maintained by the organization had not been made productive. Specifically, he pointed out that not more than 10 per cent of the total occupied lands were actually rendered productive. Several reasons were identified for this failure. First, most of the areas were heavily militarized and so the peasants could not resume their normal farming activities. Second, almost no government or private institution wanted to lend credit to the peasants occupying the lands. Third, the pool of cadres, peasants or otherwise, assigned in their communities were trained as political activists and not as business entrepreneurs or development activists who could help these communities organize viable farming enterprises. This was especially difficult because – and this is the fourth reason – the majority of the occupied lands were marginal. Fifth, and perhaps a summary of the ear-lier factors, was that when the communities started to be militarized, the peasants normally did not make an exhaustive effort to stay, perhaps partly because they felt there was not much at stake in the land: no legal titles and productive activities. In short, the KMP's land occupation campaign during the second half of the 1980s contributed to keeping the issue of land reform on the national agenda, but it failed as an alternative land reform pro-gramme that could be implemented outside the state. Internally for the ND movement, the campaign failed to create the political polarization that would be necessary to put the revolutionary movement back on track.

Meanwhile, the revolutionary land reform programme being carried out selectively in some areas where the NPA was strong suffered a fate similar to the KMP's land occupations. The communist insurgents' campaigns for land rent reduction, abolition of usury and selective land confiscation made initial and partial gains for the peasants, as some lands were redistributed to landless peasants, while land rents and loan interests were reduced in areas where the NPA was strong. But as soon as the general politico-military condition began to be unfavourable to the communist rebels in the late 1980s, most of these partial gains were rolled back as landlords later vio-lently took back their lands. The campaign to eradicate usury proved to be a very contentious issue within the revolutionary movement because in most cases where this campaign was launched, local moneylenders simply withdrew from their activities, draining the community of much-needed cash to finance rural village production. In the end, many peasants, even in the guerrilla zones, contracted loans from these moneylenders anyway but concealed them from the guerrillas (see Putzel, 1995).[9] The same ideological, political and organizational factors that accounted for the KMP's strength during its early years, especially under an authoritarian regime, led to its weakening towards the 1990s. The ND movement's static 'semifeudal, semi-colonial' analysis of Philippine society locked the KMP in a situation of inflexibility amidst a profoundly and rapidly changing context. The 'statist' and thus 'maximalist' (i.e. 'all or nothing') attitude of the ND movement in regard to the question of state power imprisoned the KMP in a situation where it was unable to take full advantage of political opportunities opened in the agrarian front. By the late 1980s, when it was clear that the mass base of the ND movement had been seriously affected by the government's counterinsurgency operations, the general call within the movement was to 'recover' the 'lost' mass base. In response, the National Peasant Secretariat (NPS) of the CPP Central Committee revised much of the orthodoxy in the strategy and tactics of the CPP. Relative to other CPP organs, the NPS came up with one of the earlier critiques of the CPP analyses and strategy. Among other key issues, the NPS called for invigorated organizing work in the more populous lowland areas (the CPP's stress was upland, mainly for guerrilla base building) through 'inclusive', 'fast-track' and 'issue-based' organizing methods aimed at achieving palpable gains for the peasants. From late 1989 until 1993, such an approach proved to be effective in recovering lost mass base areas, organizing new communities, and securing concrete socioeconomic gains for the peasants. By 1992, different 'non-KMP', 'ND-influenced' peasant organizations were formed along crops. At this point, tactical struggles for land using the positive provisions of CARP could be carried out only sporadically since the DAR bureaucracy did not want to work with progressive peasant organizations (see Franco, 1999c).

Meanwhile, many NGOs under the influence of the NPS worked along this adjusted concept of peasant work. At the height of the CPP influence, many of the well-known NGOs supporting the peasant movement had been well into the fold of the ND movement. In fact, many of the party decisions on the direction and conduct of the peasant movement had been carried out through these NGOs that were run by party intellectuals. But these same NGO-based party intellectuals, who were directly exposed to peasant struggles, were the first ones to be critical of the 'instrumentalist' attitude of the CPP towards peasant organizations and NGOs, so it was not surprising that they were the most active in the internal reorientation drive within the ND movement. At the forefront was the PEACE Foundation (Philippine Ecumenical Action for Community Empowerment).[10]

By early 1992, the KMP was already geared to 'institutionalize' the adjusted orientation in defiance of the official CPP line. However, by the end of 1992, a serious split occurred within the CPP, which had far-reaching effects in all ND organizations – open-legal and clandestine-illegal – so that the initial momentum of KMP reorientation had to be substantially realized outside the ND organizational framework. In 1993, the entire organizations of the CPP, NPA and their controlled legal organizations like KMP split over differences on political and military strategies. The CPP, NPA and the united front (NDF) and all their fraternal organizations (like KMP) split into at least four major groups. One group 'reaffirmed' the basic principles of the Marxist-Leninist-Maoist line under the leadership of Armando Liwanag. Another group came to be known as the 'third bloc', also as the 'democratic bloc', which is a highly heterogeneous group composed of various groups that had opted to undergo a process of rethinking and renewal without fixing any ideological or political line for the moment. The key leaders of the KMP, including Tadeo, its chairperson, opted to dissociate themselves from the 'reaffirmist' bloc and the tarnished name of the organization, and instead formed the *Demokratikong Kilusang Magbubukid ng Pilipinas* (DKMP, Democratic Peasant Movement of the Philippines).[11] On the one hand, the KMP retained control of a sizeable portion of the original (but largely constricted) mass base of the organization, mostly in upland interior areas. On the other, the DKMP, while taking a modest share of the original base, was composed more of local peasant organizations that emerged along cropline during the reorientation period since the late 1980s. The DKMP vowed to pursue the militant tradition of the KMP and to further develop the aborted ideological, political and organizational reorientation. Liberated from the dogmatism, the DKMP loosely identified itself with the 'third bloc'. Its first major resolution was to engage the government on the issue of land reform, using CARP as a starting point. Such opening of the DKMP was partly internally driven (the desire to continue the reorientation to reposition itself politically) and partly externally driven as political opportunities have opened up. (A few years later, DKMP would suffer massive defection by local affiliate organizations due to internal, personality-related conflicts; most of these organizations would later regroup under the banner of the National Coordination of Autonomous Local Rural People's Organizations (UNORKA) – discussed later.) At this point, the new DAR leadership was proving its reformist tendencies.

The proliferation of autonomous political organizations due to the widespread realignments of different left and centre-left political organizations marked the post-1992 period. After Ramos' election in mid-1992, the CPAR was disbanded mainly because about half of the member organizations had opted to support Ramos' presidential bid, even though he campaigned for a 50-hectare retention limit for land.[12] The demise of the CPAR and the ND split in turn created an opportunity for realignments within the broad left and centre-left peasant movement and NGO community. A new coalition of NGOs and peasant organizations was formed, namely, the Partnership for Agrarian Reform and Rural Development Services (PARRDS), which brought together the former ND peasant network (e.g. the DKMP and PEACE Foundation) and other autonomous groups. In addition, various organizations across the political spectrum began to cooperate on selected tactical issues despite the absence of formal organizational coalitions (PARRDS, 1997). Moreover, other non-ND progressive peasant organizations have become stronger and more widespread, like PAKISAMA (*Pambansang Kilusan ng mga Samahang Magsasaka*, or National Movement of Farmers' Associations) identified with the broad social-democratic political group. The emergence of these broad formations of autonomous peasant organizations, NGOs and political movements, combined with the widespread erosion of the CPP's influence both within the progressive movement's circle and in the national polity more generally, thus ushered in an era marked by a militant but pragmatic rural people's movement in the country. This had a positive impact on the implementation of CARP.

Meanwhile, the reform-oriented leadership in the DAR since 1992 has come from different progressive ideological traditions and political affinities, many of whom have been recruited by the Ramos administration from the progressive NGO community. The state reformists within the DAR have some autonomy from other anti-reform policy currents within the state and society and, at the same time, built up its capacity to implement reforms. Such capacity has been manifested in the national bureaucracy which has been beefed up by reformist and qualified officials and employees (neutralizing, if not isolating, conservative elements within the bureaucracy), the renewed interest of foreign funders in the programme, and its ability to make modest but positive 'reforms' in response to rising actual needs. Above all, these state reformists in the DAR correctly identified the role played by autonomous social movements from below. What they needed was a kind of societal group that would be militant, daring and widespread, but at the same time pragmatic enough to be able to work within the possibilities and limits of the programme.

Overall, the stage on which CARP implementation was being set has been marked since 1992 by the changing degrees of power and influence of state and societal actors, erosion of leftist hegemonic groups, flourishing of pluralist formations, alteration of alliances, and shifting terrain of struggles. These political dynamics have a far-reaching impact on CARP implementation. In March 1997, 190 DAR officials and NGO-PO (peasant organizations) community organizers and peasant leaders participated in the second national DAR-NGO-PO workshop (the first was in 1996) on how to 'fast-track' the implementation of CARP. The workshop was convened by 'National Task Force 24', an initiative of the PEACE Foundation to fast-track CARP implementation in twenty-four provinces identified as major areas of highly contested big landholdings. This evolved later into Project 40 Now!, stretching the campaign's target to forty provinces, and taking in additional peasant and non-government organizations such as the broadly known social democratic-oriented Agrarian Reform Now! group. Project 40 Now! has become the main mechanism under the Garilao DAR (1992–8) through which peasant and non-government organizations interfaced with the reformist officials of the DAR. This interface mechanism was also replicated in the lower levels of the provinces – where it had become known as ProCARRDs (Provincial Consultations on Agrarian Reform and Rural Development) and at the municipal level (MuCARRDs).

The specific examples of the pro-reform interactions between state reformists and autonomous rural social movements from above are of the more formal type. There are numerous informal positive interactions that also contribute towards the success of land reform, one example of which is the campaign against the World Bank's proposal to adopt the market-led agrarian reform (MLAR). In early 1996, the Garilao DAR was being pressured by the World Bank to stop the implementation of CARP and instead shift to MLAR. The Garilao DAR was not convinced. Top officials at the DAR secretly gave some NGOs and peasant organizations a copy of the confidential document of the World Bank that calls on the Philippine government to adopt MLAR. In turn, the NGOs and peasant organizations, especially those under the banner of the Partnership for Agrarian Reform and Rural Development Services (PARRDS), a coalition of eighteen NGOs and peasant organizations, made a high-profile campaign against MLAR and the World Bank that was given generous attention by the media. Put in a very defensive and embarrassing situation (for secretly lobbying to end CARP), the World Bank eventually recalled its proposal (see Franco, 1999a).

When the Morales leadership came into office at the DAR in mid-1998, such a consultative mechanism was not sustained. There were many reasons for the demise of ProCARRDs, but foremost was the fact that the realignment in the state actors had directly caused realignments among social movement groups. Some social movement groups had been anti-Estrada administration from the very beginning and so refused to engage the Morales DAR constructively. In turn, the Morales DAR seemed to be uninterested in constructively engaging these more critical groups on the grounds that the latter were anti-Estrada anyway. Whatever comes first, or whichever is more crucial, the result was a divided agrarian reform constituency, which did not help much in the cause of agrarian reform. Meanwhile, it was also during the Morales administration when the World Bank – again, secretly – attempted to convince the Philippine government to shift to MLAR altogether, if not, to pilot-test the MLAR on a smaller scale. Again, the rural social movement organizations were in unison in rejecting such a proposal and the process (that is, 'secret' and non-transparent) through which it was being discussed with the government (see Franco, 1999a).

During the Morales administration at the DAR, positioning by different rural social movement groups have principally been influenced by the latter's broader political stance vis-à-vis the Morales–Estrada administration. For example, in December 2000, the Morales DAR co-sponsored a major international conference on agrarian reform and rural development (ICARRDD). Instead of participating in the conference, several NGOs and peasant organizations chose to boycott the activity and held a protest rally outside the conference venue condemning the conference as a scheme by the World Bank and the DAR to 'inaugurate market-led agrarian reform (MLAR) in the Philippines'. Meanwhile, several other peasant organizations and NGOs opted to participate in the conference – and actively engaged and debated with World Bank scholars on the issue of MLAR. While both groups of NGOs and peasant organizations – both those outside and inside the conference – were against MLAR, only those inside the conference were able to confront, face-to-face, the World Bank and registered in the strongest possible terms the peasants' rejection of MLAR. At a glance, the rural social movement groups were divided between pro- and anti-MLAR during the event, but such projection had no basis in reality – the division between them was more on how to oppose the MLAR proponents, on the one hand, and the more political positions between those who were clamouring for the ousting of Morales and those who critically engaged with the then DAR leadership.

It is important to note at this point that three significant national peasant organizations were formed. The first is UNORKA, or the National Coordination of Autonomous Local Rural People's Organizations (*Pambansang Ugnayan ng Nagsasariling mga Lokal na Samahang Mamamayan sa Kanayunan*). In 2000, UNORKA was directly engaged in the struggle for land redistribution of more or less 200 000 hectares of land involving at least 90 000 landless rural poor households. UNORKA traces its roots from the national-democratic peasant movement, i.e. KMP and then DKMP. UNORKA continues the militant tradition of KMP, but explores some spaces for political pragmatism, especially with regard to land reform. It is best described as a militant-but-pragmatic peasant movement. The second one is PKSK, or the National Federation of Organizations in the Countryside (*Pambansang Katipunan ng mga Samahan sa Kanayunan*). PKSK traces its militant tradition and influence from the independent socialist group called the Union of the Advancement of Socialist Thought and Action (BISIG), and some of the NGOs over which the latter has varying degrees of influence, such as the Centre for Agrarian Reform, Empowerment and Transformation (CARET). Meanwhile, the last one is KASAMA-KA, or the Federation of People's Organizations in the Countryside (*Katipunan ng mga Samahang Magsasaka sa Kanayunan*). KASAMA-KA is a generally cooperative-oriented type of movement, but has some coalition members that are directly engaged in land struggles. It traces its progressive provenance from the earlier socioeconomic work of the Philippine Peasant Institute (PPI), and a spin-off NGO called the Philippine Network of Rural

Development Institutes (PhilNET-RDI). All these three national organizations are members of PARRDS, and all are opposed to MLAR. Furthermore, all three organizations are, to varying degrees, assertive of their autonomy from the state and other political parties.

Moreover, in recent years, the politically broad social-democratic network of rural NGOs and peasant organizations (see the earlier discussion on CPAR, as well as Putzel, 1995 and Franco, 1999c) have been able to reconsolidate (after the demise of CPAR) and even expand their ranks along the struggle for land reform within the reformist framework of CARP. These organizations grouped together and called themselves Agrarian Reform Now!, or the AR Now! national coalition – with PAKISAMA as its leading peasant organization. The peak strength and political influence of this coalition can be traced during the years between 1997 and 2000, especially during the national controversial land struggle over the case of Mapalad (in Bukidnon, Mindanao). AR Now! as a coalition has become an important player in the land reform struggle, and in the movement against the World Bank's market-led agrarian reform lobby in the Philippines. Recently, however, some internal organizational and political problems started to plague this national network, leading to relative paralysis.

After Estrada was overthrown by a popular mobilization in January 2001, Arroyo installed as DAR chief Hernani Braganza, a former student activist identified with the ND movement, and nephew of former President Fidel Ramos. Braganza has no prior background on agrarian reform work or with the peasant movement, and he has become a traditional politician representing a district in the province of Pangasinan in Congress. Immediately, it became quite clear that Braganza had failed to understand the inherently conflictive relationship between social movement organizations pushing for agrarian reform and reformist officials within government. The Braganza DAR has been intolerant of social mobilizations from below, the most basic ingredient in state reformism. For example, when 400 poor peasants from UNORKA stormed the DAR's Office of the Secretary in August 2001 (and stayed there for three days and two nights) after Secretary Braganza failed to show up at their appointed time and place, Braganza instead called in fully armed anti-riot police to try to disperse the peasants – the first time that any DAR secretary had done so since 1992.

Meanwhile, Braganza has clearly taken the market-friendly approaches to land redistribution as his main strategy. For the first time in CARP history, a DAR secretary announced that the DAR's main strategy in CARP land redistribution would be the VLT scheme. Hence, a few months after Braganza assumed office at the DAR, the overwhelming majority of peasant organizations and NGOs that have historically manoeuvred within the reform framework of CARP have called for his ousting. The pro-market stance of the Braganza DAR appears to have the full blessing of President Arroyo. For example, in addition to VLT, Arroyo favours leasehold reform because it does not require any state funds (see Borras, 2002b: 19).

In sum, the degree of unity (or division) among peasant organizations at the national level tends to be determined largely by political dynamics related to two factors: ideologically determined or influenced rural social movement networks, and changing alliances within and between rural social movements, and between them and state actors in the context of changing alliances within the state (partly influenced by electoral cycles – see Franco, 1999c, 2001a). Market-friendly land redistribution mechanisms appear to have no direct divisive and debilitating impact on rural social movements at the national level.

Market-friendly land reform mechanisms and their impact on peasant organizations: local perspectives

This section is based on four case studies in localized contexts, each one presenting and examining a particular local case that gives relevant empirical evidence to the arguments advanced in this chapter. Cases 1 and 2 are both examples where the pro-market land redistribution scheme is essentially an 'anti-reform' formula, one being controlled by a multinational company and the other by a domestic elite. Case 3 illustrates a case where the market-friendly land redistribution scheme can even exclude women from land reform benefits. Meanwhile, case 4 demonstrates how a combined political strategy of pro-reform state and societal actors can achieve tactical successes in agrarian reform policy processes and implementation.

Case 1: the Dole-DARBCI leaseback arrangement

This case involves more than 9000 hectares of government-owned land in Polomolok, South Cotabato (in Mindanao, southeastern Philippines) planted to pineapple. The government-owned National Development Corporation (NDC) leased this large, contiguous land to the Dole company years before the implementation of the Comprehensive Agrarian Reform Programme. In 1988, the government decided to redistribute the land to the more than 7000 workers employed by Dole in this pineapple plantation, becoming one of the earliest government-owned lands and MNC-controlled plantations to be placed under land reform. The awarded land-beneficiary ratio was almost a little more than a hectare per worker-beneficiary. The government required the beneficiaries to pay for the land at a price of PhP17 000 per hectare. It is not very clear why the government asked the beneficiaries to pay for land when it is a government-owned property.

The Dole company then offered a lease arrangement with the new 'owners' of the land who formed themselves into one cooperative, the Dole Agrarian Reform Beneficiaries Cooperative Incorporated (DARBCI). The cooperative, prodded by the government, decided to accept the lease offer and, in turn, opted for a collective mode of ownership of the land, i.e., the DARBCI owns the land. The lease arrangement was to run for ten years where Dole can use the land to continue its pre-CARP operation in an almost unchanged manner. In exchange, Dole would pay each beneficiary PhP3200 per hectare per year as lease rent. The government hailed the 'leaseback' arrangement as an alternative reform model where the MNC would stay in the country for its operations while securing the ownership of the land by the farmworkers, thus maintaining employment and providing additional income through lease rents. It was thought to be a viable way for the state, the rural poor and the market to come together for the common good. It would not take long for the farmworkers to realize what kind of contract they had entered into with the company.

During the ten-year lease contract in 1988–98, more or less half of the entire farmworker-beneficiaries, or about 3300 farmworkers, were retrenched from work by Dole. Since then most of these farmworkers were left without any other sources of income but the meagre PhP3200 per year per beneficiary – an amount which is not even sufficient for a month-long food need of a worker household. To make it worse, the lease rent of PhP3200 did not go directly and wholly to the beneficiary, since a portion of it was automatically deducted as payment to the government for the land. While a few thousand farmworkers were thrown out of employment, conflicts within the leadership of the cooperative started to intensify on issues of cooperative policy directions and fund management. Towards the end of 1998 when the lease agreement was to expire, the division within the DARBCI cooperative became more real than apparent, and the fault-line began to widen around the new round of leaseback arrangement. Dole offered to renew a lease agreement for twenty-five years, at PhP5000 per hectare per year. One group of the (actively) employed farmworkers endorsed and supported the proposal. Another group rejected such a proposal on the grounds that the lease rent offered was very low. Some lease arrangements in the region (banana and pineapple) plantations were already in the region of PhP30 000 per hectare per year. Thus, the second group put forward a proposal for the renewal of leaseback arrangement but with PhP30 000 per year per hectare lease rent. Legal battles as to which group is the rightful representative of the cooperative ensued. Until late 2002, the legal battle was still being fought – this time at the Supreme Court. Meanwhile, Dole had entered into a *de facto* arrangement with the first group at a lease rental agreement of PhP7500 per hectare per year for twenty-five years.

The agrarian reform-related intra-beneficiary and inter-actors conflict in this case is the most important in the history of CARP in terms of the land size and number of beneficiaries involved and affected. While the fault-line between the two broad divisions of the cooperative leadership is clear, that is, along the terms and conditions of the renewed leaseback agreement, it fails to capture key issues that may be more important for the greatest number of farmworkers affected, and for insights more relevant to other agrarian reform cases. These issues can be seen in a number of ways. First, the more than 3000 farmworker-beneficiaries who were retrenched from employment between 1988 and 1998 have no stake or interest whatsoever in any type of renewed leaseback. They will have negligible benefits under any types of leaseback since they have no regular daily sources of income. Their main interest is to get their individual parcels of land and cultivate them directly or enter into individual growership arrangements. Second, within the context of the pro-market DARBCI-Dole, collective ownership of the land is elitist, divisive and exclusionary. Individual beneficiaries who have no interests or benefits from leaseback arrangement are denied exit options. They are even threatened to be delisted from the beneficiary roll since they are 'non-working' beneficiaries, and that under the CARP law, non-working beneficiaries should be dropped from the beneficiary roll and replaced. Yet, under these circumstances, the 'non-working status' of the farmworker-beneficiaries has been induced from the outside rather than from the farmworkers' own voluntary option.

Third, Dole is reaping more profits under the leaseback arrangement compared to the pre-CARP set-up in the plantation. In fact, many MNCs have been pushing for land reform in the plantations, but trying to secure post-land transfer leaseback agreements. Going through this MNC 'trap' or the inability to resist their manoeuvres and other local elites could defeat the very essence of agrarian reform. Finally, the government has been remiss in its responsibility to protect the rights of beneficiaries over the awarded lands, or promote a more broad-based post-land transfer agricultural development. Leaving the land reform beneficiaries alone and unassisted in a non-level playing field to deal with the agricultural elites is most likely to lead to the immediate demise of agrarian reform in the context explained in this case. The state has to face its responsibility in ensuring that the social justice measure is implemented strategically amidst harsh market conditions.

Case 2: the Eduardo Cojuangco Jr. Company (ECJ) orchard 'special land reform deal'

The estate involved in this case is the more than 4000 hectares of land worked by more than a thousand workers in the province of Negros Occidental (central western Philippines). The estate used to be a sugarcane plantation owned by one of the most powerful landlord-businessmen in the country – Eduardo 'Danding' Cojuangco Jr. Danding is a cousin of ex-President Corazon Cojuangco-Aquino. However, the cousins had deep political differences since Danding was one of the closest allies (and cronies) of the Marcos dictatorship. After Marcos was overthrown in 1986, Danding had to exile abroad and went back to the country only after several years, and after some compromises were worked out with the new government. Danding was able to evade the sequestration of most of his assets (as done to some Marcos allies after 1986). The 4000 hectare farm is just one of Danding's many assets that he was able to secure away from government sequestration. Danding's political clout was even reinforced when Joseph Estrada became the country's president. They were close allies politically.

Some time in the mid-1990s, Danding stopped the operation of sugarcane plantation and instead shifted to high value crops for exports. He transformed the 4000-hectare farm in Negros into a modern fruit orchard. During the last few years of the Ramos administration (1992–8), Danding started to negotiate with the DAR on how CARP could and should be implemented in his estate. His proposal was to sell the land to his workers and then immediately place the orchard into a joint venture agreement with his company, ECJ (Eduardo Cojuangco Jr.). The terms of the joint venture were as follows: (i) the government would not spend any money in acquiring the land since it would be a direct deal between Danding and his workers in a manner akin to the market-led agrarian reform; (ii) the ECJ company would retain ownership of the newly installed modern plantation infrastructures such as irrigation pipes and farm machineries; (iii) the ECJ company would invest heavily in the installation of processing plants and set up modern management systems; (iv) the workers would continue to be employed in the joint venture company and would earn additional dividends from the profits of the joint venture; (v) the ownership of the land would be collective, and in the name of the workers' cooperative; (vi) the joint venture shares would be 30 per cent for the farmworkers and 70 per cent for the ECJ company. The latter's share is explained by its capital-intensive investments on infrastructures and management; (vii) the joint venture agreement would be for twenty-five years, renewable for another twenty-five years; and (viii) the workers' cooperative should put up its Certificate of Land Ownership Award as equity to the joint venture company. The negotiations for this special land reform deal were never completed during this period because the term of office of the Ramos administration ended in mid-1998.

A new round of negotiations started when the administration of Joseph Estrada, Danding's close ally, assumed office on 1 July 1998. Danding renewed negotiations on a special land reform deal in his estate with the new DAR leadership under Horacio Morales Jr. Danding's offer was basically the same as his offer under the Ramos administration. Two new developments, however, came in. On the one hand, Danding purged from 'his' list of beneficiaries several workers who have been critical of him. It was apparent that Danding was the one choosing who would be and who would not be the beneficiaries. It must be noted also that autonomous organizing initiatives among the workers in the estate had difficulty gaining ground because of the harassment and various manipulations carried out by the landlord. On the other hand, while Danding was all along negotiating for a purchase price of PhP300000 (roughly US$7000 at that time) per hectare of land to be paid directly by the beneficiaries within the joint venture scheme, he made a surprise announcement during the visit of President Estrada at the farm that he was going to offer his land free of charge to the workers – while the proposed terms in the joint venture agreement remained. This prompted then President Estrada to declare Danding the 'Godfather of land reform' – a pronouncement met with angry protests from rural social movement groups.

The high-profile attention given by the public to this case has brought to the surface critical questions confronting CARP implementation. First, the 4000-hectare farm should have been sequestered earlier by government because it is part of the supposedly 'ill-gotten' wealth of Marcos and his cronies. Why had the administrations of Aquino, Ramos and Estrada failed to confiscate this estate and redistribute it to the workers? Second, what made the non-land investments of the ECJ company earn the right to have a 70 per cent share in the joint venture (as proposed by Cojuangco)? Third, why a virtually lifelong length of the joint venture, that is, twenty-five years plus twenty-five years? Fourth, why should the workers' cooperative put up its CLOA as equity since if the company went bankrupt the beneficiaries would lose their land? Finally, why was Danding the one choosing who the beneficiaries would be? The DAR (under secretary Morales), reacting to the various criticisms by the public, delayed its actions on the case and instead came up with a counterproposal offered to Danding with the following features. First, the equity of the worker-beneficiaries must be the 'land use' and not the CLOAs (or title) so as to protect the ownership of the workers over the land in the event of a bankruptcy of the joint venture. Second, the government, represented by the DAR, should be allowed to be part of the joint venture with the following terms: 30 per cent share of the beneficiaries, 65 per cent share of the ECJ, and 5 per cent share of the government. This was supposed to deny the ECJ any automatic two-thirds majority vote in the company, and for the government to provide assistance and protection to the beneficiaries. Finally, the length of the joint venture must be ten years, renewable upon mutual agreement of all parties involved. Meanwhile, the DAR also released a new legal guideline on joint venture arrangements called DAR Administrative Order No. 2 series of 2000 (the infamous 'Corporative Scheme'). While this new guideline has various features relevant to other cases, one salient feature of this administrative order is the legal provision that the CLOAs of beneficiaries cannot be used as equity to any joint venture arrangements, and that only the 'land use' can be allowed as equity. Unsurprisingly, Danding has rejected the counterproposal of the DAR. The rejection led to an impasse on the case, that has remained long after Estrada was overthrown and the Arroyo administration took power.

Various critical issues should be looked into by the social movement groups in this case in the context of state–market–social movement interaction.

First, the originally (1987) reported 'sequestered' lands from Marcos' cronies have ended up within the normal CARP processes where beneficiaries have been asked to pay for the land, defeating the very essence of government sequestration processes of what was supposed to be 'ill-gotten' wealth of Marcos and his cronies. The Floirendo (banana in Davao) and Benedicto (sugarcane, Negros Occidental) cases are examples of this questionable shift under the Aquino, Ramos and Estrada administrations. Second, land acquisition and distribution have apparently become a conditional issue vis-à-vis post-land transfer joint venture arrangements, leading to legal impasse and prolonged implementation of land redistribution. The same manipulation by Danding is being done on a wider scale in banana plantations in Mindanao. Third, the state has indirectly allowed the manoeuvres of landlords to promote co-opted beneficiary organizations instead of promoting the emergence of autonomous beneficiary groups. The fate of the Danding estate in Negros remains uncertain especially given the absence of autonomous workers' and beneficiaries' organizations in the orchard and the refusal of the government to take more decisive action on the case. Meanwhile, given the impasse, it is Danding who is reaping all the benefits as he started to harvest and sell from his orchard.

Case 3: the case of 'AgriDevCo' in Mindanao[13]

The rubber–coffee plantation in this case covers 3000 hectares of land located in a predominantly Muslim part of Mindanao, southern Philippines. At the turn of the century, a foreign company, AgriDevCo, came into this part of the country, acquiring from the government this vast tract of land on which it planted rubber and coffee. When this foreign company arrived, the land was occupied by an indigenous group of Muslim subsistence farming communities. When AgriDevCo started the operation of the plantation, it had ejected the Muslim occupants and brought in Christians from different parts of Mindanao to become landworkers. There were more or less 1000 regular farmworkers in the plantation, most of them men. While men worked as rubber tappers, women worked as coffee pickers and did other maintenance work in the plantation, such as grass cutting. In addition, there were almost the same number of seasonal farmworkers, most of whom were women. The plantation continued to make money for decades.

When CARP was inaugurated in 1988, AgriDevCo voluntarily offered the plantation to the government for redistribution. The company was able to get a handsome amount of money from the land reform programme, especially since the rubber and coffee trees were already old and no longer so productive and the plantation would need immediate replanting and rehabilitation. Upon the government's acquisition of the plantation in the early 1990s, the existing union and its NGO ally immediately came up with a CARP implementation scheme in the plantation: (i) each beneficiary should get 3 hectares – the maximum size of land awarded under CARP; (ii) only the regular farmworkers were to become beneficiaries, but also those at management and supervisory levels; and (iii) the mode of land ownership would be collective, owned by the cooperative. Hence, when CARP was eventually implemented, there were 1000 beneficiaries, each having 3 hectares of land – all men. Land ownership was collective, and those who became cooperative leaders were the same union leaders plus those in the management and supervisory levels under the AgriDevCo. There are no Muslim beneficiaries. During its operation, the cooperative decided to hire as workers most of its members who were all men. The cooperative put an end to the pre-CARP plantation practice of hiring seasonal farmworkers in coffee picking and grass cutting. All available work was given to cooperative members. The net effect was that women found themselves not only denied their distinct right to become land reform beneficiaries, but they were also denied their traditional employment. Women began to assert their rights over their traditional sources of income, but the cooperative at this point was becoming financially bankrupt due to the fact that the old rubber and coffee trees were no longer producing that much. To ease the rising tension along the gender divide, the all-men cooperative offered women small projects such as baking and backyard raising of animals. However, the women were not appeased and began demanding their own share of the land. They brought the case to the government and the media, and it became a nationally controversial issue, revealing anti-women possibilities and actual currents within CARP. Yet, the financial bankruptcy of the cooperative has also complicated the problem.

Case 4: reforming agrarian reform from below: the DAR Administrative Order No. 9 s. 1998

Unlike most land reforms elsewhere, modern commercial plantations in the Philippines are covered by the CARP law. However, land acquisitions and redistribution of these plantations have been deferred for ten years, from 1988 to 1998. While there are only less than 100 000 hectares of land (and the same number of rural poor households) affected by this provision, the monetary value of export crops derived from this sector is much higher than the traditional crops. For example, the banana sector covers only about 50 000 hectares but its yearly gross value is roughly one-third of the total gross value of the coconut sector that has 3 000 000 hectares and 2 million households. There were two main reasons cited for the delay in land acquisition of these modern farms. On the one hand, the deferment is supposed to give plantation owners the time to recoup their investments, and on the other, to give time to farmworkers to undergo training in skills in order to prepare them for the eventual takeover of these plantations. Meanwhile, during the deferment period, plantation owners are required by the CARP law to give production and profit shares to their workers: 10 per cent of the yearly gross sales plus 5 per cent of the yearly net income. Many of the plantations have been redistributed to farmworkers even before the expiration of the deferment period. There are two apparent reasons for this phenomenon. On the one hand, many of these plantations were government-owned lands leased to MNCs. Realizing that there might be better profit opportunities under agrarian reform, the MNCs pushed for the early redistribution of the land and forged lease arrangements with the beneficiaries. Insights from the Dole Agrarian Reform Beneficiaries Cooperative Incorporated (DARBCI)-Dole leaseback arrangement are instructive. On the other hand, there are plantation sectors that are not performing well in the markets and require major capital reinvestments. Landlords in these plantations saw a better way out of the 'sinking' economics of their plantations, and so voluntarily offered their lands to be bought by the state under land reform. Such is the case of the rubber plantations. A few years later, most of the beneficiary cooperatives that took over these rubber plantations went bankrupt.

The case of the banana sector is different and remains a very lucrative business. In fact the global market continues to expand. Thus, it has been rare for banana plantations to be voluntarily offered by their owners for land redistribution. The banana sector, involving about 50000 hectares of land (including small farms) and 50000 farmworkers, has become one of the most contentious cases in CARP. There are a number of interrelated issues that warrant a closer look. First, between 1988 and 1998, or during the deferment period, around 20000 banana farmworkers were retrenched from employment in an apparent effort of the plantation owners to purge their companies of land and production/profit shares claim-makers. Second, a split between MNCs and local plantation elites on the issue of agrarian reform has not automatically translated to actual benefits for all farmworkers. While most local elites continue to manoeuvre to evade expropriation, MNCs have pushed for land redistribution, for the reasons cited earlier.

Meanwhile, in most cases where local elites realized the apparent eventuality of land reform in their plantations, they have desperately tried to forge different forms of joint venture agreements – but with a preference for leaseback – with the would-be beneficiaries. This has led companies to make efforts to consolidate their hold on less autonomous or outrightly company-co-opted farmworkers' unions or cooperatives. Third, in order to increase the chances that companies could forge post-land transfer joint venture agreements, farmworkers identified with the militant trade union tradition, or farmworkers who have formed autonomous organizations, have been the principal targets of earlier retrenchments. Hence, the companies have been lobbying for the exclusion of retrenched farmworkers from becoming land reform beneficiaries. Fourth, while most companies have complied with the CARP-mandated production and profit sharing scheme from 1988 to 1998, most of them had cheated the company's financial records and so paid farmworkers way below their due price. It is estimated that altogether banana companies owe farmworkers hundreds of millions of dollars in unpaid production and profit shares. Fifth, plantation owners have been asking government to pay extremely high prices for the land, ranging from PhP350 000 to PhP1 400 000 per hectare (or between US$7000 and $28 000). It must be recalled that most of the current banana companies had procured these lands from the government a few decades ago at 'give-away prices'. Finally, reluctant to antagonize banana plantation owners – most of whom are well connected politically – while facing the problem of insufficient funds to purchase expensive lands, the government has been encouraging farmworkers and plantation owners to employ the 'direct payment scheme', that is, direct market-based land purchase between farmworkers and plantation owners.

There is thus a rare confluence of events that are double-edged: possibly consolidating the economic and political power of transnational and local elites in the banana sector at the expense of the farmworkers, or perhaps opening up a path for radical change. Both scenarios, however, would depend on various factors and actors. For a more democratic path to emerge, the development of highly autonomous and highly capable farmworkers' organizations allied with reformists within the state is most likely to become a crucial factor. While there are serious reasons to be alarmed at how the market forces and the state have been trying to advance their interests at the expense of poor farmworkers, there are also reasons to hope that progressive change may also occur. The case of the DAR Administrative Order No. 9 series of 1998 is a good example of the latter.

In May 1998, a month before the Ramos administration's term of office ended, the DAR under the leadership of Ernesto Garilao issued an administrative order (AO) to guide the implementation of CARP in commercial plantations, especially the banana sector, the deferment of land reform coverage of which would expire the following month, in June 1998. While the DAR AO 6 series of 1998 has ordered the immediate expropriation of all deferred commercial plantations, the same guideline, if implemented, would have excluded from land reform all retrenched farmworkers, thousands of whom became furious about the guideline and campaigned for its recall. To these farmworkers, AO 6 would permanently institutionalize the historical injustice committed against them. For example, Enrico had worked in a banana plantation in Davao del Norte since 1974, until he was retrenched from work in 1994, having served the company for twenty years. Since he was not actively employed during the time of land reform implementation in 1998 onward, he would not, under AO 6, become a land reform beneficiary. Meanwhile, in late 1996, Pablo was employed by the banana company that used to employ Enrico. Since Pablo was actively employed in 1998 onward when land reform would have been implemented, he would have, under AO 6, become a land reform beneficiary despite having worked in the company for only just more than a year. There would have been no conflict among potential beneficiaries if there had been enough land for everyone, but there are at least two potential beneficiaries for every hectare of banana land. Hence, the critical issue of prioritizing beneficiaries.

Thousands of farmworkers – who would later form themselves under the national umbrella coalition of UNORKA – campaigned hard for the adoption of the principle of prioritizing 'those who worked the longest in the farm' regardless of their employment status at the time of the actual land reform process. Plantation owners, however, have been working behind the scenes and been lobbying for only those actively employed at the time of actual land reform coverage – and to include those who are in the management and supervisory levels of the company – to be the priority beneficiaries. It is not surprising that the most contentious division has occurred between different groups of farmworkers – a conflictive split instigated by transnational and local elites and indirectly encouraged by the ineptitude of the government.

The following month, Horacio Morales took office at the DAR. After several months of militant forms of collective action by farmworkers – both locally and nationally – the Morales DAR issued a new guideline replacing AO 6. In December 1998, the Morales DAR issued the DAR Administrative Order No. 9 series of 1998, declaring that the key guiding principle in prioritizing beneficiaries is the principle of 'those who worked the longest in the farm regardless of their employment status at the time of actual land reform process'. It was a huge victory for thousands of retrenched farmworkers. However, while it has constituted an important step of the agrarian reform, the implementation of AO 9 has not been automatic, since local DAR officials have appeared to be continuously influenced by the banana elites in circumventing the law. Yet, AO 9 has altered the terrain within which retrenched farmworkers could assert their rights.

In summary, a number of analytic issues can be discussed. First, market-friendly land redistribution mechanisms have an *exclusionary* impact on marginalized sections of the peasantry. The case of AgriDevCo demonstrates how women and Muslim farmworkers have been excluded from the land reform process in the name of maintaining economies of scale in the coffee–rubber plantation through the policy of 'one plantation–one cooperative–one collective title' controlled by male regular farmworkers through their elite leaders, many of whom were former management staff in the pre-reform plantation. Moreover, the ECJ case shows how a group of farmworkers, although a minority, who objected to a special market-based land reform in the Cojuangco orchard, were stripped of their right to own the land they tilled. Such exclusions occur horizontally as well as vertically – cutting across social classes. Second, market-friendly land redistribution schemes have the most serious *divisive* impact on peasant and farmworker organizations at the estate, plantation or landholding level. The Dole-DARBCI case demonstrates how the pro-market scheme of leaseback arrangement has seriously divided what used to be a solid cooperative of 7000 farmworker-beneficiaries. Third, the officially reported CARP accomplishments through market-friendly land redistribution are likely to be devoid of any redistributive substance. The case of Dole-DARBCI, involving 9000 hectares and 7000 farmworkers, is one classic example. Another example is the ECJ orchard involving 4000 hectares and more than 1000 farm households. More generally, the VLT and SDO cases – more or less 500 000 hectares involving at least 200 000 households nationwide – reported as an accomplishment in land redistribution in CARP are devoid of any elements of true 'redistribution' and 'reform'. Fourth, most of the cases discussed above show that the exclusionary and divisive currents brought about by market-friendly land redistribution schemes tend to have a mixed impact on rural social movement organizations. Some groups have been weakened, some demobilized and violently repressed, although some have become even more militant and persistent in their collective actions. In general, however, fragmented rural social movement groups are relatively weak. Finally, despite the exclusionary and divisive, and so weakening, impact of market-friendly land redistribution schemes on rural social movement organizations, some groups have been able to resist. The most promising approach through which subaltern groups have been able to advance pro-reform interests despite odds posed by pro-market policy currents is the sandwich or 'bibingka' strategy: the symbiotic interaction between state reformists from above and autonomous rural social movements from below (see Borras, 1999, 2001; also Fox, 1993, 1996, 2001). This is demonstrated in the case of the DAR AO 9 s. of 1998.

Conclusion

The empirical evidence presented and examined in this chapter shows four interrelated issues related to the impact of market-friendly land redistribution schemes on rural social movements and their collective actions. First, the national level rural social movement organizations appear to be not negatively affected by market-friendly land redistribution schemes: meaning, divisions within and between peasant organizations and NGOs have nothing to do with pro-market land redistribution mechanisms enshrined within CARP or with the entirely new model proposed by pro-market scholars (i.e. MLAR). In fact, ideologically diverse peasant organizations and NGOs have, at times, been united in common positions against MLAR and other market-friendly land redistribution mechanisms within CARP. Minor differences within and between these rural social movements with regard to pro-market land reform schemes do occur, but within the context of how to advance the opposition to such programmes and schemes.

Second, what the Philippine experience shows, however, is that splits and divisions within and between peasant organizations and NGOs are often caused by ideological and political differences between these rural social movement groups, as well as other internally driven differences. The changing state–society alliances, periodically determined partly by electoral cycles – is another cause of serious division among rural social movement organizations affecting their capacity to mount sustained, coherent and broad-based collective actions around the land reform issue (see Franco, 2001a and 1999c). Third, the exclusionary and divisive currents of market-friendly land redistribution schemes are most real at the local level estate, farm or landholding. It is at this level where peasant organizations are most vulnerable to being isolated and thus easily defeated by anti-reform forces. It is at this level that the anti-reform forces are most influential. It is at this level where the national leaderships of peasant organizations and NGOs that are generally opposed to market-based solutions to land problems are relatively weak. The divisions brought about by pro-market land redistribution schemes occur both horizontally and/or vertically – cutting across social classes. Fourth, empirical evidence presented and examined in this chapter shows that the officially reported land redistribution accomplishments of CARP through the market-friendly schemes are lacking any true redistributive character. This is especially the case with voluntary land transfers, stock distribution options, and leaseback arrangements.

Hence, market-friendly land redistribution schemes, even when framed within a basically state-led land reform programme have an exclusionary and divisive impact on rural social movements. This is demonstrated in the several specific local cases shown in this chapter. The outcomes of such schemes are devoid of any essence of redistributive reform. But while these market-friendly land redistribution schemes have an exclusionary, divisive and debilitating impact on rural social movement groups, some subaltern groups, under certain conditions, are able to resist the differentiating currents of such mechanisms, or even block the exclusionary and divisive market-based policies. This is partly confirmed by the modest, but significant, land redistribution accomplishment of CARP between 1992 and 2000. More specifically, the case of DAR Administrative Order No. 9 series of 1998, where retrenched farmworkers victoriously blocked previous attempts to automatically exclude them from land reform, is a good example.

Notes

1. The author would like to thank Jennifer Franco for sharing her analytic insights and many of her own field research data and documents for the full construction of this chapter. For their useful comments and suggestions on various earlier draft papers, I thank Kléber Ghimire, Jennifer Franco, Steve Quiambao and Danny Carranza. For their generous assistance during field visits, I thank the community organizers of PEACE Foundation and leaders and members of UNORKA (National Coordination of Autonomous Local Rural People's Organizations); and Cecil Lijauco and Nestor Tapia for excellent research assistance. For their extremely useful insights and information, I thank several reform-oriented officials within the Department of Agrarian Reform (DAR) who preferred to be anonymous in this chapter.

2. This section is drawn largely from Borras (2001).
3. For background analyses, see Boyce (1992), De la Rosa (1994), Aguilar (1998) and Hawes (1987).
4. For more on this, see Abinales (1998), Kerkvliet (1993), and Rutten (2000a, 2000b).
5. National regime transitions usually offer rare opportunities for popular claim-making mobilizations. For a recent contribution on this, see Houtzager (2000) in the context of rural Brazil.
6. This subsection is drawn largely from Borras (2001).
7. In some nearly bankrupt, especially rubber, plantations, landed elites were able to cash in their lands via the voluntary-offer-to-sell or VOS option; see Rimban (1997b).
8. This section draws from Borras (1999: chapter 2); see also Putzel (1995), Franco (2001a) and Feranil (2003).
9. For relevant literature, refer to KMP (1992), DKMP (1993), Padilla (1990), Canlas (1992, 1994), Kerkvliet (1993), Fuentes and Paring (1992), Rutten (2000a, 2000b).
10. See PEACE (1994), and Franco (2001b) for a comprehensive analysis of this issue.
11. For an excellent analysis, refer to Rocamora (1994).
12. Franco (1999c) offers an excellent analysis of the issue. See also Putzel (1995).
13. The names and basic data in this case have been altered in order to protect the various entities involved in the actual case. The essence, however, remains the same.

References

Abinales, Patricio (1998) *Images of State Power: Essays on Philippine Politics from the Margins*. Quezon City: University of the Philippines.

Aguilar, Filomeno Jr. (1998) *Clash of Spirits: the History of Power and Sugar Planter Hegemony on a Visayan Island*. Honolulu, HI: University of Hawaii Press.

Anderson, Benedict (1988) 'Cacique democracy in the Philippines: origins and dreams', *New Left Review*, 169, pp. 3–29.

Angeles, Leonora (1999) 'The political dimension in the agrarian question: strategies of resilience and political entrepreneurship of agrarian elite families in a Philippine province', *Rural Sociology*, Vol. 64, No. 4, pp. 667–92.

Banerjee, Abhijit (1999) *Land Reforms: Prospects and Strategies*. A paper presented at the Annual Bank Conference on Development Economics (Washington, DC, April).

Barraclough, Solon L. (2001) 'The role of the state and other actors in land reform', in K. B. Ghimire (ed.), *Land Reform and Peasant Livelihoods: the Social Dynamics of Rural Poverty and Agrarian Reform in Developing Countries*. London: ITDG Publishing.

Bernstein, Henry (2002) 'Land reform: taking a long(er) view', *Journal of Agrarian Change*, Vol. 2, No. 4, pp. 433–63.

Binswanger, Hans (1996) 'Rural development and poverty reduction', in J.v. Zyl, J. Kirsten and H. P. Binswanger (eds), *Agricultural Land Reform in South Africa: Policies, Markets and Mechanisms*. Oxford: Oxford University Press.

Borras, Saturnino Jr. (1999) *The Bibingka Strategy in Land Reform Implementation: Autonomous Peasant Movements and State Reformists in the Philippines*. Quezon City: Institute for Popular Democracy.

Borras, Saturnino Jr. (2001) 'State–society relations in land reform implementation in the Philippines', *Development and Change*, Vol. 32, No. 3, pp. 545–75.

Borras, Saturnino Jr. (2002a) 'Towards a better understanding of market-led agrarian reform in theory and practice – focusing on the Brazilian case', *Land Reform, Land Settlement and Cooperatives*, Vol. 1, pp. 33–50.

Borras, Saturnino Jr. (2002b) 'Land reform – stuck in the mud: CARP in its 14th year', *IPD Political Brief*, Vol. 10, No. 3, pp. 1–17. Quezon City: Institute for Popular Democracy (www.ipd.ph).

Borras, Saturnino Jr. (2003) 'Questioning market-led agrarian reform: experiences from Brazil, Colombia and South Africa', *Journal of Agrarian Change*, Vol. 3, No. 3, July, pp. 367–94.

Borras, Saturnino Jr. (2003) 'Questioning the pro-market critique of state-led agrarian reforms', *European Journal of Development Research*, Vol. 15, No. 2, December.

Borras, Saturnino Jr. and Manuel Quiambao (1998) 'The difficult challenge of agrarian reform, rural development and democratization in banana plantations', *Conjuncture*, Vol. 10, No. 4, pp. 8–10/12. Quezon City: Institute for Popular Democracy (www.ipd.ph).

Boyce, James (1992) 'Of coconuts and kings: the political economy of an export crop', *Development and Change*, Vol. 23, No. 4, pp. 1–25.

Bryant, Coralie (1996) 'Strategic change through sensible projects', in *World Development*, Vol. 24, No. 9, pp. 1539–50.

Canlas, Corinne (1992) 'BUGKOS and BUFFALO: two stories of peasant-initiated land occupations in Bukidnon', in F. Lim (ed.), *Waging the Battle for Land Ownership: Case Studies of Peasant Initiated Land Occupations*. Quezon City: Philippine Peasant Institute.

Canlas, Corinne (1994) 'In search of land: three cases of land occupation in San Antonio, Mandayao and Hacienda Tison in Negros Occidental', in Reyes-Cantos (ed.), *Waging the Battle for Land Ownership. Part II: Case Studies of Peasant-Initiated Land Occupations*. Quezon City: Philippine Peasant Institute.

Chalmers, Douglas, Martin Scott and Piester Kerianne (1997) 'Associative networks: new structures of representation for the popular sectors?', in D. Chalmers, C. M. Vilas, K. Hite, S. B. Martin, K. Piester and M. Segarra (eds), *The New Politics of Inequality in Latin America*. Oxford: Oxford University Press.

Cuarteros, Gladstone (2001) *Upgrading Possibilities for Philippine Banana Co-operatives* (unpublished MA Thesis). The Hague: Institute of Social Studies.

Deininger, Klaus (1999) 'Making negotiated land reform work: initial experience from Colombia, Brazil and South Africa', in *World Development*, Vol. 27, No. 4, pp. 651–72.

Deininger, Klaus and Hans Binswanger (1999) 'The evolution of the World Bank's land policy: principles, experience and future challenges', *The World Bank Research Observer*, Vol. 14, No. 2, pp. 247–76.

De la Rosa, Romulo (1994) *CAP and the European Market for Coconut Oil and Copra Meal*. Davao: Alternate Forum for Research in Mindanao.

Democratic Peasant Movement of the Philippines (DKMP) (1993) *Proceedings of the National Congress of DKMP (26–29 November 1993)* (mimeo). Quezon City: DKMP.

Department of Agrarian Reform (DAR) (2001) *Land Redistribution Status as of 31 December 2001*. Quezon City: DAR.

Dorner, Peter (2001) 'Technology and globalization: modern-era constraints on local initiatives for land reform', in K. B. Ghimire (ed.), *Land Reform and Peasant Livelihoods: the Social Dynamics of Rural Poverty and Agrarian Reform in Developing Countries*. London: ITDG Publishing.

El-Ghonemy, Riad (2001) 'The political economy of market-based land reform', in K. Ghimire (ed.), *Land Reform and Peasant Livelihoods: the Social Dynamics of Rural Poverty and Agrarian Reform in Developing Countries*. London: ITDG Publishing.

Feranil, Salvador (2001) *The Politics of Agrarian Reform in Philippine Commercial Banana Plantations: the Case of Hijo Plantation in Davao* (unpublished MA Thesis). The Hague: Institute of Social Studies.

Feranil, Salvador (2003) *The Emerging New Peasant Movement in Negros Occidental*. Quezon City: Institute for Popular Democracy.

Fox, Jonathan (1992) 'Democratic rural development: leadership accountability in regional peasant organizations', *Development and Change*, Vol. 23, No. 2, pp. 1–36.

Fox, Jonathan (1993) *The Politics of Food in Mexico: State Power and Social Mobilization*. Ithaca, NY: Cornell University Press.

Fox, Jonathan (1996) 'Does civil society thicken? The political construction of social capital in rural Mexico', *World Development*, Vol. 24, No. 6, pp. 1089–1103.

Fox, Jonathan (2001) 'Vertically integrated policy monitoring: a tool for civil society policy advocacy', *Nonprofit and Voluntary Sector Quarterly*, Vol. 30, No. 3, pp. 616–27.

Franco, Jennifer (1998a) 'Between honesty and hope on the agrarian front: wrestling with warlords in the Bondoc Peninsula', *Conjuncture*, Vol. 10, No. 4, pp. 1–4/5/8. Quezon City: Institute for Popular Democracy.

Franco, Jennifer (1998b) 'Challenging the dinosaurs: local elections and political change in San Narciso', *Conjuncture*, Vol. 10, No. 2, pp. 1–5/9/10. Quezon City: Institute for Popular Democracy.

Franco, Jennifer (1999a) 'Market-assisted land reform in the Philippines: round two – where have all the critics gone?', *Conjuncture*, Vol. 11, No. 2, April. Quezon City: Institute for Popular Democracy (see www.ipd.ph).

Franco, Jennifer (1999b) 'Post-CARP banana split turns deadly: what went wrong at Hijo Plantation?', *Conjuncture*, Vol. 11, No. 4. Quezon City: Institute for Popular Democracy.

Franco, Jennifer (1999c) *Between Uncritical Collaboration and Outright Opposition: an Evaluative Report on PARRDS*. IPD Occasional Papers. Quezon City: Institute for Popular Democracy.

Franco, Jennifer (2001a) *Elections and Democratization in the Philippines*. London/ New York: Routledge.

Franco, Jennifer (2001b) *Building Alternatives, Harvesting Change: PEACE Network and the Institutionalization of Bibingka Strategy*. Quezon City: Philippine Ecumenical Action for Community Empowerment (PEACE) Foundation.

Franco, Jennifer (forthcoming) *The Contemporary Peasant Movement in Bondoc Peninsula*. Quezon City: Institute for Popular Democracy.

Franco, Jennifer and Norman Acosta (1999) 'The Hijo banana war. Part two: conclusion', *Conjuncture*, Vol. 11, No. 5.

Fuentes, Anna Luisa and Emma Paring (1992) *Learning Lessons from Struggle: the Land Occupation of the Aquafil Estate in Occidental Mindoro*. Quezon City: Philippine Peasant Institute.

Ghimire, K. B. (ed.) (2001a) *Land Reform and Peasant Livelihoods: the Social Dynamics of Rural Poverty and Agrarian Reform in Developing Countries*. London: ITDG Publishing.

Ghimire, K. B. (2001b) 'Peasants' pursuit of outside alliances and legal support in the process of land reform', in K. B. Ghimire (ed.), *Land Reform and Peasant Livelihoods: the Social Dynamics of Rural Poverty and Agrarian Reform in Developing Countries*. London: ITDG Publishing.

Ghimire, K. B. (2001c) 'Regional perspectives on land reform: considering the role of civil society organizations', in K. B. Ghimire (ed.), *Whose Land? Civil Society Perspectives on Land Reform and Rural Poverty Reduction – Regional Experiences from Africa, Asia and Latin America*. Rome: IFAD/Popular Coalition to Eradicate Hunger and Poverty/UNRISD.

Ghimire, K. B. (ed.) (2001d) *Whose Land? Civil Society Perspectives on Land Reform and Rural Poverty Reduction – Regional Experiences from Africa, Asia and Latin America*. Rome: IFAD/Popular Coalition to Eradicate Hunger and Poverty/UNRISD.

Guererro, Amado (pseudonym) (1970) *Philippine Society and Revolution*. Oakland, CA: International Association of Filipino Patriots (IAFP).

Hawes, Gary (1987) *The Philippine State and the Marcos Regime: the Politics of Export*. Ithaca, NY: Cornell University Press.

Herring, Ronald (1983) *Land to the Tiller: the Political Economy of Agrarian Reform in South Asia*. New Haven/London: Yale University Press.

Houtzager, Peter (2000) 'Social movements amid democratic transitions: lessons from the Brazilian countryside', *Journal of Development Studies*, Vol. 36, No. 5, pp. 59–88.

Kay, Cristóbal (1993) 'For renewal of development studies: Latin American theories and neoliberalism in the era of structural adjustment', *Third World Quarterly*, Vol. 14, No. 4, pp. 691–702.

Kay, Cristóbal (1998) 'Latin America's agrarian reform: lights and shadows', *Land Reform, Land Settlement and Cooperatives*, Vol. 2, pp. 9–31.

Kerkvliet, Benedict (1990) *Everyday Politics in the Philippines: Class and Status Relations in a Central Luzon Village*. Berkeley, CA: University of California Press.

Kerkvliet, Benedict (1993) 'Claiming the land: take-overs by villagers in the Philippines with comparisons to Indonesia, Peru, Portugal, and Russia', *Journal of Peasant Studies*, Vol. 20, No. 3, pp. 459–93.

Kilusang Magbubukid ng Pilipinas (KMP) (1992) *Proceedings of KMP's Strategic Assessment and Planning, Conducted by an 'Expanded' National Council on 27–31 January 1992, Tagaytay City* (internal document). Quezon City: KMP.

Lara, Francisco Jr. (2001) *Cooperative Bias in the Redistribution of Commercial Farms and Agribusiness Plantations: the 'Illogic' of Collective Action* (mimeo).

Ofreneo, Rene (1980) *Capitalism in Philippine Agriculture*. Quezon City: Foundation for Nationalist Studies.

Padilla, Sabino Jr. (1990) *Agrarian Revolution: Peasant Radicalization and Social Change in Bicol*. Manila: Kalikasan Press.

Partnership for Agrarian Reform and Rural Development Services (PARRDS) (1997) *Executive Summary, Second DAR-NGO-PO Workshop: Fast-Tracking CARP Implementation* (mimeo). Quezon City.

Peralta, Athena (2001) *The Rise of Services in the Philippines: Productivity Impacts and Determinants, 1970–1999* (unpublished MA Thesis). The Hague: Institute of Social Studies.

Petras, James (1997) 'Latin America: the resurgence of the left', *New Left Review*, No. 223, pp. 17–47.

Petras, James (1998) 'The political and social basis of regional variation in land occupations in Brazil', *Journal of Peasant Studies*, Vol. 25, No. 4, pp. 124–33.

Philippine Ecumenical Action for Community Empowerment (PEACE) (1994) *Case Studies on Agrarian Reform and Rural Development* (mimeo). Quezon City.

Putzel, James (1992) *A Captive Land: the Politics of Agrarian Reform in the Philippines*. New York: Monthly Review Press; London: Catholic Institute for International Relations (CIIR); Quezon City: Ateneo de Manila University Press.

Putzel, James (1995) 'Managing the "main force": the Communist Party and the peasantry in the Philippines', *Journal of Peasant Studies*, Vol. 22, No. 4, pp. 645–71.

Putzel, James (1999) 'The survival of an imperfect democracy in the Philippines', *Democratization*, Vol. 6, No. 1, pp. 198–223.

Putzel, James (2002) 'The politics of partial reform in the Philippines', in V. K. Ramachandran and M. Swaminathan (eds), *Agrarian Studies: Essays on Agrarian Relations in Less-Developed Countries*. New Delhi: Tulika Books.

Riedinger, Jeffrey (1995) *Agrarian Reform in the Philippines: Democratic Transitions and Redistributive Reform*. Stanford: Stanford University Press.

Rimban, Luz (1997a) 'Women being winnowed out of agrarian reform', serialized in *The Manila Times*, 3–4 March.

Rimban, Luz (1997b) 'Dole bets on land reform and wins', serialized in *The Manila Times*, 10–11 June.

Rocamora, Joel (1994) *Breaking Through: the Struggle within the Communist Party of the Philippines*. Manila: Anvil.

Rodriguez, Joel (2000) *Agrarian Reform in Commercial Farms: Designing an Appropriate Institutional Response*. MODE Research Papers, Vol. 1, No. 3, pp. 1–40.

Rosset, Peter (2001) 'Tides shift on agrarian reform: new movements show the way', *Backgrounder*, Vol. 7, No. 1.

Rutten, Rosanne (2000a) 'High-cost activism and the worker household: interests, commitment, and the costs of revolutionary activism in a Philippine plantation region', *Theory and Society*, Vol. 29, pp. 215–52.

Rutten, Rosanne (2000b) 'Changing sides in revolutionary times: the career of a lower-class CPP-NPA leader in Negros Occidental', in A. McCoy (ed.), *Lives at the Margin: Biography of Filipinos Obscure, Ordinary, and Heroic*. Quezon City: Ateneo de Manila University Press.

Tadem, Eduardo, Johnny Reyes and Linda Susan Magno (1984) *Showcases of Underdevelopment in Mindanao: Fishes, Forests, and Fruits*. Davao: Alternate Forum for Research in Mindanao.

van Schalkwyk and Johan van Zyl (1996) 'The land market', in J. van Zyl, J. Kirsten and H. P. Binswanger (eds), *Agricultural Land Reform in South Africa: Policies, Markets and Mechanisms*. Oxford: Oxford University Press.

Vellema, Sietze (2002) *Making Contract Farming Work?: Society and Technology in Philippine Transnational Agribusiness* (PhD dissertation). Wageningen University, The Netherlands. Maastricht: Shaker Publishing.

Wurfel, David (1988) *Filipino Politics: Development and Decay*. Ithaca, NY: Cornell University Press.

9
Rural Power Structures and Evolving Market Forces in Bangladesh

Manzurul Mannan

Introduction

Contemporary rural power structures in Bangladesh have been greatly modified by the influence of globalization. Local economic activities and needs are intricately woven into a global web of cause and effect over which the rural population has less and less control. Even the most remote villages are now drawn into national and global markets. Such an integration has become possible in part because Bangladesh has been pursuing development policies aimed at achieving a higher quality of life through sustained and rapid adjustments in its society's productive capacity, and political and social organizations. However, these policies have deep implications for its social fabric, political structure and economy, as the state in general has hugely failed to mitigate the social effects and manage market economy. On the one hand, state policies put emphasis on a more democratic society with a vibrant role for civil society. On the other hand, they have failed to impede the power concentration among certain individuals and social groups – in particular those already with considerable political and economic power. These social forces have become all too powerful, frequently to the detriment of the interests of the common people.

In more recent years, although Bangladesh has rapidly changed from a state-managed mixed economic system to a market-based capitalist system, there has been no lack of emphasis on the virtue of liberal democracy and governance (Mannan, 1990a, 1990b, 1993). Indeed, the country has ritually followed the development prescription and market parameters of good governance set by the World Bank, the IMF, the European Commission and Japan. The good governance model emphasizes three axes: the role of a competitive market and the economy, government responsibility to manage the state, and the importance of private rights and individual initiatives in civil society (Archer, 1994: 7). As such, a competitive market economy is favoured

271

by government policies assisting private producers to operate more efficiently. A strong state is required to manage the market and political system. Some signs for a well-managed state are good long-term planning for macro-economic policy, financial control, efficient institutions, a good education system, human rights and rule of law. A democratic civil society is required to save its economic and political system from the distortion of powerful interest groups. Civil society opens space for the role of citizens to maintain the quality of their institutions by making them responsible. Some attributes of civil societies include the functioning of a vigorous voluntary sector or NGOs, a free press, democratic processes, change of government by free elections and entrenched rights. Thus, the good governance model remains market-driven and conception is 'consumer-led'. Since consumers and voters remain sovereign, government should rise and fall by popular judgement on their performance. Companies and economics should likewise live and die by market competition (Archer, 1994: 14). But the basic facet of this three-axis model of social structure is the free circulation of commodities and also administrative dictates of the state – strictly distinguishable from a civil society that fosters a vibrant life world of symbols and solidarities (Cohen and Arato, 1992).

This chapter seeks to advance two prominent arguments with respect to the relationship of civil society, the market and state in Bangladesh. First, both the state and market have become so forceful that civil society institutions are steadily becoming passive satellites to the detriment of the productive functioning of both institutions (cf. Anderson, 1996: 112). Second, the mutual reinforcing influence of the market and the state generates increased fragmentation and has created transactional friction in civil society instead of helping to evolve cohesiveness among civil society forces.

It has been recognized that historically Bangladesh villages have developed their own local civil society, namely, *samaj* and traditional markets (Ishihara, 1987). The reliance on the local civil society and market has meant that, for a long time, contacts with the outside world were fairly limited and mediated by the chief of the village. From time to time peasants went to town to pay taxes or purchase minimum necessities and household items. At the local level, itinerant merchants frequently supplied them with outside consumption goods while at the same time buying peasants' produce. But in recent decades the influence of donor agencies and NGO interventions, and expansion in national and global markets affecting both the state apparatus and their actions, have relegated local civil society and traditional indigenous markets to the position of insignificant agencies. The civil society institution of *samaj* has been transformed into factional and splinter groups incapable of providing the customary forms of social protection and community solidarity. Similarly, the role and scope of traditional markets which existed in the form of numerous daily and weekly markets, and annual *melas* (festivals) where peasants went regularly to meet with fellow peasants and relatives, entertain themselves, and most crucially sell their produce in exchange for outside goods or cash payment have gradually changed. Although many traditional features of social institutions and forces can still be found in most parts of Bangladesh, rural society has dramatically changed over the years and villages are no longer isolated communities.

Village power structures have evolved by encompassing impulses from both inside and outside forces. The interplay between these forces has created numerous tensions and factions and led to the emergence of convoluted forms of power structures. In particular, there are increased contacts and remodelling of relations between historically evolved local civil society (*samaj*) and global civil societies represented by NGOs as well as between external market forces represented by multinationals and historically evolved traditional markets. State institutions have greatly facilitated this process, frequently channelling the class interests of competing groups. These friction and co-optation processes have at times resulted in the formation of splinter and interest groups configured by different power elites. But, on the whole, this has resulted in local civil society, traditional markets and governance structures slowly disappearing with the co-optation and weight of the state, national/global markets and donor agencies. At the same time, no concrete form of institutions and movements has emerged to deal with the daily anxieties and structural exploitative relations in localized village contexts.

The arguments and analyses presented in this chapter are based, in large part, on a case study of four villages of Sherpur *Thana* of Bogra district where the author has been able to conduct a study over the last two years. The Korotoa River, which runs north–south, divides the Sherpur *Thana* into two topographical areas and ecological zones. Two villages are selected from the first ecological zone, which is located to the east of Korotoa River. This area is formed by silt ridges and perennially flooded depressions, and the recent deltaic alluvium and sediments form the soil. The other two villages are from the second ecological zone and located west of the Korotoa River where the land rises to an elevated terrace that is known as the Barind tract whose soil is composed of red clay from former alluvium.

The two ecological zones have several natural advantages and disadvantages. The productivity of the soil in the Barind tract is much lower than the deltaic alluvium, but the land is free from floods. The deltaic alluvium represents the quality of aquatic ecology, as it is rich in both fertile land and fish resources. As a result, the delta plain area has attracted people for land settlement, even though they are aware of the flood hazards. The history of settlement in the flood plain dates back more than 200 years, whereas selected villages of the Barind tract began to be inhabited only after the independence of Bangladesh in 1971. The settlers are mostly the victims of river erosion who, after losing arable lands in the floods, sought to develop new villages. Historically people were less willing to settle in these areas because of infertile soil and very low productivity. However, after independence with an increase in population and soaring land prices, people from neighbouring districts began to flock to these Barind villages, which resulted in a significant increase in local population.

There are significant socioeconomic inequalities among the population groups in the four villages of Sherpur *Thana*. As will be shown later, there is a large number of poor and abject poor people, with little or insecure access to land. Although land still remains a major source of livelihood, land ownership alone cannot explain the economic stratification of the peasantry. For example, many land-poor peasants commonly enter into sharecropping agreements with rich peasants beyond the boundary of their villages, although these arrangements usually remain in favour of the latter. Increasingly, also, peasant households from all tenure categories are involved in non-farm activities, including employment in urban areas and abroad. In these cases, outside income has enabled certain peasant households to purchase extra land and invest in agriculture and trading. Their economic advancement has somewhat helped to reduce the power of the traditional landed elites, although they are still able to hold onto a large number of political positions and influence institutional investment in their areas.

The chapter is also built on data and insights from several other sources. The first source of information includes the author's own observation of the transformation of rural society since 1993. Two events have captured his interest. The first event in 1993 includes the onset of religious backlash on NGOs, which has been examined in detail elsewhere (Mannan et al., 1994). The second event was the development of peasant movements in 1995, which were provoked by the fertilizer crisis. This crisis and the peasants' opposition associated with the event have been discussed in some detail by Samshir (1996), especially highlighting the social structure of the rural rebellion (Samshir, 1996).[1] These two events, albeit of different origin, had in common the generation of widespread rural hostility towards outside interference in village lives and economies. The second source of data is the qualitative information on social change and transformation in rural society generated by the application of Participatory Rapid Appraisal (PRA). PRA was carried out between the beginning of 2000 and 2003, and in order to do this, ten teams were formed, each team consisting of five members.[2] Five teams surveyed the first ecological zone of deltaic alluvium; and another five teams covered villages in the Barind tract. PRA enabled the research teams to collect information on social wealth, quality of life and ecological change since 1920 in these areas. Finally, in-depth interviews with *Chatals* (paddy and rice stockers), local informants, Union Parishad (UP) members and government contractors provided deep insights into the dynamics of the power structure.

Prime genesis of social transformation in rural Bangladesh

Bangladesh, with its 68 000 villages and 90 per cent rural population, is essentially an agrarian society. Agriculture contributes 72 per cent of gross domestic product (GDP) and 60 per cent of employment. In recent years, although several large cities and market centres have emerged, villages remain identifiable entities of physical and social importance. The villages are known as *Grama*, which refers to the social organization of kinship family groups. A village is recognized by a cluster of households physically separated, but functionally tied to each other, usually, covered by lush green trees and bushes and separated from other villages by large surrounding arable fields. All villages have a basic structure of families and social groupings made up of traditionally conferred roles and status given and accepted by members of the community. Villages also have secondary structures and organizations, which have evolved through direct interaction with outside forces to serve certain purposes and goals. Although the peasantry constitutes the lifeline of the country, the governance of politico-economic affairs of peasant communities is mediated by a complex power structure that is operational beyond the immediate boundaries of villages.

No doubt, the country has achieved remarkable advancement in a host of areas including food production, safety net programmes, rural infrastructures, credit provisions, primary education, family planning, provision of drinking water and reduction of population growth that can largely be attributed to the results of state intervention. However, once all gains have been accounted for, the net rate of reduction in poverty in the 1990s appears to be only around 1 per cent annually (Rahman, 2000). In particular, this progress has yet to resolve the twin problems of landlessness and land concentration. Furthermore, the country has to manage a population of 120 million. The modernization processes have also triggered the breaking down of extended families, giving rise to nuclear families. There has been a tremendous erosion of social values, slackening of the elders' authority and increase in rural violence.

Under the influence of globalization, village economies and their social fabric are rapidly changing. Many alterations have been injected into a semi-feudal peasantry (Mukherjee, 1957: 53–6; Mannan, 1990a, 1990b). The global forces, such as donors, multinational marketing companies and financial institutions in collaboration with the state, bear the onus of governing peasant society. In a changed reality, multiple layers of the village economy and polity are being incorporated into national and global markets. The expansion in donor-supported road infrastructure and communications across villages with a simultaneous transformation of traditional agriculture into commercialized agriculture opens up space for dominance of outside organizations such as the state administration, market and development organizations over the traditional socioeconomic and political institutions of villages. These processes generate an emerging rural–urban continuum, with numerous implications for power relations at the village level.

The development of road communications has brought a substantial amount of linkage between rural and urban areas. Since the mid-1980s, a tremendous increase in rural roads and communications has taken place.

In 1947, Bangladesh had just 459 kilometres of roads (Jansen et al., 1989: 15), whereas by 2000 there were 17 554 kilometres (BSS, 1999: 247). It now takes only four hours to travel from Bogra to the capital city, Dhaka, which took nearly twelve hours even as recently as three years ago. One in every three Bangladeshi villages is now accessible by road from their nearest regional cities. The roles of the donor-financed high profile Local Government Engineering Department (LGED) and CARE (an international NGO) are crucial in developing the road infrastructure across rural areas.

The growth of the road network has many implications at the village level. First, road communications spur rural mobility and migration along gender lines. The transformation encourages the migration of both young men and women to cities, while married women and elderly men remain in the villages (Islam and Ahmad, 1984). Adult men and young unmarried women migrate to city areas in order to work in the garment industries, public sectors and different urban occupations. The economic opportunities open up new horizons for self-advancement, notably for rural young women. Secondly, remittances from migrant workers have emerged as an important source of rural household incomes, rising from 3.7 per cent in 1987–8 to 18.5 per cent in 2000 (Hossain et al., 2001). Those who remain in rural areas, apart from the principal occupation of agriculture, today find employment opportunities in rickshaw vans, local transport and locomotives, carpentry, masonry and so forth.

Finally, a major shift has occurred in traditional peasantry with the introduction of water-seed-fertilizer technologies, known as the 'Green Revolution'. These technologies have brought a fundamental change and altered agricultural practices. With the availability of high-yielding variety (HYV) seeds, supported by the provision of fertilizer and underground water for irrigation, peasants are now able to diversify crops from the previously rain-fed practice to dry-season cultivation. In addition to draft animals, farmers are also using power tillers (Adhikary and Rahman, 1999: 7). A few development agencies, such as the Swiss Agency for Development and Cooperation (SDC), the Canadian International Development Agency (CIDA) and several NGOs have played an important role in educating peasants to diversify their crops. This has created space for multinational companies to market seeds, fertilizers, pesticides and irrigation technologies and equipment even in the remotest villages. The overall result of this crop diversification is impressive. For example, by the early 1980s, the Bogra district produced a grain surplus of 82–100 per cent over local needs (Crow, 1999: 151). The thriving agriculture offers employment throughout the year. A peasant in the district proudly told the author: 'Boro mashe tero foshol' ('We get thirteen crops in twelve months'). The development in agriculture has also increased crop trading and business transactions with the main market in Dhaka. The rise in agricultural business has led an informant to remark, 'If we stop marketing our crops, people in Dhaka would starve.'

Economic stratification of the peasantry

Two important studies have already been carried out in the villages of Sherpur. In the 1970s, Westergaard conducted a study on a Boringram village. She explained the stratification of peasantry in terms of the access to agricultural lands across four principal tenurial categories: landless peasants, marginal peasants, subsistence peasants (small and medium) and surplus peasants. The inhabitants of Boringram village had a low degree of mobility and they were reluctant to move out of the village. In the locality there were few job opportunities outside agriculture. The landless households were able to find occasional short-term employment outside the village, but most of the time they were quite highly dependent on landowners for employment (Westergaard, n.d., 1985: 111). Her study confirmed the assumption that the rural power structure was fully dominated by landed classes mustering both economic and political power. Much later Momtaz (1996) also carried out a study in Sherpur, confirming the persistence of similar patterns of agrarian relations and stratifications as highlighted by Westergaard. However, Momtaz observed an important demographic transition in that villages were experiencing an emergence of youth as an agent of change. In one village, she observed that youths had come forward as a distinct 'power group' to take control of *Krishak Samabaya Samity* (Peasants' cooperatives). Most of these youths belonged to large and middle farmer families (Momtaz, 1996: 116). Groups of young people were also on the rise elsewhere in the country, and one scholar described the youths as 'recently emerged economic elites' (Rahman, 1986: 207–8).

With the introduction of modern agricultural practices, tenure relationships have rapidly changed. In particular, there has been considerable alteration in sharecropping systems. There are three forms of tenure agreement: *Khaikhalas*,

Table 9.1   The pattern of landownership in two ecological zones

Category	No. of families (65)	Land size
Wealth ranking in deltaic plain		
Rich peasants	4 (6.15%)	35–50 Bigha*
Middle peasants	26 (40%)	25–40 Bigha
Poor peasants	20 (30.77%)	5–24 Bigha
Ultra poor	15 (23.07)	Homestead/1–4 Bigha
Wealth ranking in Barind tract		
Rich peasants	6 (8.45%)	20–35 Bigha*
Middle streasants	29 (40.84%)	10–20 Bigha
Poor peasants	15 (21.13%)	1–10 Bigha
Ultra poor	21 (29.57)	Homestead

*1 Bigha = 0.67 hectare.
Source: author's own research, 2002–3.

Borga and *Chownia*. *Khaikhalas* literally means the 'return of land to the landowner by tenants after its utilization for a fixed period of time'. In this system, the tenant is obliged to pay cash in advance to the landowner.[3] The agreement may last up to fifteen years, but nowadays people prefer the shorter period of agreement of five to seven years. This happens because land values have soared due to commercialization of agriculture and high demand for arable land. Depending on land fertility, usually it costs Taka 1000–1200 per year per *bigha* of land. Thus if one enters into *Khaikhalas* for five years, the total cost for this period would be Taka 5000–6000. *Borga* is sharecropping between a landowner and a land renter. However, seasonal variations determine the amount of sharecropping. For instance, in *Baoishak–Jaistho* (15 April–15 June), the landowner is entitled to one-third of the crops, but in *Poush–Magh* (15 December–15 February), the landowner gets 50 per cent of the crops. *Chownia* agreements take place between a landowner and a tenant against a fixed amount of crops, irrespective of the total produce. The usual custum is for the landowner to obtain 8 maunds (around 425 kg) of the International Rice Research Institute (IRRI) paddy, 4 maunds (around 212 kg) of Amon paddy, and 2.5 maunds (around 133 kg) of vegetables. The tenant bears all the input costs for the production.

A polarization is also observed among the landowning peasantry. The rich and middle peasants, or their offspring, are transforming themselves into farmers by using modern agricultural equipment such as power tillers, control over deep tubewells and water sources, etc. In addition, rather than becoming restricted to agricultural work, young people within these categories are adopting non-farm activities or migrating to urban areas to find more profitable occupations. But migration of this nature is also taking place among poor peasants, resulting in a shortage of agricultural labour and, at times, higher wages in urban areas. More importantly, workers are gradually becoming reluctant to work as daily wage labourers; increasingly, they prefer to cultivate land on their own by entering into different forms of tenure agreements.

Khaikhalas has become popular among absentee landlords as this allows them to have an important cash income at the beginning of the contract. Rich peasants may also take land from middle peasants against a *Khaikhalas* arrangement. In this situation, they can maximize the utilization of power tillers and deep tubewells. Overall, the prime beneficiary of *Khaikhalas* is usually the middle peasant. A common practice is for the middle peasants to take land against *Khaikhalas* for seven years, but then immediately renting it to poor peasants in the form of seasonal *Borga* or *Chownia*. On many occasions, when middle peasants require cash they turn not to the rich, but to the poor to give their land for *Khaikhalas* or *Chownia*. In case of cash requirements, middle-class peasants, in particular, have difficulties. They usually have trouble in obtaining loans from rich peasants and they are careful not to take loans from the *Mohazon* (moneylender) because of exorbitant rates.

Instead, they may turn for cash to poor peasants who have access to NGO credit. The poor sharecroppers could also solve their cash problem by getting easy access to NGO credit.

Borga is a popular form of tenure for those who do not hire external labour since cultivating land by employing wage labourers does not prove to be cost-effective. Thus, those middle peasants and poor peasants who use their own labour, choosing to remain in their villages, usually get involved in sharecropping in addition to self-cultivation. People enter into this form of tenure agreement because rich landowners, although having lands, face scarcity of labour with the rise of non-farm activities for village labourers and poor peasants. Supervision of wage labourers and cultivation work is also very hazardous. Owing to economic uncertainty and a relatively tough labour bargain, they prefer to lease out their land to sharecroppers. Usually sharecropping appears to be a win–win situation, although in case of floods, natural hazards and pest attacks, the sharecropper is the net loser.

Although the stratification of peasantry in relation to land ownership has not changed in any significant manner, as suggested by Westergaard and Momtaz, to stratify peasantry by merely looking into landowning size may be misleading. Upon enquiry into household incomes in the area, it was found that some poor households had extra non-agricultural incomes, at times as much as the middle peasantry (without any significant outside income). The emerging scenario is that rural society is undergoing a process of transformation as peasants adopt new non-agricultural professions. In a recent study, it was found that 33 per cent of the population were cultivators, and another 33 per cent had taken up agriculture as a principal source of livelihood, with business as a secondary occupation. The remainder combined agriculture, services and employees in different rural occupations (Adhikary and Rahman, 1999: 5). Moreover, peasants in their lifetimes take up different occupations to fit with their survival strategies. Many rich and middle peasants (particularly their offspring) now prefer to enter into various forms of sharecropping rather than self-operation as it allows them to diversify their business activities or create a wider political base.

Power structure and the market

According to rural development literature, it is often suggested that villages are more or less distant units existing independently from larger society. But this isolation has been rapidly diminishing. Even twenty years ago, the predominance of agriculture and the localized nature of work limited the mobility of village people. The land-centric prominence of economic and social activities has led to a vision of a unifocal power structure, and what may be best described as a patron–client relationship (Jansen, 1987). The patrons manage the affairs of village communities, including the *Samaj*. This high-level concentration of power in the hands of village elites, frequently based on the investigation of a single or a limited number of villages, continues to receive consideration in academic debates and policy analyses. And this is despite the fact that numerous studies on micro-level power and individual centric leadership have shown that local heroes and tribunes have always existed in Bangladeshi villages at different times (Arens and van Beurden, 1977; Bertocci, 1970; Chowdhury, 1978; Jahangir, 1979; Jansen, 1987; Karim, 1990; Thorp, 1978; Wood, 1976). According to these studies, traditional leaders in apparently self-sufficient isolated villages use their social status and economic resources to control the political structure, while formal leaders may hold positions of political power by means of their access to government administration and their ability to distribute project funds. However, these studies have overlooked the important fact that the small power structures of villages are extended beyond the immediate boundary of villages, thereby often becoming part of a larger regional and national power structure.

The notion of isolated village is perhaps borrowed from the study of Indian villages and its *Panchayat* system (Bhuiyan, 1991: 210). Bangladeshi villages, unlike Indian caste *Panchayat*, have functioned neither as collective economic units nor as administrative units; rather they exist as vibrant social units (Akbar, 1996). In a fairly sceptical way, one scholar writes, '[in] our national system we have villages and villagers but no village organism, no village community. The village organism has disintegrated into a multitude of disunited individuals, living in mutual proximity' (Haq and Husain, 2001: 27). The inherent weakness of villages to develop cohesive social and economic structures allowed both colonial and post-colonial states to extend their administrative reach and economic infrastructure by devolving local government, police administration and development interventions. The historical expansion of state administration into villages was also complemented by the penetration of external market forces shaping their economic structures. These phenomena create a typical situation whereby state and market encompass villages, rural society historically remaining alienated from the rest of society and the state (Hashmi, 1992). A reason for historical alienation is that the social and economic situation in rural Bangladesh has not undergone any major modernization process that could unleash natural forces to influence or change the system to any great extent (Chowdhury et al., 1987: 15). The persistent influence of outside forces prevents the peasantry from becoming organized as a collective change-oriented group. The alienation sanctions the state administration to restructure power relations, while external market forces are able to determine the configuration of the economic structure in rural society.

The present work is a departure from previous studies available on village power structures by stressing that contemporary villages of Bangladesh do not exist as an isolated, alienated and independent unit from larger society.

Despite the gradual engrossment of outside society, the rural sector is far from disappearing, though, and the role of agriculture in providing food security and improved living conditions for the rural poor is extremely crucial. On the contrary, villages are becoming increasingly dependent on broader society through multiple layers of power structures and economic dependence of actors. These structures and relationships operate at micro-, meso- and macro-levels. The micro-level comprises actors, land structures and organizations, all of which are visible in the villages. The actors include the landed elites, religious leaders, NGO group members, etc. who maintain close relationships with peasants. The meso-level power structure exists beyond the land-based power structure of the immediate village, and is operational at an intermediary level. The actors include local government officials, market intermediaries, NGOs, development practitioners (representative of donors), contractors (Local Government Engineering Department/LGED agents) and UP politicians (state political representatives) who enjoy influence over a large area encompassing several villages, as well as peri-urban markets. Most of these actors live outside the village but control village affairs through multiple relationships. The macro-level is operational both at the state and global echelons through multinational marketing companies, NGOs and state bureaucrats. They have structural presence in villages, but control village affairs mainly through their regulatory power. Micro-villages are integrated into macro-level power structures through meso-level organizations of the state. The three levels are represented in Figure 9.1.

In much of rural Bangladesh, global influence has proved quite powerful in steering local power structures and in forming new forces and alliances. The reconfiguration of the power structure has moved the epicentre of power structure of villages from the micro-level to the meso-level, with further integration into macro-level structures and organizations. In concrete terms, this new development has meant an important shift in the balance of power from land-based leadership to new leaders and elites at the meso-level. The new elites have the ability to maintain handy linkages with the state and market forces. The rise of the meso-level elites is also the result of the transformation of the unifocal power structure into a fluid form of the multi-focal market-oriented power structure and relations. The land-centric leaders and patrons have dominated the unifocal power structure, while the multi-focal power structure gave rise to multiple elites and patrons. The multi-focal power structures have resulted in a condition wherein neither the land-centric elites nor new elites are in a position to exert decisive influence over the governance of villages. In other words, the new rural power structure could be defined as the absence of power elites, with the rise of several spheres of power represented by respective elites. The phenomenon of the absence of power elites has demonstrated that these contending elites neutralize each other – or what has been termed as the 'Absence of Champions' (Rahman and Islam, 2002: 159). This has indeed generated new dynamics in

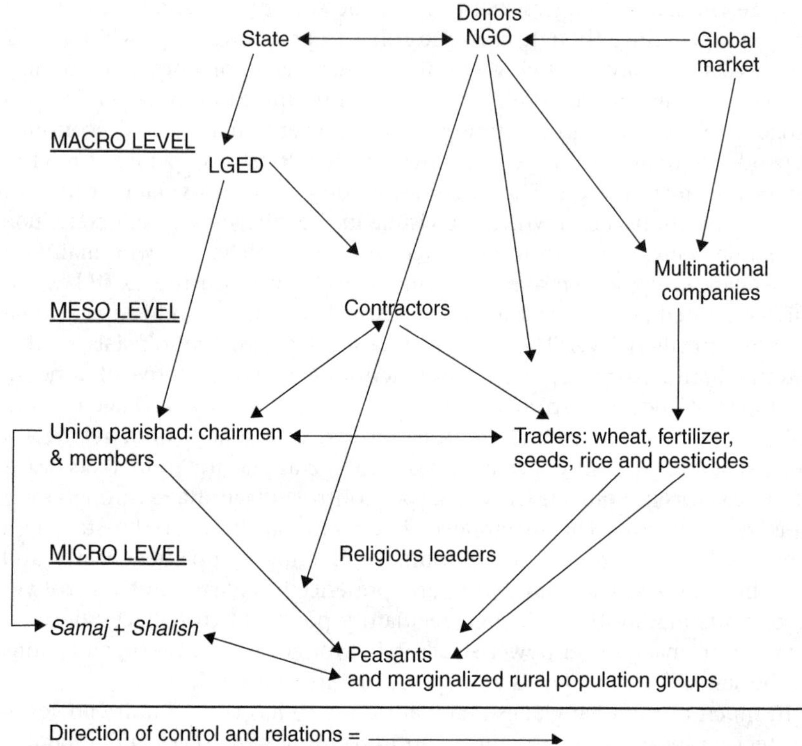

Figure 9.1   Rural power structure in Bangladesh

rural society, which have apparently interlocked powerless elites and patrons with mass peasantry. Emerging elites may enjoy their power within their particular sphere of activities affecting the community, but they do not command universal loyalties like the land-centric patrons. Thus the new leaders are unable to completely replace the role of the land-centric elites; indeed, the inability to fully dominate the power structure might thus be seen as the absence of competent heroes and champions, as indicated above.

The multi-focal power structures have evolved with the direct outcome of a growing penetration of outside forces from three directions: state administration, market forces and development interventions. These penetrations have entirely reconfigured the power structure to shape the governance of village society by relational and structural presences. The concept of 'relational presence' is taken to express the visibility of actors and patrons primarily at micro- and meso-levels. The relational presence refers to a dyadic interaction and relationships of exchange, often unequal, cultivated by villagers both with persons of equal and higher status. The dyadic relational presence could refer to a relationship between patrons and clients. Unlike the former, the structural presence is articulated not at the individual level, but at the level where actors manipulate and regulate village lives through organizational and market dynamics. The structural presence indicates the existence of elites who are operational through their contacts with the state and marketing networks and agencies. The structural presence of power actors at the macro-level shapes the 'relational presence' of actors at both meso- and micro-levels.

Erosion in the role of landed elites

These processes of change in power structures have evolved with a deep impact on traditional social organizations and institutions of *Samaj*. *Samaj* could be defined as historically developed local civil society to govern the daily functioning of villagers. Each village has one or more *Samaj*. The institutions of *Samaj* are as old as the villages themselves, and consist of a number of spatially continuous households belonging to one or more patrilineages and kinship groups. The head of *Samaj*, an elderly person in the community, is known as *Matbar*, and as well as him, the eldest members of the community also exert their influence in the decision-making of *Samaj*. *Samaj* is the most visible form of social grouping, which interlinks virtually all segments of the peasantry (Adnan, 1997: 277). The dynamics of the social organization of *Samaj* allow collective sanctions at the community level without outside interference (Kotalova, 1993). *Samaj* is also built on the lineage structure of *Bangsha* and *Gusti*.[4] Often, the courtyards of mosques become the pivotal centres for organizing *Samaj* activities, which makes the religious leader powerful by integrating *Samaj* activities into religion. *Samaj* is also an important civil society voluntary institution which takes on the role of disaster management, such as mitigating flood effects, constructing bridges, mosques, schools and so forth.

Samaj structures have experienced erosion because kinship groups and lineages are losing power due to: breakdown of joint families with the growth of nuclear families; rise of an educated class of youths; extended reach of state administration to the heart of villages; and increased scope of diversified livelihood opportunities for the poor. These changes have also brought erosion in the traditional structure of loyalties to elders and patrons who primarily exercised power by using the status of high *Bangsha* and control over lands (Jansen, 1987). The weakening of power of *Samaj* is also associated with the (i) declining centrality of land in rural life; (ii) gradual dominance of modern seed-fertilizer-irrigation technology over traditional modes of ploughing and rain-fed cultivation; and (iii) emergence of women-only associations organized by NGOs.

Historically land was not only a critical source of subsistence, but was also a symbol of wealth and prestige (Mannan, 2001: 82). However, this centrality of land has disappeared as it is neither a basis of status, nor does it represent a single livelihood source for the rural population. In a recent estimate, household income from agriculture was found to have dropped to under 50 per cent (Hossain et al., 2001: 10). This decline of household income from land is compensated with multiple livelihood systems and opportunities for the rural poor both in the agricultural and non-agricultural sectors, resulting in the circulation of money in poor households. In the case study villages, the annual income of households is Taka 30 000, which is well above the national level income, determined at Taka 19 000 per household per annum.

The second factor is the gradual importance of the mechanized tiller over the traditional plough; use of both deep and shallow tubewells that rely greatly on seasonal rain fall; use of fertilizer and pesticides instead of traditional cow manure; and replacement of traditional with a high-yielding variety of seeds. All these shifts, induced by the introduction of new technology, have brought fundamental changes to the social organization of the peasantry. The technological extension initiated by public agencies (which are now in the process of privatization) has gone hand in hand with the establishment of many peasant cooperatives that have encroached upon the scope and work of *Samaj*. This new technology has created additional arenas of contention among the peasantry, since it has become a lucrative business to gain control over mechanized tubewells and the increased quantum of water. New ties are established between people from different villages and social groups – for example, the people who have operational plots within the command area of the same tubewell. At times, heterogeneous groups are required to work out a system of joint management to reconcile various competing as well as conflicting interests (Adnan, 1997: 284).

The *Samaj* is a male-dominated organization. The emergence of NGO-sponsored 'women-only groups' has thus had an important impact on the structure and functioning of *Samaj*. Over the years, NGOs have provided services in the area of conscientization and empowerment, health and education, and credit to women. However, since 1990, NGOs have increasingly engaged in activities related to 'women-only groups' in micro-credit programmes, bringing certain changes to household relations. With access to NGO credits, female members have begun to control money and a degree of decisional space previously controlled by men (Mannan, 1997), with direct implications on the functioning of *Samaj*. The expansion of the social scale of production and micro-credit have had an effect on the cohesive structure of traditional *Samaj*, which splits into different factional groups on various issues ranging from internal to external conflicts, involving issues like access to government project funds, status configurations, marriage links, etc. Again, the conflicting factional groups may paradoxically reunite around the ambit of *Samaj*. The process of opposition and alliance thus gives rise to considerable fluidity in the structure and forms of *Samaj*.

This has also led to important changes in the scope of the *Shalish* system. This is a local-level court for dispute resolution as well as for maintaining rule and order, norms and traditions. While the cohesive structure and authority of *Samaj* have been in erosion with the rise of agricultural cooperatives and women-only associations, its *Shalish* functions have been transformed into formal institutional structures. An additional reason for becoming *Shalish* as a formal institution is the empowerment of it by government. In 1976, the government passed the Village Court Ordinance, which empowers *Shalish* with an arbitration authority to impose penalties up to 500 Taka (Hashmi, 2000: 103). This recognition has transformed *Shalish* mechanisms into administrative institutions ruled by quasi-formal procedures for dispute-resolution, thereby reducing the traditional role of *Samaj*.

Market-driven NGO sector

NGOs play a catalyst role in rural transformation. The role of NGOs is important both on traditional borders of state action and market development. NGOs perform state functions, such as providing primary education and healthcare to the grassroots level; Bangladeshi NGOs work to develop consensus among the rural poor at a level where the state has a weak presence. NGOs started their development work with a clear commitment to carry out value-driven voluntary programmes with a 'high moral ground'. This allows NGOs to represent non-market values, as well as maintain influence in the political process.

However, NGOs, despite creating an image of value-driven social movements, are always market-driven agencies seeking to provide services at a lower price than the commercial sector. Since 1990, large and small NGOs have witnessed a major transition from their earlier approach of representing non-market values (e.g. the conscientization approach) for increasing the bargaining power of poor women through micro-credit. Out of 1300 donor-supported NGOs, 800 deal with micro-credit to reconfigure their links with donor agencies, government, the market and civil society (Huq, 2000: 21). By the year 2000, NGOs disbursed micro-credit amounting to $2000 million to the poor, particularly to poor women.

In the study area, the Bangladesh Rural Advancement Committee (BRAC), Rural Development Academy (RDA), the Centre for Human Development (PROSHIKA) and Tengamara Mahila Samity (TMS) are strongly represented. Funding from NGOs has resulted in the increase of cash flows in households and the possibility for poor people to transact with money and trading. Among others, additional money inflow into households has brought changes to relationships between men and women, with women gaining some advantages. In some cases, women have themselves become mini-moneylenders. A study in the early 1990s showed that BRAC's credit had affected the informal credit system controlled by moneylenders as the latter are forced to charge a much lower rate of interest against lending money (Begum, 1994). On the whole, NGOs are able to provide the poor with a significant amount of economic comfort or at least delay the process of becoming totally destitute.

Moreover, growing NGO intervention in rural areas is helping the poor to be integrated more rapidly into market systems. Financial aid to the poor is taking place at a time when new labour opportunities are being made available for them in the non-agricultural sector. The labour market has changed at different levels. Piece-rate labour contracts and fixed rent tenancies are becoming dominant instead of the occupational hierarchy of the recent past when casual daily labour was a preferred source of employment for the poor. At the same time, as indicated earlier, the expansion of non-farm sectors, such as rural construction, transport business, trade and services, have become important sources of employment.

The dominant micro-credit ethos of NGOs has to be understood against their approach using social mobilization of the peasants and the poor to demonstrate against economic injustice and exploitative power structures.[5] NGOs began by preparing women to riposte against social prejudices and exploitation by moneylenders. One way to reduce the reliance on money lenders has been to provide money to group members. As NGOs started to lend money, they found that providing credit is a lucrative business for the organization and one which gives financial sustainability to their group members. Thus, NGOs have been providing more loans to their group associates, thereby transforming their members into actors in the market. Increasingly, NGOs have been seeing poverty as a potential business opportunity and now define their group members as market actors like customers and clients. They are not only providing credit to group members, but have also sought to create a more favourable condition for women receiving credit to enter into business transactions with NGOs. The latter sell agricultural seeds,[6] medicines, poultry products and micro-dairy goods through their groups; they prepare their group members to produce different marketable goods taking the responsibility to market the produce of their group members as an extension of NGO business; they play a catalyst role in transforming the group members into prospective entrepreneurs; and they begin businesses either independently or in partnerships with business enterprises, the latter activity being carried out by NGOs without the consent of group members. The three largest NGOs – Grameen Bank, BRAC and PROSHIKA – now dominate the information technology business in Bangladesh.

Growing role of merchants and traders

Market actors play an important role in reshaping the power structure through economic dynamics. The rural agricultural market operates through both input and output outlets. The input market actors are the traders who supply fertilizers, pesticides and seeds[7] produced by global multinationals; and the output market is influenced by *Chatals*, who control the rice market. The input market has been subjected to the influence of the government's privatization policy which has sought to spur nationwide growth in businesses dealing with fertilizers, seeds and water technology (e.g. shallow tubewell – STW; low lift pump – LLP; and deep tubewell – DTW). From 1978, under donor pressure, the government privatized the distribution of STW and LLP, and the ownership of DTW from the Bangladesh Agriculture Development Corporation (BADC). The private sector was encouraged to take a leading role in the importation and distribution of STW. At the same time, the government pursued its policy of increasing rental charges on DTW and LLP, as well as selling them to cooperatives and private individuals assisted by cheap institutional credit.

The government also relaxed the control of BADC over fertilizer distribution to private sectors. In the early 1990s, two major areas of policy change exerted a significant influence. The first policy was related to the privatization of fertilizer distribution and elimination of subsidies; and the second policy was concerned with the evolution of a minor irrigation policy towards increased private sector participation in procurement and distribution (Shahabuddin, 1999: 141). However, the government retained control over a certain category of fertilizer production. Before the completion of privatization in 1992, the government's distribution system was characterized by a shortage of supply and the existence of fairly institutionalized black markets where fertilizers from the public distribution system found their way to private traders (Adnan, 1999: 189). As such, the existent private fertilizer market was further strengthened by transforming it into a legal market with privatization of fertilizers. The government also allowed the private sector to import fertilizer. This policy had a huge impact on the proliferation of the fertilizer market. It is estimated that, by 1988, there were 8000 wholesalers and 50 000 retailers in operation. In 1992, the share of private trade went up from 75 per cent to 100 per cent (Ahmed, 1998: 54). The input market actors, particularly the fertilizer traders, are formally represented through their network of wholesalers and numerous small retailers in rural agriculture. Peasants are forced to buy fertilizers in hard cash as credit transactions are virtually absent in the fertilizer market. However, peasants can obtain loans from various sources, such as informal loan markets, NGOs and *Chatals*.

The fertilizer-seed-water technologies have contributed to the increase of agricultural output in various forms as Bangladesh has now become a surplus producer of rice. This increase of agricultural output has also led to the importance of *Chatals* and mechanized rice-milling owners in the output market. The increased volume of harvest also creates twofold problems. First, peasants do not have sufficient space for storing paddy; and, secondly, they have to parboil large volumes of paddy before processing it into rice. Again, peasants face the problem of storing parboiled rice as well as reduced access to the market. *Chatals* have thus been exploiting the vulnerability of peasants.

The relationship between *Chatals* and peasants is very complex. *Chatals* make efforts to keep up business by exerting influence on fixing and controlling prices of the harvest and rice market. They play a strategic role between peasants' production, harvesting and marketing of rice, and, over-all, have three major roles. The first is as paddy hoarders, the hoarding business being cemented by the primordial loyalty existing between *Chatals* and peasants. This loyalty is determined not on the basis of market princi-ples and exchange, but on traditional hierarchy founded on the cognition of relative ranking, which may vary with one's wealth, lineage, education and age. *Chatals* have a tricky position as they have to prove their humane face and not appear as exploiters. As such, on some occasions, *Chatals* lend money with nominal or no interest to peasants during the cultivation period and, in return, peasants commit themselves to supply paddy after harvest.

Chatals are also the employers of female labour. Traditionally women were involved in processing of paddy into rice by using *Dheki* technology, which is home-based manual rice milling, a method used in every rural household. The commercialization of agriculture, the seed-water-technology and motor-ized rice milling have completely wiped out the traditional *Dheki* sector and created female unemployment. However, poor women labourers, who had lost their traditional employment in *Dheki*, found compensation by working in the mechanized rice mills and *Chatals* (Rahman, 2001: 11). These female labourers are often the kin of peasants who maintain a primordial relation-ship with *Chatals*.

The second role of *Chatals* emanates from their control over the technology of processing paddy to rice.[8] A simple payment rule is followed in this process. The *Chatals* deduct 5 kg of rice from one *maund* (40 kg) as a pro-cessing loss in the conversion of paddy into rice. A further 5 kg is deducted as a process fee. Thus, out of one *maund* of paddy, peasants eventually receive 30 kg of rice. In practice, *Chatals* accept a processing fee either in cash or kind, whichever is more favourable to them. If *Chatals* anticipate that the price of rice is going to increase, they accept in kind (i.e. 5 kg of rice); if it is to decrease, they ask for cash (i.e. price of 5 kg of rice). The pro-duction of paddy and its impact on the rice market could be well assessed in advance by *Chatals*, determined by harvest output, pre-existing prices of rice and role of the *Chatal* association.[9]

The third role of *Chatals* is marketing rice as wholesalers. In principle, *Chatals* buy both paddy and rice from peasants at cheap prices, and supply it to the market when prices soar. They adopt different strategies to maximize their profits from both ends: during the processing of paddy, marketing of rice and during hoarding. To utilize their full hoarding capacity, the *Chatals* aim to continuously buy paddy from the peasants in order to use the store-house to its full capacity. Any excess is released into the market. The *Chatals* have to manage two situations simultaneously, i.e., first procuring the paddy, and then after processing it into rice, replacing their paddy stock with rice. Any miscalculation in this process may incur losses to the *Chatals*.

It is estimated that fifteen *Chatals* could collectively stock a minimum of 22 500 tons of rice at any given point of time for a period of 2–2.5 months. The continuing capacity to stock rice is important in order to be able to fix the price of rice on local markets to the advantage of the *Chatals*. However, such a strategy works against the peasants' interests. There is a 'price complex' that works in three phases to affect the market price of rice in relation to its stock position. The first phase is the strategy of the *Chatals* to maintain a full stocking capacity. However, they release rice beyond their stocking capacities to be taken away by peasants to sell at markets. The second phase begins when peasants try to sell rice at markets, and the *Chatals* simultaneously release the rice from their stocks. This depresses the price as the market is saturated with rice. Thus, peasants find it difficult to obtain a fair price for their produce. The lowering of prices triggers the third phase when many peasants reluctantly begin to sell rice at low prices. The *Chatals* then purchase cheap rice, through their agents, to replenish their stocks until finally exhausting the peasants' reserves. These strategies ultimately establish the monopoly of *Chatals* over rice trading by creating an artificial shortage of supply which results once again in raising rice prices. The *Chatals* thus remain in a dominant position, being able to determine rice prices to their own relative advantage.

Those peasants having the possibility to do so, and in the wake of a decline in prices, adopt the method of holding back from selling rice on the market by renting the *Chatals*' storage space. The rent is usually fixed at Taka 0.10 per kilogram against any profitable sale. Peasants can stock their rice for two months at the *Chatals*,[10] but persistence of low prices makes peasants' lives untenable, thereby allowing *Chatals* to benefit again. Peasants are prevented from both removing their stocks of rice because of transport costs and lack of space, as well as being unable to sell their rice on the market. This situation forces peasants to renegotiate with *Chatals*. The latter, however, always try to give the impression to peasants that they too incur losses because of having to buy back their rice at market prices. This helps them to ensure that the same peasants return to them during the next seasonal production cycle.

The role of the state in sponsoring market forces

In recent years, the state has expanded its administrative reach to rural areas, aiming, among other things, to develop grassroots democracy and promote the representative character of local political organs. A proper electoral representative body is seen as necessary to administer state-sponsored development activities. The local political organ is known as UPs and covers an average population of 25 000. A position in UPs provides access and linkages to the local government bureaucracy and also allows political elites to widen their power base from micro-village to meso-village higher forums.

UPs oversee both political functions and development activities. The political function of the UP chairperson and members is of strategic importance in the formation of rural power structure. The chairperson and members are elected by direct voting which gives them legitimacy to govern local political institutions. Given the importance of UPs, the subsequent political government tried to reform UPs to suit their interests. Two important policy changes in the 1990s have put a further spotlight on this organ. First, the government streamlined the representational base of the UPs by demarcating a union into nine wards instead of the previous three, with each ward having its electoral representatives. The new system broadens the base of political representation, as members are elected from constituent villages within the boundary of respective wards. Second, the government has made the representation of women mandatory in the UPs, each UP having to reserve three seats for women (Rahman, 2001: 2). However, female participation has brought critical changes in local electoral politics along gender lines.

UPs are an important power base for political parties and usually those in power attempt to command the loyalty of UP chairmen and members through allocation of development budgets and state patronage. In fact, UP actors are the principal forces behind the *Gram Unnayan* (village development) activities, which cover *Dushtha Vhata* (poverty allowance), *Bidhova Vhata* (widow grant) and *Boisko Vhata* (old age support). They also allocate scholarships amounting to Taka 20 per month to the mothers of poor students at primary schools; female students of primary schools receive support under 'food for education'. Moreover, female students from class six to class ten receive scholarships in the range of Taka 400–500.

A big stake of UP actors lies in their role of overseeing and monitoring state and donor-sponsored infrastructure development activities, such as construction and maintenance of roads and bridges, culverts, hospitals, and distribution of seeds and pesticides. These activities are subjected to approval of local members and the chairperson. They thus exert considerable influence in the distribution of resources and political authority. At times, UP members themselves become 'Project Chairmen' supported by five to seven local aides. UP actors work closely with the Local Government Engineering Department (LGED)-appointed contractors to implement development projects. Donors, notably the Asian Development Bank, finance this high-profile body. LGED carries out more than 90 per cent of development activities in rural areas. Contractors receive 'wheat' at a subsidy rate to implement different projects. They then sell wheat at the highest price on the market in collaboration with UP actors, partly to pay wages to labourers; the remainder being shared. 'Wheat' is now a catchy term implying a unique form of power nexus binding politicians, administrators and local government functionaries in a truncated vision of development built on institutionalized corruption (Rahman, 2001: 5).

Peasantry and power structure: evolving counter-tendencies

The integration of villages in larger society and the penetration of the state, market and development actors bifurcate villages along both traditional patron–client relationships (shaped by relational presence) and class relationships (shaped by structural presence of elites). Depending on the context, peasants maintain simultaneous contracts, elaborating relationships with the landed elites (for sharecropping lands), UP actors (for receiving state patronage), NGOs (for credit and other benefits), and market actors (for agricultural inputs) and *Chatals* (for agricultural outputs). The question of relationships between mass peasantry and the power structure is problematic because at least three major counter-tendencies have been observed in recent years.

Gender polarity

The rural society is witnessing polarity in gender relationships. Traditionally, women's activities were confined within the private spheres around households of the immediate neighbourhood, while men's activities are spread over a wider public sphere. Both the policies of the government and NGOs to give priority to women in politics and development projects have created a context in which women have become increasingly visible in the public sphere. In the first place, the government's electoral policy to reserve three compulsory women electoral posts in UP underlines the importance of elite women in local politics. This new female political elite relies heavily, not on men's votes, but on the votes of a large number of women. Thus, women make alliances along gender lines. NGOs are also playing an important role in canvassing village women for their parties. Furthermore, NGOs have brought qualitative changes to gender relations at the household level as women's direct access to NGO credit allows them to gain enhanced control over money and economic resources. This is a new phenomenon in village community, challenging the traditional position of men controlling money. For example, traditionally men earned money and preserved the right to spend it. Now as women earn cash and their political position is improved, men cannot ignore the power of women in household decision-making, including family expenditure (Mannan, 1997). On some occasions, as the acceptance by NGOs to provide credit to peasant women has been widely criticized by male patriarchs and privileged classes, male peasants and kin of credit-receiving households have enabled them to use a 'buffer' to protect themselves against criticism. Thus, increasingly, women seek to invest in different productive opportunities generated by market liberalization.

Evolution in patron–client relationships

Until recently, the land-based elites, through a complex patron–client relationship, held domineering positions within rural power structures. The traditional patron–client relationship is influenced by numerous factors, such as the multiple inheritance system with many heirs to a family land plot; individual property rights to land; scarcity and unequal distribution of land; lack of employment and other sources of livelihood; need for political and physical protection; and access to resources in rural areas made available by government (Jansen, 1990: 25–6). The traditional power of patron–client relationships has begun to erode with market liberalization, commercialization of agriculture, increase of employment opportunities and the subsequent rise of multi-sector elites who maintain control over their respective clients. In this new situation, the position of land-centric elites increasingly relies on the support of government officials and the urban elites. This dependency has brought a cleavage among rich peasants competing for the different segments of the power structure. A new power configuration has thus emerged among those controlling technology, owning lands, as well as those having access to government resources.

This newly gained power allows one group of elites to oppose another. At the same time, elites from different segments of the power structure make attempts to establish new forms of patron–client relationships with the peasantry, which, in turn, triggers divisions among the latter. These various power elites create a new form of dependency relationship with peasants to their own advantage. The peasants have adapted to this new situation in which dynamic relationships of agricultural society are increasingly determined by structural and class forces. This typical situation transforms broader patron–client associations with a unifocal power structure to a patron–client relationship within a multi-focal power structure in order to reproduce patron–client relationships within the framework of class relationships. The multi-focal elites while in external opposition to each other consider loyalty from the peasantry as being crucial to one another.

Peasant class consciousness

The peasants are clearly caught at the crossroads between traditional forms of loyalty based on patron–client relationships and class-based economic relationships. While elites are trying to exert their influence over multi-focal power structures, the poor peasants still reproduce patron–client values, as they need a safety net to protect their position by tagging their loyalties to one or several power elites. However, while they express their loyalty to patrons, a typical class-consciousness and differential attitude occurs among peasantry beyond their patronage system. The differential attitude of peasants towards rich patrons is linked to one's own economic interests, which, in turn, depends a great deal on how patrons form particular elites to serve the peasants' interests. This also suggests that the public expression of respectful behaviour towards peasants may not match the private disliking towards their patrons. This happens because the development of class relations has not completely eliminated age-old patron–client hierarchical values and ideology.

On the contrary, because of the absence of a clear distinction between various elite groups, it becomes difficult for the peasants to define a common enemy guilty of exploiting them (Jansen, 1990: 27). Even though the poor feel exploited by the rich, their primordial consciousness deters them from developing a class-consciousness for articulating shared needs and launching collective actions. Importantly, with the dyadic economic relations existing between the rich and the poor, there are several types of intermediate sanctions to which a client could be subjected leading their safety net to disappear if they were to break away from their respective elite patrons. Although traditional relationships are eroding, peasants continue to reconfigure relationships along established primordial traditional lines.

On the whole, peasants manifest factional loyalty towards different power elites. This fragmentation prevents peasants from working and emerging as a cohesive category. This is a reverse trend of what was observed in the 1980s when peasants would organize united actions in order to improve their bargaining position on the rural labour market (Jansen, 1990: 28). The weakness in peasants' cohesiveness prevails because of a typical situation whereby there are erosions both in areas of rules and ideology that regulate peasants and political institutions (e.g. *Shalish*) that sanction them.

Despite the dependence of peasants on elites, electoral politics has given some bargaining power to peasants. It has been observed that during both national and UP elections the patron–client relationship is increasingly challenged. Although the overall patron–client relationship is reproduced within the emerging structure of class, power elites are incapable of fully manipulating peasants. More and more, the UP political actors have to rely on peasants' votes, which tacitly recognizes the mass power of the peasantry.

Conclusion

This study has made an attempt to show the evolving nature of the relationship between the peasantry and local elites in the process of market expansion in Bangladesh. The course of action connecting rural society to wider economic dynamics is now complete. The following have been particularly instrumental in this process: state and donor policies to privatize essential agricultural inputs and services; the active role of NGOs in connecting rural producers to national and global markets through credits, seeds and market linkages; and the increased penetration of multinational companies into rural areas. Recent market expansion has produced many implications in reshaping rural power structures. Peasants too are adapting. They seek to develop a hierarchy of economic relationships and dependence with market elites, while maintaining a more or less independent path of choosing their political representatives. It may appear somewhat paradoxical that, while market forces are instrumental in remodelling power configurations, peasants enjoy relative political freedom beyond the control of the market. At the same time, ongoing trends in the make-up and function of various interest groups have led the traditional institutions of civil society (e.g. *Samaj*) to be fragmented and weak, thereby incapable of representing the interests of ordinary peasants.

Clearly, the traditional land-centric power structure has eroded with the strong presence of a market-friendly state, donor agencies, NGOs and market forces. As different groups of power elites emerge to control community affairs, many previously isolated villages are now rapidly brought into the orbit of market globalization, primarily through the spread of improved road communications, state projects and donor agencies' efforts to pump money into rural society. In this process of integration, the epicentre of the power structure has also shifted from micro-level to meso-level, resulting in the erosion of a unifocal power structure, but giving rise to a new class of elites. At the same time, many of these new elites fail to achieve a broader recognition of their roles across villages. This creates a situation whereby elites neutralize each other to create a condition described above as an absence of power or heroes. The non-existence of power is indicative of the fact that rural society has developed multi-focal power structures, which divide and compartmentalize power relations with counter-tendencies. The counter-tendencies of one power elite to oppose another have neutralizing affects. For example, NGOs work with the poor peasant women to empower them against social and economic injustices, but the same NGOs develop exploitative relationships with women through micro-credit to favour the market. *Chatals*, too, on the one hand, appear to be pro-peasant, but on the other, become benevolent exploiters.

The various roles of power elites are implicitly influenced by a zero-sum game over peasantry through the control and access to a donor-sponsored development process (e.g. NGOs and LGED), control of power over state patronage (e.g. UP members) and control of economics by market elites. The absence of power in rural societies indicates that market-based elites through their structural presence are overpowering the land-centric elites. This has somewhat developed into complex and complicated power equations among actors who keep the dynamics of power structure operational. The dominance of the elite at the meso-level is so illuminating that when peasants defended their rights to fertilizers or fair prices for their harvest, the elites of micro- and meso-levels become helpless to support their demands. As an outcome, peasants saw no viable opponents against them and were thus unable to formulate their rights. In other words, the state, donors, global market and NGOs are unable to offer an alternate forum for development by giving more political voice to the peasantry, as well as opening new prospects for sustainable and dignified economic well-being at the grassroots.

Notes

1. The peasants' unrest was the outcome of the process of transition from the public to the private sector, especially when new private entrepreneurs mismanaged the distribution of fertilizers. The markets ran short of fertilizer not because fertilizer

companies had produced less, but the distribution system collapsed as a result of transition from a public to a private distribution system. Peasants did not necessarily protest against the government's privatization policy and, in general, they were too poor and unorganized to have provided any effective political resistance to the detrimental outcome of the elimination of a subsidy on fertilizers as well as privatization of import and distribution. The underlying reason for the peasants' uprising was the 'shock effect' caused by privatization, as well as shortage in fertilizer supplies – especially to small farmers (Adnan, 1999: 216).

2. The chapter in large part is based on the qualitative data generated by the students of the Independent University, Bangladesh (IUB) between 2000 and 2003. I am grateful to students for giving me access to their study reports, as well as to the Rural Development Academy (RDA), Bogra, for providing logistic support, including lodging.

3. There are various reasons why people prefer *Khaikhalas* against hard cash money. These range from the need for cash money to arrange marriages, bear the cost of children's education, purchase of agricultural tools and so forth.

4. For a detailed discussion on *Bangsha* and *Gusthi*, see Mannan (1990b, 2002).

5. Until 1990, the dominant approach of NGOs has been social mobilization. However, under the influence of micro-credit programmes, NGOs have rapidly restructured their organizations, although, in the process, this has created cultural tension. For example, Ghimire (2001: 143–6) observed the proactive role of *Gonoshahajjo Sangstha* (GSS) in providing legal assistance to peasants and poor women, but this NGO was disintegrated and abolished when they tried to restructure the organization's role from one of social mobilization to one of a micro-financial institution.

6. Some NGOs are also aggressively promoting hybrid and terminator seeds of multinationals as well as forcing their group members to buy these seeds. This policy creates conflict with peasants when they attempt to use their own indigenous variety of seeds. Indeed, parallel movements are emerging, denouncing increased collusion between NGOs and agribusiness groups. One such association is the New Agricultural Movement, which has already helped to preserve more than 700 local varieties of seeds for use by peasants.

7. Currently, BRAC, a leading NGO in the country, is emerging as one of the leading hybrid and terminator seed suppliers to peasants.

8. The processing of paddy into rice is divided into two categories: *Chatal* and mill work. *Chatal* work includes unloading paddy from trucks, soaking it in water, parboiling, drying and then carrying it to mills. The mill work includes putting the rice into haulers and the paddy into winnowing machines for processing into rice, and then putting the rice into sacks before weighing it (Jahan, 2000: 13).

9. There are fifteen *Chatals* in Bogura district, making up the association. *Chatal* associations play an instrumental role in fixing the prices of both paddy and rice.

10. *Chatals* and peasants enter into agreement that during the stocking period if any damage is done to rice, *Chatals* would bear the loss. Usually the duration of this agreement is valid between 2 and 2.5 months.

References

Adhikary, R. C. and Rahman H. (1999) *Cultural Practices and Rice Yield: an Image of the Level Barind*. Bogra: Rural Development Academy.

Adnan, Shapan (1997) 'Class, caste and *Samaj* relations among the peasantry in Bangladesh. Mechanisms of stability and change in the Daripalla villages, 1975–86', in J. Breman, P. Kloos and A. Saith (eds), *The Village in Asia Revisited*. Delhi: Oxford University Press.

Adnan, Shapan (1999) 'Agrarian structure and agricultural growth trends in Bangladesh: the political economy of technological change and policy intervention', in B. Rogaly, B. Harriss-White and S. Bose (eds), *Sonar Bangla? Agricultural Growth and Agrarian Change in West Bengal and Bangladesh*. Dhaka: University Press Ltd.

Ahmed, Raisuddin (1998) 'Assessment of past agricultural policies', in Rashid Faruqee (ed.), *Bangladesh Agriculture in the 21st Century*. Dhaka: University Press Ltd.

Akbar, Ali Khan (1996) *Discovery of Bangladesh: Explorations into Dynamics of a Hidden Nation*. Dhaka: University Press Ltd.

Aminul Islam, A. K. M. (1978) *A Bangladesh Village: Conflict and Cohesion: Anthropological Study of Politics*. Cambridge: Schenkman Publishing Company.

Anderson, David G. (1996) 'Bringing civil society to an uncivilised place. Citizenship regimes in Russia's Arctic frontier', in Chris Hann and Elizabeth Dunn (eds), *Civil Society: Challenging Western Models*. London and New York: Routledge.

Archer, Robert (1994) 'Market and good government', in Andrew Clayton (ed.), *Governance, Democracy and Conditionality: What Role for NGOs?* Oxford: International NGO Training and Research Centre (INTRAC).

Arens, Jeneke and Joseph van Beurden (1977) *Jhagrapur: Poor Peasant and Women in a Village in Bangladesh*. Birmingham: Third World Publications.

Bangladesh Bureau of Statistics (BSS) (1999) *Statistical Year Book of Bangladesh*. Dhaka: BSS.

Begum, Shamim Ara (1994) *Grameen Mohilader Artho-Samajik Unnoyone BRAC-er Rindhan Kormochuchir Provab: Jamalpur Jillar Puchti Gramer Sommikkha*. Research Report. Dhaka: Bangladesh Rural Advancement Committee (BRAC).

Bertocci, Peter J. (1970) *Elusive Villages: Social Structure and Community Organization in Rural East Pakistan* (unpublished PhD Dissertation). East Lansing: Michigan State University.

Bhuiyan, M. A. (1991) 'Social mobility and changing power structure in a Bangladesh village', in Clinton B. Seely (ed.), *Calcutta, Bangladesh and Bengal Studies: 1990 Bengal Studies Conference Proceedings*. East Lansing: Asian Studies Center, Michigan State University.

Chowdhury, A. (1978) *A Bangladesh Village: a Study of Social Stratification*. Dhaka: Center for Social Studies.

Chowdhury, A. M., M. A. Hakim and S. A. Rashid (1987) *Changes in Land Ownership and Use in Rural Bangladesh: a Study of Seven Mouzas of Bogra District, 1920–1987*. Bogra: Rural Development Academy.

Cohen, J. and A. Arato (1992) *Civil Society and Political Theory*. Cambridge, Mass.: MIT Press.

Crow, Ben (1999) 'Why is agriculture growth uneven? Class and the agrarian surplus in Bangladesh', in B. Rogaly, B. Harriss-White and S. Bose (eds), *Sonar Bangla? Agricultural Growth and Agrarian Change in West Bengal and Bangladesh*. Dhaka: University Press Ltd.

Ghimire, K. B. (2001) 'Peasants' pursuit of outside alliances and legal support in the process of land reform', in K. B. Ghimire (ed.), *Land Reform and Peasant Livelihoods: the Social Dynamics of Rural Poverty and Agrarian Reform in Developing Countries*. London: ITDG Publishing.

Haq, M. N. and A. T. M. A. Husain (2001) *Rural Development in Historical Perspective*. Bogra: Rural Development Academy.

Hashmi, Taj I. (1992) *Pakistan as a Peasant Utopia: the Communalization of Class Politics in East Bengal, 1920–1947*. Boulder, CO: Westview Press.

Hashmi, Taj I. (2000) *Women and Islam in Bangladesh: Beyond Subjection and Tyranny*. London and New York: Macmillan Press Ltd. and St. Martin's Press, Inc.

Hossain, Mahabub et al. (2001) *Changes in Agriculture and Economy in Bangladesh, 1988–2000: Insights from a Repeat Survey of 16 Villages*. Manila: International Rice Research Institute.

Huq, Hamidul (2000) *People's Practices. Exploring Contestation, Counter-development, and Rural Livelihoods. Cases from Muktinagar, Bangladesh*. Wageningen: Grafisch Service Centrum.

Ishihara, Hirioshi (ed.) (1987) *Markets and Marketing in Rural Bangladesh*. Market and Traders in South Asia, Series No. 1. Nagoya City: Nagoya University.

Islam, Mahmuda and Parveen Ahmad (1984) 'Bangladesh: tradition reinforced', in United Nations Educational, Scientific and Cultural Organization, *Women in the Villages, Men in the Towns*. Paris: UNESCO.

Jahan, Nargis (2000) *Employment of Women in Small Scale Industries*. Bogra: Rural Development Academy.

Jahangir, B. K. (1979) *Differentiation, Polarisation and Confrontation in Rural Bangladesh*. Dhaka: Center for Social Studies.

Jansen, Eirik G. (1987) *Rural Bangladesh: Competition for Scarce Resources*. Dhaka: University Press Ltd.

Jansen, Eirik G. (1990) 'Process of polarization and the breaking up of patron–client relationships in rural Bangladesh', in O. D. K. Norbye (ed.), *Bangladesh Faces the Future*. Dhaka: University Press Ltd.

Jansen, Eirik G., Anthony J. Dolman, Alf Morten Jerve and R. Nazibor Rahman (1989) *The Country Boats of Bangladesh: Social and Economic Development and Decision-Making in Inland Water Transport*. Dhaka: University Press Ltd.

Karim, A. H. M. Zehadul (1990) *The Pattern of Rural Leadership in an Agrarian Society: a Case Study of the Changing Power Structure in Bangladesh*. New Delhi: Northern Book Centre.

Kotalova, Jitka (1993) *Belonging to Others: Cultural Construction of Womenhood in a Village in Bangladesh*. Dhaka: University Press Ltd.

Mannan, Manzurul (1990a) 'The state and the formation of a dependent bourgeoisie in Bangladesh', *South Asia Journal*, Vol. 3, No. 4, April–June. New Delhi/Newbury Park/London: SAGE Publications.

Mannan, Manzurul (1990b) *Kinship Nexus and Class-Politics: the Case of the State in the Post-Colonial Bangladesh Society* (Cand. Polit, Postgraduate Thesis). Institute of Social Anthropology, February. Bergen: University of Bergen.

Mannan, Manzurul (1993) 'An anthropology of power structure: the making of tribunes and dictators in Bangladesh', *Journal of South Asian and Middle Eastern Studies*, Vol. 16, No. 2. Villanova, USA.

Mannan, Manzurul (1997) *Culture, Cash and Credit: the Morality of Money Circulation*. Paper presented at European Network of Bangladesh Studies Workshop (16–18 April). Bath: University of Bath.

Mannan, Manzurul (2001) 'South Asia's experience in land reform: NGOs, state and donors', in K. B. Ghimire (ed.), *Whose Land? Civil Society Perspectives on Land Reform and Rural Poverty Reduction*. Rome: IFAD/PC/UNRISD.

Mannan, Manzurul (2002) '*Bangsha*: Islam, history and the structure of Bengali Muslim descent', in N. Alam (ed.), *Contemporary Anthropology of Bangladesh: Theory and Practice*. Dhaka: University Press Ltd.

Mannan, M., A. M. R. Chowdhury and F. Karim (1994) *Fatwabaz against BRAC: Are They Alone?* Dhaka: BRAC, Research and Evaluation Division.

Momtaz, Salim (1996) *Rural Development in Bangladesh: the Problem of Access.* Dhaka: University of Dhaka.

Mukherjee, Ramkrishna (1957) *The Dynamics of a Rural Society.* Berlin: Akademic-Verlag.

Rahman, Atiur (1986) *Peasants and Classes: a Study in Differentiation in Bangladesh.* London: Zed Books.

Rahman, Hossain Zillur (2000) *Poverty: the Challenges of Graduation.* Dhaka: BIDS.

Rahman, Hossain Zillur (2001) *Re-thinking Local Governance towards a Livelihoods Focus.* PPRC Policy Papers. Dhaka: Power and Participation Research Centre.

Rahman, H. Z. and S. A. Islam (2002) *Local Governance and Community Capacities: Search for New Frontiers.* Dhaka: University Press Ltd.

Samshir, Sharif (1996) *Sar Sonkote Krishak Andolon: Rajnoitic Dal O NGO-eder Bhumica* (Peasants' movement during fertilizer crisis: the role of political parties and NGOs). Working Paper No. 14, Programme for Research on Poverty Alleviation. Dhaka: Grameen Trust.

Shahabuddin, Quazi (1999) 'Agricultural growth performance in Bangladesh: a note on the recent slowdown', in B. Rogaly, B. Harriss-White and S. Bose (eds), *Sonar Bangla? Agricultural Growth and Agrarian Change in West Bengal and Bangladesh.* Dhaka: University Press Ltd.

Thorp, John P. (1978) *Power among the Farmers of Daripalla: a Bangladesh Village Study.* Dhaka: Caritus.

Westergaard, Kirsten (n.d.) *Boringram: an Economic and Social Analysis of a Village in Bangladesh.* Bogra: Rural Development Academy.

Westergaard, Kirsten (1985) *State and Rural Society in Bangladseh.* London: Curzon Press Ltd.

Wood, G. D. (1976) 'Class differentiation and power in Bandakgram: the minifundist case', in Ameerul Huq (ed.), *Exploitation and the Rural Poor.* Comilla: BARD.

10

Social Movements, Rural Poverty and Markets: the Case of India

Neil Webster

Introduction

The primary concern of the chapter is with the capacity of rural social movements to play an important role with respect to rural poverty reduction in the age of market globalization. To this end it seeks to understand how the growing complexities and diversities of local rural societies and their economies have given rise to new forms of collective action that contribute to pro-poor development. Viewing social movements as a particular form and phase of collective action, it argues that groups of the poor can enhance their bargaining positions in the markets in which they engage and, secondly, they can better intervene in public spheres in ways that can change for the better dimensions of their poverty. This is to view social movements not so much as being responses to local and global processes, but as powerful instruments for changing and directing such processes and their (local) consequences. While such change cannot be assumed to be an intended consequence of globalization, examples from India and West Bengal, in particular, are provided to illustrate how collective actions have achieved benefits for groups of the poor.

The processes and changes associated with globalization have shaped a new context for rural social movements that has led, in turn, to their revealing greater diversities and originalities in their objectives and natures today, not least as they draw upon new types of linkages and instruments. The changes have been in the political sphere of contesting forms and directions of government policies and programmes and in the economic sphere of markets. In the case of the former, social movements have become key actors in processes of democratization and poverty reduction in particular. In the case of the latter, social movements and other forms of collective action have become increasingly important means through which social groups can contest their economic condition in an increasing range of market situations.

Can it be said that social movements have taken on a new role and function in the era of globalization? The argument in this chapter is that they have to a degree, but that there is no simple causal relationship to be found between the presence and nature of rural social movements and the processes of globalization. Today we are faced with a process of globalization in which market forces, in particular, shape, contextualize and facilitate the actions of individuals and groups. However, the logic for individuals to engage in collective actions that lead to rural social movements, the chapter argues, lies in the constitution and nature of local politics and the public spheres in which these occur and are contested. There therefore remains a strong continuity with the past history of rural social movements, not least in the goals and objectives pursued by local actors in the age of market globalization. Nevertheless, the propensity for collective action and social movements in particular to effect changes in the bargaining position of social groups in markets has increased significantly with important consequences for strategies promoting poverty reduction in rural areas.

A number of issues need to be taken up in the discussion on rural social movements, not least the relationship of social movements to other forms of collective action, the role of local organizations, and how to address poverty in such a way that the strategic use of social movements by the rural poor can be better understood. Prior to this, however, it is important to address the issue of what constitutes a market and how one should approach the study of poor people's engagement in key markets.

The analysis of markets and organizing practices in and around markets provides an important point of access into researching the present for forms of collective action to bring about substantive changes for groups traditionally marginalized and exploited in markets central to their livelihoods. Linked to such an investigation in the Indian context is the potential role of local organizations, both grassroots organizations and organizations based upon external interventions (local government, NGO-based projects, etc.) in facilitating and extending the impact of such processes of change.

In such an analysis, we can see how persons both individually and collectively utilize their diverse capabilities in order to improve or defend their bargaining capacities and to secure their entitlements, e.g. for their labour, their production, etc. Similarly we can analyse the roles of institutional actors at different levels in either the structuring of a market or in affecting individuals' bargaining capacities at different points within particular markets. Both are central to any analysis of the ability of the rural poor to improve their condition economically and politically.

Such an approach to the analysis of markets is not in line with more traditional approaches in which markets are portrayed in stylized terms of innumerable voluntary actions between countless individuals and are thereby the supreme expression of individual choice. Such markets are mediated on the basis of autonomous, fully informed entities with profit-maximizing behavioural motivations, which one can freely enter or leave. Models of stylized market structures, such as an oligopoly, a monopoly or a monopsony, are produced by altering certain criteria, retaining others, and thereafter used for predicting the consequences for prices and quantities.

> These abstractions leave us not only short of the means whereby to understand not only how supply is supplied and demand is demanded, but the structure and behaviour of the real market systems which relate supply and demand. (Harriss-White, 1995: 3)

A real market is an 'economically qualified, purposeful interchange of commodities on the basis of *quid pro quo* obligations at a mutually agreed-upon exchange rate … in a cluster of exchange and rivalry relations' (Fourie, 1992: 43, 48). Here the social relations unique to market exchange require the combination of 'horizontal' and adversarial competition between populations of buyers and populations of sellers, on the one hand, and a mass of 'vertical', exclusive, bilateral transactions between one buyer and one seller, on the other. The implications of this definition (*pace* the voluntaristic definition) are that exchange rates mutually agreed on may not be mutually beneficial, that vertical contractual arrangements may prevail over horizontal competition, and that purposeful bargaining and the obligations resulting from it may rest upon and reinforce a highly unequal base or fall-back position.

From this we can conclude that: (i) policies directed at markets will not have the expected result at the expected pace of reaction as the policies operate with the narrow concept of market; (ii) the institutional analysis of markets is central – markets are bundles of institutions nested in others; (iii) markets are also structured in the same way as are production relations – key elements in the structure of a marketing system are the organization of assets and of physical activities; (iv) the analysis of markets institutionally and structurally – the involvement of, and relationship to the state, the contractual relations involved, the organization of labour within the system, the trend towards market globalization – requires an intellectual finesse so that it can also address the analysis of poverty and of poverty reduction through collective action and rural social movements in particular.

Markets are highly complex systems in which occur multiple sequences of transfers of property rights and price formation. Obviously the structure, the number of levels, etc., of markets will vary greatly and not least with the growing integration of national and international levels and with the accompanying 'demands' that impact upon the local levels where the rural poor in the south are mostly located. However, the interests of the poor in a rural Indian context can be found primarily at the point of producer-wholesaler,[1] the points of interaction at which they come to sell their commodities including labour and at the point of consumption (retailer-consumer) where they obtain food, housing, land, credit, etc. Two dimensions can then shape the interactions and the entitlements achieved by the poor: the organized capacity of the poor in the market and the broader system of institutional rules and regulations that control and regulate market behaviour.

To approach the analysis of such markets is to take up the examination of economic power. The ownership of economic assets both in the means of production and the means of distribution is perhaps the closest we can get to any measurements of power and as a basis for understanding practices and behaviour based upon bargaining advantage reflecting differences in fall-back positions, capacities to bear risks, to press decisions, constrain the choice of others, to link or segment markets, to hold stock. Thereafter, one of the most significant indicators of relative power on the part of market actors is the rate of profit in that it indicates the capacities to appropriate or redistribute producers' surplus and to generate surplus in marketing. It is not surprising that as agricultural labourers have secured increased real wages in West Bengal in the 1980s and 1990s, there has been a movement of capital away from cultivation into the trading of rice and commercial crops, for example potatoes, on the part of some wealthier villages in areas such as Bardhaman district.

Clearly, markets are dynamic, being continually reconstituted and increasingly affected by the processes associated with globalization. The latter is not least in terms of extended vertical linkages of markets, but also in the institutions and other actors that are brought into these extended market networks and in the importance attached to the public spheres at different levels in which actors seek to engage with, shape or change markets. On the one hand, there is a need to analyse this globalization of markets to understand its consequences for the livelihoods of the poor at the local level. On the other hand, there is a need to locate the public spheres in which the functioning of such markets can be shaped and regulated by collective actions emerging at the local level.

Through the institutional mapping of markets, along the lines indicated above, it is possible to move towards an understanding of the roles collective actions, including social movements, can play; where organizations of and for the poor can attempt poverty reduction; as to how movements and organizations can pursue political strategies that also embrace consequences stemming from the globalization of markets. Such a mapping of markets will also contribute to the analysis of the political space (see, for example, Webster, 2001) open to the poor and local organizations in that the economic power within the market structures is more often than not a close reflection of political power and the interests of the dominant actors at each 'level'.

The second important dimension of markets for the following discussion is that they are fields in which social identities are formed, reproduced, changed and reaffirmed. For all parties concerned at each level, in each set of transactions, these social identities are a basis for ownership, wealth, dispossession and oppression. They are also the basis for acceptance as to what is the 'norm' in these matters and, conversely, for resistance and change. One point at which these occur, the arena for strategies and tactics that draw upon social identities consciously or subconsciously, is at the point of the interchange of commodities. Another is in strategies upon which individuals or groups draw when seeking to relocate their position within existing markets or to enter new markets. Within the Indian context, practices that illustrate the existence and nature of these strategies include the payment of lower wages to female agricultural labourers, the exclusion of tribal people from forest lands, ethnic bias in public sector recruitment, and caste-based allocation of occupation. From the perspective of resistance or challenge, it includes practices such as migration to urban areas drawing upon kinship or community networks, demanding irrigation water on the basis of regional or national identity, farmers' movements against the policies of an urban/industrial state, tenancy movements, and similar.

Some of these can be described as responses from below, but the capacity of groups of the rural poor to cope with and challenge diverse dimensions of poverty goes far beyond organized rural social movements. Among the many types of collective action to be 'discovered' at the village level one can also find systems of labour exchange, cooperation in inland fishing, systems of animal share-rearing, marketing cooperatives, migrant labour gangs, and numerous institutional practices around irrigation, forests and minor forest products, and similar natural resources.

Therefore, markets can be said to generate social identities that can take an institutional or organizational form. And, conversely, social identities influence key aspects of different actors' behaviour in markets. As such, it is important to consider how the social identities that participants in an interchange of commodities possess and perceive in themselves and in others, affect the bargaining, the price paid, and the realization of an entitlement. Here lies a discussion of how groups through social movements and local organizations, not least organizations of particular groups of the poor founded in their experiences in different markets – exclusion, bias, discrimination, etc. – can begin to change the condition of these poor through a renegotiation of exchange relations on the basis of a new power position, for example, through the organization of labour or the collective cultivation of land.

Changing nature of social movements

Two significant developments have occurred with respect to rural social movements in India during the past few decades. First, their nature has changed significantly in terms of their form, objectives and the techniques practised; and, second, the way in which rural social movements are defined, located and analysed has changed quite markedly. Both reflect the new context for collective action and a restructured political space that has emerged, enabling groups of the poor especially to engage in different forms of political action, including social movements.

There is no doubt that both local and global processes have increasingly combined to affect the development trajectories of rural locales generally. While the rural poor have remained poor in the majority of countries, the nature of the processes, the institutions and organizations involved, and the relations that give rise to their poverty, have undergone many transformations. Changed perhaps to a lesser degree have been the poor's perceptions of poverty, its causes, and as to who should be held responsible for their problems. While new forms of rural social movements have emerged, the 'enemy' has tended to remain the same – as witnessed in the slogans raised and the banners displayed: 'land to the tiller', 'security to the tenant', 'power away from the moneylender', 'sack the corrupt official', 'drop the new tax', 'kick out the government', 'oppose international business' (as imperialists, foreign price fixers, etc.), and so on.

The semi-spontaneous techniques of resistance and challenge also possess a continuity with the past: administrative officials are still blockaded in their offices, angry crowds gather and proceed in demonstrations against kerosene price rises and reduced subsidies, boycotts of markets are mounted, land is occupied by squatters, non-payment of taxes and duties is practised, government financed loans are not repaid.

The more general forms of collective action have clearly changed, however. There is a clear break with the rural social movements of the first seven decades or so of the twentieth century; changes in their character, their organizational form, the forms of mobilization, the associated discourses, and the forms of actions undertaken. The terminology has changed too; peasant movements have been replaced with land movements, farmers' movements, forest dwellers' movements, environmental movements, women's movements, and indigenous peoples' movements, to name but a few.

Rural social movements whose objectives were previously concerned with the defence of a way of life, of a type of production, of a community from the intrusions and demands of a state, have been replaced with social movements that cross spatial boundaries and delineate new political and cultural spaces. Where once the state, as well as its institutions and organizations, were to be strategically contested and repelled, now the state is seen as much more fragmented in form and nature with different interests held by diverse stakeholders. Today government can be contested in elections, politicians lobbied, officials subpoenaed, changes to the constitution challenged and the rights of citizenship can be demanded. Diverse tactics, both within and outside the formal political and juridical framework, can be used at different levels of society and government, and translocal and transnational alliances can be forged. Finally the objectives of social movements are more often to change policies, their implementation and outcomes rather than to demand the retreat of state and government from 'their' locality. The idyll of a past way of life without outside incursions is no longer at the romanticized core of the associated discourse.

It is also clear that today we need to acknowledge the increased role that exposure to increasing global markets has for the rural poor and the extent to which social movements seek to contest economic control in these markets: the 'right' to determine prices of inputs or outputs; the returns to labour; the status of particular forms of labour based on gender, ethnicity, migrant status, and similar; and the use of institutional constraints to restrict market opportunities for the poor in rural economies. Again it is the diversity of rural social movements that needs to be captured; how they have become increasingly disaggregated, more specific and more nuanced in their objectives; in the means they utilize; and in the alliances of interests that they attract.

In order to understand these changes in the nature of rural social movements and in the rural actors involved, it is necessary to break with the peasantry of Shanin, Alavi, Wolf, Chayanov and so forth, as rural collective action can no longer be reduced to peasant struggles. The spatial delineation of a peasantry that once existed has been undermined through seasonal migration, the mobility of younger generations in finding new employment, the diversification and commodification of agrarian production, the emergence of new patterns of consumption with the cultural, social and economic implications that these bear, and of course the access to new forms of cultural transmission with the electronic media at the forefront.

While some speak of a new peasantry, particularly in the Latin American context, it is proposed here that the retention of the term 'peasantry' reduces the analytical strength of the concept. Not only does it amount to being little more than a descriptive category, it imputes a greater continuity with the past than contemporary rural social formations in reality possess. When viewing the diversity of contemporary rural collective actions involving the poor, it is difficult to include this within a general category of peasant movements without collapsing important analytical dimensions in the process. Attaching the term 'new' is merely confusing in its conflation of time and nature.

Retaining the terminology of 'peasant' and 'peasantry' would therefore be to leave them as loose terms for groups with common characteristics rather than as concepts to be used in a more precise analysis of rural social formations and production systems. A Goan household in southern India with a son working in an electronics shop in a Gulf state, a father working as a labourer on building sites in Mumbai, and a mother with two sons and a daughter cultivating a small plot of land with coconuts for the market and rice for household consumption, can no longer be categorized as peasant households. The household might be living in poverty, in part based upon subsistence and petty commodity land-based production, but there the similarities with yesterday's peasant household end.

Today stress needs to be placed on the multi-dimensional nature of poverty and the diversity of practices pursued in the face of such poverty. The focus on poverty as a condition has changed towards a greater emphasis on the diverse processes which give rise to poverty and the discussion now embraces the fact that rights and knowledge are central constituent elements of poverty and well-being alongside other elements such as a household's assets, its consumption, its access to common property resources and government services, and its proneness to economic and natural crises. Furthermore, the move is towards a concept of poverty in relational terms and thereby the establishment of a basis for a more open discussion of the politics of poverty.

New approaches to poverty have also had ramifications for the selection of instruments with which to intervene. Meeting the claims of sharecroppers for security of tenure, or of the landless for land redistributed from large landowners, requires a very different type of actor to an income generation project or agricultural extension work: a political party, a social movement of the landless, a radical NGO. The presence or not of these organizations, the interests they represent, the leadership they posses, their preparedness to take on different political roles, their different capabilities within the local and national public spheres, are all reflections of the changing political and social environment. These are also factors that could potentially bring about changes in economic power in the markets, changes in the distribution of resources, and in the access to resources, and in the returns to labour and production.

When the analysis of the nature of the poverty faced by the poor and their capacity to mobilize and to take action is linked to this organizational mapping of the political and social environment, it then becomes possible to explore the political space for action on the part of the poor and to identify the public spheres in which negotiation, cooperation and contestation can take place for, and by, the poor within a locality. These are also questions which go a long way towards explaining when rural collective action takes the form of a social movement. Their engagement can then take two forms: firstly, actions and activities that seek to change directly the bargaining position of a group within a particular market. Examples would be use of labour gangs and associations to secure higher wages; formation of producer cooperatives to secure better terms for inputs and better prices for products; and water user associations to resolve 'top ender' and 'bottom ender' conflicts in canal irrigation. Secondly, social mobilization and similar forms of collective action designed to bring about changes in juridical status of market entrants and to regulate markets' functioning.

To view rural social movements in this light is to bring them into the contemporary age of market globalization. Whereas previously there was a tendency to locate rural social movements within an analytical framework based upon class with a central debate on the question of whether the peasantry should be understood as a class or as divided by class, the more recent concern has been with the diversity of rural social movements, the originalities to be found in the organizing principles they draw upon, and the complex politics of 'naming' and 'claiming' that characterizes their social and political relations to other social groups and public authorities (Hammar, 2001).

The possibility of social movements changing the regulations and controls shaping markets is a consequence of the change in political space that agrarian politics and the rural poor are now located within as well as of the changes in the way such movements are studied and analysed.[2] Contesting political space concerns power. Where power lies is also changing with the demarcation of new faultlines within the social formation as interests change and allegiances shift, requiring not only new analytical approaches to these, but new political strategies on the part of the rural poor. The state is no longer categorically the enemy of the rural (peasant) poor. Its claims and interventions can no longer be denied through its overthrow or by repelling it at the borders of peasant society. This is not to deny the potential within the state for serving the interests of the wealthy against the poor, the city against the countryside, the landowner against the landless. It is, however, to accept that the state is more often than not constituted by diverse and often fragmented interests, that it exists at all levels from the national to the local, in the macro- and in the micro-levels, and, not least, that it is reproduced and contested through the actions and daily practices of social groups and individuals within rural locales.[3]

The politics and practice of the rural poor today are to engage with the state. Whether by means of conflict and open contestation or through lines of patronage and primordialism, the state is a point of focus for diverse strategies on the part of the poor. While we would not rule out that class might underlie such politics, revolutionary class action is not the characteristic of these politics of the rural poor. As outlined above, what does characterize the politics of the rural poor increasingly is political action directed at economic power and local economic power in particular. To understand these actions requires that the approach to social movements is developed to embrace the diversity and originality of these actions.

This chapter proposes that social movements be viewed as a specific form of collective action, the rise and demise of which are determined by a range of endogenous and exogenous factors. At the same time, there are many forms of collective action that are not seen to take on the forms of acts and organizational practices associated with social movements: later the discussion stresses the importance of organizing practices as pre-institutional forms of collective action. Placing social movements within a broader landscape of collective action enables the development of and different forms of social movements to be more easily placed within historical processes of development in a country or region. It also permits the phases of collective action of which a social movement is one to be examined, and it counters the tendency to treat social movements as isolated and discrete phenomena. Finally, it enables the link to be made between social movements that seek to challenge and rupture a political order and its associated socioeconomic system, and social mobilization that strives to integrate, to work within, and to reform a political order and its policies and practices.

It is in the case of the latter that reformism can be understood as a logical extension of a radical social movement within a political system experiencing a process of democratization rather than as being in some way an ideological break with a revolutionary past. India provides a good example of the transition of rural social movements from revolutionary class movements to struggles for equity and the rights of citizenship in a wide range of different public spheres. It also exemplifies the twin processes of changes in movements and changes in their interpretation and analysis.

Rural poverty and social movements in India

In the 1970s, the study of rural poverty in India could be crudely characterized as following two lines: poverty measured in terms of quantitative indicators, such as income, nutritional intake, infant mortality and life expectancy, and poverty understood in terms of relations of exploitation and the accompanying impoverishment that centred upon access to, and control over, land and the returns to one's labour. While the former reflected the dominant tendency to treat poverty as a condition, the latter reflected the form of reductionism embodied in peasant actions perceived as class actions with nothing left to lose.

India's rural poverty is recognized as being a more complex affair today, not just because the forms of poverty have changed, but because the factors and processes involved in poverty are no longer seen to be reducible to such simplistic explanations. For many, the quantitative approach to poverty is no longer tenable because of its apolitical nature and a general lack of explanatory capacity. However, the crude Marxist approach is largely rejected today for its reductionism and the negative weight of a history of failed movements launched from a variety of leftist ideological standpoints. The failure of the radical Left to find a stronger base among its natural rural constituency of poor peasants and agricultural workers in India has to be in itself a strong argument for questioning the explanatory adequacy of such an analysis of poverty and its relevance for the rural poor in India today. History raises similar questions in many African and Latin American countries.

In one sense, therefore, the problem must be seen as a definitional one; theoretical approaches being the basis from which to define and identify the poor, and with which to design and implement poverty reduction. For mainstream non-Marxist sociologists, poverty was measured by the data derived from farm management studies, nutritional studies and the occasional village study based primarily on detailed survey work. For Marxist sociologists, the concern with the rural poor was subordinated to the debate over the character and role of the Indian bourgeoisie, of the Indian state, and the best political strategy for contesting landlordism in the Indian countryside. The rural condition, and thereby the nature – and political role(s) – of the rural poor, was bound up in systems of land tenure and ownership, the forms and use of family labour, and class-based dependencies rooted in access and control over credit, irrigation, trade and other resources. Beteille, with his studies on class formation in West Bengal, was perhaps one of the few notable exceptions of the time (see Beteille, 1974).

Despite the profound theoretical and ideological differences between these two latter groups, there was a considerable degree of agreement as to what constitutes rural poverty: primarily a lack of access to, or control over, economic resources; a poor return to one's labour and productive activities; little or no access to social services; the result being poor nutrition, illiteracy, high infant mortality, low life expectancy, high indebtedness, and similar 'problems'. The main difference between them lay in the causalities argued for in the explanations of these 'facts'.

Causal simplicity in explaining poverty was particularly apparent with a particular structuralist perspective with roots in the powerful arguments of dependency theories emerging from Latin America. In this, the principal contradiction that underlay the condition of the poor was to be found at the national level in the relation between dominant and dependant nation states. While terms of trade and other relations between national developed and undeveloped economies might well have been factors in the processes leading to poverty, the solutions proposed reflected a strong faith in the willingness of national elites to pursue an autonomous national development strategy that would also serve the interests of the poor. In India the history of the past three decades suggests that the politics required for such a change were not adequately understood.

At the time, the narrow-mindedness of the analytical approaches, the strictures imposed upon the analytical work through the methodologies used, and the neglect of political and cultural issues raised little by way of critical comment. This lack of vital reflection and informed thinking paved the way for a 'subaltern backlash' in India in the attempt to fill these analytical and empirical voids. It came in diverse forms, ranging from support for participatory methodologies of Chambers (1997) to the rewriting of Indian histories (social movements, etc.) by Guha (1983) and the subaltern historians. Despite its predictability in hindsight, it remains somewhat ironic that a politics of the 'Left' that sought to advocate the cause of those 'below' could so easily fall prey to a critique that presents itself as coming from 'below'.

Today, we can see that both the 'Left' and the development orthodoxy have taken the critiques and the subsequent strategies and methodologies that have emerged to be good, albeit with varying degrees of procrastination and reluctance. In the field of poverty research, the 'voices of the poor' have served to take our understanding beyond the structural dimensions of poverty enabling a far more nuanced analysis. They have also provided the means for developing political strategies for poverty reduction that involve and engage with the poor. While, on the one hand, it is now clear that income and nutritional indicators of poverty are insufficient to understand poverty, on the other hand, it is also apparent that the pursuit of class struggle and national liberation has been insufficient for poverty reduction. The complexities of poverty and the institutional subtleties of states and markets require that alternative ways and means be sought.

The importance of new sources of knowledge and a more nuanced under-standing of socioeconomic processes is well illustrated by a study of rural poverty undertaken in West Bengal. Based upon detailed field research, Beck estimated that between 19 and 29 per cent of the poorest house-holds' incomes came from common property resources (Beck, 1994: 133). Furthermore, the poor were found to be very active in the share-rearing of cattle, based upon the availability of 'free' grazing on paddy fields between cultivation. The impact in recent years of increased cropping of land based upon increased secondary irrigation, high-yielding variety seeds, fertilizers and increased credit for farmers had been to reduce the availability of this grazing, seriously affecting the livelihoods of many of the poor. Neither conventional farm management studies nor a range of socioeconomic analyses of the consequences of the green revolution for poverty reduction had recorded such activities or the unintended poverty outcomes of other reform processes. Not only does it reveal the problems with standard assessments of poverty and impact assessments, it also demonstrates the capacity for observers to completely miss the agency of the poor in finding ways – in this case share-rearing – with which to lessen the condition of poverty.

A more frequently cited work that illustrates the importance of qualitative and more detailed research is provided by Jodha's study of two Rajasthani villages (Jodha, 1989). Surveys from 1960–2 and 1980–2 found that while real per capita incomes were lower in 1980–2 than twenty years earlier, there were nevertheless significant improvements in other qualitative indicators of economic well-being. For example, Jodha observed: (i) expanding economic opportunities, including a broad range of employment activities and sources of credit; (ii) increased consumption of goods with high-income elasticities (e.g. refined rather than unrefined sugar); (iii) investment in consumer durables; and (iv) a reduced reliance on patrons. Again it is the need to explore the different dimensions of poverty using both quanti-tative and qualitative methodologies that such research revealed. Not only does it enhance the understanding of poverty, it leads to a finer grasp of the processes giving rise to poverty and the ways in which poverty reduction strategies can build upon the perceptions and actions of the poor themselves. The fact that such appalling poverty persists in India suggests that we have not yet absorbed the lessons to be learnt from such research.[4] Poverty remains a term of general description rather than signalling the point of entry into a detailed analysis of poverty as process, embracing both local and macro-levels of policy and practice.

Linking poverty at a household and local level to the broader processes of famine and famine relief, of poverty and poverty reduction, requires knowledge of the political means present for connecting the local into the higher tiers of politics and policy-making. It is to find the connections between political action at local and macro-levels and change in a country's overall development trajectory – not least the links between social movements and poverty reduction. If the political environment for development is today characterized by democratization, and if democracy is concerned with rights with respect to control over decision-making and rights with respect to the equity of resource distribution, then poverty reduction must be seen as an objective in the struggle for democracy in India and democracy must be seen as a means to poverty reduction.

Contesting poverty through social movement

Narrowing the discussion on social movements through a focus on the underlying objective of poverty reduction requires that the analysis of poverty as a process and the diversity of poverties if it is to be capable of being linked to the diversities and originalities of social movements. Furthermore, if social movements are to be seen as an expression of poor people's agency then the analysis of poverty must include poor people's own perceptions of well-being and poverty. Finally in this age of market globalization, it must acknowledge the linkages between processes and actors at local and macro-levels.

Clearly this makes poverty analysis far more complex as it must now embrace not only economic dimensions, such as income and consumption, but also political dimensions, such as those of empowerment and rights, together with human and cultural dimensions (health, education, status and dignity). In addition, there are cross-cutting concerns, such as those of gender and environment, which also have important implications for the poor. Is it possible to bring these factors and dimensions into a coherent analytical framework and link this to the discussion of rural social movements?

Recent work by a network of European institutes, led by the Overseas Development Institute (ODI) in London, has stressed four dimensions of livelihoods, resources, knowledge and rights (Cox and Healey, 2000). Partly building upon this work, the Development Assistance Committee (DAC) Guidelines on Poverty Reduction speak of economic, human, political, social and protective capabilities, to which is added security/vulnerability (OECD, 2001). These are summarized in Box 10.1.

Box 10.1   Defining poverty: the core dimensions

Economic capabilities (ability to earn an income, to consume and to have assets, which are all key to food security, material well-being and social status).

Human capabilities (health, education, nutrition, clean water and shelter – core elements of well-being as well as crucial means to improving livelihoods).

Political capabilities (human rights, political freedoms, a voice and some influence over public policies and political priorities – powerlessness aggravates other dimensions of poverty, the politically weak have neither the voice in policy reforms nor secure access to resources required to rise out of poverty).

Sociocultural capabilities (to participate as a valued member of a community, i.e. social status, dignity and other cultural conditions for belonging to a society. Geographic and social isolation is the *main* meaning of poverty for people in many local societies).

Protective capabilities (to withstand economic and external shocks, insecurity and vulnerability due to seasonal variations, natural disasters, economic crises and violent conflicts – dynamic concepts are needed because people move in and out of poverty).

Source: OECD, 2001.

What is significant within these attempts to define poverty is, first, the multi-dimensional perspective adopted; second, the tight interlinkages between the different dimensions of poverty; third, the diversity of poverties to be found that not least permits the disaggregation of the poor as a category; and fourth, the acknowledgement of the political side to poverty and poverty reduction by a growing number of the central actors in the field of development and aid strategies. It is especially these last two – the disaggregation of the poor and the politicization of poverty – that are particularly relevant here.

Some years ago, Byres (1981), in an important article on the impact of technology and commercialization on Indian agriculture, argued that the sharecropper and the landless agricultural labourers could not be united in their agrarian struggles as their (class) interests were too opposed. Interestingly, it is an argument that has long been reflected in the organization of the main communist party in India today, the Communist Party of India (Marxist) or CPI(M): one mass organization for the poor farmers including sharecroppers and another for the agricultural labourers.[5]

The problem with such a narrow class-based approach to poverty is that it predetermines the groups to be mobilized, the basis for mobilization, and the principal objectives to be secured. While a degree of flexibility in the nature and form of contestation and negotiation might be permissible at the local level, it is the nature of the anti-poverty agenda at the national level that dominates; it is this that serves to determine the nature and cause of poverty and thereby the nature and organization of any anti-poverty movement. So while a political mobilization might be rooted in a concept of poverty as a relation (exploitation) and its goals might be to challenge key economic, social and cultural structures and hierarchies (landlords, capitalist industrialists, imperialists, etc.), the actual 'ownership' of the movement is not so clear. An exploration of the politics of mobilization, of the roles of leading organizations, the nature of the leadership at different levels, and the location of effective decision-making all too often reveal it to be a movement in the name of the poor rather than of the poor.

For its part, the more orthodox approach to poverty, which involves applying poverty lines, identifying and statistically analysing those who fall under these, and following trends in absolute and relative frequency of poverty over time, provides a detailed profile of national poverty. It also provides an important tool for comparing situations internationally and for pro-poor planning, monitoring and evaluation. But as with the class-based approach to poverty it only provides one set of answers to the question 'who are the poor?' Diversity within the poor, between different groups of the poor, and the interconnectedness between types of poverties and groups of the poor at sub-national level remain unexplored.

If rural poverty can be examined in its diversity and complexity with a multi-dimensional approach, the implications for the politics of poverty reduction are considerable. Not least, factors of gender, ethnicity, religion, culture and economic status can be explored for their local implications for social groups located in different political, social and economic contexts.

In the 1980s and 1990s, sociological analyses of rural poverty showed many of the characteristics of the theoretical impasse within the broader field of development studies and the seemingly irreconcilable divisions of the agency-structure debate. Fortunately the actions and political practices of the rural poor have continued to present a source of information and knowledge with the potential to analyse these failures and to suggest ways in which to take the demand for poverty reduction forward.[6] A growing number of authors have recognized the poor's role and agency (for example, Villareal, 2001; Long and Long, 1992; Long and Villareal, 1998; Nuitjen, 1998). However, the balance between actor and structure in the theoretical approach remains a subject of disagreement in much of the literature.

Recognition of the agency of the poor is only part of the need. It remains the case that there is still a general paucity of research-based knowledge concerning the nature and functioning of local politics with respect to poverty and poverty reduction. Not least in the present climate for promoting local development through decentralization, local NGOs and support to local social capital, the dearth of studies on the functioning and processes behind local politics is a serious lacuna in development studies. It is a problem that undermines the identification, design and implementation of poverty reduction programmes, no matter whether they are rooted in a socioeconomic analysis of class or from within the current orthodoxy of Poverty Reduction Strategy Papers (PRSPs)[7] and attempts to promote pro-poor economic growth.

The requirement is to capture the diversity of experiences and interests held by the poor and the actions that these give rise to, their political agency, while acknowledging the role of socioeconomic structures in shaping the contexts in which the poor find themselves. Political and developmental interventions can then build upon the diversities and originalities of their actions by making them intrinsic elements in strategies designed to facilitate pro-poor development.

Promoting the agency of the poor is not to argue that the poor can bring about poverty reduction on their own. A concept of poverty as relational does not permit the possibility of the poor 'pulling themselves up by their boot straps'. Rather it is to recognize the potential role such an agency can have when directed at the institutions, relations and structures that generate and reproduce their poverty, and how certain institutions and organizations can be an integral element in challenging the underlying structures involved in relations of poverty. This point is re-examined later. First it is necessary to explore further the processes involved in constituting the context within which such agency can be located.

Is market globalization *per se* a problem for the poor in India?

It has long been acknowledged that rural poverty is not constituted at the local level alone. What has not been so clearly understood is the manner in which poverty at the local level has been constituted by actors, institutions and structures whose roots and logics lie outside a specific rural locale. In the 1960s and 1970s, the state tended to be the critical actor and it was examined for its class nature and its relationship to forces of imperialism, on the one hand, and to those of progressive nationalism, on the other. Today it is clear that the state's role cannot be seen in such deterministic terms, that it is certainly more fragmented than previously argued, and that its nature and role are far more open to contest and change. It is also the case that today global actors and processes are intrinsic to the shaping and structuring of poverty at the local level.[8]

What defines market globalization for the purposes of this chapter? It is framed by a political economy perspective in which the defining features are new forms of internationalization of capital, the emergence of truly global markets, the qualitative shifts occurring in the patterns of international trade, direct foreign investment and general flows of money capital. Accompanying these are the shifts in macroeconomic policies and state reforms and in particular the 'third wave' of democratization encompassing Eastern Europe, parts of Asia, Latin America and Africa together with the transition states of the former Soviet bloc (Bernstein, 1998). The changes in financial markets, production and technology have been reflected in the reorganization and integration of economies within the international system, where states have a shrinking role in macroeconomic policy and management.

For the developing countries, it is assumed that the promise offered by globalization lies within the possibility of reforming the linkages between domestic economies and international markets, not least through structural adjustment policies. Most recently political reforms to promote democratization have also been added. Thus we find the drive to redirect domestic investment and production according to principles of comparative advantage in international trade, the subjection of macroeconomic policy and management to the discipline of international market competition and the pursuit of political liberalism to speed the transition towards democracy.

What does globalization imply for rural poverty today? In countries such as India, the liberalization policies aimed specifically at reversing exchange rate and public investment policies that supported import-substituting industrialization. The effects were to favour imports of mainly capital and intermediate goods over exports and incentives to export producers, especially in agriculture. At the same time, the rolling back of the state in terms of its size and economic role has been actively pursued to complement the structural adjustment policies. The negative impact upon the agricultural economy has been most severe for the poor, not least due to the inequities and disparities in the application and implementation of the national economic policies of neoliberalism. Patnaik notes that in the area of subsidies, 'the advanced countries organized in the Organisation for Economic Co-operation and Development (OECD), paid out 336 million dollars of farm subsidies in 1995 (considerably more than India's entire national income) to less than 20 million farmers. The United States alone paid 75 billion dollars out of its annual budget to 2.7 million full-time farmers, or an average of $28,000 per farmer' (Patnaik, 2000: 20–1). Patnaik writes of the hypocrisy and political power of the dominant economic powers in the international system, as West European and North American governments work to reduce the subsidy burden on their own budgets but do not wish to see countries like India and China emerge as global players. In the case of India, she points to the unremitting insistence that the government cuts the relatively small subsidies on power and on fertilizers designed to aid the agricultural sector and not least the rural poor. India is but one example. Across Asia, Africa and Latin America, similar stories abound and it is around these that the analyses of social movements as reactions to globalization's effects are developed (for example, see Abdel Aal, 1998, on Egypt; Gibbon, 1997, on Tanzania; Villareal, 2001, on Mexico).

However, while it is both correct and necessary to point to the inequities to be found in the domestic and foreign policies of governments in many developed countries, there is a problem when the argument subsequently proceeds to suggest that globalization itself is the problem, with the corollary argument that the critical boundaries in political terms for contesting and changing globalization as a process are national ones. Such an argument is to reiterate the argument of dependency scholars concerning the importance of the interface between dominant and dependent national entities. For the rural poor such boundaries are usually not seen as the most critical for their lives, and from a poverty reduction perspective they are probably right in most instances.

Support for this view can be found in a number of studies that have examined the political consequences of structural adjustment induced liberalization for different groups within developing countries. While they have shown that greater efficiency in the economies has not been an outcome as they opened up for international competition, they have also documented that the benefits stemming from the reforms have gone to particular political and business groups. These groups have frequently been able to augment or adapt prior rent-seeking activities or else have been able to generate new ones; a recurrent example being through the privatization of public sector enterprises (Lewis, 1994; Boone, 1994), or through changes in the marketing of their production (e.g. the case of Egypt in Abdel Aal, 1998; Bush, 1998). As Gibbon (1997: 72) describes it, liberalization has expanded the scope for certain, especially parasitic, forms of 'African capitalism' – above all those involving export and import – without enhancing the prospects of 'capitalism in Africa'.

It is argued that it is not so much globalization *per se* that is at fault, but the political nature of the system responsible for deciding upon policies, providing services and allocating resources: globalization is part of the context rather than the cause. In this way we can see that it is the possession of power found in the politics of distribution of gains and benefits rather than globalization itself that should be contested. Opposing globalization will not only fail to change the internal policies that reproduce poverty, it can promote forms of nationalist politics that serve the vested interests of those with disproportionate control over existing resources and assets within a country. Furthermore, the possibility of building transnational linkages that can serve to strengthen the political capacity of the poor to contest their poverties is lost not least in undermining support for democratization.

While juxtaposing the national to the global is somewhat naive from a political economy perspective, it is a tendency that takes considerable strength from certain arguments concerning the cultural politics of globalization. But as with the causal arguments tying economic cost and poverty to globalization, there are problems with the political argument that globalization is undermining or threatening people's cultures. Just as the economic gains and costs of globalization have been unequally shared, the cultural consequences have also been experienced in markedly different ways. Attempts to mobilize around culturally derived demands that globalization should be 'rolled back'[9] cannot be assumed to serve the interests of the poor and other marginalized groups in a country. This is not to deny the attraction of populist appeals to national cultural values and to oppose global (i.e. Western) cultural hegemony. It is, however, to recognize that the national politics of such movements rarely serve the interests of the poor and least of all the rural poor despite claims by leaders to the contrary.

Yet it is not only nationalistic leaders who appeal to such populist ideas that are to blame. On the part of academics and development practitioners, the imperative of capturing voices of the poor and of drawing upon local knowledge, local social institutions and the like has for some tended to elevate all that is deemed local to a status that serves to subordinate other forms of knowledge and other modes of explanation. Development thinking in contemporary India is no exception to this tendency. While it might be claimed with some credibility that analyses must include the voices and interpretations of the poor within a locality in any study of action and social movement, when these become the principal basis for explanation, then one must question the correctness of the approach. Unfortunately, the recent tendency for it to be politically correct to accept the validity of explanations provided by 'subaltern voices' has resulted in support being given to a politics rooted in gender, ethnic or other identity forms that is often more chauvinistic than liberal, promotes exclusion rather than inclusion, and is anti-poor in its sectarianism.[10]

Here lies a fundamental danger in the age of globalization. The globalization of the international economy and the internationalization of flows of production, consumption and communication have prompted the development of defensive nationalisms and social movements that seek to oppose the perceived threats to a specific cultural, social and territorial identity. This is as true for the developing world as it is for the developed. In its extreme form, it has resulted in a national consciousness in which nationalism leads to a country appearing to close in on itself and to reject those seen to belong to more than one society as 'strangers'; they have no unique or central identification but rather manage a plurality of identities. So it is that fear of globalization is promoting a world increasingly 'dominated by the growing dissociation between a global economy and fragmented cultural identities that are mobilized by political authorities which arrogate legitimacy to themselves' (Touraine, 1996: 16).

At the core of the problem is that globalization is blamed for the impoverishment – cultural and economic – facing national communities who then support social movements that lead to greater fragmentation of societies and polities without removing former inequalities and disparities.

To break this pattern, the conceptual need is to challenge the presentation of globalization as inherently anti-poor and to oppose a political agenda dominated by the desire to defend national interests. The political problem is that national institutions and organizations have often displayed a vested interest in mobilizing the population behind such political agendas. The search for a political exit strategy from radical nationalism has led Touraine to a focus on the potential in civil society as the place in which the articulation of the economy and cultures takes place and where the politics of fragmentation, closure and exclusion can be challenged. The problem is to find ways in which interests can be organized and mobilized to challenge policies that are anti-poor without falling back upon social and cultural identities that promote isolationism, exclusion and intolerance.

This raises the fundamental question as to whether there is a democratic path out of this particular problem. If we refrain from seeing globalization as an inherently negative factor and accept a certain 'historical inevitability', then the political need is somewhat changed. Rather than to counterpoise the national to the global the task is instead to disaggregate the different processes at work and to identify the public spheres in which institutions and instruments can be contested in order to change outcomes to the advantage of the poor and marginalized groups within a developing country. The most obvious areas for making such challenges are in the markets in which the poor most actively engage. In the agrarian economy these are around land, labour, credit, irrigation and rural employment in industries such as brick manufacturing, paddy milling and construction. To these should be added health and education provision.

The example of West Bengal

While we saw how Patnaik focused upon the Indian state at the national level and inequities and costs of globalization as experienced at the all-India level, the state of West Bengal illustrates how the introduction of a set of reforms since 1977, designed and implemented from a pro-poor perspective (decentralization of government, land reform, civil service reform and financial decentralization), has enabled the poor to benefit significantly from economic growth in the agricultural sector. Expressed in another way, a new political space for poverty reduction enabled the poor to challenge and change their poverties through a pro-poor state government. In this instance a development process that embraces and is embraced by globalization in terms of political ideas, changes in production and production technologies, movements of people and capital, has yielded pro-poor outcomes in terms of the access to, and control over, the benefits stemming from the resultant economic growth (Webster, 2001).

The changes that commenced with the election of the Left Front Government (LFG) in 1977 were rooted in a long history of social movements sometimes overtly political, as with the independence movement against the British (1930s and 1940s) or the Naxalite movement against landlords and black marketeers (late 1960s and early 1970s). Many more were more specific and more localized, such as the Canal Tax movement (1920s and early 1930s), the Tebhaga movement of sharecroppers (1940s), the Food movements (1950s) and various Hat Tola (market fee) movements (1950s). The LFG therefore carried the organized expectation of the mass associations of the CPI(M) and the CPI, but the institutional memory of the dangers of class-based radicalism; direct presidential rule from the centre was imposed three years earlier than for the rest of India with the ousting of the United Front government in which the CPI(M) was also a partner in 1972.

The reform programme launched in 1977–8 was therefore similar in many ways to a social movement, but within a constitutional framework where the appeal to democratic process could sustain the reform process. *Krisak Samitiis* (local peasant associations) mobilized to register sharecroppers and to support claims for the new minimum agricultural wage. Illegally held land was registered and distributed according to legal requirements. Women through the *Mohilla Samiti* (women's association) began to be elected to local government and to demand greater and better access to health and education for all including women and girls. Security in land tenure, improved agricultural wages, a limited redistribution of land to the landless, ownership of homestead land, improved credit provision and improved functioning of Primary Agricultural Cooperatives were a few of the achievements that collectively have raised the condition of the poor. Here the shift in economic power can be seen in material terms for the rural poor.[11] It illustrates the combination of direct action on bargaining positions in key markets and the indirect action directed at reshaping and regulation of markets through political interventions. The experience of West Bengal also illustrates the diversity of collective actions that can promote change to the benefit of the rural poor.

Organizing practices, economic power, political arenas and micro-public spheres

In the current wave of democratization, the tendency is to pose the question: if the rural poor are to bring the diversity of their situations into the public spheres of development on a daily basis, what institutional practices and organizations should be the basis for their participation? A problem with such a question is that it tends to assume that if there is no community-based organization (CBO), appropriate NGO, or political party that can be described to be either of, or for, the poor, then the poor are politically inactive and have yet to be empowered. The argument continues that new organizations of the poor need to be established and new institutional practices based upon participation and empowerment need to be developed. More often than not this is through social mobilization projects that focus upon access to credit, irrigation and clean drinking water, one of the markets in which a group has traditionally lacked economic power.

However, if it is accepted that the poor already possess a political agency, that they already engage in a variety of sociopolitical practices with which they avoid the descent into (greater) poverty or vulnerability, then the question should change. We should instead be asking: how do the rural poor engage in social action outside of clearly observable social movements? How do they organize to cooperate, negotiate and contest with others, both poor and non-poor? How do they engage with the institutions and organizations that reconstitute and secure the interest and rights of the non-poor while marginalizing or 'downgrading' those of the poor?

Poststructural organization theories (as well as postmodernist approaches) provide interesting insights on actors' actions, but they also possess significant limitations. While they meet the need to explore the ideas guiding people's organizing behaviour and enable the associated discourse to their actions and strategies to be better understood, they leave us at a level of multiplicity and fluidity in explanation that is not particularly helpful when searching for a logic that can explain the past and provide a prescriptive guide for poverty reduction in the future. One of the more serious problems with such an approach is the apparent abandonment of the study of power relations located within specific sociopolitical fields or contexts. They also neglect the logic of economic relations in which people knowingly or unknowingly find themselves located – as a sharecropper, as a female agricultural labourer, as a marginalized small farmer, etc. As Nuitjen argues, the discursive practices through which social actors decide upon a certain courses of action, the social conditions in which they are formulated and implemented, and the outcomes that they produce, are embedded within fields of power (Nuitjen, 1998: 13). But these do not always give rise to collective action with the clear organizational form of a social movement or a member-based organization.

> People often follow fragmented organizing strategies, without collective projects ever becoming crystallized. They work with one set of actors and then another, develop strategies and change them in the course of action. Another important point is that collective action has the notion of common goals and well-defined objectives. However, in many cases common goals do not exist and the objectives develop in the course of the organizing process … although these fragmented forms of action are much harder to grasp and difficult to put in place, they form an important part of the organizing process. Hence, when I talk about organizing practices, I refer to the manifold forms of organizing, whether they be individual or collective. Yet my ultimate interest lies not in the isolated organizing actions, strategies, and performances in themselves, but in understanding their logics in specific socio-political contexts. (Nuitjen, 1998: 14)

Just as social movements can be viewed in terms of the flow of action which brings rural demands around land, agricultural wage rates or agricultural input prices onto the national political agenda, so too can we study organizing practices in the flow of action through which the rural poor seek to secure their livelihoods through negotiation, cooperation and contestation in local, less visible ways. This is the study of 'small politics' and of the creativity in 'everyday organizing practices' (Nuitjen, 1998: 15). It is a study that acknowledges both the agency of the poor and the importance of the sociopolitical context in facilitating and shaping that agency. It is collective action found at the pre-social movement phase, pre-institutional in nature, or in the post-social movement phase (or after the collapse of member-based organizations such as a cooperative movement) where such practices continue to be utilized, but within a changed context.

Economically, it is to recognize that market economies are continuously being confronted and questioned with respect to their own boundaries and that the rural poor, as marginal landowners, tenants, artisans and sellers of labour, contest economic control with respect to different aspects of their livelihood activities. This can be through various forms of credit, wages, market prices, access to common resources and tenancy contracts. It is not to argue that the poor can ever attain political or economic control over their situation. On the contrary, by definition the poor would find such a task improbable.

As Villareal argues, it is important not to misconstrue the idea of economic control as there are many in the field of development who propose that the poor can gain such control through cost-efficiency formulas and budgetary measures. However, such thinking is to reify the idea that control is possessed in absolute terms and total control is therefore possible. Instead Villareal argues that economic control is only ever partial and circumstantial and that its possession is under continual negotiation. Therefore it is in fact being underrated as it is only perceived in the sphere of the powerful and the degree to which those living in poverty, in the 'margins of markets', can wield control is in reality hardly considered. If we were to change our expectations and to investigate more closely we would see that:

> People manage a degree of control in particular situations by manipulating definitions and changing interpretations, by joining unions which can represent their interests and whereby they can wield greater leverage, by networking and by playing one authority against the other. (Villareal, 2001: 3)

Research reveals that there is a wide range of such organizing practices utilized by poor people in seeking to assert, contest, negotiate or cooperate in securing assets, resources, returns to production or labour, and much more. Economic control is therefore not merely being contested from below, it is being exercised from below, albeit seemingly far away from global markets and financial circuits.

Returning to the political role of organizing practices, if we move beyond the overt challenges to policy and market structures made by social movements, how might the organizing practices of the poor enter the new political space for collective action emerging under democratization? Organizing practices on the part of the poor are as diverse as the dimensions of poverty they reflect. The politics that they can give rise to will be in the public sphere(s) that constitute the political space. At the local level, village councils, school committees, neighbourhood groups, local shopowners, cooperative societies, political parties, and branches of trade unions will constitute one or more arenas in which the politics of resource allocation, service provision and access to these on the basis of gender, age, ethnicity, economic position, etc. will be played out.

In a similar line of argument, Keane argues for the importance of public spheres found 'within the nooks and crannies of civil societies and states' (1998: 169) that provide the basis of challenging power and control.[12] While interconnected and networking in character, public spheres are seen to have a fractured quality, which is not overcome by tendencies towards greater integration, and the decline of geopolitical boundaries, as discussed by Slater (1998). Rather there are multiples of public spheres operating at different levels leading to Keane disaggregating them into micro-public spheres at the sub-state level; meso-public spheres at the level of the territorial nation-state framework; and macro-public spheres which normally encompass hundreds of millions and even billions of people enmeshed in disputes at the supranational and global levels of power.

Micro-public spheres in particular are a vital feature of all social movements. They are initial points through which large-scale institutions' capacities to secure the cooperation of subordinates can be challenged and where the 'norm' can be more easily questioned particularly in more distant rural areas. What Keane describes as the 'dominant codes of everyday life' can be called into question by submerged networks of small groups, organizations, initiatives, local contacts and friendships. Many of these are interlinked with market interactions as rural workers meet, women sit together and manufacture *biddis* (country cigarettes), marginal cultivators arrange to share the lease of an irrigation pump-set, and fishermen manage the collective lease of village ponds. Similarly, meeting at the tea stall, when taking food in the fields, and the informal gathering of friends and passers-by in the evenings are points where the cohesiveness of local societies and the economic power in local markets, the social and political institutions that sustain the economic and political powers present, the ordering of lives and the reproduction of poverty that they sustain, are potentially threatened. From these, public disputes emerge and more organized challenges can take root. Here is the political agency that feeds social movements and challenges poverty through the capacity of democratic politics to enable collective actions in pursuit of diverse but related interests. It might be in a local demand for higher wages or collective action around irrigation water, or it might be to take interests to other forums and to mobilize more broadly.

Drawing again from the experience of West Bengal in India, *Adivasi* (tribal) women have drawn upon their marginal status as women, tribals and migrant labourers to organize not only their own silkworm production cooperatives on land previously controlled by the Department of Forestry, but also to gain control of the local Forest Protection Committees established under the national programme of Joint Forest Management (Webster, 2001). Their social identities as tribals, women, agricultural labourers, and women out of the house and village without their husbands were all bases for entrenched social and economic practices that included their marginalization in markets. More importantly, they were able to secure rights to lease and own land, they pressurized government officials to provide high-quality eggs for hatching, and they pressurized the local market board to purchase their products. Thereafter demands for improved childcare, education and health were presented to the local government bodies responsible. The transfer of their organizational skills to the area of community forestry management has led to women holding rights to committee membership and to hold bank accounts into which the benefits are paid (Webster, 2001). The results of such activities have been an improvement in their economic condition, an elevation in their household status, and a marked change in their political status when dealing with both the elected and the administrative local government bodies.

Such evidence is sufficient to give recognition to the political agency of the poor as a central element in processes of poverty reduction and with a growing capacity to influence state and markets within the broader framework of politics as the political space changes. The general political environment, the attitude of government and the dominant political discourse, not least as to the nature, extent and reasons for poverty within a country, all have a strong bearing on the poor's political strategies. Institutional reform, notably democratization and decentralization, has constituted the most popular way of seeking to integrate the poor into the political system in recent years, and has been central to the success of West Bengal in achieving two decades of pro-poor economic development for the state as a whole.

Weaknesses in this reform process nevertheless remain when one takes the broader Indian scenario into account. Most significant is that not all decentralization reforms have been implemented uniformly and the majority have failed to connect the poor more directly into the functioning and practice of government at the macro-level. Power has not yet been devolved; the poor have not been politically empowered in any systematic way; and poverty has not become a priority of political, economic and social life in the majority of states despite statements to the contrary. These failures as yet do not undermine the democratic project as a means through which to pursue sustainable poverty reduction, but they do demonstrate the strength of the forces opposed to greater popular control over collective decision-making and political equality. At the local level, collective actions directed at improving market bargaining positions have a better record of success, primarily as Indian NGOs have taken up the interests of specific groups of the poor at local level and tried to improve their access to, and participation in, markets central to their livelihoods.

Conclusion

To achieve change in an individual's poverty condition requires different forms of action by either the individual or from an actor working on the individual's behalf such as an NGO or donor agency, or a combination of these. Actions will be based upon the perceived nature of the problem and the means deemed both necessary and acceptable in trying to pursue a solution. The argument in this chapter has been that two general types of actions are most important from the perspective of the poor: action that improves their bargaining position, their capacity to access resources, realize entitlements, etc.; and action that affects the policies structuring their 'rights and interests', in particular regulating and controlling market practices. Under market globalization, the role of social movements has become diversified in the ways and means that actions are formulated and undertaken in both these general types. Social movements can be seen as a form of collective action that draws upon concepts, such as those of community, ethnicity, and common dimensions of poverty, as well as drawing upon more specific associational linkages between households, sometimes referred to as forms of social capital. In the majority of cases it is to be found that social movements as collective action seek to challenge aspects of the state's and/or market's relationship to those who constitute the social movement.

Many writers concerned with globalization have seen the position of the poor worsen as the forces controlling economic and political power have become more remote from the rural localities in which the poor find themselves. The financial and production systems have become international while the poor remain fragmented as workers, consumers and producers at the local level. In this chapter the argument has been that it is not market globalization *per se*, but the politics of control that need to be the focus of our analysis. Globalization is not something that can be broken down into constituent elements and rolled back. All too often such arguments tend to focus upon the importance of national boundaries with a belief in the capacity for national elites to defend their own peoples whether for reasons of self-interest or in defence of self-determination. While in a few instances this might have been the case, these tend to have been where there were strong anti-democratic regimes whose development also fulfilled the objectives of Western powers during the Cold War. In most South Asian countries the national elites have displayed wanton disregard for the poor. So while the capacity of actors within the international system to advocate and pursue policies detrimental to the rural poor cannot be denied, the argument of this chapter has been that globalization in itself is not the cause of rural poverty and that to mobilize the poor against an 'international' enemy with possible national 'collaborators' promotes a nationalism and chauvinism that often has greatest impact upon those already economically marginalized and politically excluded within a society, namely the poor and the poorest of the poor.

Our argument here is that it is necessary to find new and better ways to contest economic and politic control at local, national and global levels and this should be according to the possibilities found in each locality and at each level of a political system.

While social movements have been traditionally seen as the most obvious option, our understanding of these has more often than not been based upon analyses that take them as isolated and discrete phenomena and not to locate them within a broader framework of collective action. By placing them within such a broader framework, it is possible, first, to stress their dynamic nature including their rise and demise; secondly, it is to stress their place within broader political and social processes within the society and polity; thirdly, it enables other forms of collective action to be brought into the analytical and political frame. The argument then follows that the diversity of poverty can be located in the diversity of actions at the point of market interfaces between buyers and sellers as illustrated at the beginning of the chapter and, more generally, through the continuing tendencies towards greater democratization, which offer political opportunities not previously present.

On this final point it can be argued that the political space present for poverty reduction has never been greater, partly as a consequence of the changing political and economic environment introduced through processes of globalization. Here the key factors are the institutional and organizational means by which the poor can engage in collective control over decision-making; the ways in which poverty is conceptualized and perceived within society generally and government in particular; and thirdly the extent to which the political agency of the poor is facilitated and acknowledged. Changes in all three are being pursued through the diverse and often original forms of collective action found in India today. The consequences are rarely those intended, but successes such as those experienced by the poor in West Bengal are being achieved.

Notes

1. This is not to ignore the fact that large numbers of the poor are also to be found at various points in the intervening levels (e.g. employment in processing or transportation).
2. The latter point is demonstrated through the diversity found today in past movements – diversities that were not previously noted or were not fully understood. See, for example, the work of Ranajit Guha (1983) and his subsequent Subaltern

Studies in (re-)discovering the voice of the colonized, the 'subalterns', and their 'histories'.

3. Foucault's discussion of power as the norm is of particular relevance here (Foucault, 1980).

4. It is interesting, and perhaps ironic, that the World Bank uses such evidence to support the case for liberalization policies in India, questioning the adequacy of comparing two observation points or of seeing well-being only in terms of income-based indicators (World Bank, 1997).

5. In West Bengal, the states's CPI(M) was allowed to have just one body representing both: the Krisak Samitiis at the local level is for agricultural labourers, sharecroppers and owner-cultivators.

6. Not least, the fact that many of the poor survive and do so on the basis of quite diverse tactics and strategies. The argument that the need for poor people as workers, credit takers, etc. is the basis for actions by the interests of capital to enable the poor to survive is not adequate in itself, although undoubtedly containing some truth in its logic.

7. PRSPs currently being produced under the auspices of the World Bank and the International Monetary Fund (IMF) in order to obtain debt relief under the HIPC (Heavily Indebted Poor Countries) initiative.

8. In both intellectual and popular discourses, the global has a prominence today that has not been matched perhaps since similar intellectual and popular concerns with imperialism and empire in the late nineteenth century. One consequence has been that the concept of globalization has attained a theoretical status that is, at times, hard to explain or justify.

9. The national culturalism in the rhetoric of economic policies by the Bharatiya Janata Party (BJP) government in India is a good example.

10. For example, the promotion of certain chauvinistic forms of Hindu politics in India has been supported by a legitimacy accorded by intellectual analyses of social movements whose aim was to contest colonial or Western constructions and interpretations. I believe similar criticisms can be made of academic work on people's movements in Central and South America and elsewhere.

11. A growing number of works have been published on the West Bengal experience; Rogaly et al. (1999) provide an important collection documenting the experience. Its comparison with the Bangladesh experience draws out the different roles of politics and that of agricultural technology.

12. A public sphere is 'a particular type of spatial relationship between two or more people, usually connected by a certain means of communication (television, radio, satellite, fax, telephone, e-mail, etc.), in which non-violent controversies erupt, for a brief or more extended period of time, concerning the power relations operating within their given milieu of interaction and/or within the wider contexts of social and political structures within which the disputants are situated. A public sphere has the effect of desacralizing power relationships. It is the vital medium for naming the unnameable, pointing at frauds, taking sides, starting arguments, inducing diffidenza (Eco), shaking the world, stopping it from falling asleep' (Keane, 1998: 169–70).

References

Abdel Aal, M. H. (1998) 'Farmers and cooperatives in the era of structural adjustment', in N. Hopkins and K. Westergaard (eds), *Directions of Change in Rural Egypt*. Cairo: American University in Cairo Press.

Alavi, H. (1973a) 'Peasants and revolution', in K. Gough and H. Sharma (eds), *Imperialism and Revolution in South Asia*. New York: Monthly Review Press.

Alavi, H. (1973b) 'Peasant classes and primordial loyalties', *Journal of Peasant Studies*, Vol. 1, No. 1, pp. 23–62.

Beck, T. (1994) *The Experience of Poverty: Fighting for Respect and Resources in Village India*. London: Intermediate Technologies Publications.

Bernstein, H. (1998) *Globalisation Rethought or Imperialism Rediscovered?* Paper presented at the Workshop on Rethinking Globalization. Berkeley, CA: University of California.

Beteille, A. (1974) *Studies in Agrarian Social Structure*. Delhi and London: Oxford University Press.

Boone, C. (1994) 'Trade, taxes and tribute: market liberalizations in West Africa', *World Development*, Vol. 22, No. 3.

Bush, R. (1998) 'Facing structural adjustment: strategies of peasants, the state, and the international finance institutions', in N. Hopkins and K. Westergaard (eds), *Directions of Change in Rural Egypt*. Cairo: American University in Cairo Press.

Byres, A. J. (1981) 'The new technology, class formation and class action in the Indian countryside', *Journal of Peasant Studies*, Vol. 8, No. 4, pp. 405–54.

Chambers, R. (1997) *Whose Reality Counts? Putting the Last First*. London: Intermediate Technology Publications.

Cox, A. and J. Healey (2000) *European Development Cooperation and the Poor*. London: Macmillan Press Ltd.

Foucault, M. (1980) in Colin Gordon (ed.), *Power/Knowledge: Selected Interviews and Other Writings 1972–77*. New York: Harvester Wheatsheaf.

Fourie, F. (1992) 'Quest for economic justice', in G. Howe and P. Le Roux (eds), *Transforming the Economy: Policy Options for South Africa*. Durban: Indicator SA (University of Nepal).

Gibbon, P. (1997) 'Prawns and piranhas: the political economy of a Tanzania private sector marketing chain', *Journal of Peasant Studies*, Vol. 25, No. 1.

Guha, R. (1983) *Elementary Aspects of Peasant Insurgency in Colonial India*. Oxford: Oxford University Press.

Hammar, A. (2001) 'Speaking with space: displacements and claims in the politics of land in Zimbabwe', in N. Webster and L. Engberg-Pedersen (eds), *In the Name of the Poor: Contesting Political Space for Poverty Reduction*. London: Zed Books.

Harriss-White, B. (1995) *Agricultural Growth and the Structure and Relations of Agricultural Markets in West Bengal* (unpublished conference paper). Copenhagen: Institute for International Studies (IIS) Library.

Jodha, N. S. (1989) 'Social science research on rural change', in P. Bardhan (ed.), *Conversations between Economists and Anthropologists*. Oxford: Oxford University Press.

Keane, J. (1998) *Civil Society: Old Images, New Visions*. Cambridge: Polity Press.

Lewis, P. M. (1994) 'Economic status, private capital and dilemmas of accumulation in Nigeria', *World Development*, Vol. 22, No. 3.

Long, N. and A. Long (eds) (1992) *Battlefields of Knowledge: the Interlocking of Theory and Practice in Social Research and Development*. London: Routledge.

Long, N. and V. Villareal (1998) 'Small product, big issues', *Development and Change*, Vol. 29, No. 4, pp. 725–50.

Nuijten, M. (1998) *In the Name of the Land: Organization, Transnationalism and the Culture of the State in a Mexican Ejido* (PhD Thesis). University of Wageningen.

Organization for Economic Cooperation and Development (OECD) (2001) *DAC Guidelines on Poverty Reduction*. Paris: OECD.

Patnaik, U. (2000) *The Impact of Globalisation on Poverty and Food Security in India*. Paper presented to the 16th EMSAS Conference (Edinburgh, 5–9 September).

Rogaly, B., S. Bose and B. Harris-White (eds) (1999) *Sonar Bangla? Agricultural Growth and Agrarian Change in West Bengal and Bangladesh*. London: Sage.

Shanin, T. (ed.) (1971) *Peasants and Peasant Societies*. London: Penguin.

Slater, D. (1998) 'Rethinking the spatialities of social movements: questions of (b)orders, culture and politics in times of global movements', in S. Alvarez, E. Dagnino and A. Escobar (eds), *Cultures of Politics, Politics of Culture*. Boulder, CO and Oxford: Westview Press.

Touraine, A. (1996) 'Nation, nationalism and citizenship', *Journal of Social Studies*, Vol. 71, January.

Villareal, M. (2001) *The Art of Coping: Debt Economies in Rural Communities of Western Mexico*. Working paper. Copenhagen: Centre for Development Research.

Webster, N. (2001) 'Local organisations and political space in the forests of West Bengal', in N. Webster and L. Engberg-Pedersen (eds), *In the Name of the Poor: Contesting Political Space for Poverty Reduction*. London: Zed Books.

Wolf, E. (1971) *Peasant Wars of the 20th Century*. London: Faber.

Wolf, E. (1990) 'Facing power: old insights, new questions', *American Anthropologist*, Vol. 92, No. 3, pp. 586–96.

World Bank (1997) *India: Achievements and Challenges in Reducing Poverty*. Washington, DC: World Bank.

Index